Power and Interdependence

Power and Interdependence

Second Edition

Robert O. Keohane
Harvard University

Joseph S. Nye
Harvard University

Scott, Foresman/Little, Brown Series in Political Science
SCOTT, FORESMAN AND COMPANY
Glenview, Illinois   Boston   London

For our parents,
with gratitude,
And our children,
with hope.

Written under the auspices of the
Center for International Affairs,
Harvard University

Library of Congress Cataloging-in-Publication Data

Keohane, Robert O. (Robert Owen), 1941-
 Power and interdependence / Robert O. Keohane, Joseph S. Nye.—
2nd ed.
     p.   cm.
 Includes bibliographical references and index.
 ISBN 0-673-39891-9
 1. International relations.   2. International economic relations.
I. Nye, Joseph S.   II. Title.
JX1395.K428   1989   88-18354
327—dc19   CIP

1   2   3   4   5   6   7   8   9   10—KPF—94   93   92   91   90   89   88

Printed in the United States of America

Preface to First Edition

As students in the late 1950s and early 1960s, we were taught to look at international politics through "realist" glasses, which emphasized the ever-present possibility of war among sovereign states. As our earlier work indicates, we soon became uneasy about this one-sided view of reality, particularly about its inadequate analysis of economic integration and of the roles played by formal and informal international institutions. Our collaboration began in 1968 when, as new members of the board of editors of *International Organization*, we decided to edit a special issue of that journal to criticize traditional views of world politics and to demonstrate the relevance of international organization broadly conceived.[1]

We decided to write the present book, after *Transnational Relations and World Politics* was published in the summer of 1971, for two main reasons. Although in that volume we had pointed out significant problems with realist theory, particularly in the area of international political economy, we had not provided an alternative theory. We still needed to fit transnational relations into a larger framework of world politics if we were to complete the analytical task we had begun. From a policy standpoint, we thought that significant improvements in American policy on issues involving transnational relations and international organizations were unlikely unless the premises of policy were changed. We believed that many of the failures of American foreign policy in

[1] *International Organization* 25, no. 3 (Summer 1971); later published as *Transnational Relations and World Politics* (Cambridge, Mass.: Harvard University Press, 1972).

these areas had their roots in the limitations of realist assumptions. For both analytical and policy reasons, therefore, we sought to write a book that would put into a broader context the classic realist analysis that Hans Morgenthau's *Politics Among Nations*, among other works, had bequeathed to the current generation.[2]

Our analytical and policy concerns help to explain the orientation of this book. Our central policy concern had to do with American foreign policy, but the book's focus is completely different from that of most books and articles on this subject. Because we are concerned with the premises of policy, our major emphasis is on the changing nature of the international system and how to understand it. Only in the last chapter do we draw lessons for foreign policy. Our two country-oriented case studies, however, are focused on the United States. Yet throughout the book, our emphasis is on theory. The cases were selected for their potential significance for theory as much as for their intrinsic policy importance. Since the United States is the most important actor in the system, our focus on American actions can be justified on theoretical as well as policy grounds. In addition, each of our major cases is examined over at least a fifty-year period to help us understand underlying forces of stability and change. Our method is not simply historical; we have analyzed the cases according to a theoretical and comparative scheme that we elaborate in chapters 1–3. This approach bears some resemblance to what our teacher Stanley Hoffmann called "historical sociology" over a decade ago.[3] We try to quantify what we can, but we stress theory over method and understanding the premises of policy over charting a detailed course of action.

In this book we try to understand world politics by developing explanations at the level of the international system. This does not mean that we regard the domestic politics of foreign policy as unimportant. Quite the contrary. Foreign policy and domestic policy, as we repeatedly emphasize, are becoming increasingly difficult to disentangle. Nevertheless, the complex relations between foreign and domestic policy make it essential to know how much one can explain purely on the basis of information about the international system. In this sense, we try to discover what cannot be explained on the basis of international factors, as well as what can be so explained. Thus, although comparative foreign

[2] Some of our thoughts on the subject of this book have appeared in earlier articles, but they have been so greatly altered in form and content that only a few fragments remain in the present volume. For these we acknowledge permission from the University of Wisconsin Press to draw from the following articles: C. Fred Bergsten, R. Keohane, and J. Nye, "International Economics and International Politics: A Framework for Analysis," *International Organization* 29, no. 1 (Winter 1975); R. Keohane and J. Nye, "Introduction: The Complex Politics of Canadian-American Interdependence," *International Organization* 28, no. 2 (Autumn 1974); J. Nye, "Transnational Relations and Interstate Conflicts: An Empirical Analysis," *International Organization* 28, no. 4 (Autumn 1974).

[3] Stanley Hoffmann, ed., *Contemporary Theory in International Relations* (Englewood Cliffs, N.J.: Prentice-Hall, 1960).

policy is not the subject of this book, we hope that students of comparative foreign policy will find our analysis useful—if only as a starting point for their attempts to explain patterns of national action.

We do not claim that our explanations of change and stability in world politics are the only ones that could be developed for this purpose, even at the international level. We have not, for example, included a Marxist formulation. Many Marxists adopt what we call an overall structure approach, although unlike realists, they accept a class theory of the foreign policy process. Some Marxists, however, focus on direct relations among capitalists: in these formulations, multinational corporations are important in their own right as political actors.[4] Yet, as far as we could determine, there is not a generally accepted and clearly articulated Marxist theory of international regime change. We are neither sympathetic enough with the Marxist perspective, nor learned enough in its subtleties, to develop a Marxist model of our own. It is to be hoped that Marxists will develop models of international regime change to compete with or complement our own.

Friends have often asked us how we have managed to collaborate so intensively over such a long period of time. The short answer is by swallowing our pride while we tore apart each other's chapters. Although collaboration invokes occasional frustration, it produces the keen intellectual pleasure of rapid response and exploration of ideas. By and large, we have enjoyed the process. The theoretical chapters have gone through so many drafts that it is virtually impossible to identify the source of particular ideas. Keohane took primary responsibility for the case studies on money and Australia; Nye, for oceans and Canada. Even here, however, the initial division of labor does not accurately reflect the equality of our contributions to the final version.

Our transcontinental collaboration would not have been possible without the support of a Ford Foundation grant. In addition, over the last five years, financial help was provided to Nye by the Rockefeller Foundation and to Keohane by the University Consortium for World Order Studies, the Johnson

---

[4] This statement certainly applies to much of the literature on "international dependency," which focuses on relations between developed and underdeveloped countries (but which is by no means exclusively Marxist in character). Apart from this dependency literature, explorations of this theme from a Marxist point of view can be found in Stephen Hymer, "The Internationalization of Capital," *Journal of Economic Issues* (March 1972); and Ernest Mandel, *Europe vs. American Contradictions of Imperialism* (New York: Monthly Review Press, 1970), especially chapters 1–6, pp. 7–67. In the literature on dependency, the following are notable: Stephen Hymer, "The Multinational Corporation and the Law of Uneven Development," in Jagdish Bhagwati (ed.) *Economics and World Order from the 1970s to the 1990s* (New York: The Free Press, 1972), pp. 113–140; Johan Galtung, "A Structural Theory of Imperialism," *Journal of Peace Research* (1972): 81–117; Osvaldo Sunkel, "Transnational Capitalism and National Disintegration in Latin America," *Social and Economic Studies* (University of West Indies) 22, no. 1 (March 1973): 132–176; and Robert R. Kaufman et al., "A Preliminary Test of the Theory of Dependency," *Comparative Politics* (April 1975).

Foundation, and the Stanford University Center for Research in International Studies. Nye is also grateful to Carleton University in Ottawa and to the Royal Institute of International Affairs in London and its staff. We are both grateful to the Harvard Center for International Affairs and its two directors, Robert R. Bowie and Raymond Vernon, tireless and enormously supportive critics, without whose help it is hard to imagine this book. It is also hard to imagine this book without the comments we received from so many critics and friends (the two categories are not mutually exclusive!). We particularly wish to thank Graham Allison, Jonathan Aronson, Robert Art, Francis Bator, Dan Caldwell, Stephen Cohen, Jorge Dominguez, Linda Cahn, Dan Fine, Alexander George, Robert Gilpin, Crauford Goodwin, Ernst Haas, Roger Hansen, Jeff Hart, Barbara Haskell, Fred Hirsch, Stanley Hoffmann, Cavan Hogue, Ann Hollick, Ray Hopkins, Peter Jacobsohn, Robert Jervis, John Q. Johnson, Peter Katzenstein, James Keeley, Janet Kelly, Peter Kenen, Nannerl Keohane, Charles Kindleberger, Stephen Krasner, James Kurth, David Laitin, Peter Lange, Charles Lipson, Peyton Lyon, Rachel McCulloch, Michael Mandelbaum, Edward Miles, Theodore Moran, John Odell, Van Doorn Ooms, Rob Paarlberg, Wynne Plumptre, Richard Rosecrance, John Ruggie, Robert Russell, Philippe Schmitter, Ian Smart, Louis Sohn, Susan Strange, Harrison Wagner, and Dan Yergin. Ava Feiner, Robert Pastor, Debra Miller, Alison Young, Kenneth Oye, and Constance Smith greatly helped our research on the case studies. Numerous officials of the American, Australian, and Canadian governments gave generously of their time in interviews. Emily Hallin supervised the reproduction and transmission of innumerable drafts at the Stanford end of this transcontinental relationship. Beverly Davenport, Amy Gazin, and Amy Contrada ably managed the typing of the manuscript and administrative chores at Harvard. The contributions of Nannerl Keohane and Molly Nye would require another book, not a mere preface, to recount.

No author is an island. We gladly toll our bell of thanks.

Preface to Second Edition

Theorists of international relations suffer from being too close to the events they discuss. When we wrote *Power and Interdependence* in the mid-1970s, dramatic changes were taking place in world politics. By the beginning of the decade the Vietnam War had become highly unpopular in the United States, and detente seemed to have reduced the importance of the U.S.–Soviet nuclear competition. At the same time, international trade was growing more rapidly than world product; transnational corporations were playing dramatic political roles; and from 1971 on the international monetary system was in flux. Meanwhile, the relative economic predominance of the United States was declining as the European and Japanese economies grew at more rapid rates. President Nixon and Secretary of State Kissinger spoke of the development of a five-power world, and futurologists such as Herman Kahn predicted the imminent arrival of a multipolar international system.[1]

On top of this came the oil crisis of 1973, in which some very weak states extracted enormous resources from the strong. Hans Morgenthau wrote of what he called an unprecedented divorce between military and economic power based on the control of raw materials.[2] The vulnerability of Western societies at a period of high commodity prices encouraged many less developed countries to believe that a greater transformation of power had occurred than

[1] Herman Kahn and B. Bruce-Briggs, *Things to Come* (New York: Macmillan, 1972).
[2] Hans J. Morgenthau, "The New Diplomacy of Movement," *Encounter* (August 1974): 56.

was actually the case. Many theorists reflected on these concerns. A representative view among the modernist writers of the 1970s was that:

The forces now ascendant appear to be leaning toward a global society without a
dominant structure of cooperation and conflict—a *polyarchy* in which nation-states,
subnational groups, and transnational special interests and communities would all be
vying for the support and loyalty of individuals, and conflicts would have to be resolved
primarily on the basis of ad hoc bargaining in a shifting context of power relationships.[3]

   By the late 1970s the mood began to change, both in the United States and in
the United Nations. The United States Government became more concerned
about Soviet policy, and less sensitive to the policies and complaints of governments of less developed countries. The experience of the Carter administration illustrates this point. While campaigning in 1976, Jimmy Carter promised
to reduce the defense budget, but by 1980 he was closer to Ronald Reagan's
position than to his own previous view. Reagan's election accentuated these
trends. American policy focused on East-West confrontation and scaled down
North-South issues and the role of multilateral institutions. The defense budget
increased in real terms for five straight years, and the United States was more
willing to use military force (albeit against extremely weak states such as Grenada and Libya). Arms control was downgraded and the modernization of
nuclear forces was intended to restore an "edge" for additional utility of military force. This shifting agenda was accompanied by a resurgence of realist
analysis, for history seemed to have vindicated the realist model.
   Just as some analysts in the 1970s overstated the obsolecence of the nation
state, the decline of force, and the irrelevance of security concerns, others in
the early 1980s unduly neglected the role of transnational actors and economic
interdependence. Contrary to the tone of much political rhetoric and some
political analysis, however, the 1980s did not represent a return to the world of
the 1950s. Just as the decline of American power was exaggerated in the 1970s,
so was the restoration of American power exaggerated in the 1980s. Looking
carefully at military and economic indices of power resources, one notes that
there was far more change in psychology and mood than in true indicators of
power resources. The diffusion of power continued as measured by shares in
world trade or world product. Economic interdependence as measured by
vulnerability to supply shocks eased in a period of slack commodity markets
(but it could change if markets tighten again and growth of economic transactions continues). Sensitivity to exchange-rate fluctuations remained high. The
costs of the great powers' use of force remained higher than in the 1950s.
Moreover, despite rhetoric, the relations between the superpowers did not
show a return to the Cold War period. Not only were alliances looser, but

[3] Seyom Brown, *New Forces in World Politics* (Washington: Brookings Institution, 1974), p. 186.

transactions were higher and the relations between the superpowers reflected a fair degree of learning in the nuclear area.[4] In our view, therefore, the analysis that we put forward in *Power and Interdependence* has not been rendered irrelevant by events. The real questions are not about obsolescence, but about analytical cogency.

In a sense, the 1970s and 1980s were merely the latest instance of a recurring dialectic between the two main strands in what has been called the "classical tradition" of international-relations theory. Realism has been the dominant strand.[5] The second strand is the "liberal" or "Grotian tradition," which tends to stress the impact of domestic and international society, interdependence, and international institutions. In their simplest forms, liberal theories have been easily discredited. The proposition that gains from commercial transactions would overcome the problems inherent in the security dilemma and make war too expensive was belied in 1914. Hopes that a system of international law and organization could provide collective security to replace the need for self-help inherent in the security dilemma were disappointed by 1939. Nonetheless, the sharp opposition between realist and liberal theories is overstated. In fact, the two approaches can be complementary. Sophisticated versions of liberal theory address the way interactions among states and the development of international norms can interact with the domestic politics of the states in an international system to transform how those states define their interests. Transnational as well as interstate interactions and norms lead to new definitions of interests as well as new coalition possibilities for different interests within states.

Power and Interdependence sought to explain the patterns of change that we observed during the early to mid-1970s by integrating aspects of the realist and liberal traditions. Thus our core argument in Chapter 1, that asymmetrical interdependence can be a source of power, links the liberal stress on interdependence with the realist focus on power. Yet as we noted in our Preface to the first edition, we were taught as students to see the world through "realist" glasses, and our book reflected our struggle to see a more complex vision. Thus, realism bore the brunt of our critique, and our quarrels with aspects of liberalism were subdued. As a result of our rhetorical barbs at realism, our approach is sometimes labeled simply as "liberal." Yet this characterization of *Power and Interdependence* is highly misleading, since we stressed the importance of governments' wielding of power in pursuit of their conceptions of self-interest, and we declared in Chapter 1 that "military power dominates

---

[4] Joseph S. Nye, Jr., "Nuclear Learning and U.S.–Soviet Security Regimes," *International Organization* (Summer 1987).

[5] K. J. Holsti, *The Dividing Discipline: Hegemony and Diversity in International Theory* (Boston: Allen & Unwin, 1985).

economic power in the sense that economic means alone are likely to be ineffective against the serious use of military force" (p. 16).

We have quite a bit to say, after more than a decade, both about how commentators construed or misconstrued our work, and about our own shifts in perspective. We could have changed the text of our book, but this would not have enabled us to respond to our critics, and it would have concealed our own amendments, shifts in point of view, and second thoughts. We could have written a long Preface—indeed, we drafted one—but our astute editor pointed out that this would encumber the reader unacquainted with our book with commentary before he or she had read the original text. In this edition we have therefore left the original text as it was written and have added only a brief new Preface. We have, however, added an Afterword, which provides a fuller discussion of how we see our work, as contrasted with the perspective of commentators.[6]

In Chapter 8 of *Power and Interdependence* we drew some implications from our analysis for policy. In our view, many of our judgments remain valid—for instance, we argued that reducing the United States' vulnerability to external shocks could be part of a strategy of policy coordination and international leadership. Building an American oil stockpile and taking the lead in the International Energy Agency have indeed been the two key components of the successful international energy policy which has helped to transform international energy politics since the 1970s. Furthermore, they have been, as we suggested, complementary, rather than alternative, policies. We also argued for effective international policy coordination on ecological issues—as lovers of wild lands we could not ignore this dimension of global politics—but suggested that cooperation on such issues would be difficult. In general, we called for "international surveillance and collective leadership" (p. 232), which we still believe to be crucial if urgent world problems are to be addressed.

These prescriptions, however valid, were mostly quite general. In 1985 we sought to make more specific recommendations, using not only the analysis of *Power and Interdependence* but also that of subsequent work on international regimes. The article that we produced, "Two Cheers for Multilateralism," is reprinted from *Foreign Policy* at the end of this volume, following the Afterword.

In the eleven years since we completed *Power and Interdependence*, our professional paths have diverged and then converged again. Robert O. Keohane has concentrated on interpreting patterns of international cooperation and discord in light of social science theory; Joseph S. Nye has served in government and published works on nuclear deterrence, ethics and international

---

[6] Most of the Afterword appeared as an article entitled "*Power and Interdependence* Revisited," published in *International Organization* 42, no. 4 (Autumn 1987): 725–753.

relations, and U.S.–Soviet relations. Since 1985 we have been colleagues at Harvard University, giving us the opportunity to discuss analytical and policy issues intensively again, both in seminars and in personal conversations. We have gained enormously from our intellectual companionship and deeply satisfying personal friendship, which now extend over twenty years. If our readers also benefit, we will be doubly pleased.

Contents

PART I

Understanding Interdependence

Chapter 1 | INTERDEPENDENCE IN WORLD POLITICS

We live in an era of interdependence. This vague phrase expresses a poorly understood but widespread feeling that the very nature of world politics is changing. The power of nations — that age-old touchstone of analysts and statesmen — has become more elusive: "calculations of power are even more delicate and deceptive than in previous ages."[1] Henry Kissinger, though deeply rooted in the classical tradition, has stated that "the traditional agenda of international affairs — the balance among major powers, the security of nations — no longer defines our perils or our possibilities. . . . Now we are entering a new era. Old international patterns are crumbling; old slogans are uninstructive; old solutions are unavailing. The world has become interdependent in economics, in communications, in human aspirations."[2]

How profound are the changes? A modernist school sees telecommunications and jet travel as creating a "global village" and believes that burgeoning social and economic transactions are creating a "world without borders."[3] To greater or lesser extent, a number of scholars see our era as one in which the territorial state, which has been dominant in world politics for the four centuries since feudal times ended, is being eclipsed by nonterritorial actors such as multinational corporations, transnational social movements, and international organizations. As one economist put it, "the state is about through as an economic unit."[4]

Traditionalists call these assertions unfounded "globaloney." They point to the continuity in world politics. Military interdependence has always existed, and military power is still important in world politics — witness nuclear deterrence; the Vietnam, Middle East, and India-Pakistan wars; and Soviet influence in Eastern Europe or American influence in the Caribbean. Moreover, as the Soviet Union has shown, authoritarian states can, to a considerable extent, control telecommunications and social transactions that they consider disruptive. Even poor and weak countries have been able to nationalize multinational corporations, and the prevalence of nationalism casts doubt on the proposition that the nation-state is fading away.

Neither the modernists nor the traditionalists have an adequate framework for understanding the politics of global interdependence.[5] Modernists point correctly to the fundamental changes now taking place, but they often assume without sufficient analysis that advances in technology and increases in social and economic transactions will lead to a new world in which states, and their control of force, will no longer be important.[6] Traditionalists are adept at showing flaws in the modernist vision by pointing out how military interdependence continues, but find it very difficult accurately to interpret today's multidimensional economic, social, and ecological interdependence.

Our task in this book is not to argue either the modernist or traditionalist position. Because our era is marked by both continuity and change, this would be fruitless. Rather, our task is to provide a means of distilling and blending the wisdom in both positions by developing a coherent theoretical framework for the political analysis of interdependence. We shall develop several different but potentially complementary models, or intellectual tools, for grasping the reality of interdependence in contemporary world politics. Equally important, we shall attempt to explore the *conditions* under which each model will be most likely to produce accurate predictions and satisfactory explanations. Contemporary world politics is not a seamless web; it is a tapestry of diverse relationships. In such a world, one model cannot explain all situations. The secret of understanding lies in knowing which approach or combination of approaches to use in analyzing a situation. There will never be a substitute for careful analysis of actual situations.

Yet theory is inescapable; all empirical or practical analysis rests on it Pragmatic policymakers might think that they need pay no more heed to theoretical disputes over the nature of world politics than they pay to medieval scholastic disputes over how many angels can dance on the head of a pin. Academic pens, however, leave marks in the minds of statesmen with profound results for policy. Not only are "practical men who believe themselves to be quite exempt from any intellectual influences" unconscious captives of conceptions created by "some academic scribbler of a few years back," but increasingly the scribblers have been playing a direct role in forming foreign policy.[7] Inappropriate images and ill-conceived perceptions of world politics can lead directly to inappropriate or even disastrous national policies.

Rationale and rationalization, systematic presentation and symbolism, become so intertwined that it is difficult, even for policymakers themselves, to disentangle reality from rhetoric. Traditionally, classical theories of world politics have portrayed a potential "state of war" in which states' behavior was dominated by the constant danger of military conflict. During the Cold War, especially the first decade after World War II, this conception, labeled "political realism" by its proponents, became widely accepted by students and practitioners of international relations in Europe and the United States.[8] During the 1960s, many otherwise keen observers who accepted realist approaches were slow to perceive the development of new issues that did not center on military-security concerns.* The same dominant image in the late 1970s or 1980s would be likely to lead to even more unrealistic expectations. Yet to exchange it for an equally simple view — for instance, that military force is obsolete and economic interdependence benign — would condemn one to equally grave, though different, errors.

What are the major features of world politics when interdependence, particularly economic interdependence, is extensive?[9] This is one of the two major questions we address in this book. In Chapter 2 we explore this question in general terms; in Chapter 5 and part of Chapter 7 we investigate it further in four case studies; and Chapter 8 examines the implications for American foreign policy. To lay the groundwork for these analyses, in the rest of this chapter we define what we mean by interdependence, differentiate its major types, and relate them to the concept of power, which remains fundamental to the analysis of world politics.

Interdependence affects world politics and the behavior of states; but governmental actions also influence patterns of interdependence. By creating or accepting procedures, rules, or institutions for certain kinds of activity, governments regulate and control transnational and interstate relations. We refer to these governing arrangements as *international regimes.* The second major question of this book is, How and why do international regimes change? Chapter 3 develops a set of explanations for the development of international regimes, and their eventual decline. In Chapter 6 we apply these explanations to issues of oceans and money, and in Chapter 7 we use them to understand some features of Canadian-American and Australian-American relationships.

* In *The Troubled Partnership* (New York: McGraw-Hill for the Council on Foreign Relations, 1965) Henry A. Kissinger discussed alliance problems with hardly a reference to economic issues, although economic issues were beginning seriously to divide the NATO allies.

But interdependence is not simply an analytical concept. It is also a rhetorical device employed by publicists and statesmen. For the statesman, eager to increase the number of people marching beneath his banner, vague words with broad appeal are useful. For the analyst, such vagueness is the path to a swamp of confusion. Before we can construct usable concepts, much less increase our understanding of interdependence and regime change, we must clear a way through the rhetorical jungle. Our task is to analyze the politics of interdependence, not to celebrate it.

THE NEW RHETORIC OF INTERDEPENDENCE

During the Cold War, "national security" was a slogan American political leaders used to generate support for their policies. The rhetoric of national security justified strategies designed, at considerable cost, to bolster the economic, military, and political structure of the "free world." It also provided a rationale for international cooperation and support for the United Nations, as well as justification for alliances, foreign aid, and extensive military involvements.

National security became the favorite symbol of the internationalists who favored increased American involvement in world affairs. The key foreign policy coordinating unit in the White House was named the National Security Council. The Truman administration used the alleged Soviet threat to American security to push the loan to Britain and then the Marshall Plan through Congress. The Kennedy administration employed the security argument to promote the 1962 Trade Expansion Act. Presidents invoked national security to control certain sectoral economic interests in Congress, particularly those favoring protectionist trade policies. Congressmen who protested adverse economic effects on their districts or increased taxes were assured — and in turn explained to constituents — that the "national security interest" required their sacrifice. At the same time, special interests frequently manipulated the symbolism of national security for their own purposes, as in the case of petroleum import quotas, promoted particularly by domestic oil producers and their political allies.[10]

National security symbolism was largely a product of the Cold War and the severe threat Americans then felt. Its persuasiveness was increased by realist analysis, which insisted that national security is the primary national goal and that in international politics security threats are permanent. National security symbolism, and the realist mode of analysis that supported it, not only epitomized a certain way of reacting to events, but helped to codify a perspective in which some changes, particularly those toward radical regimes in Third World countries, seemed inimical to national security, while fundamental changes in the economic relations among advanced industrialized countries seemed insignificant.

As the Cold War sense of security threat slackened, foreign economic competition and domestic distributional conflict increased. The intellectual ambiguity of "national security" became more pronounced as varied and often contradictory forms of involvement took shelter under a single rhetorical umbrella.[11] In his imagery of a world balance of power among five major centers (the United States, the Soviet Union, China, Europe, Japan), President Nixon tried unsuccessfully to extend traditional realist concepts to apply to the economic challenge posed by America's postwar allies, as well as the political and military actions of the Soviet Union and China.

As the descriptive accuracy of a view of national security dominated by military concerns declined, so did the term's symbolic power. This decline reflected not only the increased ambiguity of the concept, but also American reaction to the Vietnam imbroglio, to the less hostile relationship with Russia and China summed up by the word *detente,* and to the misuse of national security rhetoric by President Nixon in the Watergate affair. National security had to share its position as the prime symbol in the internationalists' lexicon with *interdependence.*

Political leaders often use interdependence rhetoric to portray interdependence as a natural necessity, as a fact to which policy (and domestic interest groups) must adjust, rather than as a situation partially created by policy itself. They usually argue that conflicts of interest are reduced by interdependence, and that cooperation alone holds the answer to world problems.

"We are all engaged in a common enterprise. No nation or group of nations can gain by pushing beyond the limits that sustain world economic growth. No one benefits from basing progress on tests of strength." [12] These words clearly belong to a statesman intending to limit demands from the Third World and influence public attitudes at home, rather than to analyze contemporary reality. For those who wish the United States to retain world leadership, interdependence has become part of the new rhetoric, to be used against both economic nationalism at home and assertive challenges abroad. Although the connotations of interdependence rhetoric may seem quite different from those of national security symbolism each has often been used to legitimize American presidential leadership in world affairs.

Yet interdependence rhetoric and national security symbolism coexist only uneasily. In its extreme formulation, the former suggests that conflicts of interest are passé, whereas the latter argues that they are, and will remain, fundamental, and potentially violent. The confusion in knowing what analytical models to apply to world politics (as we noted earlier) is thus paralleled by confusion about the policies that should be employed by the United States. Neither interdependence rhetoric nor national security symbolism provides reliable guidelines for problems of extensive interdependence.

Rhetoriticians of interdependence often claim that since the survival of the human race is threatened by environmental as well as military dangers, conflicts of interest among states and peoples no longer exist. This conclusion would only follow if three conditions were met: an international economic system on which everyone depended or our basic life-supporting ecological system were in danger; all countries were significantly vulnerable to such a catastrophe; *and* there were only one solution to the problem (leaving no room for conflict about how to solve it and who should bear the costs). Obviously these conditions are rarely all present.

Yet balance of power theories and national security imagery are also poorly adapted to analyzing problems of economic or ecological interdependence. Security, in traditional terms, is not likely to be the principal issue facing governments. Insofar as military force is ineffective on certain issues, the conventional notion of power lacks precision. In particular, different power resources may be needed to deal with different issues. Finally, in the politics of interdependence, domestic and transnational as well as governmental interests are involved. Domestic and foreign policy become closely linked. The notion of national interest — the traditionalists' lodestar — becomes increasingly difficult to use effectively. Traditional maxims of international politics — that states will act in their national interests or that they will attempt to maximize their power — become ambiguous.

We are not suggesting that international conflict disappears when interdependence prevails. On the contrary, conflict will take new forms, and may even increase. But the traditional approaches to understanding conflict in world politics will not explain interdependence conflict particularly well. Applying the wrong image and the wrong rhetoric to problems will lead to erroneous analysis and bad policy.

INTERDEPENDENCE AS AN ANALYTIC CONCEPT

In common parlance, *dependence* means a state of being determined or significantly affected by external forces. *Interdependence*, most simply defined, means *mutual* dependence. Interdependence in world politics refers to situations characterized by reciprocal effects among countries or among actors in different countries.

These effects often result from international transactions — flows of money, goods, people, and messages across international boundaries. Such transactions have increased dramatically since World War II: "Recent decades reveal a general tendency for many forms of human interconnectedness across national boundaries to be doubling every ten years." [13] Yet this interconnectedness is not the same as interdependence. The effects of transactions on interdependence will depend on the constraints, or costs, associated with them. A country that imports all of its oil is likely to be more dependent on a continual flow of petroleum than a country importing furs, jewelry, and perfume (even of equivalent monetary value) will be on uninterrupted access to these luxury goods. Where there are reciprocal (although not necessarily symmetrical) costly effects of transactions, there is interdependence. Where interactions do not have significant costly effects, there is simply interconnectedness. The distinction is vital if we are to understand the *politics* of interdependence.

Costly effects may be imposed directly and intentionally by another actor — as in Soviet-American strategic interdependence, which derives from the mutual threat of nuclear destruction. But some costly effects do not come directly or intentionally from other actors. For example, collective action may be necessary to prevent disaster for an alliance (the members of which are interdependent), for an international economic system (which may face chaos because of the absence of coordination, rather than through the malevolence of any actor), or for an ecological system threatened by a gradual increase of industrial effluents.

We do not limit the term *interdependence* to situations of mutual benefit. Such a definition would assume that the concept is only useful analytically where the modernist view of the world prevails: where threats of military force are few and levels of conflict are low. It would exclude from interdependence cases of mutual dependence, such as the strategic interdependence between the United States and the Soviet Union. Furthermore, it would make it very ambiguous whether relations between industrialized countries and less developed countries should be considered interdependent or not. Their inclusion would depend on an inherently subjective judgment about whether the relationships were "mutually beneficial."

Because we wish to avoid sterile arguments about whether a given set of relationships is characterized by interdependence or not, and because we seek to use the concept of interdependence to integrate rather than further to divide modernist and traditional approaches, we choose a broader definition. Our perspective implies that interdependent relationships will always involve costs, since interdependence restricts autonomy; but it is impossible to specify *a priori* whether the benefits of a relationship will exceed the costs. This will depend on the values of the actors as well as on the nature of the relationship. Nothing guarantees that relationships that we designate as "interdependent" will be characterized by mutual benefit.

Two different perspectives can be adopted for analyzing the costs and benefits of an interdependent relationship. The first focuses on the joint gains or joint losses to the parties involved. The other stresses *relative* gains and distributional issues. Classical economists adopted the first approach in formulating their powerful insight about comparative advantage: that undistorted international trade will provide overall net benefits. Unfortunately, an exclusive focus on joint gain may obscure the second key issue: how those gains are divided. Many of the crucial political issues of interdependence revolve around the old question of politics, "who gets what?"

It is important to guard against the assumption that measures that increase joint gain from a relationship will somehow be free of distributional conflict. Governments and nongovernmental organizations will strive to increase their shares of gains from transactions, even when they both profit enormously from the relationship. Oil-exporting governments and multinational oil companies, for instance, share an interest in high prices for petroleum; but they have also been in conflict over shares of the profits involved.

We must therefore be cautious about the prospect that rising interdependence is creating a brave new world of cooperation to replace the bad old world of international conflict. As every parent of small children knows, baking a larger pie does not stop disputes over the size of the slices. An optimistic approach would overlook the uses of economic and even ecological interdependence in competitive international politics.

The difference between traditional international politics and the politics of economic and ecological interdependence is *not* the difference between a world of "zero-sum" (where one side's gain is the other side's loss) and "nonzero-sum" games. Military interdependence need not be zero-sum. Indeed, military allies actively seek interdependence to provide enhanced security for all. Even balance of power situations need not be zero-sum. If one side seeks to upset the status quo, then its gain is at the expense of the other. But if most or all participants want a stable status quo, they can jointly gain by preserving the balance of power among them. Conversely, the politics of economic and ecological interdependence involve competition even when large net benefits can be expected from cooperation. There are important continuities, as well as marked differences, between the traditional politics of military security and the politics of economic and ecological interdependence.

We must also be careful not to define interdependence entirely in terms of situations of *evenly balanced* mutual dependence. It is *asymmetries* in dependence that are most likely to provide sources of influence for actors in their dealings with one another. Less dependent actors can often use the interdependent relationship as a source of power in bargaining over an issue and perhaps to affect other issues. At the other extreme from pure symmetry is pure dependence (sometimes disguised by calling the situation interdependence); but it too is rare. Most cases lie between these two extremes. And that is where the heart of the political bargaining process of interdependence lies.

POWER AND INTERDEPENDENCE

Power has always been an elusive concept for statesmen and analysts of international politics; now it is even more slippery. The traditional view was that military power dominated other forms, and that states with the most military power controlled world affairs. But the resources that produce power capabilities have become more complex. In the eyes of one astute observer, "the postwar era has witnessed radical transformations in the elements, the uses, and the achievements of power." [14] And Hans Morgenthau, author of the leading realist text on international politics, went so far in his reaction to the events of the early 1970s as to announce an historically unprecedented severing of the functional relationship between political, military, and economic power shown in the possession by militarily weak countries of "monopolistic or quasi-monopolistic control of raw materials essential to the operation of advanced economies." [15]

Power can be thought of as the ability of an actor to get others to do something they otherwise would not do (and at an acceptable cost to the actor). Power can also be conceived in terms of control over outcomes. In either case, measurement is not simple. [16] We can look at the initial power resources that give an actor a potential ability; or we can look at that actor's actual influence over patterns of outcomes. When we say that asymmetrical interdependence can be a source of power we are thinking of power as control over resources, or the *potential* to affect outcomes. A less dependent actor in a relationship often has a significant political resource, because changes in the relationship (which the actor may be able to initiate or threaten) will be less costly to that actor than to its partners. This advantage does not guarantee, however, that the political resources provided by favorable asymmetries in interdependence will lead to similar patterns of control over outcomes. There is rarely a one-to-one relationship between power measured by any type of resources and power measured by effects on outcomes. Political bargaining is the usual means of translating potential into effects, and a lot is often lost in the translation.

To understand the role of power in interdependence, we must distinguish between two dimensions, *sensitivity* and *vulnerability*. Sensitivity involves degrees of responsiveness within a policy framework — how quickly do changes in one country bring costly changes in another, and how great are the costly effects? It is measured not merely by the volume of flows across borders but also by the costly effects of changes in transactions on the societies or governments. Sensitivity interdependence is created by interactions within a framework of policies. Sensitivity assumes that the framework remains unchanged. The fact that a set of policies remains constant may reflect the difficulty in formulating new policies within a short time, or it may reflect a commitment to a certain pattern of domestic and international rules.

An example of sensitivity dependence is the way the United States, Japan, and Western Europe were affected by increased oil prices in 1971 and again in 1973–74 and 1975. In the absence of new policies, which could take many years or decades to implement, the sensitivity of these economies was a function of the greater costs of foreign oil and the proportion of petroleum they imported. The United States was less sensitive than Japan to petroleum price rises, because a smaller proportion of its petroleum requirements was accounted for by imports, but as rapid price increases and long lines at gasoline stations showed, the United States was indeed sensitive to the outside change. Another example of sensitivity interdependence is provided by the international monetary situation prior to August 15, 1971. Given the constraints on policy created by the rules of the International Monetary Fund (IMF), European governments were sensitive to changes in American monetary policy, and the United States was sensitive to European decisions whether or not to demand the conversion of dollars into gold.

Sensitivity interdependence can be social or political as well as economic.* For example, there are social "contagion effects," such as the trivial but rapid spread of the fad of "streaking" from American to European society in 1974, or, more significant, the way in which the development of radical student movements during the late 1960s was reinforced by knowledge of each other's activities. The rapid growth of transnational communications has enhanced such sensitivity. Television, by vividly presenting starvation in South Asia to Europeans and Americans about to sit down to their dinners, is almost certain to increase attention to and concern about the issue in European and American societies. Sensitivity to such an issue may be reflected in demonstrations or other political

---

* Since we are referring to the sensitivity of economies and polities to one another, not merely to price sensitivities or interest rate sensitivities as used by economists, our definition builds on, but differs from, that of Richard Cooper, *The Economics of Interdependence* (New York: McGraw-Hill, 1968).

action, even if no action is taken to alleviate the distress (and no economic sensitivity thereby results).

Using the word *interdependence*, however, to refer only to sensitivity obscures some of the most important political aspects of mutual dependence.[17] We must also consider what the situation would be if the framework of policies could be changed. If more alternatives were available, and new and very different policies were possible, what would be the costs of adjusting to the outside change? In petroleum, for instance, what matters is not only the proportion of one's needs that is imported, but the alternatives to imported energy and the costs of pursuing those alternatives. Two countries, each importing 35 percent of their petroleum needs, may seem equally sensitive to price rises; but if one could shift to domestic sources at moderate cost, and the other had no such alternative, the second state would be more *vulnerable* than the first. The vulnerability dimension of interdependence rests on the relative availability and costliness of the alternatives that various actors face.

Under the Bretton Woods monetary regime during the late 1960s, both the United States and Great Britain were sensitive to decisions by foreign speculators or central banks to shift assets out of dollars or sterling, respectively. But the United States was less vulnerable than Britain because it had the option (which it exercised in August 1971) of changing the rules of the system at what it considered tolerable costs. The underlying capabilities of the United States reduced its vulnerability, and therefore made its sensitivity less serious politically.

In terms of the costs of dependence, sensitivity means liability to costly effects imposed from outside before policies are altered to try to change the situation. Vulnerability can be defined as an actor's liability to suffer costs imposed by external events even after policies have been altered. Since it is usually difficult to change policies quickly, immediate effects of external changes generally reflect sensitivity dependence. Vulnerability dependence can be measured only by the costliness of making effective adjustments to a changed environment over a period of time.

Let us illustrate this distinction graphically by imagining three countries faced simultaneously with an external event that imposes costs on them — for example, the situation that oil-consuming countries face when producers raise prices.

Figure 1.1 indicates the sensitivity of the three countries to costs imposed by such an outside change. Initially, country A has somewhat higher sensitivity to the change than B and much higher sensitivity than C. Over time, furthermore, C's sensitivity falls *even without any policy changes*. This change might be caused by price rises in country C, which gradually reduce oil consumption, and therefore reduce imports. The total

FIGURE 1.1 Sensitivity of three
countries (assume policies unchanged)

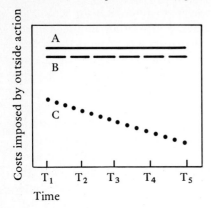

FIGURE 1.2 Vulnerability of three
countries (assume policy changed)

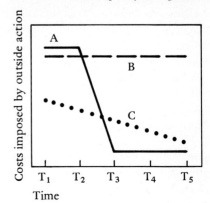

sensitivity of each country over the time covered by the graph is represented by the area under its respective line.*

Suppose we now alter this picture by assuming that each country tries
to change its policies in order to reduce the costs imposed by outside
actions. In our oil example, this attempt might involve deciding to incur
the high domestic costs of rationing or developing expensive internal
energy sources. The extent of these costs and the political willingness to
bear them would be the measure of vulnerability. The vulnerability of a
country such as Japan is imposed primarily by that country's physical en-
dowments and is virtually inescapable without drastic costs. For other
countries, such as the United States, physical vulnerability is not so great,
but sociopolitical constraints on policy change may cause vulnerability.
For instance, American efforts to formulate a new energy policy after
1973 were slowed by the lack of domestic consensus on the issue.

In Figure 1.2, depicting vulnerability, we can see that country *A*'s
vulnerability is much less than its sensitivity. A policy change at the
beginning of the second time period allows that country, by the third
period, to reduce costs imposed by external change almost to the vanishing
point. Country *A*'s diminished vulnerability would reflect an effective
policy to become actually or potentially self-sufficient in petroleum. For
instance, it might possess new sources of energy that could be developed
by the government. *B* and *C* are less able to alter their situations by
changing policy, thus remaining vulnerable to costs imposed by outside
events.

* Our example is deliberately simplified. Among other things, the costs of the situation
at later points would, of course, have to be reduced by an appropriate discount rate.

The sensitivity dependence of the three countries at the time of the first external event is not, therefore, the same as their vulnerability dependence at that time. Measures of the immediate effects of changes will not precisely indicate long-term sensitivities (note that C's sensitivity declines naturally over time), but they are likely to be even less accurate in measuring long-term vulnerabilities, which will depend on political will, governmental ability, and resource capabilities. In our example, although country A is more sensitive than country B, it is much less vulnerable.

Vulnerability is particularly important for understanding the political structure of interdependence relationships. In a sense, it focuses on which actors are "the definers of the *ceteris paribus* clause," or can set the rules of the game.[18] Vulnerability is clearly more relevant than sensitivity, for example, in analyzing the politics of raw materials such as the supposed transformation of power after 1973. All too often, a high percentage of imports of a material is taken as an index of vulnerability, when by itself it merely suggests that sensitivity may be high. The key question for determining vulnerability is how effectively altered policies could bring into being sufficient quantities of this, or a comparable, raw material, and at what cost. The fact that the United States imports approximately 85 percent of its bauxite supply does not indicate American vulnerability to actions by bauxite exporters, until we know what it would cost (in time as well as money) to obtain substitutes.

Vulnerability applies to sociopolitical as well as politico-economic relationships. The vulnerability of societies to transnational radical movements in the late 1960s depended on their abilities to adjust national policies to deal with the change and reduce the costs of disruption. When Sweden criticized American policy in Vietnam, its vulnerability to a possible American suspension of cultural contacts would have depended on how it could adjust policy to the new situation. Could exchange professors and tourists be attracted from elsewhere?[19]

Let us look again at the effects on the United States of a famine in South Asia. The vulnerability of an American administration to domestic protests over its lack of a food aid policy would depend on the ease with which it could adjust policy (for instance, by shipping more grain to India) without incurring other high political or economic costs.

How does this distinction help us understand the relationship between interdependence and power? Clearly, it indicates that sensitivity interdependence will be less important than vulnerability interdependence in providing power resources to actors. If one actor can reduce its costs by altering its policy, either domestically or internationally, the sensitivity patterns will not be a good guide to power resources.

Consider trade in agricultural products between the United States and the Soviet Union from 1972 to 1975. Initially, the American economy was highly sensitive to Soviet grain purchases: prices of grain rose dramatically in the United States. The Soviet Union was also sensitive to the availability of surplus American stocks, since its absence could have internal political as well as economic implications. The vulnerability asymmetries, however, ran strongly in favor of the United States, since its alternatives to selling grain to the USSR (such as government storage, lower domestic prices, and more food aid abroad) were more attractive than the basic Soviet alternative to buying grain from the United States (slaughtering livestock and reducing meat consumption). Thus, as long as the United States government could retain coherent control of the policy — that is, as long as interest groups with a stake in expanded trade did not control it — agricultural trade could be used as a tool in political bargaining with the Soviet Union.

Vulnerability interdependence includes the strategic dimension that sensitivity interdependence omits, but this does not mean that sensitivity is politically unimportant. Rapidly rising sensitivity often leads to complaints about interdependence and political efforts to alter it, particularly in countries with pluralistic political systems. Textile and steel workers and manufacturers, oil consumers, and conservatives suspicious of radical movements originating abroad are all likely to demand government policies to protect their interests. Policymakers and policy analysts, however, must examine underlying patterns of vulnerability interdependence when they decide on strategies. What can they do, at what cost? And what can other actors do, at what cost, in response? Although patterns of sensitivity interdependence may explain where the shoe pinches or the wheel squeaks, coherent policy must be based on an analysis of actual and potential vulnerabilities. An attempt to manipulate asymmetrical sensitivity interdependence without regard for underlying patterns of vulnerability is likely to fail.

Manipulating economic or sociopolitical vulnerabilities, however, also bears risks. Strategies of manipulating interdependence are likely to lead to counterstrategies. It must always be kept in mind, furthermore, that military power dominates economic power in the sense that economic means alone are likely to be ineffective against the serious use of military force. Thus, even effective manipulation of asymmetrical interdependence within a nonmilitary area can create risks of military counteraction. When the United States exploited Japanese vulnerability to economic embargo in 1940–41, Japan countered by attacking Pearl Harbor and the Philippines. Yet military actions are usually very costly; and for many types of actions, these costs have risen steeply during the last thirty years.

Table 1.1 shows the three types of asymmetrical interdependence that we have been discussing. The dominance ranking column indicates that the power resources provided by military interdependence dominate those

TABLE 1.1   ASYMMETRICAL INTERDEPENDENCE AND ITS USES

Source of interdependence	Dominance ranking	Cost ranking	Contemporary use
Military (costs of using military force)	1	1	Used in extreme situations or against weak foes when costs may be slight.
Nonmilitary vulnerability (costs of pursuing alternative policies)	2	2	Used when normative constraints are low, and international rules are not considered binding (including nonmilitary relations between adversaries, and situations of extremely high conflict between close partners and allies).
Nonmilitary sensitivity (costs of change under existing policies)	3	3	A power resource in the short run or when normative constraints are high and international rules are binding. Limited, since if high costs are imposed, disadvantaged actors may formulate new policies.

provided by nonmilitary vulnerability, which in turn dominate those provided by asymmetries in sensitivity. Yet exercising more dominant forms of power brings higher costs. Thus, *relative to cost,* there is no guarantee that military means will be more effective than economic ones to achieve a given purpose. We can expect, however, that as the interests at stake become more important, actors will tend to use power resources that rank higher in both dominance and cost.

A movement from one power resource to a more effective, but more costly, resource, will be most likely where there is a substantial *incongruity* between the distribution of power resources on one dimension and those on another. In such a situation, the disadvantaged actor's power position would be improved by raising the level at which the controversy is conducted. For instance, in a concession agreement, a multinational oil company may seem to have a better bargaining position than the host government. The agreement may allow the company to set the level of output, and the price, of the petroleum produced, thus making government revenues sensitive to company decisions. Yet such a situation is inherently unstable, since the government may be stronger on the vulnerability dimension. Once the country has determined that it can afford to alter the agreement unilaterally, it may have the upper hand. Any attempt by the company to take advantage of its superior position on the sensitivity dimension, without recognizing its weakness at the vulnerability level (much less at the level of military force) is then likely to end in disaster.

We conclude that a useful beginning in the political analysis of international interdependence can be made by thinking of asymmetrical interdependencies as sources of power among actors. Such a framework can be applied to relations between transnational actors (such as multinational corporations) and governments as well as interstate relations. Different types of interdependence lead to potential political influence, but under different constraints. Sensitivity interdependence can provide the basis for significant political influence only when the rules and norms in effect can be taken for granted, or when it would be prohibitively costly for dissatisfied states to change their policies quickly. If one set of rules puts an actor in a disadvantageous position, that actor will probably try to change those rules if it can do so at reasonable cost. Thus influence deriving from favorable asymmetries in sensitivity is very limited when the underlying asymmetries in vulnerability are unfavorable. Likewise, if a state chafes at its economic vulnerabilities, it may use military force to attempt to redress that situation as Japan did in 1941; or, it may subtly threaten to use force, as did the United States in 1975, when facing the possibility of future oil boycotts. But in many contemporary situations, the use of force is so costly, and its threat so difficult to make credible, that a military strategy is an act of desperation.

Yet this is not the whole story of power and interdependence. Just as important as understanding the way that manipulation of interdependence can be an instrument of power is an understanding of that instrument's limits. Asymmetrical interdependence by itself cannot explain bargaining outcomes, even in traditional relations among states. As we said earlier, power measured in terms of resources or potential may look different from power measured in terms of influence over outcomes. We must also look at the "translation" in the political bargaining process. One of the most important reasons for this is that the commitment of a weaker state may be much greater than that of its stronger partner. The more dependent actor may be (or appear to be) more willing to suffer. At the politico-military level, the United States' attempt to coerce North Vietnam provides an obvious example.

Yet the point holds even in more cooperative interstate relations. In the Canadian-American relationship, for example, the use or threat of force is virtually excluded from consideration by either side. The fact that Canada has less military strength than the United States is therefore not a major factor in the bargaining process. The Canadians can take advantage of their superior position on such economic issues as oil and natural gas exports without fearing military retaliation or threat by the United States. Moreover, other conditions of contemporary international interdependence tend to limit the abilities of statesmen to manipulate asymmetrical interdependence. In particular, the smaller state may have greater internal political unity than the larger one. Even though the more powerful state may be less dependent in aggregate terms, it may be more fragmented internally and its coherence reduced by conflicts of interest and difficulties of coordination within its own government.

We will explore this question further in Chapter 7 when discussing our findings on Canadian-American and Australian-American relations between 1920 and 1970. What we have said is sufficient to indicate that we do not expect a measure of potential power, such as asymmetrical interdependence, to predict perfectly actors' successes or failures at influencing outcomes. It merely provides a first approximation of initial bargaining advantages available to either side. Where predictions based on patterns of asymmetrical interdependence are incorrect, one must look closely for the reasons. They will often be found in the bargaining process that translates power resources into power over outcomes.

INTERNATIONAL REGIME CHANGE

Understanding the concept of interdependence and its relevance to the concept of power is necessary to answering the first major question of this book — what are the characteristics of world politics under conditions of extensive interdependence? Yet as we have indicated, relationships of interdependence often occur within, and may be affected by, networks of rules, norms, and procedures that regularize behavior and control its effects. We refer to the sets of governing arrangements that affect relationships of interdependence as *international regimes*. Although not so obvious as the political bargaining process, equally important to understanding power and interdependence is our second major question: How and why do regimes change?

In world politics rules and procedures are neither so complete nor so well enforced as in well-ordered domestic political systems, and the institutions are neither so powerful nor so autonomous. "The rules of the game include some national rules, some international rules, some private rules — and large areas of no rules at all." [20] The weakness of international organizations and the problems of enforcing international law sometimes mislead observers into thinking that international regimes are insignificant, or into ignoring them entirely. Yet although overall global integration is

weak, specific international regimes often have important effects on interdependent relationships that involve a few countries, or involve many
countries on a specific issue. Since World War II, for instance, specific
sets of rules and procedures have been developed to guide states and
transnational actors in a wide variety of areas, including aid to less developed countries, environmental protection, fisheries conservation, international food policy, international meteorological coordination, international
monetary policy, regulation of multinational corporations, international
shipping policy, international telecommunications policy, and international trade.[21] In some cases these regimes have been formal and comprehensive; in others informal and partial. Their effectiveness has varied
from issue-area to issue-area and from time to time. On a more selective
or regional level, specific groups of countries such as those in the European Community or the Organization for Economic Cooperation and
Development (OECD) have developed regimes that affect several aspects
of their countries' relationships with each other.

International regimes may be incorporated into interstate agreements
or treaties, as were the international monetary arrangements developed at
Bretton Woods in 1944, or they may evolve from proposed formal arrangements that were never implemented, as was the General Agreement on
Tariffs and Trade (GATT), which derived from the International Trade
Organization proposed after World War II. Or they may be merely implicit, as in the postwar Canadian-American relationship. They vary not
only in their extensiveness but in the degree of adherence they receive
from major actors. When there are no agreed norms and procedures or
when the exceptions to the rules are more important than the instances
of adherence, there is a *nonregime* situation.*

To understand the international regimes that affect patterns of interdependence, one must look, as we will in Chapter 3, at structure and process
in international systems, as well as at how they affect each other. The
structure of a system refers to the distribution of capabilities among similar units. In international political systems the most important units are
states, and the relevant capabilities have been regarded as their power
resources. There is a long tradition of categorizing the distribution of
power in interstate systems according to the number and importance of
major actors (for instance, as unipolar, bipolar, multipolar, and dispersed)
just as economists describe the structure of market systems as monopolistic, duopolistic, oligopolistic, and competitive.[22] Structure is therefore

---

* We are concerned in this book with the general question of adherence to specified
basic norms of the regimes we examine. Regimes can also be categorized in terms of
the degree and type of political integration among the states adhering to them. See J.
S. Nye, *Peace in Parts* (Boston: Little, Brown, 1971), Chapter 2, for discussion of
measurement of the integrative and institutional dimensions of regimes.

distinguished from *process*, which refers to allocative or bargaining behavior within a power structure. To use the analogy of a poker game, at the process level analysts are interested in how the players play the hands they have been dealt. At the structural level they are interested in how the cards and chips were distributed as the game started.

International regimes are intermediate factors between the power structure of an international system and the political and economic bargaining that takes place within it. The structure of the system (the distribution of power resources among states) profoundly affects the nature of the regime (the more or less loose set of formal and informal norms, rules, and procedures relevant to the system). The regime, in turn, affects and to some extent governs the political bargaining and daily decision-making that occurs within the system.

Changes in international regimes are very important. In international trade, for example, an international regime including nondiscriminatory trade practices was laid down by the General Agreement on Tariffs and Trade (GATT) in 1947. For almost three decades, the GATT arrangements have constituted a relatively effective international regime. But the last decade, particularly since the first United Nations Conference on Trade and Development in 1964, has been marked by the partly successful efforts of less developed countries to change this regime. More broadly, by the mid-1970s, the demands of less developed countries for a New International Economic Order involved struggles over what international regimes should govern trade in raw materials and manufactures as well as direct foreign investment.

In the two issue areas that we will investigate in Part II — money and oceans — some regime changes have been rapid and dramatic whereas others have been gradual. Dramatic changes took place in international monetary policy in 1914 (suspension of the gold standard); 1931 (abandonment of the gold-exchange standard); 1944 (agreement on the "Bretton Woods System"); and 1971 (abandonment of the convertibility of dollars into gold). Rules governing the uses of the world's oceans changed more slowly, but with significant turning points in 1945 and after 1967. Yet we have no theory in the field of international relations that adequately explains such changes. Indeed, most of our theories do not focus on this question at all.

In Chapter 3, we shall look closely at the problem of explaining the change or persistence in the patterns of norms, rules, and procedures that govern interdependence in various issues. There we will lay out four models, or intellectual constructs, designed to explain regime change, and examine their strengths and weaknesses. The models rest on different assumptions about the basic conditions of world politics. Since world politics varies, over time and from place to place, there is no reason to believe that a single set of conditions will always and everywhere apply, or that any one model is likely to be universally applicable. Thus, before examining the explanatory models, we shall establish the conditions under which they can be expected to apply. As we indicate in the next chapter, in periods of rapid change such as the current one, assumptions about the conditions of world politics can differ dramatically.

Chapter 2 | REALISM AND COMPLEX INTERDEPENDENCE

One's assumptions about world politics profoundly affect what one sees and how one constructs theories to explain events. We believe that the assumptions of political realists, whose theories dominated the postwar period, are often an inadequate basis for analyzing the politics of interdependence. The realist assumptions about world politics can be seen as defining an extreme set of conditions or *ideal type*. One could also imagine very different conditions. In this chapter, we shall construct another ideal type, the opposite of realism. We call it *complex interdependence*. After establishing the differences between realism and complex interdependence, we shall argue that complex interdependence sometimes comes closer to reality than does realism. When it does, traditional explanations of change in international regimes become questionable and the search for new explanatory models becomes more urgent.

For political realists, international politics, like all other politics, is a struggle for power but, unlike domestic politics, a struggle dominated by organized violence. In the words of the most influential postwar textbook, "All history shows that nations active in international politics are continuously preparing for, actively involved in, or recovering from organized violence in the form of war."[1] Three assumptions are integral to the realist vision. First, states as coherent units are the dominant actors in world politics. This is a double assumption: states are predominant; and they act as coherent units. Second, realists assume that force is a usable and effective instrument of policy. Other instruments may also be employed, but using or threatening force is the most effective means of wielding power. Third, partly because of their second assumption, realists assume a hierarchy of issues in world politics, headed by questions of military security: the "high politics" of military security dominates the "low politics" of economic and social affairs.

These realist assumptions define an ideal type of world politics. They allow us to imagine a world in which politics is continually characterized by active or potential conflict among states, with the use of force possible at any time. Each state attempts to defend its territory and interests from real or perceived threats. Political integration among states is slight and lasts only as long as it serves the national interests of the most powerful states. Transnational actors either do not exist or are politically unimportant. Only the adept exercise of force or the threat of force permits states to survive, and only while statesmen succeed in adjusting their interests, as in a well-functioning balance of power, is the system stable.

Each of the realist assumptions can be challenged. If we challenge them all simultaneously, we can imagine a world in which actors other than states participate directly in world politics, in which a clear hierarchy of issues does not exist, and in which force is an ineffective instrument of policy. Under these conditions — which we call the characteristics of complex interdependence — one would expect world politics to be very different than under realist conditions.

We will explore these differences in the next section of this chapter. We do not argue, however, that complex interdependence faithfully reflects world political reality. Quite the contrary: both it and the realist portrait are ideal types. Most situations will fall somewhere between these two extremes. Sometimes, realist assumptions will be accurate, or largely accurate, but frequently complex interdependence will provide a better portrayal of reality. Before one decides what explanatory model to apply to a situation or problem, one will need to understand the degree to which realist or complex interdependence assumptions correspond to the situation.

THE CHARACTERISTICS OF COMPLEX INTERDEPENDENCE

Complex interdependence has three main characteristics:

1. *Multiple channels* connect societies, including: informal ties between governmental elites as well as formal foreign office arrangements; informal ties among nongovernmental elites (face-to-face and through telecommunications); and transnational organizations (such as multinational banks

or corporations). These channels can be summarized as interstate, transgovernmental, and transnational relations. *Interstate* relations are the normal channels assumed by realists. *Transgovernmental* applies when we relax the realist assumption that states act coherently as units; *transnational* applies when we relax the assumption that states are the only units.

2. The agenda of interstate relationships consists of multiple issues that are not arranged in a clear or consistent hierarchy. This *absence of hierarchy among issues* means, among other things, that military security does not consistently dominate the agenda. Many issues arise from what used to be considered domestic policy, and the distinction between domestic and foreign issues becomes blurred. These issues are considered in several government departments (not just foreign offices), and at several levels. Inadequate policy coordination on these issues involves significant costs. Different issues generate different coalitions, both within governments and across them, and involve different degrees of conflict. Politics does not stop at the waters' edge.

3. Military force is not used by governments toward other governments within the region, or on the issues, when complex interdependence prevails. It may, however, be important in these governments' relations with governments outside that region, or on other issues. Military force could, for instance, be irrelevant to resolving disagreements on economic issues among members of an alliance, yet at the same time be very important for that alliance's political and military relations with a rival bloc. For the former relationships this condition of complex interdependence would be met; for the latter, it would not.

Traditional theories of international politics implicitly or explicitly deny the accuracy of these three assumptions. Traditionalists are therefore tempted also to deny the relevance of criticisms based on the complex interdependence ideal type. We believe, however, that our three conditions are fairly well approximated on some global issues of economic and ecological interdependence and that they come close to characterizing the entire relationship between some countries. One of our purposes here is to prove that contention. In subsequent chapters we shall examine complex interdependence in oceans policy and monetary policy and in the relationships of the United States to Canada and Australia. In this chapter, however, we shall try to convince you to take these criticisms of traditional assumptions seriously.

Multiple Channels

A visit to any major airport is a dramatic way to confirm the existence of multiple channels of contact among advanced industrial countries; there is a voluminous literature to prove it.[2] Bureaucrats from different countries deal directly with one another at meetings and on the telephone as well as in writing. Similarly, nongovernmental elites frequently get together in the normal course of business, in organizations such as the Trilateral Commission, and in conferences sponsored by private foundations.

In addition, multinational firms and banks affect both domestic and interstate relations. The limits on private firms, or the closeness of ties between government and business, vary considerably from one society to another; but the participation of large and dynamic organizations, not controlled entirely by governments, has become a normal part of foreign as well as domestic relations.

These actors are important not only because of their activities in pursuit of their own interests, but also because they act as transmission belts, making government policies in various countries more sensitive to one another. As the scope of governments' domestic activities has broadened, and as corporations, banks, and (to a lesser extent) trade unions have made decisions that transcend national boundaries, the domestic policies of different countries impinge on one another more and more. Transnational communications reinforce these effects. Thus, foreign economic policies touch more domestic economic activity than in the past, blurring the lines between domestic and foreign policy and increasing the number of issues relevant to foreign policy. Parallel developments in issues of environmental regulation and control over technology reinforce this trend.

Absence of Hierarchy among Issues

Foreign affairs agendas — that is, sets of issues relevant to foreign policy with which governments are concerned — have become larger and more diverse. No longer can all issues be subordinated to military security. As Secretary of State Kissinger described the situation in 1975:

progress in dealing with the traditional agenda is no longer enough. A new and unprecedented kind of issue has emerged. The problems of energy, resources, environment, population, the uses of space and the seas now rank with questions of military security, ideology and territorial rivalry which have traditionally made up the diplomatic agenda.[3]

Kissinger's list, which could be expanded, illustrates how governments' policies, even those previously considered merely domestic, impinge on one another. The extensive consultative arrangements developed by the OECD, as well as the GATT, IMF, and the European Community. indicate how characteristic the overlap of domestic and foreign policy is among developed pluralist countries. The organization within nine major departments of the United States government (Agriculture, Commerce, Defense, Health, Education and Welfare, Interior, Justice, Labor, State, and Treasury) and many other agencies reflects their extensive international commitments. The multiple, overlapping issues that result make a nightmare of governmental organization.[4]

When there are multiple issues on the agenda, many of which threaten the interests of domestic groups but do not clearly threaten the nation as a whole, the problems of formulating a coherent and consistent foreign policy increase. In 1975 energy was a foreign policy problem, but specific remedies, such as a tax on gasoline and automobiles, involved domestic legislation opposed by auto workers and companies alike. As one commentator observed, "virtually every time Congress has set a national policy that changed the way people live . . . the action came after a consensus had developed, bit by bit, over the years, that a problem existed and that there was one best way to solve it."[5] Opportunities for delay, for special protection, for inconsistency and incoherence abound when international politics requires aligning the domestic policies of pluralist democratic countries.

Minor Role of Military Force

Political scientists have traditionally emphasized the role of military force in international politics. As we saw in the first chapter, force dominates other means of power: *if* there are no constraints on one's choice of instruments (a hypothetical situation that has only been approximated in the two world wars), the state with superior military force will prevail. If the security dilemma for all states were extremely acute, military force, supported by economic and other resources, would clearly be the dominant source of power. Survival is the primary goal of all states, and in the worst situations, force is ultimately necessary to guarantee survival. Thus military force is always a central component of national power.

Yet particularly among industrialized, pluralist countries, the perceived margin of safety has widened: fears of attack in general have declined, and fears of attacks *by one another* are virtually nonexistent. France has abandoned the *tous azimuts* (defense in all directions) strategy that President de Gaulle advocated (it was not taken entirely seriously even at the time). Canada's last war plans for fighting the United States were abandoned half a century ago. Britain and Germany no longer feel threatened by each other. Intense relationships of mutual influence exist between these countries, but in most of them force is irrelevant or unimportant as an instrument of policy.

Moreover, force is often not an appropriate way of achieving other goals (such as economic and ecological welfare) that are becoming more important. It is not impossible to imagine dramatic conflict or revolutionary change in which the use or threat of military force over an economic issue or among advanced industrial countries might become plausible. Then realist assumptions would again be a reliable guide to events. But in most situations, the effects of military force are both costly and uncertain.[6]

Even when the direct use of force is barred among a group of countries, however, military power can still be used politically. Each superpower continues to use the threat of force to deter attacks by other superpowers on itself or its allies; its deterrence ability thus serves an indirect, protective role, which it can use in bargaining on other issues with its allies. This bargaining tool is particularly important for the United States, whose allies are concerned about potential Soviet threats and which has fewer other means of influence over its allies than does the Soviet Union over its Eastern European partners. The United States has, accordingly, taken advantage of the Europeans' (particularly the Germans') desire for its protection and linked the issue of troop levels in Europe to trade and monetary negotiations. Thus, although the first-order effect of deterrent force is essentially negative — to deny effective offensive power to a superpower opponent — a state can use that force positively — to gain political influence.

Thus, even for countries whose relations approximate complex interdependence, two serious qualifications remain: (1) drastic social and political change could cause force again to become an important direct instrument of policy; and (2) even when elites' interests are complementary, a country that uses military force to protect another may have significant political influence over the other country.

In North-South relations, or relations among Third World countries, as well as in East-West relations, force is often important. Military power helps the Soviet Union to dominate Eastern Europe economically as well as politically. The threat of open or covert American military intervention has helped to limit revolutionary changes in the Caribbean, especially in Guatemala in 1954 and in the Dominican Republic in 1965. Secretary of State Kissinger, in January 1975, issued a veiled warning to members of the Organization of Petroleum Exporting Countries (OPEC) that the United States might use force against them "where there is some actual strangulation of the industrialized world."[7]

Even in these rather conflictual situations, however, the recourse to force seems less likely now than at most times during the century before 1945. The destructiveness of nuclear weapons makes any attack against a nuclear power dangerous. Nuclear weapons are mostly used as a deterrent. Threats of nuclear action against much weaker countries may occasionally be efficacious, but they are equally or more likely to solidify relations between one's adversaries. The limited usefulness of conventional force to control socially mobilized populations has been shown by the United States failure in Vietnam as well as by the rapid decline of colonialism in Africa. Furthermore, employing force on one issue against an independent state with which one has a variety of relationships is likely to rupture mutually profitable relations on other issues. In other words, the use of force often has costly effects on nonsecurity goals. And finally, in Western democracies, popular opposition to prolonged military conflicts is very high.[8]

It is clear that these constraints bear unequally on various countries, or on the same countries in different situations. Risks of nuclear escalation affect everyone, but domestic opinion is far less constraining for communist states, or for authoritarian regional powers, than for the United States, Europe, or Japan. Even authoritarian countries may be reluctant to use force to obtain economic objectives when such use might be ineffective and disrupt other relationships. Both the difficulty of controlling socially mobilized populations with foreign troops and the changing technology of weaponry may actually enhance the ability of certain countries, or nonstate groups, to use terrorism as a political weapon without effective fear of reprisal.

The fact that the changing role of force has uneven effects does not make the change less important, but it does make matters more complex. This complexity is compounded by differences in the usability of force among issue areas. When an issue arouses little interest or passion, force may be unthinkable. In such instances, complex interdependence may be a valuable concept for analyzing the political process. But if that issue becomes a matter of life and death — as some people thought oil might become — the use or threat of force could become decisive again. Realist assumptions would then be more relevant.

It is thus important to determine the applicability of realism or of complex interdependence to each situation. Without this determination, further analysis is likely to be confused. Our purpose in developing an alternative to the realist description of world politics is to encourage a differentiated approach that distinguishes among dimensions and areas of world politics — not (as some modernist observers do) to replace one oversimplification with another.

THE POLITICAL PROCESSES OF COMPLEX INTERDEPENDENCE

The three main characteristics of complex interdependence give rise to distinctive political processes, which translate power resources into power as control of outcomes. As we argued earlier, something is usually lost or added in the translation. Under conditions of complex interdependence the translation will be different than under realist conditions, and our predictions about outcomes will need to be adjusted accordingly.

In the realist world, military security will be the dominant goal of states. It will even affect issues that are not directly involved with military power or territorial defense. Nonmilitary problems will not only be subordinated to military ones; they will be studied for their politico-military implications. Balance of payments issues, for instance, will be considered at least as much in the light of their implications for world power generally as for their purely financial ramifications. McGeorge Bundy conformed to realist expectations when he argued in 1964 that devaluation of the dollar should be seriously considered if necessary to fight the war in Vietnam.[9] To some extent, so did former Treasury Secretary Henry Fowler when he contended in 1971 that the United States needed a trade surplus of $4 billion to $6 billion in order to lead in Western defense.[10]

In a world of complex interdependence, however, one expects some officials, particularly at lower levels, to emphasize the *variety* of state goals that must be pursued. In the absence of a clear hierarchy of issues, goals will vary by issue, and may not be closely related. Each bureaucracy will pursue its own concerns; and although several agencies may reach compromises on issues that affect them all, they will find that a consistent pattern of policy is difficult to maintain. Moreover, transnational actors will introduce different goals into various groups of issues.

Linkage Strategies

Goals will therefore vary by issue area under complex interdependence, but so will the distribution of power and the typical political processes. Traditional analysis focuses on *the* international system, and leads us to anticipate similar political processes on a variety of issues. Militarily and economically strong states will dominate a variety of organizations and a variety of issues, by linking their own policies on some issues to other states' policies on other issues. By using their overall dominance to prevail on their weak issues, the strongest states will, in the traditional model, ensure a congruence between the overall structure of military and economic power and the pattern of outcomes on any one issue area. Thus world politics can be treated as a seamless web.

Under complex interdependence, such congruence is less likely to occur. As military force is devalued, militarily strong states will find it more difficult to use their overall dominance to control outcomes on issues in which they are weak. And since the distribution of power resources in trade, shipping, or oil, for example, may be quite different, patterns of outcomes and distinctive political processes are likely to vary from one set of issues to another. If force were readily applicable, and military security were the highest foreign policy goal, these variations in the issue structures of power would not matter very much. The linkages drawn from them to military issues would ensure consistent dominance by the overall strongest states. But when military force is largely immobilized, strong states will find that linkage is less effective. They may still attempt such links, but in the absence of a hierarchy of issues, their success will be problematic.

Dominant states may try to secure much the same result by using overall economic power to affect results on other issues. If only economic objectives are at stake, they may succeed: money, after all, is fungible. But economic objectives have political implications, and economic linkage by the strong is limited by domestic, transnational, and transgovernmental actors who resist having their interests traded off. Furthermore, the international actors may be different on different issues, and the international organizations in which negotiations take place are often quite separate. Thus it is difficult, for example, to imagine a militarily or economically strong state linking concessions on monetary policy to reciprocal concessions in oceans policy. On the other hand, poor weak states are not similarly inhibited from linking unrelated issues, partly because their domestic interests are less complex. Linkage of unrelated issues is often a means of extracting concessions or side payments from rich and powerful states. And unlike powerful states whose instrument for linkage (military force) is often too costly to use, the linkage instrument used by poor, weak states — international organization — is available and inexpensive.

Thus as the utility of force declines, and as issues become more equal in importance, the distribution of power within each issue will become more important. If linkages become less effective on the whole, outcomes of political bargaining will increasingly vary by issue area.

The differentiation among issue areas in complex interdependence means that linkages among issues will become more problematic and will tend to reduce rather than reinforce international hierarchy. Linkage strategies, and defense against them, will pose critical strategic choices for states. Should issues be considered separately or as a package? If linkages are to be drawn, which issues should be linked, and on which of the linked issues should concessions be made? How far can one push a linkage before it becomes counterproductive? For instance, should one seek formal agreements or informal, but less politically sensitive, understandings? The fact that world politics under complex interdependence is not a seamless web leads us to expect that efforts to stitch seams together advantageously, as reflected in linkage strategies, will, very often, determine the shape of the fabric.

The negligible role of force leads us to expect states to rely more on other instruments in order to wield power. For the reasons we have already discussed, less vulnerable states will try to use asymmetrical interdependence in particular groups of issues as a source of power; they will also try to use international organizations and transnational actors and flows. States will approach economic interdependence in terms of power as well as its effects on citizens' welfare, although welfare considerations will limit their attempts to maximize power. Most economic and ecological interdependence involves the possibility of joint gains, or joint losses. Mutual awareness of potential gains and losses and the danger of worsening each actor's position through overly rigorous struggles over the distribution of the gains can limit the use of asymmetrical interdependence.

Agenda Setting

Our second assumption of complex interdependence, the lack of clear hierarchy among multiple issues, leads us to expect that the politics of agenda formation and control will become more important. Traditional analyses lead statesmen to focus on politico-military issues and to pay little attention to the broader politics of agenda formation. Statesmen assume that the agenda will be set by shifts in the balance of power, actual or anticipated, and by perceived threats to the security of states. Other issues will only be very important when they seem to affect security and military power. In these cases, agendas will be influenced strongly by considerations of the overall balance of power.

Yet, today, some nonmilitary issues are emphasized in interstate relations at one time, whereas others of seemingly equal importance are neglected or quietly handled at a technical level. International monetary politics, problems of commodity terms of trade, oil, food, and multinational corporations have all been important during the last decade; but not all have been high on interstate agendas throughout that period.

Traditional analysts of international politics have paid little attention to agenda formation: to how issues come to receive sustained attention by high officials. The traditional orientation toward military and security affairs implies that the crucial problems of foreign policy are imposed on states by the actions or threats of other states. These are high politics as opposed to the low politics of economic affairs. Yet, as the complexity of actors and issues in world politics increases, the utility of force declines and the line between domestic policy and foreign policy becomes blurred: as the conditions of complex interdependence are more closely approximated, the politics of agenda formation becomes more subtle and differentiated.

Under complex interdependence we can expect the agenda to be affected by the international and domestic problems created by economic growth and increasing sensitivity interdependence that we described in the last chapter. Discontented domestic groups will politicize issues and force more issues once considered domestic onto the interstate agenda. Shifts in the distribution of power resources within sets of issues will also affect agendas. During the early 1970s the increased power of oil-producing governments over the transnational corporations and the consumer countries dramatically altered the policy agenda. Moreover, agendas for one group of issues may change as a result of linkages from other groups in which power resources are changing; for example, the broader agenda of North-South trade issues changed after the OPEC price rises and the oil embargo of 1973–74. Even if capabilities among states do not change, agendas may be affected by shifts in the importance of transnational actors. The publicity surrounding multinational corporations in the early 1970s, coupled with their rapid growth over the past twenty years, put the regulation of such corporations higher on both the United Nations agenda and national agendas.

Politicization — agitation and controversy over an issue that tend to raise it to the top of the agenda — can have many sources, as we have seen. Governments whose strength is increasing may politicize issues, by linking them to other issues. An international regime that is becoming ineffective or is not serving important issues may cause increasing politicization, as dissatisfied governments press for change. Politicization, however, can also come from below. Domestic groups may become upset enough to raise a dormant issue, or to interfere with interstate bargaining at high levels. In 1974 the American secretary of state's tacit linkage of a Soviet-American trade pact with progress in detente was upset by the success of domestic American groups working through Congress to link a trade agreement with Soviet policies on emigration.

The technical characteristics and institutional setting in which issues are raised will strongly affect politicization patterns. In the United States, congressional attention is an effective instrument of politicization. Generally, we expect transnational economic organizations and transgovernmental networks of bureaucrats to seek to avoid politicization. Domestically based groups (such as trade unions) and domestically oriented bureaucracies will tend to use politicization (particularly congressional attention) against their transnationally mobile competitors. At the international level, we expect states and actors to "shop among forums" and struggle to get issues raised in international organizations that will maximize their advantage by broadening or narrowing the agenda.

Transnational and Transgovernmental Relations

Our third condition of complex interdependence, multiple channels of contact among societies, further blurs the distinction between domestic and international politics. The availability of partners in political coalitions is not necessarily limited by national boundaries as traditional analysis assumes. The nearer a situation is to complex interdependence, the more we expect the outcomes of political bargaining to be affected by transnational relations. Multinational corporations may be significant both as independent actors and as instruments manipulated by governments. The attitudes and policy stands of domestic groups are likely to be affected by communications, organized or not, between them and their counterparts abroad.

Thus the existence of multiple channels of contact leads us to expect limits, beyond those normally found in domestic politics, on the ability of statesmen to calculate the manipulation of interdependence or follow a consistent strategy of linkage. Statesmen must consider differential as well as aggregate effects of interdependence strategies and their likely implications for politicization and agenda control. Transactions among societies — economic and social transactions more than security ones — affect groups differently. Opportunities and costs from increased transnational ties may be greater for certain groups — for instance, American workers in the textile or shoe industries — than for others. Some organizations or groups may interact directly with actors in other societies or with other governments to increase their benefits from a network of interaction. Some actors may therefore be less vulnerable as well as less sensitive to changes elsewhere in the network than are others, and this will affect patterns of political action.

The multiple channels of contact found in complex interdependence are not limited to nongovernmental actors. Contacts between governmental bureaucracies charged with similar tasks may not only alter their perspectives but lead to transgovernmental coalitions on particular policy questions. To improve their chances of success, government agencies attempt to bring actors from other governments into their own decision-making processes as allies. Agencies of powerful states such as the United States have used such coalitions to penetrate weaker governments in such countries as Turkey and Chile. They have also been used to help agencies of other governments penetrate the United States bureaucracy.[11] As we shall see in Chapter 7, transgovernmental politics frequently characterizes Canadian-American relations, often to the advantage of Canadian interests.

The existence of transgovernmental policy networks leads to a different interpretation of one of the standard propositions about international politics — that states act in their own interest. Under complex interdependence, this conventional wisdom begs two important questions: which self and which interest? A government agency may pursue its own interests under the guise of the national interest; and recurrent interactions can change official perceptions of their interests. As a careful study of the politics of United States trade policy has documented, concentrating only on pressures of various interests for decisions leads to an overly mechanistic view of a continuous process and neglects the important role of communications in slowly changing perceptions of self-interest.[12]

The ambiguity of the national interest raises serious problems for the top political leaders of governments. As bureaucracies contact each other directly across national borders (without going through foreign offices), centralized control becomes more difficult. There is less assurance that the state will be united when dealing with foreign governments or that its components will interpret national interests similarly when negotiating with foreigners. The state may prove to be multifaceted, even schizophrenic. National interests will be defined differently on different issues, at different times, and by different governmental units. States that are better placed to maintain their coherence (because of a centralized political tradition such as France's) will be better able to manipulate uneven interdependence than fragmented states that at first glance seem to have more resources in an issue area.

Role of International Organizations

Finally, the existence of multiple channels leads one to predict a different and significant role for international organizations in world politics. Realists in the tradition of Hans J. Morgenthau have portrayed a world in which states, acting from self-interest, struggle for "power and peace." Security issues are dominant; war threatens. In such a world, one may assume that international institutions will have a minor role, limited by the rare congruence of such interests. International organizations are then clearly peripheral to world politics. But in a world of multiple issues imperfectly linked, in which coalitions are formed transnationally and transgovernmentally, the potential role of international institutions in political bargaining is greatly increased. In particular, they help set the international agenda, and act as catalysts for coalition-formation and as arenas for political initiatives and linkage by weak states.

Governments must organize themselves to cope with the flow of business generated by international organizations. By defining the salient issues, and deciding which issues can be grouped together, organizations may help to determine governmental priorities and the nature of interdepartmental committees and other arrangements within governments. The 1972 Stockholm Environment Conference strengthened the position of environmental agencies in various governments. The 1974 World Food Conference focused the attention of important parts of the United States government on prevention of food shortages. The September 1975 United Nations special session on proposals for a New International Economic

Order generated an intragovernmental debate about policies toward the Third World in general. The International Monetary Fund and the General Agreement on Tariffs and Trade have focused governmental activity on money and trade instead of on private direct investment, which has no comparable international organization.

By bringing officials together, international organizations help to activate potential coalitions in world politics. It is quite obvious that international organizations have been very important in bringing together representatives of less developed countries, most of which do not maintain embassies in one another's capitals. Third World strategies of solidarity among poor countries have been developed in and for a series of international conferences, mostly under the auspices of the United Nations.[13] International organizations also allow agencies of governments, which might not otherwise come into contact, to turn potential or tacit coalitions into explicit transgovernmental coalitions characterized by direct communications. In some cases, international secretariats deliberately promote this process by forming coalitions with groups of governments, or with units of governments, as well as with nongovernmental organizations having similar interests.[14]

International organizations are frequently congenial institutions for weak states. The one-state-one-vote norm of the United Nations system favors coalitions of the small and powerless. Secretariats are often responsive to Third World demands. Furthermore, the substantive norms of most international organizations, as they have developed over the years, stress social and economic equity as well as the equality of states. Past resolutions expressing Third World positions, sometimes agreed to with reservations by industrialized countries, are used to legitimize other demands. These agreements are rarely binding, but up to a point the norms of the institution make opposition look more harshly self-interested and less defensible.

International organizations also allow small and weak states to pursue linkage strategies. In the discussions on a New International Economic Order, Third World states insisted on linking oil price and availability to other questions on which they had traditionally been unable to achieve their objectives. As we shall see in Chapters 4 through 6, small and weak states have also followed a strategy of linkage in the series of Law of the Sea conferences sponsored by the United Nations.

Complex interdependence therefore yields different political patterns than does the realist conception of the world. (Table 2.1 summarizes these differences.) Thus, one would expect traditional theories to fail to explain international regime change in situations of complex interdependence. But, for a situation that approximates realist conditions, traditional theories should be appropriate. In the next chapter we shall look at the problem of understanding regime change.

TABLE 2.1 POLITICAL PROCESSES UNDER CONDITIONS OF REALISM AND COMPLEX INTERDEPENDENCE

	Realism	Complex interdependence
Goals of actors	Military security will be the dominant goal.	Goals of states will vary by issue area. Transgovernmental politics will make goals difficult to define. Transnational actors will pursue their own goals.
Instruments of state policy	Military force will be most effective, although economic and other instruments will also be used.	Power resources specific to issue areas will be most relevant. Manipulation of interdependence, international organizations, and transnational actors will be major instruments.
Agenda formation	Potential shifts in the balance of power and security threats will set the agenda in high politics and will strongly influence other agendas.	Agenda will be affected by changes in the distribution of power resources within issue areas; the status of international regimes; changes in the importance of transnational actors; linkages from other issues and politicization as a result of rising sensitivity interdependence.
Linkages of issues	Linkages will reduce differences in outcomes among issue areas and reinforce international hierarchy.	Linkages by strong states will be more difficult to make since force will be ineffective. Linkages by weak states through international organizations will erode rather than reinforce hierarchy.
Roles of international organizations	Roles are minor, limited by state power and the importance of military force.	Organizations will set agendas, induce coalition-formation, and act as arenas for political action by weak states. Ability to choose the organizational forum for an issue and to mobilize votes will be an important political resource.

Chapter 3 | EXPLAINING INTERNATIONAL REGIME CHANGE

International regimes help to provide the political framework within which international economic processes occur. Understanding the development and breakdown of regimes is central to understanding the politics of interdependence. Why do international regimes change?

In this chapter we shall present four models based respectively on changes in (1) economic processes, (2) the overall power structure in the world, (3) the power structure within issue areas, and (4) power capabilities as affected by international organization. We shall begin with the first two models, because they are the simplest and most familiar. We shall then add complexity by considering the more novel issue structure and international organization models.

AN ECONOMIC PROCESS EXPLANATION

Many observers have pointed to the increased importance of economic issues in international politics. Indeed, struggles over the governance of economic issues are responsible for much of the increased attention to interdependence. The contemporary Western science of international economics, however, does not have a theory of international regime change. Neoclassical economic analysis was developed not as a faithful description of reality, but as a simplified explanation that would also suggest policies for increasing economic efficiency and welfare. Quite deliberately, economic theorists have abstracted away from politics in order to achieve more precise and elegant economic explanations. Thus we cannot blame economists for not providing a model of regime change from conventional economic theory, because their questions are different from political scientists'. Political scientists tend to focus on power, whereas, "if we look at the main run of economic theory over the past hundred years we find that it is characterized by a strange lack of power considerations." [1]

The fact that a particular activity is characterized by nonpolitical behavior — for instance, transactions carried on through a competitive price system — does not imply that political power is unimportant. The effect of politics may be indirect; it may determine the relationships within which day-to-day economic processes take place. Critics of pluralistic approaches to local and national politics have pointed out that this second "face of power" is extremely important in determining which issues are raised for political decision.[2]

For example, the major economic features of the postwar period — rapidly expanding and generally nondiscriminatory trade, large-scale and rapid movements of funds from one center to another under fixed exchange rates, and the rapid growth of huge multinational enterprises — depended on a political environment favorable to large-scale internationalized capitalism. Moreover, economic bargaining is affected by the uneven distribution of effective demand — the wealthiest consumers have the most votes in the market — and by the rules and institutions that reflect past patterns of strength.

A departure from perfect competition *always* introduces political factors into the analysis. Once firms can exercise some control over their environments, problems of bargaining, strategy, influence, and leadership immediately arise. Although economic analysis can provide important insights into regime change, no sophisticated observers, including neoclassical economists, would propose it as an adequate explanation. To explain regime change, we will have to use models with explicit political assumptions. But we will also have to include insights about changing economic processes.

A model of regime change based on economic processes would begin with this century's many technological and economic changes. Particularly during the last thirty years, economic growth in the industrialized world has proceeded at an unprecedented pace. World trade has grown by more than 7 percent per year and has become a larger proportion of gross national product for most major countries of Europe and North America. Direct foreign investment and overseas production have grown even faster.[3] Behind these changes lie remarkable advances in transportation and communications technology, which have reduced the costs of distance. Using communications satellites, the cost of telephoning a person

12,000 miles away is the same as that of telephoning someone much closer. Supertankers and other innovations in shipping technology have reduced the costs of transporting goods. And over the same period, governments have been drawn into agreements, consultations, and institutions to cope with rapidly expanding transactions.

The first premise of an economic process model of regime change is that technological change and increases in economic interdependence will make existing international regimes obsolete. They will be inadequate to cope with the increased volume of transactions or new forms of organization represented, for instance, by transnational corporations. Established institutions, rules, and procedures will be threatened with ineffectiveness or collapse.

The second premise is that governments will be highly responsive to domestic political demands for a rising standard of living. National economic welfare will usually be the dominant political goal, and a rising gross national product will be a critical political indicator. The third premise of this model is that the great aggregate economic benefits provided by international movements of capital, goods, and in some cases labor will give governments strong incentives to modify or reconstruct international regimes to restore their effectiveness. Governments will argue over the distribution of gains and complain about the loss of autonomy entailed in rising economic interdependence (vulnerability as well as sensitivity); but they will generally find that, when there are domestic political demands for greater economic welfare, the welfare costs of disrupting international economic relations, or allowing them to become chaotic, are greater than the autonomy benefits. Reluctantly, they will permit economic interdependence to grow, and even more reluctantly, but inexorably, they will be drawn into cooperating in the construction of new international regimes by creating integrated policy responses. Thus, regime change will be a process of gradually adapting to new volumes and new forms of transnational economic activity. Governments will resist the temptation to disrupt or break regimes, because of the high costs to economic growth.

On the basis of an economic process model, one should therefore expect international regimes to be undermined from time to time by economic and technological change; but they will not disintegrate entirely, at least not for long. They will quickly be reconstructed to adapt to economic and technological conditions.

This simple economic process model does not correspond exactly to the views of any sophisticated theorist, although it seems to exert a powerful influence on the views of many people. Projections that in the year 2000 a handful of multinational corporations will control most of world production, and wield greater power than governments, or assertions that increases in interdependence make greater international integration inevitable, reflect recent trends of rising interdependence. Part of the appeal of this approach is its grasp of the importance of technological change in explaining developments over the last century.

Political reality, however, often diverges from expectations based simply on technological and economic trends. Quite evidently, governments continually sacrifice economic efficiency to security, autonomy, and other values in policy decisions. Furthermore, this simple economic growth model skims over the difficulty of moving from one equilibrium situation to another and thus does not confront the inevitable political questions about adjustments. In politics, adjustment is crucial — indeed, power has been defined by one political scientist as "the ability not to have to adjust to change." [4] In policymaking adjustment is critical because the views of powerful interests about the costs of change and their distribution largely determine the support a policy will command.

Rapidly rising economic interdependence can create fear and insecurity among politically important groups. Labor unions and local community leaders may fear that a corporate decision to shift production abroad or trends toward greater imports could cause severe unemployment and social distress. Industries threatened by imports press for governmental protection. Thus, protectionism may increase as economic interdependence becomes more extensive. Protectionism has always been with us. But as the technology of communication and large-scale corporate organization have reduced the natural buffers between markets, many domestic groups have turned to government to establish political buffers. Even when a country is not threatened by increased vulnerability, the sensitivity of its interest groups can stimulate it to adopt policies that restrict international transactions.

The conflicts generated by increased interdependence have contributed to controversy over international regimes, which often erupts quite suddenly. Yet a simple economic growth approach is not very effective in explaining variations, since its major explanatory variable is a long-term secular trend (technological change reducing costs of transnational activity over great distances, and therefore increasing such activity, and leading to greater sensitivity). Why have international regimes been developed and maintained at some times, whereas at other times, no regime can be successfully instituted? If economic growth were a sufficient explanation, one would expect international economic interdependence successively to "outgrow" regime constraints, and new regimes, better adapted to the new situation of interdependence, quickly to replace them. Increased sensitivity would lead to new issues and new problems; but a problem-solving orientation would lead policymakers to new regime solutions.

Yet such an explanation obviously abstracts from interests, which may diverge sharply from group to group, sector to sector, or country to country. It also assumes that international politico-military policy decisions are separate from economic ones. In 1945, international institutional decisions created a two-track or multitrack regime in which economic and security issues were kept fairly separate in day-to-day political processes.[5] They were usually linked only hierarchically in domestic politics, through appeals to common security goals as a means of limiting economic conflicts, or potential conflicts with the goals of subnational groups. Yet this separation and depoliticization of economic issues is not the norm in world politics. Indeed, it may well have been an anomaly, dependent on postwar United States economic and military dominance and alliance leadership. Because the extent of interdependence and its effects depend to a considerable extent on high-level political decisions and agreements, traditional approaches to international politics, which have concentrated on these high-level decisions and the overall power structure, should contribute to an adequate explanation.

OVERALL POWER STRUCTURE EXPLANATION

Eroding Hegemony

There is nothing new about certain kinds of interdependence among states. Athens and Sparta were interdependent in military security at the time of Thucydides. The United States and the Soviet Union have been similarly interdependent throughout the postwar period. Not only are the two countries sensitive to changes in each other's security policies, but they are also vulnerable to each other's security decisions. Exactly this high level of interdependence in one issue area — military security — coupled with mutual antagonism has been at the heart of traditional analyses of world politics. Under such circumstances security issues take precedence over others, and the distribution of military power (with its supporting economic basis) determines the power structure. War is the most important and dramatic source of structural change. Our own era, for instance, still bears the marks of the outcome of World War II.

In the traditional view, powerful states make the rules. As Thucydides put it, "the strong do what they can and the weak suffer what they must." [6] In bilateral relations, the traditionalists expect that the stronger of two states will usually prevail when issues arise between them. Within a system, the structure (that is, the distribution of power among the states in it) determines the nature of its international regimes. And the most important power resources are military.

The appeal of the traditional approach based on the overall power structure lies in its simplicity and parsimonious prediction. Judgments of relative power seem easy to make on the basis of military strength, and it is possible to calculate a rational course of action in any given situation:

We assume that statesmen think and act in terms of interest defined as power, and the evidence of history bears that assumption out. That assumption allows us to retrace and anticipate, as it were, the steps a statesman — past, present, or future — has taken or will take on the political scene. We look over his shoulder when he writes his dispatches; we listen in on his conversation with other statesmen; we read and anticipate his very thoughts.[7]

In its more extreme formulations, this realist approach deprecates domestic politics by suggesting that the national interest must be calculated in terms of power, relative to other states, and that if it is not, the result will be catastrophic. There is little margin for choice. If domestic politics interferes with diplomacy, disaster will follow. Less drastic expositions of the traditional view allow for the effect of domestic politics, but the principal focus of the theory — and the segment of it that provides its explanatory power — centers on competition among states. It is competition among autonomous actors that provides the basic driving force of world politics.

The traditional view does not have a thoroughly articulated and agreed-on theory of regime change. Its emphasis on state power and international structure — defined in terms of power capabilities — does, however, provide the basis for developing such a theory on realist premises. The basic dynamic is provided by the assertion that as the power of states changes (that is, as the structure changes), the rules that comprise international regimes will change accordingly. This dynamic is at the heart of our model of regime change based on the overall power structure.

This overall structure approach does not differentiate significantly among issue areas in world politics. On the contrary, it predicts a strong tendency toward congruence of outcomes among issue areas. Since power, like money, is considered fungible, power resources will be shifted by major states to secure equal marginal returns in all areas. When outcomes on one issue area are markedly different from those on others, we should expect shifts to make outcomes in the deviant area more consistent with the world structure of military and economic power. It follows from this view, for instance, that after 1973 the incongruity between power in petroleum politics and power generally in world politics was a source of instability. It was to be expected that the United States and other industrialized countries would attempt to reduce the incongruity in their favor by mutual aid, encouragement of new sources of supply, and even by threats of military force. Nor was it surprising that oil-exporting states, linked in the Organization of Petroleum Exporting Countries (OPEC), would try to resolve the tension in their favor by increasing their strength through arms purchases, alliances with other Third World countries for a new international economic order, deals with individual consumer countries, and ambitious long-term development plans. Because of the overall power disparities, however, traditional theory would give the OPEC states less chance of success.

These expectations about which side will prevail may or may not be confirmed, but the realist insight is important: we should examine closely situations in which the distribution of power between issue areas is uneven. Tensions develop at these points of incongruity. Crucial political struggles take place to determine whether changes in the power structure of one issue area will spread to the system as a whole, or be suppressed.

Even in the absence of war or the overt use of force, traditional views stressing the overall power structure can be adapted to explain changes in international regimes. If the strong make the rules, then shifts in politico-military power should affect economic regimes. The overall structure approach directs our attention to hegemony and leadership. Economists have argued that stable economic regimes require leadership — that is, willingness to forego short-term gains in bargaining in order to preserve the regime — and that an actor is most likely to provide such leadership when it sees itself as a major consumer of the long-term benefits produced by the regime.

Realists would add that such leadership in maintaining a regime would be most likely in a hegemonial system: that is, when one state is powerful enough to maintain the essential rules governing interstate relations, and willing to do so. In addition to its role in maintaining a regime, such a state can abrogate existing rules, prevent the adoption of rules that it opposes, or play the dominant role in constructing new rules. In a hegemonial system, therefore, the preponderant state has both positive and negative power.

In a realist world, such a condition would imply military preponderance, but not necessarily frequent use of military force. In the nineteenth century, Britain occasionally used its preponderant naval power to force free trade in South America or to protect freedom of the seas from the encroachment of coastal states, but generally such actions were unnecessary. A hegemonial power can change the rules rather than adapt its policies to the existing rules. Britain's position as defender of freedom of the seas, for example, did not deter her from interfering with neutral shipping when she was at war. But during peacetime, the British government led in regime maintenance by scrupulously enforcing free seas rules against its own domestic interests, which attempted to assert broader coastal jurisdiction.

When the hegemonial power does not seek to conquer other states, but merely to protect its favored position, other states may benefit as well. The Pax Britannica is often celebrated. Charles Kindleberger has argued that during the last century international economic systems with one leader have been more stable than other systems, and they have been associated with greater prosperity.[8] In the nineteenth century the financial strength of Great Britain provided the basis for a monetary system that was centered principally, although not entirely, on London. From World War II through the 1960s, the economic preponderance of the United States enabled it to manage monetary relations among noncommunist countries through the Bretton Woods system. By contrast, as we shall see in more detail later, the unhappy international monetary experience of the interwar period occurred when the United States was unwilling to exercise strong leadership and Britain was unable to do so.[9]

Hegemonial powers do not, therefore, always exploit secondary powers economically. During the heyday of the sterling standard, industrial production in France, Germany, Russia, and the United States increased from 50 percent to 400 percent faster than in Britain.[10] Although the United States dominated the monetary system of the postwar period, Europe and Japan grew more rapidly than it did. Even so severe a critic of American hegemony as David Calleo admits that "it was difficult to argue that the dollar system was causing economic harm to its members." [11]

Why then do hegemonial systems and their corresponding economic regimes collapse? War or major shifts in the overall balance of power are the dramatic causes. But these systems may also be undermined by the very economic processes they encourage. Ironically, the benefits of a hegemonial system, and the extent to which they are shared, may bring about its collapse. As their economic power increases, secondary states change their assumptions. No longer do they have to accept a one-sided dependence which, no matter how prosperous, adversely affects governmental autonomy and political status. As autonomy and status become possible, these values are taken from the closet of "desirable but unrealizable goals." At least for some leaders and some countries – such as France in the 1920s and 1960s – prosperity is no longer enough.[12]

Thus, as the rule-making and rule-enforcing powers of the hegemonic state begin to erode, the policies of secondary states are likely to change. But so are the policies of the hegemonic state. An atmosphere of crisis and a proliferation of ad hoc policy measures will seem not only undignified but unsettling to many. Dissenters will begin to wonder about the costs of leadership. Further, this leadership will less and less appear to guarantee economic and political objectives, as other states become more assertive. The renewed emphasis of these secondary governments on status and autonomy adds a further complication, since these values have a zero-sum connotation that is much less pronounced where economic values are involved. More status for secondary states means less for the dominant power; increases in weaker powers' autonomy bring concomitant declines in the positive influence of the system's leader.

Thus the systemic orientation natural to a hegemonial power — which identifies its interests with those of the system it manages — is challenged by a more nationalistic perspective at home and abroad. Bilateralism and autarky, formerly rejected as inefficient, are once again recommended. Their adherents stress the benefits of economic security, or risk aversion. When power seems to ensure that risks are minimal, this argument carries little weight; but when cracks appear in the hegemonial construction, prudence counsels what efficiency formerly proscribed.

When this point is reached on both sides, the hegemonic equilibrium has been broken and a spiral of action and counteraction may set in. As the system changes, assumptions change; considerations of risk aversion on one side and greater independence on the other counsel policies with less international or less systemic implications. The uncertainty thus created may be difficult to stop; a cycle of disintegration can readily set in.

From a traditional perspective, this portrait of economic processes eroding overall hegemony has a certain appeal. By adding a few assumptions, it provides an explanation based on the overall power structure that accounts for changes in economic regimes, despite the absence of major war or major shifts in the balance of power. Applying this model to the postwar period, one can argue that international economic regimes that accompanied the "Imperial Republic" or the "American Empire" are collapsing due to the "decline of American power." [13]

Limitations of an Overall Structure Explanation

Carefully defined, the concept of hegemony and analysis of its erosion by economic processes can help to explain regime change. But this overall structure explanation is more ambiguous than it first appears, and can lead to facile descriptions of change. We must specify what resources are considered effective in establishing hegemonic power, and to what range of phenomena it is meant to apply.

The simplest and most parsimonious version of the eroding hegemony thesis would be that international economic regimes directly reflect politico-military patterns of capability: high politics dominates low politics. Changes in international economic relations are explained by shifts in military power. This simple version explains the broad features of the postwar economic order, particularly its basic divisions. Although Soviet or Chinese purchases and sales can affect world markets, these planned economies are separate enough that it is more accurate to think of three distinct economic systems, corresponding to the three major (but unequal) sources of politico-military power.

Yet the most parsimonious explanation breaks down when one moves from explaining overall structure to explaining change. The United States' position in the world economy, and its dominance in policymaking, both within the industrialized areas and with the Third World, have clearly declined since 1944 or 1950. Yet during this period the United States has remained, militarily, the most powerful state in the world; and its military lead over its major economic partners (Japan, Canada, and Europe) has been steadily maintained if not increased.

Thus, although the distribution of military power affects the international economic order, by itself it provides only a small part of the explanation. Three other major factors must be added for an adequate overall structure explanation, thus reducing its simplicity but increasing its fit with the facts of postwar change in international economic regimes: (1) changes in perceptions of the threat of military aggression; (2) changes in the relative *economic* strength of the United States and its trading and investment partners; and (3) changes in hierarchical patterns involving Europe and the Third World.

Concern about a communist military threat helped stimulate Americans to make short-run economic sacrifices (that is, to exercise leadership) to develop and preserve the liberal postwar economic regimes that contributed to European and Japanese recovery. Many of the major advances in international economic relations came during the long period of maximum Cold War tension between 1947 (the Truman Doctrine) and 1963 (the Test Ban Treaty). In these years, the International Monetary Fund (IMF), World Bank (IBRD), General Agreement on Tariffs and Trade (GATT), and Organization for Economic Cooperation and Development (OECD) began to function; currency convertibility was achieved and major tariff cuts implemented; and the Common Market was established. United States security leadership was prized by its allies, and the American perception of high threat from the Soviet Union encouraged United States policymakers to grant various economic concessions to the Europeans and the Japanese. The sharp reductions in perceived threats in recent years have certainly helped to reduce the United States' ability subtly to translate its military leadership of the alliance into economic leadership without resorting to overt and highly resented linkages. American allies became less willing to act as junior partners once they perceived the external threat as diminished. At the same time, American willingness to accept economic discrimination or unfavorable exchange rates was also declining.

These changes in perceptions were reinforced by increases in European and Japanese economic capabilities relative to those of the United States. In the early postwar period, Europe was largely supine, and although it was able to bargain and resist on some issues, it complied with United States leadership within an overall economic structure. Later, the tremendous European economic recovery and the confidence it gave, at least on economic issues, provide the primary explanation for the Dillon Round tariff cuts, currency convertibility and subsequent reduced reliance on the dollar, and the construction of the Common Market. The latter steps were motivated by a desire to boost the political as well as economic strength of Europe, so that it could better stand on its own against the Soviet Union (and later, the United States).

This situation created an opportunity for linkage and trading-off of military and economic advantages, which became more tempting to the United States as its economic preponderance eroded. It is worth noting that the disruption of the economic order was not caused by an erosion of American military power in the 1960s, but by a decline in American concern that such disruption would threaten vital security relationships.

The third factor needed to fit a theory of eroding hegemony to the facts of change lies not in American relations with other countries, but in the relations of Europe to the Third World.[14] Before 1960, most of Africa, along with other now independent countries, remained under colonial rule. Since then, about fifty countries have become independent, and over time these former colonies have become more assertive. After the abortive British-French Suez invasion of 1956 and the withdrawal of most British forces east of Suez in the late 1960s, it was obvious that Europe would no longer play a major role in controlling events outside that continent. The erosion of European colonial hegemony, not American military power, added to the complexity of world politics and to the pressure on the United States as well as the other industrialized countries for economic regime change.

In short, the theory of eroding hegemony, though a useful part of the explanation of postwar economic regime change, is not as neat an overall structure explanation as it first appeared to be. Nor is it a very good basis for prediction. The apparent inevitability of decline, portrayed by the eroding hegemony model (even with these qualifications), may to some extent be an illusion, precisely because of the inadequacy of its assumptions about domestic politics, interests, and issues. In the leading state, interests in maintaining systemic leadership and in paying the cost will persist, particularly among multinational corporations based there, the financial elite, and governmental bureaucracies charged with maintaining good relations with allies. In the governments of secondary powers, as well, no firm consensus is to be expected. Dependency may provide comforts for some parties, necessities for others. There may be coalitions across national boundaries for preserving international economic regimes. Regime maintenance may not require military hegemony, but may rest on vested interests in several countries. Foreign policy may respond to particular interests — which sometimes may favor regime maintenance.

The argument about eroding hegemony also suffers from its disinclination to differentiate among issue areas. Yet dominant rule-making power in one area does not necessarily imply effective control over other areas as well. American dominance has eroded more rapidly on petroleum issues than it did on issues of international monetary policy or trade in manufactured products. Where the use or threat of force is ineffective, it will be more difficult for a major power, in what would formerly have been a hegemonial position across the board, to influence policy in one issue area by using resources not specific to that area. This difficulty was particularly evident in the petroleum crisis of 1973–74: although the United States was much stronger militarily and economically than the Middle Eastern oil producers, it was unable to persuade them to reduce oil prices.

Finally, the eroding hegemony argument ignores the complications introduced by multiple channels of contact among societies — in the form of multinational firms and other transnational actors, or informal, transgovernmental contacts among bureaucracies. Some of the domestic political reactions against an open, internationalist policy result largely from the real or perceived effects of foreign investments by multinational firms. In their activities abroad, multinationals are likely to increase the appearance of United States dominance, due to their visibility and their role as carriers of American popular culture, but it is at best uncertain whether they really contribute to United States power overseas.[15] Thus they introduce new ambiguities into the calculation of power, and possible disjunctions between the reality of power and its appearance.

ISSUE STRUCTURE

The elegance of the overall structure model derives from its basis on a simple interpretation of structure as the distribution of power capabilities, in the aggregate, among states. On the basis of these distributions, it promises significant predictions about patterns of behavior.[16] However, one must assume that there is a hierarchy of issues, with military security at the top, and that force is usable, since otherwise one could find very different patterns of politics, and regimes, for different issue areas. The overall structure explanation assumes that power, like water, will find a common level: discrepancies between which states are dominant on one issue and which predominate on others will be eliminated in important cases by linkages drawn by powerful states through the use or threat of force. Insofar as an issue is relevant to military security the most powerful states, in the aggregate, will be able to control it.

These assumptions can be challenged. After 1973, for instance, it became obvious that power in petroleum issues was distributed very differently than in other issue areas of world politics, and the discrepancy has continued to persist up to this writing. To explain such a situation, one could turn to an issue structure model in which force is usable only at high cost, and military security is not at the top of a clear hierarchy of issues for governments. From these assumptions the issue structure model infers that linkages will not be drawn regularly and effectively among issue areas. Power resources, it holds, cannot under these circumstances easily be transferred. Power will not be fungible, as in the overall structure model; military capabilities will not be effective in economic issues, and economic capabilities relevant to one area may not be relevant to another.

Observation of contemporary world politics lends general plausibility to this formulation. It is clear that different issue areas often have different political structures that may be more or less insulated from the overall distribution of economic and military capabilities. They differ greatly in their domestic politics, in their characteristic patterns of politicization, and in the interest groups that are active. For instance, small numbers of bankers, who control huge financial institutions, are very influential on international monetary issues; whereas influence on trade is much more broadly shared.[17] In oceans politics the pattern is complex, with coastal fishermen, distant-water fishermen, scientists, oil and hard minerals companies, and navies all involved. Saudi Arabia, Libya, Iran, and Kuwait may be very important on petroleum issues but virtually inconsequential on questions relating to the international regime for the oceans, world food problems, or GATT rules for trade in manufactured products. Likewise a major food producer such as Australia or an important trading country such as Sweden may not play a significant role on petroleum issues.

Yet, though issue structuralism differs in important ways from the traditional overall structure explanations, it has a similar form of argument about regime change: the strong states (in an issue area) will make the rules. A basic assumption of the issue structure model, however, is that although states may be tempted to draw linkages among issues, such linkages will be generally unsuccessful. The premise of issue structuralism is that power resources in one issue area lose some or all of their effectiveness when applied to others. Thus, unlike the overall structure explanation, issue structuralism does not predict congruence of power across issues. On the whole, then, analysis of politics will have to be conducted by issue area. Within each issue area one posits that states will pursue their relatively coherent self-interests and that stronger states in the issue system will dominate weaker ones and determine the rules of the game.

Issue structuralism thus is capable of generating clear predictions for particular situations. Yet as a theory, it is less *powerful* than the overall structure explanation because the analyst needs more information: he or she needs to know not only the overall structure of military, or military and economic, power; but how that power is distributed by issue area. Although it is less powerful, issue structuralist theory is more *discriminating*, since it can distinguish among issue areas that are crucial in analyzing much of contemporary world politics, particularly the politics of international economic relations. The two assumptions of the complex interdependence model that it incorporates therefore increase the closeness of fit of its predictions with some aspects of reality, at only partial sacrifice of predictive power.

Like the overall structure explanation, an issue structure explanation of the politics of economic regime change in a specific issue system such as oceans or money, distinguishes between activity taking place within a regime and activity designed to influence the development of a new regime. In the former case, the international regime for the issue is regarded as legitimate by major actors, although minor disagreements may exist. National policy options are constrained by the regime. Politics takes place within the ground rules laid down by the regime, and generally is directed toward small advantages, favorable adjustments, or exceptions to the rules. Politics within the General Agreement on Tariffs and Trade (GATT) during much of the 1950s and 1960s conformed to this picture. Participants accepted GATT rules but attempted to secure waivers for specific interests of their own.[18] Within the European Economic Community, the "politics of regional implementation" exhibits similar characteristics: the legitimacy of the rules is not challenged, but the members may seek to bend or delay them.[19] Governments attempt to take advantage of asymmetries in sensitivity, but do not manipulate vulnerabilities very much — since the regime itself constrains policy change.

In rule-making (the second aspect of political activity in an issue area), what is challenged is not merely a set of effects implied by rules but the rules themselves. The nature of the regime is questioned by major participants, and the political struggle focuses on whether, and in what ways, the regime will be restructured. Thus the concept of vulnerability interdependence is most appropriate here.

This distinction is important for issue structure explanations because power resources that provide influence in political activity often differ with the two aspects of the problem. Where the rules are taken for granted, they may create asymmetries in sensitivity interdependence. For instance, as long as traditional international laws requiring prompt and adequate compensation for the nationalization of foreign investment were in effect, small host countries with weak economies and administrations tended to be more sensitive to the decisions of foreign investors (and the home governments) than the investors were to their decisions.

When the rules are questioned, or the international regime is changed unilaterally, the principles that channeled sensitivity interdependence no longer confer power benefits on the actors that had benefited by them. At this point, politics begins to reflect different power resources, relative vulnerability, not sensitivity, or what can be considered as the underlying power structure in the issue area. On foreign investment issues, for instance, governments gained power as inhibitions against expropriation declined. The power resources that affect rule-*making* allow their holders to implement alternatives and to challenge assumptions about the current use of influence in an issue. Issue structuralism allows us to predict that when there is great incongruity in an issue area between the distribution of power in the underlying structure, and its distribution in current use, there will be pressures for regime change.

Both aspects of power are important, but for the issue structure model the underlying power structure is more basic, since breaking or creating regimes means changing the rules that channel the patterns of sensitivity interdependence. To a considerable extent, regime change occurs because of the difference between the influence and benefits under an existing regime and the expectations of dissatisfied states about the effects of new rules. When there is an incongruity between the influence of a state under current use rules, and its underlying sources of power to change the rules, issue structuralism predicts sharp rather than gradual regime change. For example, in 1971 the incongruity between American sensitivity to declining monetary reserves (under rules about fixed exchange rates) and its underlying rule-making power (based on the importance that American GNP conferred on the dollar) led to a sharp break of regime.

Limitations of Structural Explanations

Issue structuralism is often useful when the costliness of force or the absence of a major security concern limits the validity of explanations based on the overall power structure. But to the extent that linkages of issues are successful, the explanatory value of the issue structure model is reduced, since political outcomes in particular issue areas will no longer be accounted for simply by political resources in those areas. Moreover, in some situations linkages may come not from states with great overall power, but from poor, weak states. In the bargaining over the law of the sea, for example, much of the linkage has come "from below," as poor, weak states find it to their advantage in conference diplomacy. This linkage from below is an anomaly which neither structural model adequately explains.

Another problem with both structural explanations is their exclusive focus on the power capabilities of states; they ignore domestic and transnational political actors. We have already shown how this focus limits the overall structure explanation of postwar regime change. That limitation is not overcome by an issue-specific formulation of the structural argument. Some regimes — for example in trade among major industrial countries — have persisted despite shifts in the underlying power structure; others — as we shall see in our study of oceans policy — have changed despite continuity of power.

More generally, understanding the changing regimes that govern international interdependence requires an understanding of both structure and process. International structural explanations are generally inadequate unless coupled with an account of political process. In terms of the distinction developed in the previous chapter, there is likely to be a discrepancy between the structure of power as resources (whether military as in a stark realist formulation or economic as in the issue structure approach), and power as control over outcomes and measured by the pattern of outcomes. The translation from capabilities to outcomes depends on the political process. Skill in political bargaining affects the translation. States with intense preferences and coherent positions will bargain more effectively than states constrained by domestic and transnational actors. And even states with coherent positions may find their bargaining position weakened by the institutions and procedures that characterize a given regime, as Figure 3.1 illustrates.

FIGURE 3.1 Structural models of regime change

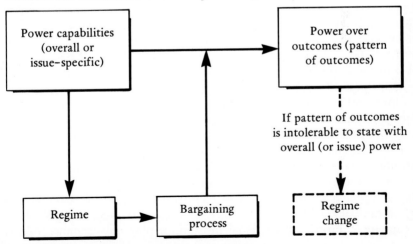

In the simplest (and least interesting) structural explanations, a shift of overall or issue-specific capabilities (for example, caused by a war) leads directly to regime change. In the more sophisticated structural explanations indicated in the diagram, a regime creates a bargaining process, which leads to a pattern of outcomes. If that pattern is incongruous with the overall power structure (or in the issue-specific model, the underlying power structure in the issue area) and is intolerable to the strongest states, there will be a regime change to reduce the incongruity. The structural approach views the regime and the bargaining process as having no autonomy. The validity of that assumption depends on the conditions of world politics that we examined in the last chapter.

In conclusion, our criticism of the structural explanations does not mean that we reject them. On the contrary, their simplicity makes them the best starting point for analyzing regime change. Our care in elaborating the structural models of economic regime change — including the traditional model, whose proponents have often portrayed it as universally valid but neglected to relate it carefully to economic regime change — indicates that we believe they have some explanatory power under certain explicitly stated conditions. Our purpose is not to demonstrate the incorrectness of international structural theory but to indicate that, even when carefully reformulated, it provides only a partial explanation.

AN INTERNATIONAL ORGANIZATION MODEL

One way to think of the structure of world politics is in terms of the distribution of capabilities (overall or within issue areas) among the major actors of world politics. This is the concept of structure used in the overall structure and issue structure models. It is also possible, however, to define another kind of structure. One can think of governments as linked not merely by formal relations between foreign offices but also by intergovernmental and transgovernmental ties at many levels — from heads of government on down. These ties between governments may be reinforced by norms prescribing behavior in particular situations, and in some cases by formal institutions. We use the term *international organization* to refer to these multilevel linkages, norms, and institutions. International organization in this sense is another type of world political structure.

In our international organization model, these networks, norms, and institutions are important independent factors for explaining regime change. One may even have international organization in this sense without any specific formal institutions: one can speak of the international organization of Canadian-American relations even though, as we shall see in Chapter 7, formal international institutions play only a minor role in the relationship. International organization in the broad sense of networks, norms, and institutions includes the norms associated with specific international regimes, but it is a broader category than regime, because it also includes patterns of elite networks and (if relevant) formal institutions. Thus, the Bretton Woods international monetary regime prescribed countries' financial dealings with one another; but the international organization of the monetary issue area during that period also included formal organizations such as the International Monetary Fund and networks of ties among national treasuries and central banks. And this international organization of the monetary issue area existed within a broader pattern of international organization, including both the formal institutions of the United Nations and informal networks of ties among governments, particularly among governments of advanced industrial societies belonging to the OECD.

The international organization model assumes that a set of networks, norms, and institutions, once established, will be difficult either to eradicate or drastically to rearrange. Even governments with superior capabilities — overall or within the issue area — will find it hard to work their will when it conflicts with established patterns of behavior within existing networks and institutions. Under these conditions the predictions of overall structure or issue structure theories will be incorrect: regimes will not become congruent with underlying patterns of state capabilities, because international organizations as defined above will stand in the way.

Thus, the international organization model will help to account for failures of the basic structural models of regime change. Regimes are established and organized in conformity with distributions of capabilities, but subsequently the relevant networks, norms, and institutions will themselves influence actors' abilities to use these capabilities. As time progresses, the underlying capabilities of states will become increasingly poor predictors of the characteristics of international regimes. Power over outcomes will be conferred by *organizationally dependent capabilities,* such as voting power, ability to form coalitions, and control of elite networks: that is, by capabilities that are affected by the norms, networks, and institutions associated with international organization as we have defined it. In the United States General Assembly, for instance, one cannot predict resolutions correctly by asserting that the most powerful states in the international system (such as the United States and the Soviet Union) will generally prevail. Instead, one has to examine governments' abilities to influence, and benefit by, the one-state-one-vote system by which the formal decisions of the assembly are made.

Thus the international organization model helps to resolve some of the puzzles that could arise for someone who believes in the overall structure or issue structure model. Some regimes may not change as rapidly as underlying power capabilities; for these regimes and others, we will be unable to predict patterns of outcomes simply from a knowledge of the distribution of capabilities among governments. The international organization model provides a dynamic of regime change, as well as an explanation, in certain instances, of inertia. As we noted before, international organization in our sense provides the context within which regimes operate. International organization — either in issues quite apart from the issue area of a regime, or within that issue area — may affect the regime. The networks, norms, and institutions of the United Nations, for instance, have affected the international trade regime, particularly since the formation of the United Nations Conference on Trade and Development in 1964. Similarly, the practices of the United Nations system affected the influence of various governments over General Assembly resolutions demanding a new international economic order. Such an order, developed through the United Nations, would be likely to affect the international trade regime, and, more important, to influence the IMF-centered international monetary regime and perhaps eventually to stimulate the development of an international regime to control direct investment. The general point is clear: international regimes can be changed by decisions that are themselves affected by international organization in our sense.

Figure 3.2 is a diagram of the international organization model. Existing norms and networks, as well as underlying capabilities, influence organizationally dependent capabilities, which in turn affect outcomes. If one

FIGURE 3.2 An international organization model of regime change

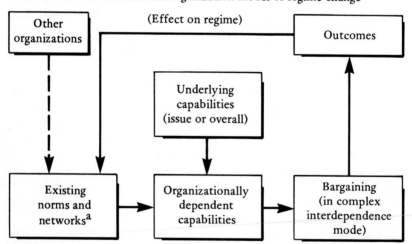

[a] At the beginning, the organization of a regime is affected by underlying capabilities of states, but not on a continuous basis.

considers only the solid lines in the diagram, this system could be self-perpetuating, with considerable stability, yet not determined entirely by underlying patterns of capabilities. The dotted line indicates the major source of change: other networks, norms, and institutions may interfere with the specific organizational configuration under consideration, thus affecting the nature of the regime. As we shall see in the next chapters, the rules, norms, and procedures of the United Nations have had such an effect on regime change in the oceans issue area: the organizational context within which decisions were made greatly affected the rules about the use of oceans space and resources.

Although the international organization model includes important factors that are ignored or downplayed by the basic structural models, it has some significant limitations of its own. It is more complicated than the basic structural approaches, requiring more information. It does not predict how international regimes will change from a single variable such as international structure. Indeed, its focus on the political processes associated with international organization implies that actors' strategies, and their cleverness in implementing them, can substantially affect the evolution of international regimes. Furthermore, it is much less deterministic than the basic structural models, leaving wide latitude for choice, decision, and multiple-level bargaining.

The factors on which the international organization model depends are also more temporary and reversible than those of the basic structural models. *If* powerful governments decide to destroy the existing regimes, and have the determination as well as the ability to do so, the regimes and their associated organizations will no longer have lives of their own. The international organization model postulates that the costs of destroying a regime will be high when well-integrated elite networks exist on many levels among countries. Nevertheless, the costs of an adverse regime could become so great that some states would resolve to destroy it even though that meant disrupting those networks. At this point the basic structural models would become more relevant than the international organization model.

We expect that under realist conditions, as described in Chapter 2, the underlying distribution of power is likely to be dominant (particularly since force is usable), and the international organization model is not likely to add significantly to explanations of regime change. Under complex interdependence, however, we expect international organizational norms and procedures and their associated political processes to affect patterns of regime change.

Please remember that the international organization model is only likely to apply under complex interdependence conditions, and that even then, its predictions could be rendered invalid by the actions of governments determined to exercise their underlying power to change regimes. The latter point can be related to our discussion in Chapter 1 of sensitivity and vulnerability interdependence as power resources. The international organization model is based on the assumption that the regime will be stable; that is, policy changes disrupting it will not be possible. Actors will manipulate each other's sensitivity dependence for their own gain; and they may make marginal policy shifts to improve their vulnerability positions. But there is a limit to their manipulation of vulnerability interdependence; if they change policy too much, the regime itself will be challenged and destroyed.

The validity of the model depends on its assumption that actors will not destroy the regime by attempting to take advantage of one another's vulnerability dependence. If, on the contrary, this occurs, underlying power resources within issue areas or overall will once again become most important, and structural models will be better guides than the international organization model to regime change. The two structural models therefore dominate the international model in the same way that vulnerability interdependence dominates sensitivity interdependence as a power resource. Above a certain level of conflict the international organization model and sensitivity interdependence become largely irrelevant.

COMBINING EXPLANATIONS

No single model is likely adequately to explain world politics. Conditions vary too greatly. You may therefore be tempted to say that everything is relevant, and indiscriminately combine all of the factors we have discussed. By doing so, you would beg the questions, however, of which factors are most important and how they should be combined. You must also abandon hope for simpler explanations, even when they are appropriate. All problems would be approached at the same level of complexity.

Because of the drawbacks of a single complex synthesis, it is better to seek explanation with simple models and add complexity as necessary. For economic issues, we can begin with the economic process model, which ignores international political structure entirely and predicts regime change on the basis of technological change and growing economic interdependence. If such a model really explains behavior, we can omit all the complexities of determining the relevant structure of power.

We believe that this will rarely, if ever, be successful. The next analytical step, therefore, will be to add politics in the simplest possible way by seeing whether the overall structure model, alone or in conjunction with the economic process model, can explain regime change. Using the overall structure model, we expect a tendency toward congruence across issues. We would expect, therefore, that actors strong on military-security, high politics issues would create linkages to important economic issues if they found themselves in weak positions on the latter.

If our arguments in this and the previous chapter are correct, however, even this approach will often be insufficient. The next step, therefore, would be to turn to an issue structure approach. Using this model, we assume that power resources are quite specific by issue area and linkage will be slight. Within issue areas, power resources related to vulnerability will dominate resources relevant to sensitivity within a regime. When the regime produces outcomes contrary to what we would expect on the basis of fundamental power resources, we would expect states powerful at the vulnerability level to force changes in the regime.

Sometimes even this refinement will not explain regime change, and one will have to turn to the international organization model and examine how norms, networks, and institutions benefit some actors rather than others — in setting the agenda, in creating presumptions or patterns of behavior that make certain bureaucracies within governments especially active on particular issues. We will also need to ask how international regimes acquire an inertial force, which allows them to persist after the conditions that brought them into being have disappeared.

We shall show in later chapters that each model helps in explaining regime change or persistence during part of the time for at least one of our four cases (oceans, money, and Canadian-American and Australian-American relations). In some cases we shall need to combine two or three models for a full explanation. In several cases we shall require a sequence of models. One model may apply quite well for one period, but poorly for another. It would not be wise to develop a single amalgamated model; but under different conditions, different combinations of the models will provide the best explanations of international regime change and political outcomes.

Our ability to combine models depends, however, on a clear understanding of their differences. Table 3.1 summarizes the assumptions of the models about three key questions. For the structural model, underlying power can be translated into changes in international regimes without high translation costs. Thus the states with significant power capabilities, overall or within issue areas, will determine the nature of international regimes. For the international organization model, this is not the case; furthermore, in this model the costs of disrupting regimes and associated policy networks will be so high that regimes will tend to persist even when their patterns of outcomes are not in line with underlying power capabilities. The economic process model argues that the economic costs of disrupting interdependence will be great, and that under high economic

TABLE 3.1 SOME KEY ASSUMPTIONS OF THE FOUR
MODELS OF REGIME CHANGE

	Overall structure	*Issue structure*	*International organization*	*Economic sensitivity*
Can underlying sources of power be translated at low cost into changes in international regimes?	Yes	Yes	No	—
Are the costs of disrupting policy networks high?	No	No	Yes	—
Are the economic costs of disrupting patterns of economic interdependence high?	(No)[a]	(No)	—	Yes

a. Parentheses indicate an *implied* answer.

sensitivity states will therefore be reluctant to disrupt international regimes.

We are now ready to consider our case studies. Before proceeding, however, we must state two caveats. First, the case studies are not representative of all of world politics. We chose them for theoretical reasons that will be explained in Parts II and III. Second, as we said at the beginning of Chapter 2, none of our models is expected to apply universally. We anticipate that the closer a situation is to complex interdependence, the more the issue structure and international organization models will apply, and the less accurate will be the overall structure model. When realist conditions pertain, the reverse is expected. The economic process model needs political specification before it can be an accurate guide.

If the overall power structure in world politics determined patterns of regime change, we would not need to have introduced such a complex set of models. World politics would be like a single great lake: often turbulent, but with a uniform level. Changes in the amount of water flowing into one part of the lake quickly have effects on the whole body of water. We assume, however, that world politics is highly differentiated rather than homogeneous. The appropriate image for our analysis is therefore not a single lake, but a river divided by sets of dikes, dams, and locks, which separate and connect various levels and "lakes." We have developed our models to attain a better understanding of the heights and strengths of the various types of dikes, dams, and locks in world politics, and to learn more about their architects, engineers, and lock-keepers, and the fees they charge.

PART II | Regime Change in Oceans and Money

Chapter 4

THE POLITICS OF OCEANS AND MONEY: HISTORICAL OVERVIEW

The Pax Britannica of the nineteenth century is sometimes seen as the golden age of international order. International economic interdependence was governed by regimes that were largely established and enforced by Great Britain. Despite the mythology of laissez-faire, Britain applied military force when necessary to maintain such norms as free trade and freedom of the seas. But the regimes were generally acceptable to other major powers. Naval power allowed Britain to dominate the world's peripheries, though the balance of power in Europe was multipolar. In the words of an important British memorandum, the regimes she policed were "closely identified with the primary and vital interests of a majority, or as many as possible, of the other nations [who were thus] less apprehensive of naval supremacy in the hands of a free trade England than they would be in the face of a predominant protectionist Power." [1]

Two of the key issue areas in the Pax Britannica were monetary affairs and oceans space and resources. We have chosen these two for detailed exploration and comparison in the next three chapters because their continued importance from the nineteenth century to the present allows us to test the applicability of our models of regime change under changing political and economic conditions. We shall first describe and then explain changes in international regimes for the oceans and monetary issues between World War I and the present. We expect no single explanatory model or combination of models to be superior for that entire period. Such dramatic changes have taken place in communications and transportation patterns, ocean shipping, fishing, and mining activity, and in international money markets and banking systems, that one would expect equally striking changes in political behavior. Indeed, we began this study believing that our conditions of complex interdependence would be more closely approximated in the 1960s and 1970s than earlier, and that traditional models of world politics would therefore become less relevant over time. As we shall see in Chapter 5, to some extent this is the case — but with important qualifications.

Except for the overall structure approach, our models predict major differences in patterns of politics *among* issue areas as well as, over time, within them. Thus, we chose international monetary and oceans issues, not just for their intrinsic importance, but for their differences, which suggested to us that the patterns of change for their respective regimes would also be quite different. Both issue areas seemed to meet the conditions of complex interdependence to some extent, yet there were significant contrasts. In both, multiple channels of contact exist between societies, and transnational actors are prominent. Force, however, plays a greater direct role in oceans questions than in money. Navies, after all, still patrol the seas, and occasionally attempt to reinforce national jurisdictional claims. But despite the role of force, oceans issues are more diverse and less closely linked, functionally, than international monetary issues. However, political actors may see relationships among oceans issues and may therefore group them. For instance, there is very little direct functional relationship between fishing rights of coastal and distant-water states and rules for access to deep-water minerals on the seabed; yet in conference diplomacy they were increasingly linked together as oceans policy issues. Finally, the issues differ in the geographical fixedness of the goods involved. Money is one of the most fungible of items; and banks, businesses, and governments have well-developed networks for moving it rapidly across borders. Oceans policy issues largely involve questions of legal jurisdiction over resources that are specific to particular geographical areas.

The applicability of the conditions of complex interdependence to the two issue areas will be explored in Chapter 5. In this chapter we shall describe major events in oceans and monetary affairs between 1920 and 1975, emphasizing changes in the nature of the international regimes for these issue areas.

Before we can analyze political processes by issue area, we must define "issue"; that task is more difficult than it may at first appear. Policy issues are not the same as objective problems, such as whether life in the oceans is being destroyed by pollution, or whether the international monetary system can finance growing volumes of international trade and investment. Issues are problems about which policymakers are concerned, and which they believe are relevant to public policy. Thus a policy issue is partly subjective. The problem must be perceived as relevant to policy by people with influence over policy.

Since issues are defined subjectively, so are issue areas. When the governments active on a set of issues see them as closely interdependent, and deal with them collectively, we call that set of issues an issue area.* When we do so, we are making a statement about actors' beliefs and behavior, not about the objective reality of the problems themselves. We noted earlier that international monetary issues are much more closely linked functionally than oceans issues, which are connected largely by the perceptions of actors that issues involving oceans should be treated together. Yet as long as oceans issues are considered collectively, an oceans issue area in our terms exists.

It is difficult precisely to define the boundaries of an issue area; this difficulty is complicated by the fact that these boundaries can change over time as issues, and their groupings, change. We therefore begin our discussions of the international monetary issue area, and the oceans policy issue area, by discussing their boundaries as we perceive them.

THE INTERNATIONAL MONETARY ISSUE AREA

People concerned with international monetary affairs frequently assume that everyone knows the boundaries of their subject, so they often do not define the issue area involved. To say that international financial affairs are being discussed is taken as definition enough. As one might expect, this lack of attention to definition reflects a great consensus on what is involved in this issue area, and a considerable agreement, therefore, on its boundaries. Richard Cooper takes the major dimensions of an international monetary regime to be: "(1) the role of exchange rates, (2) the nature of the reserve asset(s), and (3) the degree of control of international capital movements." [2] Few authorities would disagree.† *Within* an international

---

* This definition is not meant to imply that the political analyst can ignore objective reality. Presumably, political actors who misperceive reality are not likely to achieve their goals unless they adjust their perceptions. In the long run, some congruence can be expected between perceptions and reality. Nevertheless, it is on the basis of subjective perceptions, not on the basis of an objective reality that no one understands in a definitive way, that actions are taken. For a given situation, we *begin with perceptions;* to predict outcomes, or future perceptions, it may be highly useful to have further information about the reality being perceived.

† For instance, under the Bretton Woods regime, which was in operation (with some qualifications) during the 1960s, United States dollars and gold were the major reserve assets; exchange rates were fixed and were not to deviate more than 1 percent from

monetary regime, however, other issues can arise, in particular, problems of *liquidity, adjustment,* and *confidence.* *

It is very important to keep in mind this distinction between issues that focus on what *kind* of international monetary regime should exist, and those centering on relationships within a given regime. Discussions of the extent to which exchange rates should fluctuate, or the role of gold as a monetary asset, clearly belong in the former category; problems of whether the sterling-franc rate was correct in the late 1920s, or whether enough liquidity existed in the early 1960s, fall into the latter set. Although the distinction is not perfect, we emphasize questions of regime change rather than details of the political process within an established regime.

We define the international monetary issue area as the cluster of issues seen as relevant by policymakers to decisions about what kind of international arrangements should exist on exchange rates, reserve assets, and control of international capital movements, *along with* issues seen as relevant to adjustment, liquidity, and confidence within a given regime or nonregime.

To what extent are the international monetary policy themes clear and consistent throughout the period? Since the Treasury Department has the major responsibilities for the United States in international financial policy, we examined United States Treasury Department *Annual Reports* for four years in each of the decades since 1920, and including 1972. Conventional categories such as "money," "trade," "foreign loans," "aid," and "private investment," along with items having to do with taxes, almost covered the

---

par except when official devaluations took place; and international capital movements were, for the most part, unrestricted (although several exceptions could be noted). Since the late 1960s, Special Drawing Rights (SDRs) created by intergovernmental agreement, have become reserve assets in addition to gold and foreign exchange (which refers to holdings by a given country of other countries' convertible currencies — currencies that can be exchanged for other currencies, if not for gold). Exchange rates among major currencies are usually not fixed, and therefore fluctuate daily; and on the whole, international capital movements are still unrestricted.

* Conventionally, problems arising with international monetary regimes are classified under these headings. *Liquidity* refers to the value of international money (gold, foreign exchange, and now SDRs) in circulation in the system. If there is too little liquidity, international financial flows may be unduly restricted; if there is too much, inflationary tendencies may manifest themselves. *Adjustment* refers to ways in which countries can change the relationships of their economies to the outside world to more nearly balance their payments. Adjustment measures can be either internal (such as domestic "austerity" programs) or external (such as changes in exchange rates). *Confidence* refers to the attitudes of holders of liquid financial resources toward currencies: if confidence in the current value of a currency is low, it is likely to be sold on balance by private parties, thus putting downward pressure on its value. For a full discussion of international monetary relations in the 1960s, see Richard N. Cooper, *The Economics of Interdependence* (New York: McGraw-Hill, for the Council on Foreign Relations, 1968).

pages of the treasury's reports devoted to international questions. Furthermore, within the international monetary area, seven key phrases accounted for over three-quarters of the total headings. As Table 4.1 shows, concern with gold (particularly gold movements) was prominent throughout the half century. Since these concerns and those having to do with foreign exchange are closely related, and since both are also related to what we now call balance of payments issues, the table actually understates the continuity in the reports. Clearly problems of flows of financial assets (foreign exchange and gold) and the balance of payments situations associated with such flows have been perceived as important throughout the half century. Generally, the policy issues at the core of the international monetary issue area have remained remarkably consistent.

Not only do policymakers perceive the international monetary issue area as tightly connected; many functional linkages seem, in fact, to exist. Although sensitivity between monetary events taking place between any two major countries has varied, it has always been significant between 1920 and 1976, except when exchange controls have been very tight, particularly during World War II. This issue area does not necessarily include all countries in the international political system; currently, it does not include the Soviet Union, China, and other states whose governments have tried to isolate themselves from the effects of international financial flows. Nevertheless, because diverse international monetary activities are connected functionally, the issue area does not exist merely in the eyes of its beholders. Perceptions of policymakers can profoundly affect the monetary system, but they did not create it, and, short of major political upheavals, changes in those perceptions cannot destroy it.[3]

The International Gold Standard before 1914

Discussions of international monetary regimes since 1920 invite comparisons with the pre–World War I gold standard, which was viewed by contemporary bankers and officials as an automatically self-equilibrating system. It is difficult to understand later events without realizing that the minds of officials in the 1920s and even thereafter were cluttered with images of the prewar system, which many saw as an ideal to which the world should return.

The classic interpretation of how the gold standard operated was presented by the Cunliffe Committee, established by the British government toward the end of World War I. This committee argued that the Bank of England *reinforced* the effects of gold movements by raising the discount rate when a gold drain reduced its ratio of reserves to liabilities, thus restricting credit and reducing prices, economic activity, and employment. It commented:

TABLE 4.1 INTERNATIONAL MONETARY POLICY: ISSUES FOR U.S. GOVERNMENT, 1920–72

	1920	23	25	28	30	33	35	38	40	43	45	48	50	53	55	58	60	63	65	68	70	72
Gold[a]	x	x	x	x		x			x			x	x	x	x	x	x	x	x			
Balance of payments[a]														x	x	x	x	x	x	x	x	x
Foreign exchange						x												x	x	x	x	x
Stabilization (of exchange):																						
U.S. Treasury											x		x	x	x	x	x	x	x	x	x	x
International monetary cooperation									x	x	x											
IMF												x	x	x	x	x	x	x	x	x	x	x
OECD (monetary issues and Working Party Three)																		x	x	x	x	x

Note: The table indicates the key phrases that appeared in headings or subheadings of at least three U.S. Treasury *Annual Reports,* for the first, fourth, sixth, and ninth years of each decade (counting 1920 as the first year of its decade). For the years surveyed, over three-fourths of the headings in Treasury *Annual Reports* that were considered to refer to international monetary policy contained these phrases. All of the headings without these phrases could easily be classified into sets, relating closely to phrases 1–3 (unilateral U.S. actions and general developments); 4 (bilateral agreements); or 5–7 (multilateral actions).

a. Between 1953 and 1965, "gold" and "balance of payments" appear in a single heading, "balance of payments and gold movements," or "balance of payments and gold and dollar movements."

There was therefore an automatic machinery by which the volume of purchasing power in this country was continuously adjusted to world prices of commodities in general. Domestic prices were automatically regulated so as to prevent excessive imports; and the creation of banking credit was so controlled that banking could be safely permitted a freedom from State interference which would not have been possible under a less rigid currency system.[4]

In the official view, this self-equilibrating system was an excellent device. Little concern was expressed that under this interpretation the burden of adjusting to change — especially through unemployment — was borne by the working class, in particular its most marginal members.

More recent analysis has thrown considerable doubt on this interpretation of the gold standard system. Arthur Bloomfield has shown that central banks were more active than the Cunliffe report allowed, and that they used a greater variety of techniques:

Unquestionably, convertibility was the dominant objective; and central banks invariably acted decisively in one way or another when the standard was threatened. But this did not imply unawareness of, or indifference to, the effects of central bank action upon the level of domestic business activity and confidence, or neglect of considerations of central bank earnings and other subsidiary aims, or sole reliance upon movements of the reserve ratio in deciding upon policy. . . . Far from responding invariably in a mechanical way, and in accord with some simple or unique rule, to movements of gold and other external reserves, central banks were constantly called upon to exercise, and did exercise, discretion and judgment in a wide variety of ways. Clearly, the pre-1914 gold standard system was a managed and not a quasi-automatic one, from the viewpoint of the leading individual countries.[5]

Although the Cunliffe Committee had emphasized domestic effects of Bank of England policy, by 1931 dominant opinion about the prewar gold standard increasingly stressed the effects of British discount rates on *international* flows of capital. As the Macmillan Report indicated in that year:

The automatic operation of the gold standard . . . was more or less limited to the sphere of the Bank of England and was satisfactory in its results only because London was then by far the most powerful financial centre in the world . . . and could thus by the operation of her bank rate almost immediately adjust her reserve position. Other countries had therefore in the main to adjust their conditions to her.[6]

London was not the only major financial center — Berlin and Paris were also important — but it was certainly the most important. Increases in British interest rates, or reductions in the flow of new loans to peripheral areas, greatly affected short- and long-term capital flows, and thus balances of payments, not only of Britain but of states dependent on her. These effects occurred even if several central banks all raised their rates proportionately to the rise in British interest rates, because tighter monetary conditions stimulated shifts toward liquid assets, which meant increased balances of key currency countries at the expense of minor centers.[7] Control was thus asymmetrical, as Britain shifted the burden of adjusting to change to peripheral countries such as Argentina, which depended heavily on British trade. The secondary key currency centers, Berlin and Paris, acted similarly: the hierarchical system allowed them to draw funds from lesser centers, as Britain was drawing funds from them. Thus the system was remarkably stable, though it was not nearly as thoroughly dominated by Britain, and by sterling, as earlier writers had thought:

The extra control of the Bank of England over the sterling-mark exchange might conceivably have placed excessive strain on German reserves as money grew tighter in London. The financial structure was such, however, as to give the Reichsbank a similar advantage in moving the exchange rates on smaller neighboring countries in favor of Germany. This hierarchy of short-run financial influence, through which funds moved from lesser to greater financial centers as interest rates rose everywhere, helped to minimize monetary friction among major centers by passing the short-run financial adjustment burden along to the peripheral countries. It provides a striking contrast to the tendency of New York and London to compete for the same mobile funds in later years without either center's having decisive drawing power over funds from Continental countries in payments surplus.[8]

The impressive degree of British control is illustrated by the small amounts of gold that the Bank of England and the British Treasury were required to hold. Confidence in sterling was so great that in 1913 the Bank of England held only about $165 million worth of gold, or less than 4 percent of the total official gold reserves of thirty-five major countries at that time. Britain's holdings of gold were less than 15 percent of those of the United States and less than 25 percent of those of either Russia or France; they were also exceeded by the official gold holdings of Germany, Italy, Austria-Hungary, and Argentina.[9] The need to hold so little non-interest-bearing gold was a mark of strength, not weakness:

London could economize on her gold holdings, like any good banker, because of the quality of her other quick international assets, her institutional structure, and because, such was the power of Bank rate and the London Market rate of discount, gold would always flow in the last resort from other monetary centres.[10]

The stability of this system rested on its hierarchical structure and on financiers' confidence in the continued convertibility of sterling, and other major currencies, into gold at par value. Liquidity was increased not merely by new gold discoveries and by diverting monetary gold stocks into official reserves, but also by increasing holdings of foreign exchange. Whereas world official gold reserves approximately doubled between 1900 and 1913, official holdings of foreign exchange increased more than fourfold; by 1913 foreign exchange accounted for 16 to 19 percent of total reserves.[11]

Financial hierarchy was reinforced by political hierarchy. Britain was not militarily dominant over either Germany or France, but she had access to much more extensive and prosperous areas overseas. This advantage was reflected in other countries' holdings of the foreign exchange of the three key states: Britain, France, and Germany. Only about 18 percent of European holdings of these three currencies in 1913 were in sterling, whereas over 85 percent of non-European holdings of those currencies were held in sterling.[12]

Peripheral countries generally allowed their money supplies to be influenced strongly by actions of central banks in the center countries. Even for advanced small states with well-developed banking systems, the movement of short-term funds "was undoubtedly much more responsive to changes in the discount rates of the Bank of England and other large central banks than to changes in their own."[13] Argentina, which depended heavily on Britain, allowed its gold flow to determine its money supply; it had no effective central bank to control the process. Thus Argentina "could not nullify the negative effects of changes in British interest rates on its own economy." It is not at all clear, indeed, that the peripheral states' governments understood the processes that were going on or the disadvantageous position that they occupied. The absence of balance of payments statistics, and the lack of knowledge of the extent to which the system was managed by key central banks, rather than being "natural," probably helped to maintain the system's stability by making the inequality and its causes less visible. In addition, local oligarchies in the peripheries benefited from the system.[14]

Although often viewed as a very long period extending into the murky past, the international gold standard's life span was actually less than half a century. Some authorities date its beginning from the 1870s, when France, Holland, the Scandinavian countries, and the United States discontinued the use of silver coins and tied their currencies to gold; others date it from 1880 or even 1900, reflecting the adherence of Austria-Hungary, Russia, and Japan to the system during the 1890s.[15]

Moreover, the international gold standard did not operate as smoothly as has sometimes been supposed. The central banks were not particularly sensitive to the international effects of their actions. They did not cooperate to manage the international gold standard in the general interest (although the central banks of England and France did cooperate somewhat). Yet by the end of the period, the need for such cooperation was increasingly apparent as a result of the growth and volatility of short-term capital. After 1907, "there was a growing sentiment in certain quarters in favor of some kind of systematic international monetary cooperation, the absence of which was a conspicuous feature of the pre-1914 arrangements, in order to minimize undue shocks to the payments system from these and other sources." [16]

Thus the prewar gold standard was by no means immutable. Foreign exchange was being used increasingly in reserves; capital movements were becoming more disturbing; and the need for cooperation was increasingly evident. More fundamental political changes were also taking place. As the working class gained political power it would be able to fight adjustment policies that caused unemployment and wage cuts, as the British strikes of 1926 later indicated. As peripheral countries became somewhat more automonous, their policies would become less passive. And perhaps most important, the United States was becoming more prominent in the international economy. Even without the stimulus of World War I, it would eventually have begun to compete with London for funds, and the hierarchy would have been broken.[17]

The end of the international gold standard in its well-functioning phase came with the beginning of World War I. But the trends we have just enumerated, which were intensified by the war, were by no means created by it. One can therefore assume that eventually the international gold standard would have collapsed or have been transformed, even without the war; however, the conditions under which that would have taken place, the form it would have taken, and its effects can never be known.

In practice, therefore, the prewar gold standard was short-lived, managed (although with national orientations rather than an international one), and highly subject to change. It rested on political domination — the domination of the wealthy classes in Britain over less prosperous groups, and of Britain, France, and Germany over peripheral countries. Thus the reality diverged substantially from the myth of an eternal, automatic, stable, and fair system, which could only be damaged if tampered with by politicians. Yet in later years, the myth was in many ways more powerful, in its effects on behavior, than the reality itself. The rules of the old regime were no longer being followed — indeed, they had never been followed as perfectly as people imagined — but they remained the standard of behavior for statesmen and bankers, particularly in central countries such as Britain.

International Monetary Regimes, 1920–76

You will recall that we distinguish regimes from one another on the basis of their formal or de facto rules and norms governing the behavior of major actors. When shifts in rules and norms are very sharp, regime periods can be distinguished without difficulty; but sometimes changes are gradual or sequential, and then the choice of periods inevitably becomes somewhat arbitrary. This is particularly the case when, as in the 1920s, a series of countries joins a par value system sequentially, rather than as a result of general agreement, or when, as in the early 1930s, countries sequentially leave such a system. In such cases we have defined the regime periods in terms of the behavior of the key currency countries — Great Britain until 1931 and the United States thereafter. Following this convention, we have divided the fifty-six years from 1920 to 1976 into seven periods, as shown in Table 4.2. For each period we have indicated whether an international regime existed, and the action at the period's beginning that is considered to have brought the new regime into being or destroyed the old one.

The following pages briefly describe the rules and norms characterizing each period; the degree to which they were adhered to; and the reasons for our choices of beginning and end-points for these regimes. The dates we selected are not necessarily self-evident, and any such periodization does some violence to the flow of history. This review, although not a comprehensive description of political or economic processes in this issue area over the last fifty-five years, much less an explanation of regime change, will give readers unfamiliar with the history of international monetary affairs a general description of developments, and therefore facilitate the analysis of political processes and regime change that follows.

During World War I gold exports from Great Britain virtually ceased. Although the international gold standard was never formally renounced during this period, it lapsed in effect. The pound and dollar were pegged together at $4.77, about 2 percent below par.[18] British citizens were encouraged to sell their foreign securities to provide foreign exchange for the war effort. By 1919, it was clear that Britain had been seriously weakened economically by the war, and that at least for the time being, no return to the 1914 parity of $4.86, with free movements of international capital, was possible. Thus, in March 1919, the gold-dollar peg lapsed, and from early 1920 through 1924, "the rate fluctuated almost completely free from official intervention."[19] The pound reached a low in early 1920 of $3.18, and remained below $4.00 until about the end of 1921, rising to approximately the prewar parity by the end of 1924, in expectation of return to a par value system.

TABLE 4.2   INTERNATIONAL REGIMES IN THE MONETARY
POLICY ISSUE AREA, 1920–75

Period	Years	Regime situation	Action at beginning of period
I	1920–25	*Nonregime*: floating rates, currency depreciation.	Beginning of period surveyed.
II	1925–31	*International regime (de facto)*: Gold-exchange system focused on sterling-dollar convertibility.	Britain's return to gold: April 1925.
III	1931–45	*Nonregime*: floating rates, currency depreciation, exchange controls (especially important after 1939).	Britain leaves the gold standard: September 1931.
IV	1946–58	*Recovery regime*: internationally agreed-on system, but with ad hoc modifications allowed; exchange controls, inconvertibility of European currencies.	Bretton Woods Agreement of 1944 becomes operative.
V	1959–71	*International regime*: fixed but adjustable parities; dollar convertible into gold.	Convertibility of major European currencies achieved: December 1958.
VI	1971–75	*Nonregime*: no stable set of of rules, despite fourteen-month period of fixed rates for many currencies and increased central-bank coordination toward end of the period.	United States actions making dollar inconvertible into gold: August 1971.
VII	1976–	*International regime*: based on flexible exchange rates and SDRs, with central bank and governmental coordination on exchange rate policies.	Interim Committee agreement to amend IMF Articles of Agreement: January 1976.

Rates for continental currencies, which were also floating, showed greater volatility and less strength than the pound. After rising from 6.25 to 9.23 American cents from April 1920 to April 1922, the French franc declined rather steadily, reaching a low point of 2.05 cents in July 1926, before being stabilized de facto at the end of that year at 3.92 cents — about one-fifth of prewar parity.[20] Under the impact of German inflation, the mark fell from about two cents in 1920 to virtually nothing by 1923.[21] Many observers took these results as evidence of the dangers inherent in floating exchange rates. The League of Nations study conducted by Ragnar Nurkse and published in 1944 argued that although short-term capital movements were at first equilibrating in this period, in expectation of returns to prewar parities, as Continental exchange rates continued to fall, disequilibrating speculation set in: increases in interest rates, or exchange depreciation, rather than attracting funds, increased speculation against the currency, as each depreciation provided evidence for the imminence or at least eventuality of another.[22] Thus speculators' psychology, in this view, became a factor in governmental decisions.[23]

The situation from 1920 to 1925 was not considered desirable by any major government involved. The Cunliffe Committee's description of the prewar gold standard was regarded, at the Genoa Conference of 1922, not only as an accurate description of previous reality but as a desirable state of affairs to which the world should return as quickly as feasible, although with some modifications to reduce the deflationary effect of such a change. The major powers at Genoa agreed to establish a gold exchange standard, in which currencies would be exchanged at fixed parities, but in which most countries would be encouraged to hold part of their reserves in liquid claims on the international gold centers.[24] The gold exchange standard was designed to economize on gold; although it was seen as a major innovation, it in fact merely legitimized and extended a practice that was becoming increasingly widespread before 1914.[25] Central banks, which should be "free from political pressure," were to co-operate closely, in order to maintain currencies at par as well as to prevent "undue fluctuations in the purchasing power of gold." [26]

Unlike the Bretton Woods Conference of 1944, however, the Genoa Conference of 1922 does not signal a change in the international regime for monetary affairs. It became clear, particularly to Benjamin Strong of the Federal Reserve Bank of New York, that stabilization of the mark would have to precede reconstruction of the monetary order. Yet in late 1922, Germany defaulted on its reparations obligations; in early 1923 French and Belgian troops occupied the Ruhr; and the mark subsequently collapsed. Only after German stabilization in late 1923, supported by the Dawes loan a year later, could monetary stability return.[27]

The significance of the Genoa Conference is that its proposals fore-shadowed the system that central bankers attempted to put into effect after Britain's return to gold in April 1925, at the prewar parity of $4.86 per pound. Authorities agree that the return to gold was a decisive event that changed the nature of the international monetary regime,[28] although most also agree that it was a disastrous mistake. As the historian of this decision puts it, the decision to return to gold was "unfortunate and, de-spite all the emphasis on the long run, represented a triumph of short-term interests and conventional assumptions over long-term considerations and hard analysis." [29] A return to the gold standard at other than prewar parity was not seriously considered, although in retrospect it is clear that sterling was overvalued by about 10 percent at that rate. Yet "gold at any rate other than $4.86 was unthinkable." [30]

Chancellor of the Exchequer Winston Churchill was uneasy about the decision, and asked some searching questions in a predecision memoran-dum, but

he was in a difficult situation, for intellectually he could see no alternative to a policy of drift, and politically he had to rely on support in official circles, the City, business and the country which was almost unanimous in its desire for the policy actually chosen. . . . Thus Churchill really had little alternative but to accept the advice generally offered, shortsighted though it was, and to adopt the gold standard at $4.86.[31]

The British return to gold in 1925 was influenced by international as well as domestic pressures. Britain was seen as the keystone of the system, and a British decision to return to gold as a critical step in restoring in-ternational monetary stability. Small countries such as Sweden strongly urged return; more important, the United States pressed for speedy and decisive action. As the major international creditor, and the only major country to remain on the gold standard throughout this postwar period, the United States was quite influential, despite its reluctance to make official commitments.[32]

The British decisions, added to the previous German stabilization and the French actions of the following year, marked the beginning of an inter-national regime that lasted until 1931. The regime was established by a series of unilateral actions, rather than by international conference or by systematic alignment of exchange rates on technical grounds. It was a genuine international regime, with known rules, much communication among central bankers, and a good deal of cooperation, especially between the United States and British central banks. But it was weak politically as well as economically, reflecting Britain's diminished postwar position.

From 1931, when Britain left the international gold standard, until the

Bretton Woods Agreement of 1944 became effective at the beginning of 1946, there was no comprehensive and agreed-on set of rules or norms governing international monetary arrangements. The United States, which would have had to assume international leadership, did not do so for the first five years of the period. American officials insisted that there was no connection between war debts to the United States and reparations payments due to its former allies; "the effort to develop a cooperative approach to world economic recovery was thus soured by the continued war-debt conflict." [33] The United States went off the gold standard effectively in April 1933, without consulting even the British and while Prime Minister Ramsey MacDonald was at sea on his way to visit President Roosevelt.[34] During the summer of 1933, Roosevelt virtually forced the adjournment, without significant agreements, of the London Economic Conference. To the consternation of his representatives there he opposed, in a public message, the plan of conferees to ensure exchange rate stability as "a purely artificial and temporary expedient affecting the monetary exchange of a few nations only. . . . The old fetishes of so-called international bankers are being replaced by efforts to plan national currencies with the objective of giving those currencies a continuing purchasing power." [35]

Although France, Belgium, Holland, and Switzerland attempted to cling to old parities in a so-called gold bloc, the domestic economic and political results were sharply adverse. Belgium devalued in 1935, followed by Holland and Switzerland; France finally followed suit in 1936, and in 1937 let the franc float for almost a year.[36] Fluctuations in currency values were severe. The situation at least until 1936 was one of a pure nonregime, with virtually no international cooperation. The central bankers who had previously worked closely with one another, if not always in perfect harmony or with much success, had been greatly discredited by the depression, particularly in the United States. Politicians, disenchanted with orthodox opinion, were searching, almost in the dark, for panaceas or at least for stop-gap national solutions.

As a judgment on the entire period, this description must be qualified, since the Tripartite Monetary Agreement of 1936 (between France, Britain, and the United States) was at least a symbolic step in the direction of new rules, although it provided few concrete measures for cooperation. The treasuries of the three countries — not the central banks, as would have been the case in the 1920s — agreed to hold the exchange for twenty-four hours. In addition, "the French gained assurance that the United States and Britain would not indulge in competitive exchange depreciation," [37] although there was no agreement to stabilize currency values in terms of one another.

Nevertheless, the Tripartite Agreement was not much more than a faint precursor of the international cooperation evidenced at Bretton Woods, in 1944 and thereafter. Hot-money movements played havoc with exchange rates even after the agreement, particularly in 1938, the first half of which saw a speculative outflow of funds from the United States, and the second half, the reverse. Throughout the period, monetary cooperation was hindered by economic nationalism as reflected by trade barriers, German exchange controls, and a variety of bilateral clearing and payments agreements. Governments tried to manipulate exchange rates to their advantage; indeed, *freely* fluctuating exchange rates were rather rare. In a period of worldwide economic collapse and political disintegration, it would have been surprising had international monetary relations been anything but chaotic.[38]

The onset of World War II did bring changes in arrangements governing monetary affairs; in particular it brought "stricter rate pegging, tightened controls, and further displacement of ordinary commercial practices by intergovernmental arrangements." [39] These arrangements did not constitute an international regime with agreed-on rules and procedures. Formal agreement was reached at the Bretton Woods Conference in 1944, but was not fully implemented until more than a decade later. The postwar economic plight of Europe meant, particularly after the failure of attempted sterling convertibility in 1947, that the European Recovery Program became the center of attention. The IMF "sat patiently on the sidelines, guarding its resources," as the Marshall Plan was used to rehabilitate Europe.[40] Only in late 1958, when currency convertibility was achieved in Europe, did the recovery regime give way to full implementation of the regime agreed to at Bretton Woods in 1944.

Long and sometimes difficult negotiations begun in 1941 led to the Anglo-American Joint Statement in April 1944, which became the basis for the negotiations at Bretton Woods and the Articles of Agreement of the International Monetary Fund. Other allied countries had been consulted during 1943 and 1944. France and Canada produced draft plans, and at Bretton Woods the United States and Britain had to contend with the Soviet Union (which eventually did not join either the IMF or the World Bank) as well as with several small countries. Nevertheless, although forty-four countries attended the Bretton Woods Conference (as compared to thirty-three at Genoa in 1922 and sixty-six in London in 1933), the Bretton Woods Agreement was essentially an American-British creation.[41]

In contrast to the practices of the 1920s, at Bretton Woods the international monetary issue area was not left primarily to central banks and private bankers; indeed, United States Treasury Secretary Henry Morgenthau's objective was to create international financial institutions that would be instruments of governments rather than of private financial interests. To the annoyance of the American banking community, Morgenthau saw the issue as "a question of whether the Government should control these things or a special country club of business and the Federal Reserve." [42] Within the United States government, the Treasury Department took the lead, although conflict with the State Department erupted from time to time between the beginning of discussions, in 1942, and the abandonment of plans for immediate convertibility of sterling in 1947.[43]

The core of the regime designed at Bretton Woods was the provision that countries belonging to the International Monetary Fund would set and maintain official par values for their currencies, which were to be changed only to correct a "fundamental disequilibrium" in a country's balance of payments, and only in consultation with the fund. Thus currency convertibility was to be ensured. Great Britain had sought greater freedom of action for individual countries, but the United States had resisted this suggestion. The IMF was to help countries maintain par values by arranging to lend them needed currencies, up to amounts determined in a complex scheme based on countries' subscription quotas to the IMF. But on the insistence of the United States, members were not to have automatic access to the resources of the IMF, beyond their own subscriptions. The IMF retained discretion in judging the validity of members' requests, and certain other limitations were imposed.

The IMF was given considerable nominal powers; but it was itself to be controlled by member countries with the largest quotas, since votes in the IMF were stipulated to be roughly proportional to quotas. The United States therefore had over 33 percent of the voting power in the IMF in 1946; Britain held almost 16 percent. These proportions fell over the years, but throughout the life of the IMF, the United States has been assured of a veto over most important IMF decisions.[44]

When these arrangements were concluded, allowance was made for a transitional period, during which the full obligations of the regime would not apply. Members could retain restrictions on financial transactions until three years after the IMF began to operate; then the IMF would report annually on them. After five years the members were to consult with the fund on the retention of restrictions.[45] Although the transitional period was left undefined, it was generally expected not to last long: "Until early 1947, when the Truman administration shifted course, planners thought other countries would make a relatively smooth and swift transition, lasting no longer than five years, from bilateralism to convertibility." [46]

The transition actually lasted over thirteen years from the end of the war and twelve from the beginning of fund operations. In 1947 Great Britain's efforts to resume convertibility of sterling lasted barely more than a month, at a cost of about $1 billion worth of gold and dollars. Exchange controls were then reinstated, the Marshall Plan went into effect, European currencies were devalued, and the United States accepted measures that discriminated against the dollar. The International Monetary Fund played a small role in this period.

The recovery regime that came into being during 1947 bore little resemblance to the arrangements that had been designed at Bretton Woods. Worried about what they perceived as a critical Soviet threat to Western Europe, United States leaders — prompted by the State Department and followed somewhat more reluctantly by the Treasury — gave increasing aid and sympathy for Europe's financial troubles.[47] This support was accompanied by an impressive array of institutional innovations: bilateral clearing arrangements were followed by the development of the European Payments Union (EPU) and the Organization for European Economic Cooperation (OEEC). A common sense of military threat, which manifested itself most obviously in the development of the North Atlantic Treaty Organization (NATO), gave the United States an incentive to behave generously toward Europe, and the Europeans the willingness to follow the American lead. Within the framework of a political consensus, governments could allow the volume of transnational economic relations to expand while retaining control over them.

The success of this recovery regime was shown by movements toward currency convertibility during the 1950s, culminating in the formal adoption of convertibility by major European countries in December 1958.[48] The beginning of 1959 therefore marks the start of a new international regime, the full-fledged Bretton Woods regime, which lasted until the United States suspended the convertibility of the dollar into gold on August 15, 1971. Economically, the transition was made possible by the economic recovery of Europe and by American financial policies that had produced large payments deficits, furnishing dollars to a formerly dollar-short world. In the late 1950s and into the 1960s, world exports grew at the spectacular rate of 7 percent per year; and United States direct investment in manufacturing abroad increased dramatically. Politically, the transition was marked not only by the hegemony of the United States, but by the development of networks of ties between central bankers as well as between treasuries. The Bank for International Settlements was the technical agent for the European Payments Union, and central bankers "participated along with treasury officials in the managing board of the EPU, which was itself an agency of the Organization for European Economic Cooperation in Paris. These institutions brought the senior European financial officials into regular working contact." [49]

Yet the Bretton Woods regime had hardly been put into full operation before it faced serious tests. The price of gold in London rose in the autumn of 1960, indicating speculators' lack of confidence that the United States government would continue to support the dollar at 1/35 of an ounce of gold. The first result was an informal Anglo-American agreement to maintain the gold price at $35 per ounce: "The Bank of England was assured of access to New York to recompense any gold it used to meet speculative demand in London." [50] This result was followed by an international gold pool under which central bankers agreed to coordinate their gold dealings. In 1961, the central bankers developed a series of swap agreements, providing for mutual support in the event of speculation against particular currencies. Had the spirit as well as the letter of the Bretton Woods agreements been followed, the speculative crises that began in 1960–61 would have been met by expansion of IMF resources; but expansion was resisted by the Continental European countries that would have been the chief creditors. Thus, in the General Arrangements to Borrow of 1962, the members of the Group of Ten (the major advanced industrial countries) contracted to provide resources to the fund when needed, if they first agreed collectively to do so, in order to "forestall or cope with an impairment of the international monetary system." [51] Multiple networks of formal arrangements and informal agreements were developed within a variety of organizations in addition to the IMF. Important links were maintained among central bankers and, through the Group of Ten and Working Party Three of the Organization for Economic Cooperation and Development, among treasuries and economics ministries, as well. [52] To increase world liquidity, members of the International Monetary Fund agreed in 1967 to create Special Drawing Rights as a reserve asset. By 1971, the quotas of the IMF were double those of ten years earlier. [53]

Thus the Bretton Woods regime went through a continual process of political and institutional, as well as financial adaptation. The institutional imagination and flexibility shown by the regime's managers contrasted sharply with the rigidity of currency values that member states sought to maintain. Political innovations helped to maintain a system that had essentially been designed two decades before.

Yet the pressure on the regime continued to grow, particularly after 1967, when Great Britain finally devalued the pound sterling. The pegged-rate system became more and more difficult to maintain as the volume of short-term capital movements grew dramatically. The growth of the Euro-dollar * market constrained the United States as well as European countries. With a weekly flow of approximately $5 billion in each direction between the Eurodollar market and the United States, American financial

---

* "Eurodollars are dollar-denominated deposits in banks outside the United States, including the foreign branches of U.S. banks. More than half of them were created outside the United States (in the world banking system) in a process that is not controlled by the Federal Reserve System or by any other central bank." A. James Meigs, *Money Matters* (New York: Harper and Row, 1972), p. 212.

institutions could "ease out from under the restraints of the Federal Reserve System at least for a limited period of time." [54]

The sensitivity of economic transactions between nations increased, most strikingly with respect to short-term capital flows:

[As] the barriers of ignorance and cost in undertaking international transactions have fallen, the potential speculative movement of funds has increased enormously. . . . A crude quantitative indicator of these developments is provided by contrasting the maximum daily speculation of under $100 million against the pound sterling, in the "massive run" of August 1947, with the maximum daily speculation of over $1.5 billion into Germany in May 1969, and the movement of over $1 billion into Germany in less than an hour in May 1971. Moreover, as the barriers of ignorance fall further, there is no reason why $1.5 billion should not rise to $15 billion or even to $50 billion, in a day. [55]

The other major difficulty was that basic adjustment problems, involving particularly the undervaluation of the German mark and Japanese yen, were not satisfactorily addressed within the system. German and Japanese resistance to revaluation was coupled with the inability of the United States, as the source of the key currency of the system, to devalue the dollar without obtaining the consent of Japan and major European governments to change the rules. As a result, between 1959 and April 1971, the dollar actually appreciated in relation to other major currencies by 4.7 percent. [56]

The United States measures of August 1971 formally terminated the American commitment to maintain the parity of the dollar at a fixed price, on demand of foreign official institutions. But such an undertaking "had in fact been largely inoperative for some time." [57] As a result of American balance of payments deficits, the value of dollars in foreign official hands had grown so much larger than American gold stocks that it was clear to all that massive demands for gold by dollar holders would not be met by the United States. [58] Thus to some extent the Nixon-Connally measures of August 1971 merely formalized a situation that had emerged gradually over the previous decade. Ever since the early 1960s, the United States had devised ingenious schemes to improve the nominal position of the dollar. It had also twisted its allies' arms (particularly the Germans') to persuade them to help protect the dollar, and had made it quite clear that its willingness to abide by its Bretton Woods commitments would depend largely on European and Japanese cooperation with its policy.

The gradual erosion of the Bretton Woods regime reminds us that international regimes do not usually start or stop neatly on a given date. A purist might date the "death of the Bretton Woods regime" earlier, perhaps even with the Interest Equalization Tax imposed by the United States in 1963, which discouraged some capital outflows. Nevertheless, we can see that August 15, 1971, marked the end of an international monetary regime as clearly as did 1914 or 1931. The Bretton Woods regime had operated under conditions of de jure currency convertibility obligations for less than thirteen years. For most of this time it was supported by an elaborate but essentially ad hoc network of informal and institutional arrangements; and for the last few years its status was clearly precarious. Yet by historical standards, its longevity is quite impressive for an international monetary regime.

The four years following the August 15, 1971, actions by the United States were times of turmoil for the world economy. The Smithsonian Agreement never restored convertibility between the dollar and gold, nor did it significantly interrupt the sequence of foreign exchange crises that had foreshadowed the demise of the Bretton Woods regime. The dollar was under pressure in February and March of 1972; sterling was devalued in June of that year; and the dollar was devalued by 10 percent in February 1973, on top of its approximately 8 percent devaluation in December 1971. Since this devaluation failed to restore calm to the markets, they were closed. When they reopened in March, the major currencies were effectively floating against one another. During the subsequent months, values of the major currencies fluctuated widely.[59]

As the post–March 1973 "learning period" continued, treasury officials and bankers began to feel more comfortable about, and even to favor, flexible rates. The governmental officials — in finance ministries and central banks — no longer faced the impossible task of defending artificial rates against speculation; the bankers saw their foreign exchange profits soar.[60] Gradually, central banks began to intervene in the markets and to coordinate their interventions with one another. After the Organization of Petroleum Exporting Countries sharply increased oil prices in late 1973, sending shocks through the world economy, it was often remarked that flexible rates had saved the international monetary system from a massive exchange rate crisis.

Perceptive observers had discerned the direction a reformed system would take. In a world of uncertainty and huge magnitudes of easily movable funds, there would be no return to fixed rates. Fred Hirsch commented in August 1972 that "the operative issue on exchange rates is not the grand arguments between fixed and flexible, but the form that a system of controlled flexibility should take."[61] By 1975, Marina V. N. Whitman was able, in an article reviewing the experience with floating rates, to state flatly that "there can be no alternative to rate flexibility in the presence of high and widely divergent rates of inflation among nations."[62] On the other hand, the wide cyclical fluctuations in currency values between 1971 and 1975 and the involvement of central banks after 1973 indicated clearly that the extreme free-market position — that governments should avoid intervention entirely and let the market find its own level — was untenable. Expectations of self-denial by politicians seeking support from business and labor and with an eye on reelection were politically unrealistic; and absolute restraint no longer seemed economically sound. A "paucity of continuous stabilizing speculation," meant excessive fluctuations in currency values.[63]

Efforts to design a new international monetary regime took place at a time of economic uncertainty and highly publicized failures of several large banks. Yet policy coordination among central banks, and eventually among foreign ministries, increased between 1971–72 and 1973–75. In a sense therefore, a new regime emerged informally between 1973 and 1975. The formal agreement on such a regime, however, did not occur until 1976.

Between September 1972 and June 1974, the formal process of reform focused on the Committee on Reform of the International Monetary System and Related Issues (known as the Committee of Twenty), established by the Board of Governors of the IMF. The United States had urged the formation of this group, within the IMF structure, to dilute the power of European countries in the Group of Ten, which had drawn up the Smithsonian Agreement. Yet the committee's original purpose rapidly became obsolete; it had been created to restore "stable but adjustable rates," but by 1973–74 this goal had clearly become unobtainable for the foreseeable future. Nevertheless, the committee's activity moved reform ahead in two important ways. Although its basic objective was still to return to stable but adjustable rates, all principal countries agreed that floating rates would prevail in the indefinite future. Thus, a detailed set of guidelines for floating was adopted. Second, the committee agreed that Special Drawing Rights (SDRs) would be valued in terms of the by-then-obsolete official price of gold. Thus it took a step toward reducing the role of gold in the international monetary system. The committee responded to demands of less developed countries by suggesting that advanced countries show greater willingness to provide resources for poor countries seriously hurt by increases in the price of oil and related products. Finally, the committee proposed that the IMF be given more influence over national financial conduct.

Beginning in September 1974, reform was centered in an Interim Committee of the Board of Governors on Reform of the International Monetary System, although politically the major actors were the United States and France. In December 1974, France in effect agreed that currencies would not, in a reformed system, be linked to gold, and that there would be no official gold price; the United States agreed that gold could be realistically valued (in line with market prices) and made available to governments with balance of payments deficits. In November 1975, France

agreed to accept flexible exchange rates in the context of close cooperation by central banks and monitoring by finance ministry officials. This
agreement became the basis for a common position of the Group of Ten
in December and an agreement on reform issues by the Interim Committee in January 1976.[64]

The fact that complete accord was reached on formal amendment of the
Articles of Agreement of the International Monetary Fund in January
1976, suggests that this date can be taken as the beginning of a new
international monetary regime. The United States under secretary of the
treasury for monetary affairs declared that "we have a monetary system
again"; the French finance minister welcomed the agreement as "the end
of a debate lasting three years"; and the chairman of the session called it
"the end of a very long road to monetary reform that was achieved thanks
to the political will to succeed." [65] United States Treasury Secretary William E. Simon said that he did not expect any further "major initiatives"
of world monetary reform.[66] Choosing a precise date for the formation of
the new regime is somewhat arbitrary, since it did come into practice
gradually, but only by early 1976 were all the pieces for an agreement in
place. This agreement was vague on many key points, and in some ways
constituted only a commitment to consult; nevertheless, it provided the
outline of a new international monetary regime.

The Interim Committee took the following major actions to establish an
international monetary regime: [67]

1. Floating rates were legalized, under a series of conditions that emphasize the responsibility of member governments "to collaborate with
   the Fund and other members to assure orderly exchange arrangements and to promote a stable system of exchange rates." Countries
   were permitted to establish par values for their currencies, but this
   was no longer a requirement, although it could be reinstated by the
   vote of members holding an 85 percent majority of the IMF's voting
   power. (In practice this allows a United States veto.)
2. Various measures were taken to ensure that SDRs would be the
   principal reserve assets in the system, and "in order to ensure that
   the role of gold in the international monetary system would be gradually reduced."
3. The International Monetary Fund was charged with exercising "firm
   surveillance over the exchange rate policies of members," under
   guidelines that it would subsequently adopt.

The committee also agreed to establish a trust fund for poor countries,
to be financed with profits from the sale of the fund's gold and augmented
with voluntary contributions, and to liberalize credit facilities so that

assistance to developing countries in balance of payments difficulty could be more readily extended. The caucus for the less developed countries made easier credit terms a condition for agreement on the reform of the international monetary system. This linkage was the final issue that had to be settled before agreement could be reached.[68]

Implementation of these provisions would produce quite a novel international monetary regime. Historically, only pegged exchange rates have been associated with general international agreement on monetary arrangements. The January 1976 agreement, by contrast, provides for extensive international policy coordination to regulate a system based on flexible exchange rates. It is not possible for us, writing only weeks after this agreement, to predict its success. In view of the extent of liquid assets in private hands, and the great divergence in rates of inflation among major industrialized countries, it would be foolish to predict a new era of harmonious monetary stability. Furthermore, the IMF has been weakened greatly by the disruptive events of the last five years, and it remains to be seen whether it can be effective under a system of flexible but presumably partially managed exchange rates.[69] Much will depend on the patterns of informal policy coordination that develop as attempts are made further to define and implement the agreement.

THE OCEANS ISSUE AREA

Nearly three-fourths of the earth's surface is ocean. For centuries people have used oceans space for two main purposes: fishing and navigation. The oceans have been one of the "global commons" beyond the jurisdiction of any single state, somewhat like the common pastures in medieval villages that were open for all villagers to use.* And just as medieval village commons were eventually fenced off in response to economic change, so states today are "fencing off" larger parts of the oceans as technological and economic change have increased the uses of the oceans. During negotiations at the United Nations Conference on the Law of the Sea in the 1970s, the idea of allowing states to claim 200-mile exclusive economic zones in the oceans off their coasts received wide support. Under this plan, nearly a third of the world's oceans would come under national jurisdictions. "What the 200-mile zones are mainly about is oil and fish. They would take in four-fifths of the world's sea fisheries and nearly all its exploitable offshore oil." [70]

Until recent decades, ocean space and resources seemed so vast that they could be treated in general as a public good, which one country

---

* Other global commons are Antarctica and the atmosphere.

could use without diminishing what was available to others. Of course there were specific disputes over fisheries and navigation rights, but these could be treated as exceptions to the rule. In recent decades, however, technology has increased mankind's ability to exploit oceans' space and resources, thus raising questions of scarcity and stimulating countries' efforts to widen the area under their jurisdiction in order to exclude other countries from the resources. In fisheries, for example, the number of countries with fishing fleets has increased, and new techniques such as sonar fish-finding devices and factory ships, which process the catch at sea, have increased efficiency. As a result, the annual global fish catch rose from 20 million tons in the late 1940s to 70 million tons in the early 1970s, and several major species of fish were seriously depleted. Economic and technological change in shipping was also dramatic. The world's merchant shipping fleet expanded from 78 million tons in 1947 to 311 million tons in 1974. In 1946, the world's largest oil tanker was 18,000 tons. Over the next twenty years there was a twentyfold growth, to 326,000 tons; and even larger tankers were planned. States became increasingly concerned about the ecological effects of shipping accidents along their coastlines, and thus demanded restrictions on freedom of navigation.

Not only did postwar technical and economic change increase the traditional uses of the oceans; they also led to new uses. In particular, technology has added a third dimension — the bottom of the sea — to the issue of ocean space and resources. The costs of drilling for oil in the continental shelf that lies submerged increase rapidly with the depth of the water. The technology of offshore drilling developed rapidly in the postwar period, and the proportion of the world's oil that comes from under the sea grew from virtually nothing in the prewar era to nearly 20 percent in the 1970s.* Most oil drilling occurs in waters only a few hundred feet deep. Even more fascinating is the development of the technology for mining the potato-sized manganese nodules that lie on the deep seabed at depths of 12,000 to 18,000 feet. The existence of these deposits has been known for a long time, but only since the 1960s have techniques been developed that promise to make available the vast amounts of manganese, nickel, copper, and cobalt which the nodules contain.[71]

Defining the Issue Area

It is not surprising, then, that attention to oceans politics has dramatically increased since 1967, when a speech by Arvid Pardo, Malta's ambassador

* In 1975, offshore oil production was worth $40 billion, or as much as all commercial ocean shipping and four times the value of oceans fisheries ($10 billion). (*Business Week,* March 22, 1976.)

to the United Nations, dramatized the prospects of great wealth from the deep seabed and the need for a new regime. Indeed, oceans politics is sometimes regarded as new and unique. The 1972 president's *Report on Foreign Policy for the 1970's* includes the oceans under "new dimensions of diplomacy." In the view of one former American official, "by 1971, in the short space of five years, the scientific, economic, social, legal, military and political questions were uncritically homogenized and being examined energetically in every possible international forum." [72] When the United Nations Conference on the Law of the Sea convened in Caracas in 1974, more than 2,000 delegates from 137 states faced an agenda of over 100 items. Figure 4.1 presents this postwar increase as portrayed by the attention given to oceans issues in the United States *Department of State Bulletin.*

Although technological change has brought about new uses of the oceans and consequent challenges to customary law, many of the postwar challenges had antecedents earlier in this century. The interwar decades

FIGURE 4.1 Annual references to seven oceans space and resource issues

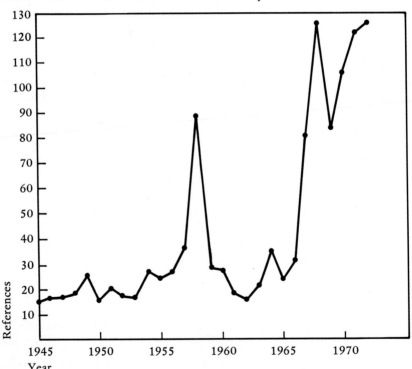

Source: Statistics are derived from *Department of State Bulletin, 1945–72.*

were marked by such familiar "current" phenomena as conferences to save whales from extinction; efforts to deal with oil pollution at sea; at least two dozen claims of jurisdiction over contiguous zones; United States protests over Latin American extensions; United States congressional pressures for extension of jurisdiction over fisheries and shelf resources. At The Hague in 1930, an international conference failed to agree on revising the law of the sea. Postwar conferences held in Geneva in 1958 and 1960 produced four major legal conventions on the oceans, though they narrowly failed to reach agreement on the precise limits of coastal states' jurisdiction.

The oceans policy issue with which we are concerned is the peacetime use and regulation of oceans space and resources. A peacetime oceans regime has two major dimensions: (1) the nature and extent of states' jurisdiction over the oceans adjoining their coasts; and (2) the ownership, use, and regulation of space and resources beyond national jurisdiction. This distinction separates the core problems of the oceans policy system from such related but broader issues as merchant marine policy, maritime labor policy, and naval armaments. It does not totally exclude the use of force as a naval role. "The term 'peacetime' now defines only the absence of *general* hostilities conducted at a *high* level of intensity." [73] As we shall see in Chapter 5, navies have played an important part in the political bargaining over oceans policy in peacetime.

The peacetime oceans issue area includes both "physical" relationships (for example, fisheries and navigation), and political ones (for example, attempts by actors to influence each others' policies towards oceans space and resources). Geography provides the oceans issue with fairly well demarcated boundaries. As one congressman put it, "While it is true that oil, fish, ships, lawyers, scientists, engineers, and admirals is a strange mix, the common denominator is seawater." [74]

The issue area of oceans space and resources has traditionally consisted of weakly related issues such as fishing, commercial navigation, offshore drilling, and military uses. As we have indicated, issue areas can be distinguished by the degree to which the subissues or relationships are linked functionally (for intrinsic technical reasons) or perceptually (through the actions and perceptions of political groups or government officials). Although some oceans issues are linked functionally (conflicting uses of oceans space for navigation versus drilling; or waste disposal versus fishing), political and legal perceptions provide much of the important linkage. These linkages stem both from legal structures and from bargaining tactics. Legal norms about one use of oceans space frequently become precedents for similar norms about other uses. The possibility of "creeping jurisdiction" strongly affected American views of oceans policy issues. As an assistant secretary of defense told Congress in 1969, "the overriding concern of the Defense Department is that the eventual legal regime for the seabeds have no effect on the traditional freedom of the seas. All too often, we have seen legal regimes applicable to one area spill over into others." [75] Both legal and bargaining linkages have been increased by conference diplomacy. As a National Academy of Sciences report noted,

Wholly different fields of ocean activity are becoming more and more inseparable in negotiating situations. Even when actual physical interactions between disparate activities are minimal, the activities tend to be considered together because of this close legal and political relationship. [76]

The Classical Free Seas Regime

The classical regime that was generally accepted for the governance of oceans space and resources since the mid-nineteenth century can be loosely termed freedom of the seas. The high seas were treated as non-appropriable *res nullius*, and coastal state jurisdictional claims were narrowly restricted. Freedom of use occasionally led to conflict, and some international principles of priority and general standards were developed to regulate conflicting uses. Traditionally, navigation was the preferred use. [77] As expressed in a 1958 Geneva convention, "the high seas being open to all nations, no State may validly purport to subject any part of them to its sovereignty." According to a Danish lawyer present at Geneva in 1958, this "cardinal principle . . . serves the interest of all states and was never contested at the Geneva Conference." [78]

The principle of freedom of the seas is often associated with the writings of Hugo Grotius whose treatise on the subject in 1609 was a defense of Dutch commercial navigational interests against Portuguese efforts at exclusion. The principle was frequently abridged in practice. By the nineteenth century, however, the free seas regime was closely associated with the interests and power of the major maritime country, Great Britain. In 1815, the British navy was larger than all the world's other navies combined. [79] Customary law was enforced by the maritime powers, particularly Britain. Maritime powers,

having no great interest in the extension of their own territorial waters owing to the *de facto* superiority that their means of action give them over vast expanses of ocean, . . . object to establishing the exclusive jurisdiction of other states over parts of the high sea, where, in peace, their ships are subject only to the law of the flag, while in time of war their fleets exercise rights there that would be restricted by any extension of the zone of neutrality. Defense of the principle of freedom of the sea was thus for them a matter of national interest. [80]

At the turn of the century, states claiming jurisdiction beyond three miles from the coast (Scandinavia, Iberia, Mexico, Uruguay) accounted for little of the world's coastline and less than 10 percent of world shipping.* In 1902, after the American victory over Spain, Mexico reluctantly went from a nine- to a three-mile limit. In 1905, British protests led Uruguay to release a ship seized for fishing in its contested waters, and in 1909 British diplomatic pressure led Portugal to accept a three-mile fishing jurisdiction. In 1915, Germany enforced a three-mile limit against Sweden.[81]

The one issue in which the classical freedom of the seas regime did not command full adherence was wartime shipping. Although naval blockades of belligerents were accepted under international legal doctrine, it was impossible to develop agreement about interference with ships from neutral nations. Despite efforts to establish rules for the use of oceans space during wartime (conferences were held in Paris in 1856, The Hague in 1907, and in London in 1909), the great powers lacked the similarity of interest necessary to make limitations work during wars.

We should note, however, that interference with shipping during wartime had little effect on adherence to the regime for other uses during wartime or during the ensuing periods of peace. The major dispute between the United States and Britain over freedom of the seas, which Woodrow Wilson enshrined as a principle in his Fourteen Points during World War I, was over these wartime exceptions, not over the legitimacy of freedom of the seas as the basis of the normal regime to govern the use of oceans space and resources.[82] In large part this situation reflected Britain's hegemonic position in oceans issues. As prime protector and enforcer of the principle of freedom of the seas, Britain could grant itself de facto exceptions by interfering with neutral shipping during wartime while continuing to uphold the principle during peace. In peacetime, Britannia ruled the waves; in wartime, she waived the rules.

Britain was careful to abide by the rules in peacetime, allowing other states to fish and navigate close to her coasts. Between 1876 and 1883, Britain adopted legislation which "intentionally limited herself to a three-mile limit for all purposes." [83] One American commentator even argued that,

in reality, the moderation and wisdom with which England has used her authority are more responsible than the strength of her fleets for the length of time that she has been supreme and for the relatively few times in the past when her control has been really threatened, or indeed, advisedly questioned.[84]

In a way strikingly similar to the politics of money under the gold standard that we discussed earlier in this chapter, the pre-1914 peacetime

* The three-mile limit was supposedly set by the distance which an eighteenth-century cannon could reach.

oceans regime was hierarchical and stable, and depended on British domination externally and, to an extent, on the strong position of certain interests inside British politics — in this case the navy and shipping interests.

Regime Periods, 1920–75

In the half century following World War I, the principle of freedom of the seas has declined from the status of a regime almost fully adhered to by all relevant states (until 1945) to a strong quasi regime in which most states adhered to the principle but strong challenges existed (1946–66); to a weak quasi regime in which the challenges have become so great that the status of the rules is open to question (1967 to date). Unlike the politics of money, in which foreign exchange crises frequently provided sharp turning points in regimes, the principle of freedom of the seas has eroded gradually, making the identification of regime periods somewhat more arbitrary. Nonetheless, two turning points — the Truman Declaration and Pardo's speech — are sufficiently prominent to allow us to identify the three regime periods outlined in Table 4.3.

TABLE 4.3   INTERNATIONAL REGIMES IN THE OCEANS
POLICY ISSUE SYSTEM, 1920–75

Period	Years	Regime situation	Action at beginning of period
I	1920–45	Free seas regime	Britain reasserts leadership after World War I.
II	1946–66	Strong quasi regime	1945 Truman Declarations and Latin American extensions.
III	1967–75	Weak quasi regime	Pardo's 1967 UN speech.

The overall regime structure based on freedom of the seas was not at issue between 1920 and 1945. With the destruction and dispersal of the German and Russian navies, Britain emerged from World War I with an even greater proportion of total world fleet tonnage (47 percent in 1921) than she had had on the eve of the war (32 percent in 1914). On the other hand, the United States, which had gone into the war with only 11 percent of world fleet tonnage, was second with 24 percent in 1921 (compared to second-ranked Germany's 14 percent in 1914).[85] Moreover, Britain viewed the American shipbuilding program as a challenge. Although an incipient naval arms race was curtailed in a 1922 treaty on naval arms limitation, the United States won a treaty from a reluctant Britain that allowed it to extend its policing jurisdiction on the high seas out to "one hour's steaming time" from the shore to curb smugglers during Prohibition.[86]

Despite the antismuggling exception, which they won for themselves, the Americans generally supported the free seas regime with narrow territorial limits. Indeed, the only major deviant state was Soviet Russia, whose effect on the regime was small, because its oceans capabilities at that time were very limited.[87] The League of Nations conference called at The Hague in 1930 to codify international law reaffirmed the principle of freedom of the seas. Although one can argue that the very fact of holding a conference in which small states had a voice and vote helped to call the three-mile limit into question, and precipitated some two dozen efforts at special extensions in the 1930s, the overall regime (as contrasted with the specific rule of the three-mile limit) was not called into question.[88]

Although the 1930 Hague Conference was unable to agree on exact limits, twenty states representing 80 percent of shipping tonnage supported a three-mile territorial limit.[89] Those states included all the major powers except the USSR (twelve miles) and Italy (six miles). Twelve states supported a six-mile limit. Efforts by Ecuador, Mexico, and Iran to extend jurisdiction in the 1930s were not recognized by the major maritime states. And as we have seen, even when disputes arose in such sub-issues as antismuggling zones and fisheries arrangements between the United States and Japan in the 1930s, the disputing parties explicitly accepted the legitimacy of the overall regime.

Ironically, it was at the end of World War II, when the United States was the leading naval power, that the Americans inadvertently sowed the seeds of the gradual postwar destruction of the regime. The turning point in the transition from the free seas regime to a strong quasi regime came with the Truman Declaration of 1945. In response to changing technologies of fishing and offshore oil drilling, President Truman unilaterally established fishery conservation zones off the United States coast and asserted American jurisdiction over the adjacent underwater continental shelf "appertaining to the United States" out to a depth of 200 meters. The United States deliberately used limited and ambiguous phrasing to formulate its claims, hoping to avoid damaging the overall regime. These subtleties, however, were obscured as Latin American states, following the great power's example, asserted their own claims to extended jurisdiction. Countries such as Ecuador, Peru, and Chile along the west coast of South America, where there is very little continental shelf, argued that a depth criterion was unfair to them and claimed jurisdiction in terms of distance on the surface. Thus extensions of shelf and fishery jurisdiction, which the United States tried to keep separate from other issues, precipitated both the broader claims by Latin American states and the subsequent seizures of American fishing boats and other difficult diplomatic incidents.[90]

During this second period, the overall regime was not fundamentally challenged, but there were signs of erosion caused by challenges in particular issues. As a result, the major maritime powers, particularly the United States and Great Britain, led efforts to reform, codify, and protect the weakened regime at two United Nations conferences on the law of the sea convened in Geneva in 1958 and 1960. More than twice as many states were represented at Geneva than had been at The Hague Conference in 1930. During the first period, Britain and the Netherlands had controlled nearly 50,000 and 18,000 miles of the world's coastline; but as decolonization progressed their dominance receded, and more and more states became involved in oceans issues during the second period.[91]

The Geneva conferences were only partly successful in bolstering the quasi regime. Four major conventions were signed at Geneva, and no government found it possible or expedient to attack the principle of freedom of the seas directly. But

what happened at the Geneva conference was that the freedom of the high seas was attacked indirectly by claims to extend the limits of the territorial sea, which would have submitted vast areas of what has traditionally belonged to the high seas, including important sea lanes, to the sovereignty of the coastal state.[92]

In 1960, Canada and the United States proposed a compromise formula for limits of six miles territorial sea plus an additional six miles fisheries jurisdiction, including recognition of countries' right to continue to fish where they had historically fished. This compromise proposal came within a single vote of the necessary two-thirds majority, and in retrospect 1960 turned out to be the high point of legal agreement in the second period. In general, there were few claims to exclusive sovereignty or regulation in the high seas beyond twelve miles — a limit preferred by the USSR and only twelve other states in 1960.[93] Although the North-South cleavage between rich and poor states that was to dominate the third period was already visible in 1960, the East-West Cold War cleavage was the dominant political concern during the second period.

In contrast, since 1967 there has been a weak quasi regime; the freedom of the seas itself has been challenged. Ambassador Pardo's 1967 speech helped to touch off a period of intense conference diplomacy. More important, it dramatized the prospect of enormous seabed wealth and focused attention on ocean resource and distributional issues. Since then, the oceans have been treated less as a public highway from whose efficient management all states can gain; instead, one state's gain is often seen as another state's loss.

New states, unbound by the earlier Geneva conventions, entered the game. One hundred and forty-nine states attended the New York sessions of the Law of the Sea Conference in 1976, but only 51 had adhered to the 1958 Geneva Convention on the High Seas (42 adhered to the territorial sea convention; 34 to the fisheries convention; and 50 to the continental shelf convention). The issues of deep seabed resources and the technical developments in offshore drilling and tanker construction raised new problems about the "middle and bottom" of the oceans. Less developed countries, fearing that the global commons would be exploited solely by the technologically advanced countries under a laissez-faire regime, tended to stress broad extension of national jurisdiction or a strong international regulatory body. The United Nations General Assembly declared the deep seabed to be the "common heritage of mankind." China argued that the freedom of the seas was upheld by both superpowers merely as a pretext for superpower "hegemony and expansionism in the oceans and their plunder of the marine resources of other countries." [94] Countries like Canada and Australia, which during the Cold War era were closely allied with the maritime powers on oceans questions, switched to a more coastal view of their interests. And even in the United States and Britain, important groups like oil companies and coastal fishermen gradually gained support for wide extension of jurisdiction. Although only a quarter of all coastal states claimed jurisdiction of twelve miles or beyond in 1960, more than half claimed such jurisdiction in 1970. Between 1968 and 1972 alone, the number of states claiming twelve-mile territorial seas increased from thirty-one to fifty-two, and the number of states claiming two hundred-mile territorial seas increased from five to ten.[95]

As important, however, as the extension of jurisdiction in the third period, was the challenge to the very principle of freedom of the seas. The situation after 1967 was not merely one of "cheating on the regime," but of pressure for an alternative regime. The principle of *res nullius* was challenged. The most influential broad notion that evolved over the last decade was "the claim to ocean space" conveniently expressed in the 1970 Montevideo Declaration, which states that "all nations have the right to claim as much of the sea and seabed near their coasts as they deem necessary to protect their actual and potential offshore wealth." [96] In accord with the dominant international philosophy of developmentalism, new goals such as potential national wealth rather than tradition, defense, or general world welfare were asserted as the basis of rights in the use of oceans space and resources.

As Ecuador's foreign minister said in 1976 on hearing that the American Senate had passed a bill broadening American fisheries jurisdiction to 200 miles, "For Ecuador it is highly satisfactory to see it becoming clearer in the international conscience that it is the sovereign right of each country to fix the limits of its jurisdiction off its coasts with the purpose, among others, to make use of and to protect ocean riches." [97] Although the major maritime powers did not accept this view of the situation, by the mid-1970s, it had become increasingly clear to both the United States and Britain (which was involved in the third of a series of fishing disputes with Iceland known as the cod wars) that whatever the prospects for a formal treaty eventually coming out of the prolonged United Nations Conference on the Law of the Sea, at least one of the major dimensions of the traditional free seas regime — narrow coastal jurisdiction — would never be the same again. Whether by international treaty or by unilateral decisions, the result of conference diplomacy in the third period was sure to be an extension of coastal jurisdiction to 200 miles, thus fencing off a third of the world's oceans.

The Changing Agenda of Oceans Politics

Unlike the money issue area, in which there was considerable continuity in the issues on the policy agenda for the United States (see Table 4.1), the oceans issue area became more complex in the postwar period. This complexity contributed to the pressures for regime change. As we have seen, the oceans were traditionally regarded as so vast that nations could appropriate oceans resources with only minimal effects on each other, and users of the oceans would only rarely interfere with each other. Technological change challenged this traditional assumption, and conflicts involving different uses and use by many nations increased. These conflicts in turn led to a shrinkage of policy space or diminution of isolation among users of the oceans. This shrinkage of policy space not only reflected real competitive uses (sea lanes and drilling platforms; pollution and fishing) but to a large extent was reflected in and amplified by the politics of conference diplomacy.

Growth in the number and linkage of issues involved in oceans policy is reflected both in the oceans policy agenda and the way that agenda has been set for the United States over the three periods. (See Table 4.4.) * From 1920 to 1945, the United States rather than other countries tended to take the initiatives that put oceans policy issues on the United States foreign policy agenda. In two major issues of the prewar era (smuggling, coastal fisheries), the United States government was responding to transnational activity. In addition, the International Law Committee of the League of Nations, searching for topics "ripe for codification," set the agenda for the 1930 Hague Conference in which the United States participated.

* There is no equivalent in oceans, for example, to the Treasury Annual Reports used in Table 4.1.

TABLE 4.4   STATUS OF OCEANS ISSUES IN
UNITED STATES FOREIGN POLICY

Ocean policy issue	1920–45	1945–65	1966–74
Anti-smuggling jurisdiction	Major		
Coastal fisheries	Major	Major	Major
Distant water fisheries		Major	Major
Shelf resources		Major	Major
Overall regime structure	Major	Major	Major
Seabed resources			Major
Pollution	Minor	Minor	Major
Scientific research		Minor	Minor
Navigation restrictions	Minor	Minor	Major

Source: Foreign Relations of the United States (Washington, D.C.: U.S. Government Printing Office, annually); Council on Foreign Relations and Royal Institute of International Affairs (London) newspaper clipping files.

Early in the second period, United States government initiatives, responding to anticipated offshore drilling and pressures by coastal fishermen, caused problems demanding attention. Subsequently Latin American and other extensions of jurisdiction began to set the policy agenda. More formally, the International Law Commission prepared the agenda of the 1958 Geneva Conference, and though the United States helped to set the conference agenda, it was unable to keep items separate or to speed up the process.

In the third period, the United States oceans policy agenda became more complex and reflected a number of sources. Much of the agenda, however, stemmed from less developed and coastal states' efforts to control transnational activities, and from the dramatization of potential economic activity by the United Nations General Assembly. Efforts by other states to control transnational fishing; to benefit from private offshore drilling; to control pollution, particularly in the transport of oil; and to regulate and benefit from transnational scientific research politicized some issues. Others, like the debate on seabed resources and seabed arms control, arose primarily from activity in United Nations conference diplomacy. The issues that received the greatest increase in attention in the *Department of State Bulletin* were minerals, pollution, oil, and overall regime structure. There was more than an eightfold increase in attention to overall regime structure. (This increase occurred both in routine references and in important statements.) * No longer was oceans politics a simple issue of navigation and fisheries dominated by naval interdependence. Modern maritime policymakers could only look nostalgically on days of British naval dominance as the bygone era of fish and ships.

CONCLUSION

In this chapter we have reviewed, but not attempted to explain, the changes in international monetary and oceans regimes since 1920. The monetary issue area is a well-defined, clearly bounded system: a tight area, with a high degree of functional linkage. Oceans space and resources has been a looser issue area with fewer functional linkages, but it has become more closely knit over time. In the international monetary issue area between 1920 and 1975 we identified three international regimes (not including the one that formally came into being in January 1976), and three periods during which an established international regime had broken down and nothing had yet appeared to take its place. In the peacetime use of oceans space and resources, there have been three major regime periods, during which a strong freedom of the seas regime has declined to a situation in which the basic principle was threatened. One dimension of that principle — narrow limits on coastal states' jurisdiction — has been profoundly altered, regardless of the formal outcome of the United Nations Law of the Sea Conference.

* Important statements are White House and departmental speeches, statements, announcements, orders, and authored articles. This category excludes press releases, texts of resolutions, treaty information, and so forth.

Chapter 5 | COMPLEX INTERDEPENDENCE IN OCEANS AND MONEY

Substantial changes have taken place in the politics of oceans and money over the last half century. In this chapter we shall investigate the extent to which political processes in each issue area correspond to the ideal type of complex interdependence, and whether such an approximation has changed over time. In the first half of this chapter we shall discuss how well oceans and monetary politics have conformed to the three conditions of complex interdependence: (1) minor role of military force; (2) multiple issues, not arranged hierarchically; and (3) multiple channels of contact among societies. In the second half we shall ask how well our expectations about the politics of complex interdependence, outlined in Chapter 2, fit patterns of behavior in oceans and monetary politics.

THE CONDITIONS OF COMPLEX INTERDEPENDENCE

The Role of Force

In a pure situation of complex interdependence, force would not be significant. It would be extraordinary if this condition were entirely realized for any major issue area of world politics. Nevertheless it makes sense to ask whether reality comes closer to the pole of complex interdependence (no force) than to the pole of realism (force the dominant instrument). If complex interdependence reflects significant aspects of reality, the realist formulation and realist predictions will require substantial modification. We should also ask whether world politics in the two issue areas is changing. Has force become less useful during this century?

In the oceans space and resources issue area, force plays a much more direct role than in the monetary realm. And because force in the oceans area has traditionally been used overtly, through the exercise of naval power, changes in its use are easier to discern.

The oceans issue area, as we have defined it, is centered on the peacetime use and regulation of oceans space and resources. It does not include those aspects of strategic politics between major powers that take place on or in the high seas except as they affect the peacetime use of oceans space. Clearly, the oceans are a crucial arena both in the nuclear balance between the United States and the Soviet Union and for projecting conventional force to distant areas. Missile-carrying submarines, free to hide in the vast oceans space, are necessary for a second-strike capability. According to one source, "since 1945, the U.S. Navy has exercised active suasion . . . on more than seventy occasions at all levels of intensity and upon areas of the globe ranging from the Caribbean to North Korea through Trieste." [1] The visit of the battleship *Missouri* to Turkey in 1946, the blockade of Cuba in 1962, and the movement of the Sixth Fleet during the Jordanian crisis of 1970 are three prominent examples of the successful American use of naval forces to achieve security objectives in the postwar period. Recently, the Soviet Union has enlarged its surface navy, apparently trying to improve its ability to intervene militarily or to show the flag for political purposes in widely scattered areas of the world.[2]

These important military uses of naval forces obviously intrude on the bargaining over a regime for oceans space and resources. The 1958 Geneva Conference essentially sidestepped the issue of nuclear testing at sea; and both the 1971 treaty on the peaceful uses of the seabed and the Law of the Sea Conference avoided restricting underwater listening devices used in antisubmarine warfare. On the other hand, potential restrictions on naval navigation on the surface and on submarines through straits have been important in bargaining, being treated as nonnegotiable by the United States and Soviet Union. But although naval interests remain powerful in determining the position of the superpowers, navy dominance, at least in the United States, has declined somewhat since 1970. The American position announced in May 1970, with its strong free seas orientation, bore a strong navy imprint that became blurred as domestic economic interests became more assertive.

The long-term trends in the use of force in these two issues have been different for large and small states. At the beginning of this century, force was used infrequently but effectively by great powers, particularly Britain

THE CONDITIONS OF COMPLEX INTERDEPENDENCE | 101

and the United States, to deter smaller states that might have wished to make incursions on the free seas regime. During the interwar period, conflict arose between the two major naval powers, when the United States used force to curtail transnational smuggling. Britain compromised on the resulting American extension of antismuggling jurisdiction. Sometimes great powers used naval force against smaller ones: Britain used force to ensure the passage of food ships through a Spanish blockade during the Spanish Civil War.[3] Yet, more significant in light of future trends was the use of force by weaker naval powers in disputes with Britain and the United States. The Soviet Union used force against British trawlers off its coast. Canada seized four American trawlers, which, along with the American sinking of a Canadian ship, created difficult disputes in Canadian-American relations in the 1930s. Ecuador levied fines on an American ship in 1935; the United States did not use force to reply, because it saw the Ecuadorian Foreign Ministry as a transgovernmental ally against the Ecuadorian War Office.[4]

Since World War II, the large powers generally have not used force in conflicts with small states over oceans resources. And although on several occasions the great powers used force or threats of force to defend their military navigational rights, these efforts have not always been successful. In 1946, a British naval force made a costly effort to assert that the Corfu Strait off Albania was international waters. In 1958, the United States sent a naval force through the straits of Lombok to protest Indonesia's claim that it was territorial waters.[5] The United States and Soviet Union have refused to recognize Indonesian and Malaysian jurisdiction over the straits of Malacca. Between 1957 and 1967, Britain and the United States used naval gestures to counter Egyptian restrictions on Israel's navigation, particularly in the Straits of Tiran, but these efforts were not successful. As one observer wrote in 1967, "The threat of purposeful force (described by the Egyptian Foreign Minister as gunboat diplomacy) was not pursued and, in the event, did more harm than good to British and American interests." [6]

In 1968, the United States failed to respond with force to North Korea's seizure of the electronic surveillance ship *Pueblo;* but in 1975 it responded with force to the Cambodian seizure of the freighter *Mayaguez.* The special circumstances of the *Mayaguez* case illustrate the limits as well as the possibility of the use of force to defend navigational rights. Force was used by a great power that refused to recognize an extended territorial claim by a small power, but the political costs were fairly low. The United States had no diplomatic or other relations with the new Cambodian government that would be jeopardized, and large segments of domestic opinion, resenting a recent defeat, were ready to support rather than criticize a short, sharp retaliatory measure. Indeed in the *Mayaguez* case, force may have been used less to defend the rights of American merchant ships on the high seas than to indicate continued United States determination to defend its interests in the wake of the defeat in Vietnam. If that was the case, then oceans space and resources were only tangential issues.

In contrast, small states have rather frequently used force to extend exclusive coastal state fishing rights further and further from the coast, or to assert extensive jurisdiction over large areas of adjacent ocean for economic or environmental purposes. "Gunboat diplomacy" by great powers has largely been replaced by the gunboat diplomacy of small powers. Seizures of American tuna boats by Ecuador and Peru or Icelandic harassment of British trawlers — rather than naval demonstrations by Her Majesty's Navy — have become symbolic of the use of force on oceans space and resources issues. Indeed, Britain found its mild use of force both costly and ineffective in its cod war disputes with Iceland.[7] In addition to the cases already mentioned, force was used successfully in postwar fishery disputes by Brazil against France; by Argentina against the Soviet Union; and by Korea, China, and the USSR against Japan. A 1969 naval display by the USSR off the coast of Ghana was at least partly designed to speed release of Russian trawlers that Ghana had held for four months.[8] In general, however, the experience of Soviet willingness to use force in securing its oceans interests is a "fairly consistent record of accepting the seizure of property and the expulsion and even loss of personnel in the interests of longer term foreign policy objectives."[9]

Although political processes are usually more complicated than statistics indicate, in eighty instances of postwar use of naval force up to 1970 (according to one admittedly incomplete list) fourteen were over the peacetime use of oceans space and resources. Of these fourteen, small powers used force successfully in slightly more instances than did great powers.[10] Such numbers can be misleading, for where deterrence is at issue, the absence of incidents may be a tribute to the effectiveness of force. Nevertheless, the fact that both small-power extensions of jurisdiction and incidents over such extensions increased indicates a decline in deterrence by the great naval powers, which had earlier preserved the peacetime oceans regime.

The changing role of force in peacetime oceans issues and the contrary trends for large and small states corresponds to our general discussion in Chapter 2. One cause is military technology. Not only are nuclear powers deterred by risks of escalation, but more recently the possession of surface-to-surface antiship missiles by some forty coastal countries has raised the potential military costs of action by distant-water fleets. General norms against the use of force are a second cause of the change. A forceful response by a big state in a fishery dispute often makes it appear as an unreasonable bully, as the British discovered in the cod wars. Finally, and perhaps most important, the great powers' attempts to use force often hinder the attainment of their extensive goals outside, as well as within, the oceans issue area. This effect inhibited the United States' use of force in its fishing disputes with Ecuador and Peru, and seems to have affected Soviet behavior as well.

Thus the role of force has changed in the oceans issue area. It is less central and no longer reinforces the dominance of powerful states. The erosion of the free seas regime enforced by great naval powers has not only given small states some leeway for using force; it has allowed them to raise additional issues of resource exploitation that were discouraged under the old regime. Technological change has contributed to the development of other issues, having to do with recovery of minerals from the seabed, oil drilling, and protection of the oceans environment — none of which have been resolved by force.

The conclusion to be drawn about trends in the use of force is complex. The oceans remain strategically important, and this use has indirectly but strongly affected bargaining on issues of oceans space and resources. Military force also continues to directly affect these issues, although here the dramatic change is from the use of force by great powers to reinforce a regime (and therefore to maintain deterrence) to the use of force by small states to erode the established free seas regime by extending their jurisdiction. In recent years, however, many issues have arisen, partly because of technological change and partly because of the erosion of the established regime, on which force is not effective.

The complexity of these patterns means that any general judgment about the role of force in oceans issues must be heavily qualified. Nevertheless, one can conclude that the actual situation in the oceans issue area lies somewhere between complex interdependence and realism: force is useful on particular questions, occasionally, but is not the predominant factor determining outcomes. In addition, force seems to be important on fewer oceans issues than it was before 1945, and on many conflicts it is not usable at all. Thus this condition of complex interdependence is approximated more closely for the oceans issue area since 1967 than earlier, particularly than before World War II.

The use or threat of force has always been less evident in international monetary issues than in oceans space and resources. In this respect, the politics of money has always approximated complex interdependence better than the politics of oceans space and resources. There is no evidence, for instance, that governments during peacetime have ever threatened the direct use of force to change exchange rates, to induce other independent governments to hold particular currencies, or to secure support for preferred monetary regimes. That is, the aggressive use of force — directly threatening to attack a country if it does not follow particular international monetary policies — seems to be exceedingly rare if not nonexistent.

On the other hand, the politics of money is not completely isolated from the politics of military force. Monetary instruments have occasionally been used to achieve political and security goals. Jacob Viner concluded that there was substantial truth in the generalization, for the pre-1914 period, that "diplomacy exercised a controlling influence over prewar international finance." [11] Germany's economic dominance in southeastern Europe in the 1930s was used to reinforce its political and military power.[12] The United States' 1947 decision to cease demanding full convertibility of the pound and to provide increased aid for the British economy was motivated largely by security concerns.[13] Conversely, in 1956 during the Suez invasion, the United States refused to support the hard-pressed British pound unless Britain changed its Suez policy.[14]

Occasionally, the links have gone the other way. Military instruments have indirectly been used to achieve international monetary objectives. While Britain retained its empire, the colonies were a source of strength for the pound, since London essentially determined their monetary policies. According to Susan Strange, in 1957 Britain directly linked military protection of newly independent Malaya to Malayan support for the pound.[15] In 1966 and thereafter, the United States linked its continued military role in Europe with German support for American international monetary policy.[16]

These cases indicate that international monetary issues are not entirely divorced from military security politics. Yet the uses or threats of force (or the threat of withdrawing military protection) are few. Much more frequently, the policy instruments used in bargaining over international monetary issues have come from within the issue area itself or from closely associated areas such as trade policy. In the 1920s, when the Bank of France put pressure on the pound, the British Treasury hinted that it might present the entire war debt of France to Britain for collection. As Governor Moreau of the Bank of France confided to his diary: "The Bank of France incontestably dominates the Bank of England, but the British Treasury dominates the French Treasury, so that when we put pressure on the institution of Threadneedle Street, M. Churchill threatens M. Poincaré." [17]

In the 1930s, monetary and trade measures were closely linked; at the London Economic Conference, trade issues could not be settled until monetary uncertainties were cleared up.[18] After World War II this connection continued, as the United States sought *both* a nondiscriminatory trading system and currency convertibility at pegged rates. In 1971, President Nixon and Treasury Secretary Connally employed both monetary and trade instruments to compel a devaluation of the dollar; but they used no explicit threat of force or of withdrawal of military protection from America's allies. Throughout the fifty-six years under review, economic instruments — within the monetary issue area or in related areas — have been more useful than force in international monetary affairs. Thus, regarding the role of force, the international monetary issue area conforms more closely to complex interdependence than to the realist ideal type; but no clear or dramatic change has taken place over time.

Absence of Hierarchy among Issues

The oceans issue area has not exhibited a consistent hierarchy of issues. Coastal interests were powerful in the interwar period, and led to the 1945 Truman declarations. Although security concerns were dominant during the Cold War, the hierarchy of goals has been challenged by new issues that different organizations or groups regard as more important. The navy's desire for freedom of action, for example, has not always had higher priority than economic interest in exploiting oceans resources or ecological concerns about pollution. The navy, large oil corporations, and the Sierra Club often disagree; and the United States government has not been able to maintain a consistent hierarchy among the various issues.[19]

The increased complexity of oceans space and resources issues is indicated by the agendas of international conferences over the past half century. There were six substantive agenda items at the 1930 Hague Conference. The 1958 Geneva Conference, which produced four major conventions, was based on an International Law Commission draft with seventy-three prepared articles. At Caracas in 1974, there were about twenty-five major items and nearly a hundred subissues. Moreover, there were more contentious items at Caracas.

The increased number of oceans issues is also evident from the perspective of American foreign policy. As Table 4.4 showed, from 1920–45 the issue area for the United States consisted of two major issues (coastal fisheries and infringement of navigation to enforce antismuggling measures) and a half dozen minor ones. From 1946 to 1966, smuggling dropped out, but continental shelf resources, distant water fisheries, and breadth of the territorial sea brought the total of major issues to five. From 1967 to 1972, as Table 5.1 indicates, attention to oil, deep seabed resources, pollution, and overall regime questions increased dramatically.

These issues have become more closely interrelated in the most recent period. There has been a compression of policy space as more agencies become involved. In 1968, the Interagency Task Force on the Law of the Sea consisted of three departments: defense, interior, and state. By 1975, thirteen agencies were involved.[20] There are two major reasons for this growth and linkage of issues: technological change and international regime change. Figure 5.1 illustrates the role of regime change. Based on

TABLE 5.1   AVERAGE ANNUAL REFERENCES TO
SEVEN OCEANS ISSUES

	1946–66	*1967–72*	*Percentage of increase between periods*
Regime	1.7	14.5	852
Fish	10.4	26.3	252
Navigation	8.3	15.5	186
Pollution	1.5	13.8	920
Science	4.2	13.3	317
Oil	.6	4.5	750
Minerals	.9	10.3	1144
Total	27.6	98.2	363

Source: Statistics are calculated from *Department of State Bulletin*, 1946–72.

FIGURE 5.1   Percentage of references to six oceans issues including linkages to other oceans issues

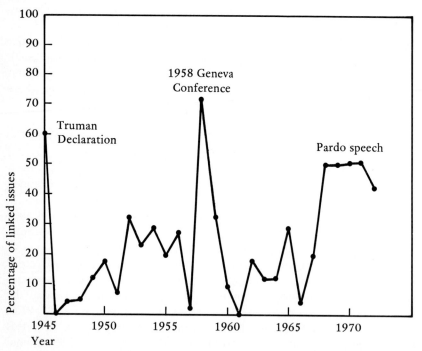

Source: Statistics are derived from *Department of State Bulletin*, 1945–72.

all oceans references in the *Department of State Bulletin* since World War II, it shows how simultaneous references to different issues rise during periods of international negotiation over regime change.

As indicated in Chapter 4, the international monetary system also involves technically complex issues. However, the issues in this issue area have generally been more tightly linked and have been very consistent over time. The 1972 Annual Report of the United States Treasury Department, for instance, listed the following five issues as needing world decision at that time:

1. Means of defending stable exchange rates and convertibility.
2. Proper role of gold, reserve currencies, and Special Drawing Rights in the system.
3. The appropriate volume of liquidity.
4. The permissible margins of fluctuation around exchange rates.
5. Other measures dealing with liquid capital movements.[21]

With the exception of Special Drawing Rights, all of these issues were important in the international monetary deliberations of the 1920s and 1940s. In the 1970s however, poor countries proposed that the international monetary system be used to transfer resources, by linking drawing rights and aid, using the sale of gold from IMF stocks to assist less developed countries in balance of payments difficulty, and liberalizing the rules for borrowing from the IMF. Although the United States and other major industrialized countries regarded these issues as being of secondary importance in creating a new monetary regime, they took up increasing time in the 1970s. Indeed, in January 1976, provisions to accommodate the demands of less developed countries were among the most controversial issues facing the Interim Committee of the IMF.

Over the long term, some changes have taken place in the relative importance of different types of issue. These changes are shown in Table 5.2, in which the concerns expressed in United States Treasury reports are in three clusters: (1) financial flows in the international monetary system, other countries' actions, and unilateral United States actions (here the United States is an observer of the system, and an actor; but principal emphasis is not on its cooperation with other actors); (2) United States bilateral agreements and arrangements; and (3) multilateral agreements, institutions, and arrangements.

Several trends are noticeable from Table 5.2. Most dramatically, the proportion of attention devoted to multinational affairs has risen from zero in the reports of the 1920s and 1930s to about one-quarter in the 1940s and 1950s, 35 percent in the 1960s, and over half in 1970–72. Bilateral agreements, which received considerable attention in the 1930s,

TABLE 5.2   ATTENTION TO THREE TYPES OF ISSUES IN U.S.
TREASURY ANNUAL REPORTS (BY NUMBER OF PAGES)

Type of issue [a]	1920s	1930s	1940s	1950s	1960s	1970s
Flows	2.65 (100)[b]	0.17 (46)	2.45 (52)	2.50 (57)	5.78 (59)	7.10 (46)
Bilateral	0.0	0.2 (54)	1.05 (23)	0.60 (14)	0.55 (6)	0.20 (1)
Multilateral	0.0	0.0	1.10 (24)	1.25 (29)	3.43 (35)	8.30 (53)

a. See text for definitions of these types
b. Number in parentheses is the percentage of total for that decade.

1940s, and 1950s, have been relegated to a minor role. In general, emphasis on the *regimes,* and how to improve or construct them, has increased, as opposed to the earlier focus almost exclusively on financial flows and American actions with regard to them.*

On the whole, however, foreign policy agendas have been affected less by the proliferation of international monetary issues or by a loss of hierarchy among them than by variations in their *salience* over time. When these questions, and other economic issues, have been less controversial, military security has tended to dominate foreign policy and a clear hierarchy of issues appears to exist. On the whole, issues were ordered this way during the 1940s and 1950s, but that was an exceptional period. In the 1920s, international monetary policy was the subject of major political decision in Britain and France, and a significant source of contention between them. In the 1930s it became highly salient politically for the United States, too. In 1933, as Herbert Feis comments, it was the "storm center of our foreign relations." [22] Despite the very important deliberations at Bretton Woods in 1944, international monetary affairs were eclipsed during the 1940s by World War II, and later (after a short period in which security fears were somewhat muted) by the Cold War.

---

* Discussions in the U.S. Treasury Department annual reports were also coded according to whether they referred entirely to direct United States concerns with balance of payments, the value of the dollar, and other national issues, or whether they dealt with questions of the international monetary regime and schemes for its reform. Systemic reform references were nonexistent until 1940, but between 1943 and 1955 always constituted (in terms of pages) at least a quarter of the attention paid in the reports to international monetary affairs. They then disappeared from the reports until 1965, after which they rose rapidly to hold, by 1972 (the last year reviewed), the most space in the section on international monetary relations.

During the past decade, political attention to monetary issues has been at an historic high. From the viewpoint of the agenda of American foreign policy, and the agendas of other major capitalist countries, this emphasis contributed to the apparent proliferation of "new issues." In the monetary area, the issues are not new but have become highly salient after a period of dormancy. At times of major decisions and crisis, such as 1925, 1933, and 1971, international monetary policy has always been high politics. But when crises subside and new regimes, or new national policies, are devised, the salience of these issues declines. Thus patterns of hierarchy among issues change as periods of crisis come and go.*

Multiple Channels of Contact

In both the oceans and monetary issue areas, opportunities for interaction between governments, at various levels, have increased dramatically since 1920. In the 1920s most relationships in these areas were bilateral. Few officials from major countries knew each other well and met frequently. Only a few governments were involved, and their bureaucratic structures in these issue areas were quite simple. Over the next fifty years, multilateral ties, often through international organizations, proliferated; the bureaucracies concerned with these issues grew much larger, and, in the oceans case, much more numerous. Intergovernmental channels of contact therefore increased dramatically.

The number of international organizations involved in the oceans issue area nearly quadrupled, from five during the first period to nineteen at the beginning of the third. The number in 1975 was close to thirty if one includes regular conferences, interagency coordinating bodies, and minor fisheries commissions.[23] In the monetary area, the proliferation of organizations was less striking, but the growth of communications networks among officials even more so. By the late 1960s and early 1970s four important intergovernmental organizations operated in the monetary area: the Bank for International Settlements (BIS), founded in 1930; the International Monetary Fund (IMF), founded in 1944; the Organization for Economic Cooperation and Development (OECD), founded in 1961 in a reorganization of the old Organization for European Economic Cooperation (OEEC); and the Monetary Committee of the EEC. As important for

* Major political figures in the governments concerned, including heads of government, have always been involved in monetary issues at these times. An analysis of the relative attention paid to international monetary issues in the *New York Times* since 1913, however, indicates that the attention paid to those issues in the late 1960s and early 1970s was the highest, by far, during the period (as measured by the proportion of space in the *New York Times Index* devoted to the issue). Similar results are found for the U.S. Treasury Department annual reports for the same period; and for the *Department of State Bulletin* since 1947. Data are available from authors on request.

policy as any of these was the less formally constituted Group of Ten, a combination of the major OECD countries who participated in the General Arrangements to Borrow in 1962.[24] Because the IMF and OECD created committees and working parties from time to time, and because memberships — both for states and individuals — on the various bodies overlapped, the elite network structure was actually much more complex and the opportunity for transgovernmental contacts was greater than this listing of the organizations indicates. In view of the complexity of arrangements, and the multiple roles of participants, it is not surprising that negotiations on monetary reform are sometimes characterized as being a "financial circus." [25]

Nongovernmental channels of contact have also increased in both areas. Before 1945, the major nongovernmental interests on oceans issues were those of fishermen (who traditionally have been nationally oriented) and shipping firms, which were organized transnationally into liner conferences and other cartel-like arrangements. Since 1945, multinational oil companies and mining firms, as well as transnational groups devoted to science, ecology, and world order, have joined the traditional shippers and fishers both in using the oceans and in making political demands on governments. There has been a rapid growth and diffusion of transnational activity in the oceans, particularly since 1945.

As transnational economic activity increased, so did transnational political activity and contacts. In the 1920s and 1930s, smugglers had unintended political effects, and coastal fishermen deliberately influenced policy, but neither were transnational organizations. The Institute of International Law and the International Law Association publicly supported a three-mile limit. The International Maritime Committee organized discussions that helped to resolve the less controversial legal issues related to navigation and shipping.

In the second period, transnational political activity became more extensive. Oil companies worked through their lawyers' membership in the International Law Association, which influenced the International Law Commission's work on draft conventions for the 1958 conference. Scientists organized transnationally in the Scientific Committee on Oceans Research (SCOR) and successfully pressed their governments to create the International Oceanographic Commission (IOC) to coordinate large-scale oceanographic research. World order groups worked transnationally to promote a stronger international regime.

Since 1967, there has been even more political activity by transnational organizations. Oil and mining companies have lobbied in various countries for their policy preferences. The International Law Association has taken stands very close to the positions of these two industries. Joint ventures have been started by mining companies in order to broaden their political support in major countries as well as to spread their economic risks.[26] Scientists have done some cautious lobbying, and groups promoting world order goals have organized various unofficial conferences and discussions to disseminate their views.[27]

In the monetary issue area, on the other hand, we do not find such steady growth in the importance of transnational actors and contacts. Transnational actors were already very important in the 1920s. American bankers were prominent actors on the international scene, floating publicly offered foreign capital issues in the United States between 1920 and 1931 of over $11 billion.[28] Politically, they were equally important, because of the official disinterest of the United States government in getting formally involved with European reconstruction. J. P. Morgan and Company was a major actor in the monetary history of the 1920s: as one author puts it, "The vacuum left by the United States authorities was filled by J. P. Morgan & Co." [29]

After the 1929–31 crash, the importance of bankers such as Morgan fell dramatically and transnational relations remained clearly subordinate to government policies for over a quarter century. Only in the late 1950s and 1960s did the large-scale return of American banks to Europe, and the spectacular growth of multinational enterprises, return transnational actors to great prominence in the international monetary system. The growth of the Eurodollar market to the vicinity of $220 billion in 1974, and the growth in deposits of the top twenty American multinational banks to $57.9 billion (30 percent of the combined head office and branch total) in 1972, indicate the magnitude of the phenomenon. Furthermore, the change had been rapid: ten years earlier, the Eurodollar market was miniscule, and in 1965 only 6 percent of the deposits of those twenty banks were held abroad.[30]

The monetary area, like the oceans issue area, shows a clear trend toward the increased importance of large, sophisticated organizations in transnational activity. Banks and multinational corporations have become more significant. In the 1960s, the expansion of American banks abroad was particularly rapid. Among banks, there is great diversity, from huge banks such as First National City Bank, with hundreds of branches around the world, to smaller banks that participate only peripherally in the international monetary system through correspondent relationships. The largest banks influence the operation of the monetary system most strongly and have the greatest stakes in it, rather than individual speculators. Finally, from time to time, transnational networks of professional economists have played a significant role in the international monetary system. In the 1960s and early 1970s economists seem to have legitimized the idea of flexible exchange rates to bankers and policymakers, partly through conferences held in European spas, and partly as a result of the fact that major policymakers, such as United States Treasury Secretary George Schultz, were economists themselves.[31]

Money, Oceans, and Complex Interdependence

Table 5.3 summarizes the closeness of the international monetary and oceans issue areas to complex interdependence, and the significant changes that have taken place in this regard over the past half century. In the 1970s, both issues lie closer to complex interdependence than to realism, though neither corresponds purely to the ideal type. In particular, force has some effect in each area, particularly in oceans politics; and the diffusion of issues in the oceans area and the difficulty in ordering them hierarchically are not paralleled for international monetary politics. Since 1920, the oceans issue area has changed more than has money on all three dimensions, but particularly on multiple issues and multiple channels of contact.

THE POLITICAL PROCESS
IN MONEY AND OCEANS

"Complex interdependence" describes a set of conditions that contrast strongly with the "state of war" on which theorists of world politics have traditionally concentrated. Thus, opportunities and constraints for decision-makers will be different under complex interdependence than in a traditional realist world. When the use of force by others is an imminent danger, as it is under realist assumptions, survival may depend on the ability to react quickly to external events. Wise statesmen will therefore attempt to insulate themselves from the vagaries of domestic politics. Often they will try to follow well-tested balance of power or realpolitik maxims, which focus entirely on external events and ignore domestic constraints. As in any other strategic situation in which maneuverability and surprise are important, the exact behavior of the actors will be somewhat unpredictable. However, each will be preoccupied with its security dilemma, as well as with power aspirations, and thus considerations of military force will weigh heavily on policy choices.

The negligible role of force under complex interdependence relaxes these constraints. No longer must states adjust every major foreign policy action to the balance of military power and the nature of military alignments. On the other hand, the emergence of multiple channels of contact between countries, on multiple and nonhierarchic issues, increases the opportunities for influence. Points of conflict as well as points of coopera-

TABLE 5.3   CHANGES IN COMPLEX INTERDEPENDENCE
FOR MONEY AND OCEANS ISSUES, 1920s–1970s

Dimensions of complex interdependence	How closely does the situation correspond to the complex interdependence model in the 1970s?	Have the patterns changed over time toward the complex interdependence model?
Oceans		
Negligible role of force	Weak approximation to complex interdependence; role of force still significant.	Yes, with qualifications: force now used *more* by weak nations, but force is not effective on many issues, especially for the great powers.
Lack of hierarchy among issues	Close approximation to complex interdependence; hierarchy difficult to maintain.	Yes.
Multiple channels of contact	Close approximation to complex interdependence.	Yes.
Money		
Negligible role of force	Fairly close approximation, although there are some linkages with force.	No. The role of force has always been minor and no clear trend is evident.
Lack of hierarchy among issues	Weak approximation to complex interdependence. Within the issue area, issues remain quite closely linked and functionally related to one another; but when monetary issues are salient, as in 1970–75, the foreign policy agenda as a whole is characterized by a less clear hierarchy of issues. (Military security no longer is automatically dominant.)	No. The pattern of close linkage among issues within the monetary area persists over time. Whenever monetary issues have become "high politics," the overall foreign policy hierarchy has been weakened—in 1933 as well as in 1971.
Multiple channels of contact	Close approximation to complex interdependence.	Yes, but the pattern is not linear. Channels of contact were reduced in the early 1930s, but by the 1960s had reached unprecedented high levels.

tion increase. The total foreign policy situation becomes more complex. As a result, the bargaining choices for states become richer. They can choose which issues to emphasize, and which to ignore; on which issues to demand concessions, and on which to compromise. With fewer constraints and more opportunities, the range of feasible policy becomes larger.

Were we to assume that states are autonomous entities, whose policies are determined by rational calculation of statesmen, we would have to conclude that complex interdependence increases the range of choice open to policymakers. Old constraints have been eroded and new opportunities have emerged. Unfortunately for the policymakers, however, other aspects of complex interdependence introduce new forms of constraint — less predictable than the constraints of the "state of war," but often equally binding. The multiple channels of contact that emerge between societies not only provide levers of influence for governments, but levers for influence on governments by nongovernmental actors. Transnational organizations such as multinational corporations are the most important of these actors. Multiple channels of contact also imply increased transgovernmental relationships, with adverse effects on the coherence of governmental policy. The growth of interdependence between societies, combined with increased governmental supervision of the society and the economy, is likely to lead first to indirect policy interdependence (in which governments inadvertently affect one another adversely), then to direct policy interdependence. New issues may arise, not from any deliberate decision by the policymakers, but from domestic pressures or in response to transnational interactions that are regarded by powerful groups as having harmful effects.

In Chapter 2 we argued that the realist and complex interdependence ideal types implied different expectations about five aspects of the political process: (1) actors' goals, (2) instruments of state policy, (3) agenda formation, (4) linkages of issues, and (5) roles of international organizations. Earlier in this chapter we concluded that both the oceans and international monetary issue areas conform more closely to complex interdependence than to the realist image, but that neither issue area conforms exactly to complex interdependence conditions. Now we explore the correspondence between the expectations about political processes discussed in Chapter 2 and the reality that we find in money and oceans. Are the expectations of complex interdependence more accurate than those of realism?

Goals of Actors

On the basis of complex interdependence, we expect that the goals of states will vary by issue area; that transnational actors' goals will differ by issue area; and that transgovernmental politics will hinder states from pursuing coherent objectives.

On a superficial level, the first part of this tripartite proposition must almost necessarily be true. After all, the problems that arise in oceans are not the same as in monetary politics. The key distinction between realist and complex interdependence expectations, however, rests on whether military security goals override others in both areas. During the Cold War these goals were dominant in oceans politics; but during the last five years economic and other goals have frequently overridden military security goals, not only in many small or middle-sized countries but in the world's greatest naval power, the United States. The navy has been less able to establish its objectives as the national interest. Although it has been able to maintain free passage through straits as a top priority, it has been unable to maintain the overall priorities in oceans policy that it helped to establish in President Nixon's policy statement of May 1970. For example, the firm navy position of 1969 that "the narrowest definition of the continental shelf would be best . . . both from a national security point of view and in keeping with the freedom of the seas attitude" has been successfully challenged by other interests.[32]

In monetary politics, security goals have periodically been relevant, but they have not been determining. The United States did not abandon its war in Vietnam for balance of payments reasons, but neither did it devalue the dollar in 1965 or 1968 to finance the war. It attempted unsuccessfully to pursue both goals — victory in Vietnam and the maintenance of a stable value for the dollar. Security considerations influenced negotiations about the extent of devaluation in 1971, yet the impetus for the Nixon-Connally actions seems to have been principally economic. Indeed some commentators were concerned that American economic bullying was weakening the Western alliance. The *New York Times,* for example, complained editorially about the treatment of our allies by the agriculture, commerce, and treasury departments.[33]

The second proposition, that transnational actors pursued different goals in the two issue areas, is clearly correct, although hardly surprising. Different transnational organizations, and different networks of elites, were involved.

The most important proposition derived from complex interdependence about actors' goals is the third: that transgovernmental politics will make it difficult for states to pursue clearly specified goals. Although it is difficult to secure systematic information about transgovernmental politics (since much of it is necessarily *sub rosa*), what evidence we have suggests that, as expected, transgovernmental politics often takes place when complex interdependence conditions apply — in the monetary system when multiple channels of contact were greatest (the 1920s and 1960s) and in the oceans issue area since the late 1950s.

Some transgovernmental relations in oceans politics take place directly between governmental subunits. The British and American navies regularly keep each other informed.[34] Osgood reports that Indonesia and the United States have probably avoided a confrontation over straits by close navy-to-navy relations.[35] Close navy-to-navy relations also helped prevent escalation in the Brazil–United States dispute over shrimp fishing in the early 1970s.[36] As we saw above, in an earlier period, the United States geared its actions to a split within the Ecuadorian government over extended limits. In the antismuggling dispute with Britain in the 1920s, both the British and American governments were internally divided, and there may have been some transgovernmental coordination among "soft-liners." [37]

It is large-scale conference diplomacy, however, that has created many, perhaps most, of the opportunities for transgovernmental relations in the oceans area. As oceans issues became politically more salient, a wide range of groups and agencies from pluralist industrial societies increased their pressure for representation on delegations. At the Caracas law of the sea meetings, the United States delegation numbered 110 (of which only 20 were from the State Department) — a virtual conference within a conference. The efforts of the secretary of state to cut the size of the delegation still left a delegation of over eighty at Geneva in 1975. The ability of the United States government to bargain effectively was limited by these transgovernmental contacts: "Some U.S. delegates have misrepresented views of foreign governments within the delegation, others have taken positions with foreign delegates contrary to official policy. Unauthorized leaks of U.S. fallback positions have not been uncommon." [38] Somewhat more subtly, the various "clubs" of delegates with similar functional interests in fishing, navies, oil, mining, and so forth that were established as part of the informal conference diplomacy set up regular channels of communication that cut across and created tension within the already fragmented national positions. Many of the smaller and poorer states had simpler positions, which were thus less affected by these transgovernmental contacts. In large-scale conference diplomacy, transgovernmental contacts helped the small and poor to penetrate the large and strong more than vice versa.

As expected, in the international monetary issue area transgovernmental relations were most prominent in the 1920s, and then again in the 1960s and 1970s. During the 1920s, the most important transgovernmental relations took place between Montagu Norman, governor of the Bank of England, and Benjamin Strong, who headed the Federal Reserve Bank of New York.[39] * Both men believed in the gold standard and in the propo-

* The Bank of England at that time was still privately owned, but it clearly performed a governmental function and was part of the British policymaking network. Thus interactions between Strong and Norman are considered "transgovernmental."

sition that central banks, working together independently of central governmental control, should make international monetary policy. These common beliefs provided a strong basis for their cooperation, but brought them into periodic conflict with their treasuries. The central bankers favored generally restrictive monetary policies, but feared that domestic political pressures would prevent such policies. Yet such pressures could be ameliorated by cooperation among them. In December 1924, for example, Strong cabled Norman about a possible ½ percent rise in the New York Federal Reserve Bank discount rate, asking whether Norman preferred to go first. Norman replied that he preferred to follow New York (he would raise his rate 1 percent to New York's ½ percent) "and so appear to have our hand forced by you." [40] In 1930, when the Bank for International Settlements (BIS) was being established, Norman tried to "work out some form of words that would place the Bank beyond the reach of Governments." [41]

Both the extent to which central bankers thought in transgovernmental terms, and their increasing ineffectiveness as governments took greater control of policy in the 1930s and as problems involving military force arose, are illustrated poignantly in a reminiscence from Hjalmar Schacht:

The more conditions in Germany approached a climax, the greater my desire to make use of my connections in Basle as a means of preserving peace. In the course of the summer [of 1938] therefore I asked my British colleague, Montagu Norman, whether it would not be possible to bring British policy more into line with my efforts to maintain peace. Hitherto, Britain's policy had appeared to be to leave Hitler a free hand in foreign affairs. When I met Norman again four weeks later, he said:
"I discussed your suggestion with Neville Chamberlain."
"And what was his reply?"
"His reply was, 'Who is Schacht? I have to deal with Hitler.'"
This answer caused me considerable astonishment.[42]

Transgovernmental activity seems to have declined precipitously during the 1930s. Crises forced governments to turn their attention to international monetary policy; and the depression discredited bankers, including central banks. National policies, directed and implemented by politically responsible officials, became predominant. The importance of treasury departments waxed; that of central banks waned.[43]

The network of ties among international monetary officials, which was revised slightly in the late 1930s, began to be rebuilt during the war years, when plans for postwar reconstruction were made in Washington and at Bretton Woods.[44] As the Bretton Woods system was gradually implemented ties among financial officials increased. Deputy central bank governors met frequently at the BIS; they and their counterparts in finance ministries got together under the auspices of the Group of Ten, the OECD, and the Monetary Committee of the EEC. Strong personal friendships were developed both at this level and among finance ministers themselves; and considerable collegiality and esprit de corps seems to have developed.[45]

As monetary issues became more politicized during the late 1960s, transgovernmental coalitions became more difficult to maintain. As Russell comments, "Central bank cooperation and transgovernmental coalitions of central bankers receded into the political background as governments became directly and intensively engaged in bargaining over exchange rates." [46]

A low point of transgovernmental cooperation among treasury officials was reached during John B. Connally's tenure as United States secretary of the treasury. Connally's description to a congressional committee of the 1971 Smithsonian negotiations gives some indication of how far his approach was from the collegial norm:

> In the Rome meeting when I suggested the possibility, not necessarily offered it, when I merely suggested the possibility of a ten percent devaluation, there was a stunned silence for 40 minutes by the clock. Not a word was said, in an entire room full of people. Not a word.
> Finally one of the ministers spoke up and said that is totally unacceptable; we can't agree to that; 5 percent would be the most we would be willing to accept. . . . So then we went from there to where we finally wound up in the Smithsonian at 8.57 percent.[47]

But neither Connally nor Connallyism lasted very long. Connally's successor, George Schultz, had much closer relations with his counterparts. Transgovernmental policy coordination among finance ministers continued, and the network of ties among central bankers remained. Even in the autumn of 1971, there was some truth in the jest of a British minister that "whatever differences we Finance Ministers may have, to be together with one's fellow sufferers and far away from one's spending colleagues at home is a most agreeable experience." [48] Richard Cooper has argued that the subsequent deliberations of the Committee of Twenty on reform of the international monetary system were organized partly to facilitate and legitimize a transgovernmental coalition of finance-oriented ministers against more expansionist domestic pressures.[49]

This discussion indicates that our expectation from complex interdependence — that transgovernmental politics would make it difficult for states to pursue clearly specified goals — needs qualification. Under some circumstances — when domestic interests are sharply divided, issues are diverse, and the attention of top political leaders is not focused on the issues — transgovernmental coalitions can make state goals difficult to define. We saw this effect in the international monetary area in the 1920s and in oceans during the late 1960s and 1970s. Yet when domestic interests are fairly consistent and the top political leaders highly concerned about the issues, governments still may pursue coherent policy goals, even under conditions of complex interdependence. The coherence of state goals is made more problematic by complex interdependence; but it is by no means excluded. Transgovernmental policy coordination seems to be inherent in complex interdependence; but transgovernmental coalitions — in which different sectors of government work for conflicting policy goals by aligning themselves with agencies from other governments — are found only under some conditions.[50]

Instruments of State Policy

Under realist conditions, one expects military force, whether used directly or by linkage, to be the most effective instrument of state policy. Under conditions of complex interdependence, manipulation of economic interdependence in the issue area and of international organizations and transnational actors are expected to be more important for achievement of states' goals.

As we have seen, although force remains a potential instrument of state policy in oceans issues, its use has become less frequent, particularly by large states. The fishery dispute between the United States and several South American states is illustrative. The smaller states frequently used force in the fishery dispute, but generally against transnational actors (fishing companies) rather than other states. The United States also tried to manipulate the transnational actors. For example, the Fisherman's Protective Act of 1954 and its subsequent amendments were designed as an alternative to using naval force to protect the American tuna fleet. By compensating fishermen for fines paid when their boats were seized, the United States government diminished their incentive to purchase Peruvian or Ecuadorian fishing licenses that might have implied acceptance of the South American claims to extended jurisdiction.

The smaller states proved more adept, however, in manipulating transnational actors. Not only did the seizure and fine procedure develop into a game in some instances, but Ecuador and Peru were able to use American fishing companies (half of Ecuador's tuna industry was American-owned) and oil companies as hostages and allies. For example, "the oil companies lobbied vigorously for Washington to reduce tensions over the fishing dispute for the companies' sake."[51] When the United States attempted to apply economic sanctions, such as curtailing aid, the South Americans escalated the issue — for example, expelling diplomats and using the Organization of American States to rally diplomatic condemnation of American "economic aggression." Because Americans were reluctant to escalate, the greater commitment of the South Americans allowed them to manipulate economic interdependence more successfully in the political bargaining.

More broadly, faced with the erosion of one regime, the great powers have tried to negotiate an alternative through international organization rather than unilateral measures backed by force. Within the context of conference diplomacy, the United States stimulated the formation of informal groups of delegates in an effort to "educate" delegates from less developed countries to the true nature of their specific functional interests. As we have seen, however, these transgovernmental contacts were used more successfully by small states than by the United States. More generally, as we will explore below, smaller and poorer states have used international organization as a means of agenda setting and linkage in political bargaining. Although the residual possibility of the use of force by the great powers has affected bargaining in oceans issues, the threat of force has not been the most useful instrument of states' policies.

In monetary affairs, as we have seen, force has sometimes been linked with other issues to affect state policy. In the 1960s, in particular, the United States linked the protective role of force to monetary policy in order to affect European policies. By and large, however, other instruments have been more effective. In the 1960s, the United States tried to counter pressure on its balance of payments by issuing guidelines designed to influence the behavior of American multinational corporations. France, meanwhile, was converting its excess dollars into gold to influence the United States by manipulating sensitivity interdependence under the rules of the Bretton Woods regime. Later, in 1971, the United States manipulated asymmetries in underlying vulnerability interdependence when it ended the convertibility of the dollar into gold. After 1971, American refusal or reluctance to support the dollar in foreign exchange markets was often taken as part of a strategy to force other countries to agree to international monetary reforms favored by the United States. International organizations have not been as important in money as in oceans, as we will see below, but states have struggled to improve their bargaining positions by changing membership and weighted voting formulas in international organizations, and by steering issues into (or out of) particular organizational forums. In short, force has been linked with other issues to affect monetary politics, but, as in oceans, it has not been the most important instrument.

Agenda Formation

Under realist conditions we expect the agenda in an issue area to be determined by security threats and shifts in the balance of power. But under complex interdependence, it will be affected principally by changes in the distribution of resources within issue areas as well as by a variety of processes: the evolution of international regimes, and their ability to cope with changing economic and technological circumstances; changes in the importance of transnational actors; linkages from other issues; and politicization as a result of domestic politics. How well is this expectation borne out for the monetary and oceans issue areas?

For international monetary issues the agenda has largely been dominated by problems of building or maintaining international regimes. As the *New York Times* has editorialized,

The international monetary system is a matter of great public interest only when it is working badly — when the exchange rates of currencies are shooting up or down, when funds are being shifted massively by speculators or businesses, when nations are being whipsawed into booms or busts by monetary instability. By that standard, one could say that the basic aim of international monetary reform is to make the world monetary system as uninteresting to the general public as possible.[52]

When there have been no established regimes, attention has usually been centered on ways to reconstruct orderly patterns of rules and norms, as in 1920–25; 1936–46; and 1971–76. In 1930–31 and 1965–71, existing fixed rate regimes became increasingly inadequate as the positions of the key currencies weakened (the British pound in the first case; the United States dollar in the second). As the regime's deficiencies became more visible, monetary issues rose on state agendas, and after the collapse of the regime they remained pressing for some time. In the 1960s, increases in the importance of multinational corporations and banks, by facilitating flows of funds, contributed to these agenda changes.

In short, agenda change has come from poor operation of a regime in a coherent and functionally linked issue area. The postwar process in money contrasts with the situation in trade, in which the agenda is set, in the United States at least, by a combination of liberalizing initiatives by presidents requesting legislative authority to lower tariffs and other trade barriers, and protectionist moves by groups that have been adversely affected by imports.[53] It also contrasts with agenda-setting of oceans issues. The oceans agenda has been strongly influenced by economic and technological changes that have presented new threats and opportunities to domestic groups. Coastal fishermen, affected by the technological advances of competitors, have agitated for protection; tuna fishermen have lobbied for retaliatory measures; and other groups, such as oil companies, deep sea mining firms, ocean-going scientists, and ecologists have all made their claims felt. Whereas the international agenda on oceans questions has in part been determined by unilateral claims of other governments to increased jurisdiction, the Truman Proclamation of 1945 was a response to domestic fishing and oil interests.[54] Increasingly, however, the agenda has been affected by international conferences, at which governments of poor countries, in particular, have agitated for new arrangements that will more fully take into account what they perceive to be their interests.

In the oceans issue area, domestic and international political agitation about distributional questions raised by technological change contributes greatly to agenda formation. In the international monetary area, increased political salience seems to result largely from crises in the international regime. In the United States at any rate, fewer domestic interests are mobilized, and the control of policy has remained chiefly with the Treasury and State departments within the government, and the financial community outside it. But for oceans issues, fragmented interests — domestic and transnational — seem to have had more influence in bringing about agenda changes.

In both issue areas our general expectation — that security threats will not be a major source of agenda change — is borne out. But within complex interdependence many patterns are possible. Agendas in different issue areas do not all change in the same way. This variation will become even more apparent when we analyze changes in international regimes in the next chapter. At this point it should at least be clear that patterns of agenda change among issue areas vary considerably, even when complex interdependence is fairly well approximated.

Linkages of Issues

Under realist conditions, one expects linkages between issues to be made principally by strong states, using their power in one area of world politics (particularly their military power) to coerce other states on other issues. Under complex interdependence, however, one expects linkages by strong states to be more difficult to make, since force will be ineffective. Nevertheless, a variety of linkages will be made, frequently by weak states through international organizations.

This process is strongly reflected in oceans politics during the past decade. In the Geneva conferences in 1958 and 1960 several linkages were made, both between issues that were functionally connected and between those that were not. After 1967, linkages became even more intense, partly because of increased functional interdependencies among issues. In contrast to the assumption of unlimited resources that underlay the old regime, a sense of actual and potential competitive use developed. Reinforcing this impetus toward linkage was the inclination, particularly of Third World majorities at international conferences, to link issues to secure satisfactory overall bargains.

The major new issue since 1967, deep seabed resources, helped to precipitate this linkage. The promise of vast treasure at the bottom of the sea increased the number of countries interested in the oceans issue area far beyond the major or moderate users of the oceans. With general rather than issue-specific interests, these new actors were a major source of linkage. The Seabed Committee established by the General Assembly in 1968 expanded from the original thirty-five members to ninety-one members by 1971. Learning of their technological disadvantage on the seabed issue, the less advanced countries "doggedly introduced considera-tion of other maritime legal regimes related to the breadth of territorial sea rights of passage through straits and fishing practices, all of which added not only new dimensions of complexity but also of controversy." [55] The United States and the Soviet Union both tried at first to keep the sea-bed issue separate from the others, but without success. Subsequently the United States linked economic zone concessions to free passage for mili-tary vessels, but generally speaking, at the conferences held on oceans questions since 1967, linkage has indeed become an instrument of the weak.

The linkage process has been quite different in monetary politics. In the first place, functional linkages are much more important. On many occasions during the last half century, United States Treasury Department reports have emphasized the obvious connection between international monetary and trade policies.[56] International monetary policy is integral to macroeconomic policy and is therefore necessarily linked to other eco-nomic areas.

Second, linkages have been drawn in the international monetary realm by the powerful as well as by the weak. In constructing the Bretton Woods system, the United States used foreign aid to affect the monetary as well as trade systems; Britain's promise to restore convertibility of sterling in 1947 was a condition for the American loan of 1946.[57] After the breakdown of the "two-track" system, in which financial and military is-sues were handled separately among the Western allies,[58] it was once again the United States that most frequently demanded the linkage of issues. This time, trade and monetary affairs were linked by Nixon and Connally; and in discussions with Europe in the early 1970s, the United States sought general agreement on a set of closely connected issues. This linkage was justified in functional terms, but the orientation was nonetheless clear: "The political, military, and economic issues in Atlantic relations are linked by reality, not by our choice nor for the tactical pur-pose of trading one off against the others." [59]

In the 1970s, less developed countries did try to link agreement on a new international monetary regime to concessions by the major powers. They did not achieve this objective, but they did receive some concessions, in the Jamaica agreement of January 1976, on the sale of IMF gold to benefit Third World members, and a liberalization of credit facilities. Yet their influence was clearly less strong in the IMF than in the Law of the Sea Conferences. Not only were their votes fewer; they had fewer bargaining resources in the monetary issue area. On oceans, they could always make trouble by declaring extended jurisdiction and harassing anyone who violated their newly declared area of control; on monetary issues, their only weapon was the costly one of default.

Our expectations about complex interdependence are confirmed for the oceans area: linkages by weak states are important parts of the political process. But they have been less important in the international monetary area, where great powers continued to hold most of the political resources.

Roles of International Organizations

We have seen that international organizations involved in the oceans issue area have proliferated over the last few decades and that transgovernmental policy coordination and coalition-building can take place within these international organizations. It is not rare to observe such behavior. In the International Maritime Consultative Organization (IMCO), officials from transport ministries sought to broaden the organization's jurisdiction to include all pollution rather than just oil pollution, although this action was against the position of the foreign offices of some of their governments.[60] We have also noted that, as expected under conditions of complex interdependence, international organizations have been significant agenda-setters.

Even more important, the politics of rule-making in the oceans issue area has become closely associated with international organizations. The procedures of international organizations in this area emphasize sovereignty and state equality. In the nineteenth century, it was unthinkable that a landlocked state would participate in rule-making for the oceans. But at the Hague Conference convened by the League of Nations in 1930, Czechoslovakia had equal voice and vote. The codification conference dramatized the importance of deviant states and weakened the normative dominance of the great powers.[61]

Even so, the pattern of world communications in the 1930s was what Galtung calls feudal, with vertical communication between powerful and weak states, but little horizontal communication among the weak.[62] In the 1930s, states like Ecuador, Turkey, and Iran, whose efforts to extend their jurisdiction brought forth great power protests, were diplomatically quite isolated. Now common membership in an international organization would transform their potential diplomatic coalition into an active one.

In recent decades, international organizations have politicized oceans issues and have greatly increased the number of states active in these questions. Even without significant oceans-related capabilities, except for coastlines, governments of less developed countries have become influential on these issues. The major maritime powers have been definitely on the defensive in the United Nations Law of the Sea Conference. The fact that questions of oceans resources were raised in the United Nations General Assembly in 1967 activated a set of potential coalitions in an arena where majoritarian voting was the norm. The rules and practices of a general-purpose institution — the General Assembly — thus affected deliberations on the rules and practices that would constitute a new oceans regime. The fact that the rules of the international organization favored less developed countries gave those countries additional influence. The expectations of our complex interdependence ideal type are therefore confirmed in this case.

The situation in the monetary issue area is somewhat different. Transgovernmental networks were developed within international organizations such as the BIS, the IMF, and the OECD. But the interstate policy agenda was largely shaped by the condition of the international regime. In the 1970s, the less developed countries had some success in attaching their own preferred issues to the deliberations, but that success was limited. Most important, international organizations have not contributed to an explosive growth of Third World participation and influence, as they have in the oceans area.

Monetary issues have been preempted by the International Monetary Fund and by smaller, more select "clubs" of industrial capitalist countries. They have not been decided at general United Nations forums.[63] In contrast to the oceans area, the international monetary area in the 1960s already had an established set of international organizations, with membership by most Third World states under *inegalitarian* conditions, with votes in approximate proportion to quotas in the IMF.[64] Furthermore, elite networks of central bankers and finance ministry officials — including bankers and officials from Third World countries — were already in place. It is true that as a result of European-American disagreements in 1971, Third World states gained a greater role in deliberations for a new international monetary regime, but this role did not make them major actors. Financial resources remained the keys to influence. After the price rises of 1973 made major oil-exporting countries suddenly much richer, their IMF quotas were soon increased, but the increase reflected their new financial eminence rather than the norms or procedures of an international organization.

Once again we find a contrast between political processes in the oceans and monetary issue areas. International organizations are significant in both areas. But in the international monetary area they serve chiefly as instruments for the coordination of policy among countries with financial resources. They *reflect* power resources more than exercising a significant influence on outcomes. In the oceans area, by contrast, international organizations have increased the influence of small and otherwise weak states, at the expense of the major maritime powers.

CONCLUSION

Table 5.4 summarizes the extent to which our expectations about the political processes of complex interdependence, as discussed in Chapter 2, are borne out for oceans and money in the 1970s. In both cases the political processes were closer to those expected under complex interdependence than to those expected under realist conditions; but the correspondence of results in our expectations was much greater in the oceans than in the international monetary issue area. In particular, less developed countries had more influence in the oceans area, and they used international organizations more effectively.

Over a longer period, the oceans case supports the proposition that as conditions in an issue area become closer to those of complex interdependence, political processes will change accordingly. The exercise of force by great powers declined, increasing small states' maneuverability. Multiple issues and multiple channels of contact among societies rose. There were increases in politicization, bargaining linkages among issues, opportunities for small states, and involvement of international organizations in oceans issues. Direct policy interdependence increased, as a result both of increased societal interdependence and of increasing awareness of indirect interdependence, particularly when unilateral claims of jurisdiction or control were made. The political process became increasingly complex, with more government agencies involved, and more opportunities for transgovernmental as well as intergovernmental relations.

In the international monetary area, on the other hand, we found considerable continuity in the issues and in the governmental agencies that dealt with them. Transnational actors became very important during the last fifteen years of the period; but up to that time, their greatest importance had been at the beginning of the period, in the 1920s. The most important change in the monetary issue system was not in the *conditions* of complex interdependence (which were present in large degree throughout much of the period) but in governmental activities. Governments became much more active on international monetary questions — particularly the United States government, which had been extraordinarily passive in the 1920s. Politically responsive agencies such as the Treasury Department gained influence at the expense of the Federal Reserve Board and New

TABLE 5.4 POLITICAL PROCESSES OF COMPLEX
INTERDEPENDENCE: OCEANS AND MONEY, 1970–75

	Expectations under complex interdependence conditions	*Borne out in oceans area?*	*Borne out in monetary area?*
Goals of actors	Goals of states will vary by issue area; transgovernmental politics will make goals difficult to define; transnational actors will pursue their own goals.	Yes.	To some extent; but under some conditions policy coherence is greater than the complex interdependence ideal type would suggest.
Instruments of state policy	Manipulation of economic interdependence; international organizations and transnational actors will be the major instruments.	Yes, though force is sometimes used.	Yes, though there was linkage to the protective role of force in the 1960s.
Agenda formation	The agenda will be affected by changes in the distribution of resources within issue areas, the status of international regimes, changes in the importance of transnational actors, linkages from other issues, politicization as a result of domestic politics, and the politics of international organizations.	Yes: international organizations and domestic politics especially important.	Yes: status of the international regime especially important.
Linkages of issues	Linkages by strong states will be difficult to make; but a variety of linkages will take place. They will often be made by weak states through international organizations, eroding rather than reinforcing hierarchy.	Yes: both parts of prediction are borne out.	No: linkages are made, but as much by the strong as by the weak.
Roles of international organizations	Significant as agenda-setters, arenas for coalition formation, and as arenas for political action by weak states. The ability to choose organizational forum for an issue and to mobilize votes will be an important political resource.	Yes, in all three ways.	Of lesser significance; important as arenas for coalitions and as coordinating devices, less so as agenda-setters or as arenas for political action by weak states.

York Federal Reserve Bank, which were not directly under presidential control. Issues became politicized domestically in the late 1960s and early 1970s to an unprecedented degree, and international organizations became more important, at least as forums, than in the prewar period. At times of decision, splits within the United States government were repeatedly evident. Bargaining linkages appeared at times of sharp conflict, and tended to increase, not so much because the number of issues increased, but because governments, particularly that of the United States, used manipulation of linked interdependencies as an important policy instrument.

We have not yet explained the changes in international regimes in the oceans and monetary issue areas. That comes next. At this point it is sufficient simply to note once again the *differences* between the two areas, both in the 1970s and in their evolution over the half century before that. Under conditions approaching those of complex interdependence, international politics is different than in the realist world; but it is not by any means uniform.

Chapter 6 | # THE POLITICS OF RULE-MAKING IN OCEANS AND MONEY

In Chapter 3 we asked how and why regimes change and presented four explanatory models. We suggested that analysis should begin with the simplest, or most parsimonious, explanation of regime change and that one should add complexity as necessary. As we saw in Chapter 3, the simplest explanation of regime change would emphasize economic growth processes. That is where we shall start.

ECONOMIC PROCESSES AND REGIME CHANGE

The economic process model of regime change is based on welfare-oriented responses to economic and technological change. In it, international and transnational economic relations will tend to outgrow international regimes: the superstructure of world politics will no longer be able to cope with changes in the basic relations of production and exchange. In one way or another, the regime will have to be adapted or be broken. This model implies that governments will be reluctant to deny themselves the welfare benefits of economic interdependence, and that they will therefore be under pressure to adapt the regime or quickly to construct a new one. It ignores questions about the international distribution of power. Thus this model explains both the decline of international regimes (due to technological change and the growth of interdependence) and the re-

TABLE 6.1 REGIME CHANGE: ECONOMIC PROCESS MODEL

Date	Issue area	Description of change	Accounted for by economic process model?
Regime Establishment or Reconstitution			
Pre-1920	Oceans	Britain established free seas regime.	Partially. Economic model explains the benefits of a free seas regime for Britain.
1925	Money	Britain returned to gold standard.	Partially. The return to peacetime economies made it possible. But misconceptions and the decision-making process are crucial to explanation.
1944–48	Money	Bretton Woods regime established but held in abeyance by agreement.	Partially. Interdependence was at a low ebb. Perceptions of future benefits from interdependence did have an effect.
1958	Money	Bretton Woods regime fully implemented.	Partially. Economic recovery made the implementation of Bretton Woods possible. But the politico-military role of the U.S. was also very important.
1976	Money	Kingston Agreement.	Partially. Benefits of trade and capital flows created an incentive for agreement, but close political relations among major countries also played an important role.
Regime Weakening or Breakdown			
1931	Money	Britain departed from gold standard.	Partially. Economic changes were crucial given a fragile political structure and previous political decisions.
1945	Oceans	Extensions following Truman Proclamation.	Partially. Technological change led to the incentive to appropriate additional jurisdiction over the seabed. Timing is not explained.
1967	Oceans	Pardo speech; UN became involved.	Partially. Perceptions of benefits due to technological change were important. Timing again is not explained.
1971	Money	Bretton Woods regime collapsed.	Partially. Technological and economic changes led to increased flows of funds with increased speed, and basic economic shifts to Europe and Japan were important. Timing, and the fact that the U.S. took the initiative, are not explained.

construction or adaptation of such regimes (in response to the perceived threat that welfare benefits will be lost otherwise).

Table 6.1 indicates the five occasions on which regimes were established or reconstituted and the four points at which regimes have broken down or weakened sharply in the monetary and oceans areas since 1920. The economic process model predicts that regime breakdown will be accounted for by technological and economic change, and that regimes will be established or reestablished to ensure the welfare benefits of interdependence. As Table 6.1 shows, the economic process model explains some aspects of every regime change. Technological changes have been rapid in both issue areas, and changes in economic processes have been important. The benefits of cooperating to manage interdependence have also been obvious, even though it has not always been possible to agree on how cooperation should take place.

But as we said in Chapter 2, the economic process model does not provide a *sufficient* explanation of any change. In every change international political factors were at least as important as economic processes. Perhaps this model is best for explaining Britain's 1925 return to the gold standard after peacetime conditions had been established, and its departure from gold in 1931 under the stress of the banking collapse and worldwide depression. But even then, political factors were important. Britain's leaders had a conception of their role in 1925, derived from Britain's traditional hegemonic position as well as from their economic beliefs, that contributed to their decision. Similarly, we cannot explain the events of 1931 adequately without considering the lack of a coherent political framework among the major Western countries and the actions of France, in particular, against sterling in the preceding years.[1]

The economic process model also predicts some turning points that did *not* occur. After the disaster of 1931, this model would have led one to anticipate success at the 1933 London Economic Conference, because the costs of competitive exchange rate manipulation and trade barriers were evident to all. Yet the conference collapsed — as proponents of an overall structure model, pointing out the absence of hegemony or effective leadership, would have predicted. It is true that greater cooperation among the United States, Britain, and France was evident by 1936 in the Tripartite Agreement, but its provisions were quite limited. Only after World War II created the political and, to some extent, the economic conditions for cohesion among the major capitalist countries, was substantial progress toward a new international monetary regime made.

The economic process model provides necessary but not sufficient conditions for regime change in the monetary and oceans issue areas. Any complete explanation will have to include the distribution of power. The

simplest explanation in terms of power is the overall structure model —
traditional high politics — to which we turn next.

OVERALL STRUCTURE AND REGIME CHANGE

The overall structure model rests on the premise that the strong make the
rules. International regimes must be consistent with the interests of the
most powerful states in the system. As aggregate power relations change,
international regimes change in corresponding ways. Because military
power is dominant when constraints on its costs are removed, wars tend
to create regime change. However, in Chapter 3 we also developed a
model of eroding hegemony to explain the collapse of international regimes
in the absence of war. When overall power in an international system
becomes dispersed, international regimes break down. When power becomes more concentrated, new regimes, favorable to the powerful states,
will be developed.

The simplest version of an overall structure approach uses the distribution of military power to explain the nature of international regimes. Our
investigations found, however, that, with some exceptions, the distribution
of military power does not provide very good explanations. For example,
Britain's dominance of the oceans before World War I was more pronounced than her general politico-military position in relation to other
great powers. Between the wars, British leadership in maintaining a free
seas regime was not accounted for by its *general* military position, which
had been seriously weakened by World War I. After World War II,
American dominance of the seas was much stronger than its margin of
military and political superiority over the Soviet Union. In no case was
the military power structure blatantly inconsistent with the oceans regime; but in each case there were considerable discrepancies between
rule-making authority and overall levels of military power.

A similar incomplete relationship between the structure of the military
system and the ability to determine the rules is evident in the monetary
issue area. Before the mid-1930s, the United States had less influence than
one would have predicted from its military capabilities, and Great Britain
had more. After World War II, the outstanding anomaly is the Soviet
Union. In the international monetary system, Soviet influence has been
virtually nil, because its economic system does not permit it to participate
actively in international economic affairs under the rules of the IMF or
the GATT. Influence over international monetary affairs has been concentrated among major capitalist countries.

As we argued in Chapter 3, the shifts in the distribution of military
power only partly explain the erosion of the Bretton Woods regime during

the 1960s and its eventual demise. Changes in perceptions of military threats, in the relative economic strength of the United States and its partners, and in hierarchical patterns involving Europe and the Third World all had an effect. When these variables are added, the explanatory power of the overall structure model is much improved. The more sophisticated overall structure model is particularly good at explaining the early erosion of the free seas regime and the postwar establishment and implementation of the Bretton Woods monetary regime.

Erosion of the Oceans Regime

In the aftermath of World War I, a weakened Britain had to make concessions to the United States over pursuit of smugglers on the high seas. By 1945, the overall power of the United States meant that the extensions outlined in the Truman Proclamation went uncontested. The Truman Proclamation was worded in a way that the United States hoped would avoid any further erosion of the regime, but many of the subsequent claims went much further than the Truman Proclamation. Despite the United States' naval preponderance and the fact that many of the offending states were in Latin America, an area of alleged American hegemony, the United States was unable to prevent further erosion of the regime.

The overall power structure explains much of this situation. Between 1945 and the 1960s, American dominance on the seas was significantly tempered by the facts that the United States was engaged in a global struggle with the Soviet Union and that its overall military strength was not as obviously superior as its naval power. Two factors are important: Soviet policy, which was influenced by its global politico-military position, and American attempts at alliance leadership.

Until the 1960s the Soviet Union held revisionist attitudes toward some important aspects of the oceans regime. As a continental power with a weak navy since its defeat by Japan at the beginning of the century, Russia had continually pressed for extended jurisdiction to protect its coasts. Indeed, from 1917 until the early 1960s, it regarded the law of the sea as "a set of rules to push others away from Soviet coasts." [2] In the postwar period, it not only claimed and defended a twelve-mile territorial sea, but also "closed" important adjacent seas.[3] Although it had a weak navy, its position as a nuclear power allowed it to deter any significant naval challenge to its coastal claims. In the International Law Commission and at the 1958 United Nations Conference on the Law of the Sea, the Soviet Union encouraged other states to join it in opposing the three-mile limit. It was not until the 1960s that the Soviet and American positions began to converge.

Second, the bipolar power structure in the military system made the

United States the leader of a global anticommunist alliance. During the period of tight bipolarity when the perceived security threat from the Soviet Union was particularly strong, the United States placed security concerns and alliance maintenance at the top of its priorities. For example, in 1954, shortly after Peru successfully used force against the Onassis whaling fleet (which the United States protested diplomatically), it was American policy to avoid a confrontation that would disrupt alliance relationships. Instead it tried to "put an end to what it considers exaggerated claims of territorial rights" through "piece by piece discussion of high seas problems" in the UN General Assembly. Yet in describing the agenda, a State Department official admitted that the oceans question was not vital compared with the disarmament and atoms-for-peace issues.[4] In 1956, when the United States found itself isolated on a vote by the Inter-American Council of Jurists to recognize each state's right to set its own limits, it resorted to bilateral diplomacy in Latin American capitals. It emphasized the threat that extended limits would pose to Western defense, but the result was merely an ambiguous formula at the next OAS conference.[5] On a personal visit to Peru, Secretary of State Dulles won agreement in principle on a fisheries pact, but his attention was subsequently diverted by the impending Suez crisis.[6]

In the meantime, the United States had passed the Fisherman's Protective Act, under which the United States Treasury reimbursed fines paid by tuna fishermen for fishing without licenses while maintaining the legal position of nonrecognition of extended jurisdiction. The United States had decided that it was cheaper to maintain its legal position by manipulating the domestic end of a conflictual transnational system than by curtailing the system or by intervening abroad. Whatever the legal effect, the international political effect was to weaken the credibility of American efforts to deter extended claims to oceans space. When the alliance leader confronted its weak allies in the oceans issue area, it was the superpower that blinked. As *The Oil Forum* explained to its clientele, in prewar days military reprisals would have been taken, but the government was afraid that a local confrontation might become "an awful atomic war"; and "we needed friendly relations with South America."[7] As a nuclear superpower concerned with alliance leadership in a bipolar military system, the United States had less leeway in exercising its potential naval hegemony than had Britain. In the multipolar military system of the nineteenth century, she had not had to worry about objections from allies or nuclear threats.

International Monetary Regimes

The sophisticated version of an overall structure model has a mixed record of predicting regime change in the international monetary area. It does not explain the fact that in the 1920s Britain regained its position as the center of international financial relations, and that the Bank of England became the acknowledged leader in the international monetary system. Indeed, because the United States had the most overall military and economic power after World War I, the overall structure explanation would have predicted an American-centered postwar regime.* *Changes* in the overall power structure did not precipitate the collapse of the monetary regime in 1931, although Britain's weakness made the regime more vulnerable to pressures created by the world depression. The overall structure model would not have allowed us to predict the international monetary regime of 1925–31, but once it had emerged, this model would have correctly anticipated the regime's short life.†

The overall structure model is most successful in the international monetary area for the immediate postwar period. American military and economic dominance played an important part in the development of the Bretton Woods recovery regime (1944–48) and in the full implementation of Bretton Woods in the years after 1958. It was also significant though less overwhelming in events leading to the 1971 regime change and in negotiations between 1971 and 1976.

The development of bipolarity and the perception of a Soviet threat explain American willingness to hold certain rules in abeyance for the sake of European recovery. The change around 1947 toward a more generous, even paternalistic, American policy toward Europe and later toward Japan, was affected by the changing perceptions toward the Soviet Union. Fear of the Soviet Union, even as early as the spring of 1946, was crucial in increasing support in Congress for the loan to Britain. The next April, the State Department was busily organizing generous measures for Britain, whereas the Treasury Department, less responsive to political and military trends, was being tight and bankerlike, as before.[8] Massive Ameri-

---

* American bankers sought in 1918–20 to ensure that New York would replace London as the major international financial center, but disagreed on whether this should be done by competing directly with British banks or by gradually "Americanizing" and dominating the facilities of the British financial system. Disagreements among bankers, and lack of strong support from the government, helped to prevent American dominance from being attained during the 1920s. See Joan Hoff Wilson, *American Business and Foreign Policy, 1920–1933* (Lexington: University of Kentucky Press, 1971), pp. 14–17. See also Carl P. Parrini, *Heir to Empire: United States Economic Diplomacy, 1916–1923* (Pittsburgh: University of Pittsburgh Press, 1969).

† No structure model can be expected to predict actions based on misperceptions of reality as the 1925 British return to gold was. Britain's leaders overestimated their own resources and underestimated the stresses that the international economy would experience during the next decade. The fact that ultimately the British effort to lead without sufficient political resources failed, as an overall structure theory would predict, can be seen as evidence *for* the importance of this theory in explaining long-run change.

can aid, which had not been in prospect before the Soviet threat was perceived, despite the economic arguments that could sensibly be made for it, poured out to Europe, and to some extent Japan. After the fiasco of Britain's attempted resumption of convertibility in 1947, the United States not only tolerated European discrimination against the dollar but also provided the European Payments Union with $350 million in working capital to establish a scheme, based on such discrimination, that would increase intra-European trade.[9] Throughout most of the 1950s the United States looked benignly on its persistent balance of payments deficits. In 1950 the Treasury welcomed a net gold outflow as indicating an improvement in other countries' positions. In 1955 the American liquidity deficit was cited as helping other countries relax their exchange restrictions.[10]

Thus in the late 1940s and early 1950s, fear of the Soviet Union and military bipolarity helped to increase the willingness of the United States Congress and the Treasury Department to make concessions to European countries (and later to Japan) on international economic issues. This in turn provided American diplomats with instruments that could be used to work gradually toward implementation of the open, multilateral trade and payments issues of the Bretton Woods regime. Developments in the military system thus reinforced American political leadership as well as assisting America's partners economically. They therefore helped to ensure that the United States would use its capabilities actively in the monetary system, rather than adopting the more passive or nationalistic policies of the interwar years.

The rise in the economic capabilities of Europe and Japan clearly contributed to the collapse of the Bretton Woods regime in 1971. Yet the frequently proclaimed American economic decline was hardly precipitous: between 1957 and 1972, the United States' share of world trade only fell from 16.8 percent to 14.4 percent (see Table 6.3, on p. 141). This gradual change hardly seems sufficient to explain the collapse of the Bretton Woods regime. Furthermore, the eroding hegemony model does not explain why the United States, rather than its challengers, precipitated the regime's end on August 15, 1971. After all, it had tried during the Kennedy and Johnson presidencies to maintain the regime, and had used both financial ingenuity and politico-military power. Thus the overall structure model gives us important background for understanding the 1971 regime change; but it does not completely explain the change.

Nor does the overall structure approach explain how a new regime of flexible rates and coordinated intervention could be agreed on in 1976, without the United States' return to economic as well as military dominance or another power's rise to preeminence. We should have expected that if the United States were not strong enough to maintain the Bretton Woods regime (due to erosion of its dominance), it should hardly have been able to impose a new regime. And without a dominant leader, there should have been no agreement on reform. Instead, there should have been a prolonged period of no effective rules, and perhaps even the trade wars, monetary manipulations, and new mercantilism that were so widely predicted between 1971 and 1974.*

Table 6.2 shows how adequate we found the overall structure model to be for explaining our nine cases of regime change. We found it to be an adequate and elegant explanation of three cases. It is most valuable, as the table shows, for the 1945–46 modification of the oceans regime, and for the international monetary regime in the decade and a half following World War II.

ISSUE STRUCTURE AND REGIME CHANGE

According to an issue structure model, the strong make the rules; but it is strength within the issue area that counts. Changes in regime reflect shifts in the distribution of power within the issue area. It is important in discussing power in an issue area to recall the distinction in Chapter 2 between two levels of action in world politics. At the first level, the international regime is accepted as legitimate, with perhaps some minor disagreements, by all major actors, and politics takes place within the ground rules that it provides. Effective power over outcomes under such conditions will therefore depend on the nature of the regime as well as on underlying economic capabilities. Within an effective nondiscriminatory trading regime, for example, the ability to impose discriminatory trading restrictions without effective retaliation (that is, comparative *invulnerability* on this dimension) will not be a usable power resource in bargaining within the rules of the system.

The second level of political behavior is rule-making; actions at this level challenge the regime itself. In such a situation, the rules of the game are questioned by major participants. The regime is no longer a constant

---

* The events of 1971–76 are so recent that any interpretation of them can only be tentative. Some informed observers have taken a much more skeptical view of the Jamaica agreements than we do. See, for instance, Tom de Vries, "Jamaica, or the Non-Reform of the International Monetary System," *Foreign Affairs* 54, no. 3 (April 1976), 577–605. Although no definitive judgment about the value or permanence of the new regime can be made at this time, future developments will provide an interesting test of an overall structure model. If the Jamaica agreements collapse, and competitive manipulations of exchange rates or great instability become prevalent, the expectations of an overall structure model will be realized. We could then infer that there was not enough central power to make the regime work. Conversely, if the Jamaica accords succeed and coordination is fairly effective, the overall structure model will seem less valid in this case.

TABLE 6.2 REGIME CHANGE:
OVERALL STRUCTURE EXPLANATION

Date	Issue area	Description of change	Accounted for by changes in overall power structure?
Regime Establishment or Reconstitution			
Pre-1920	Oceans	Britain established free seas regime.	Only partially. Britain's naval power, not overall military power, allowed her to set the rules.
1925	Money	Britain returned to gold standard.	No. The shift in overall military and economic power should have predicted U.S.-centered regime.
1944–48	Money	Bretton Woods regime established, but held in abeyance by agreement.	Yes. U.S. economic and military dominance was reflected at the Bretton Woods Conference and subsequently.
1958	Money	Bretton Woods regime fully implemented.	Partially. U.S. dominance explains to a considerable extent the implementation of the Bretton Woods regime, formed by the U.S. Yet the economic recovery of Europe was a necessary condition for doing so.
1976	Money	Kingston Agreement.	No. Changes in overall power structure, toward somewhat greater diffusion of power, would under the overall structure model predict no agreement, with hegemony eroded and unitary leadership impossible.
Regime Weakening or Breakdown			
1931	Money	Britain departed from gold standard.	No. Economic changes precipitated the event. Changes in overall world power relations were not pronounced, although the weakness of Britain's position helps to account for the regime's vulnerability.
1945–46	Oceans	Extensions following Truman Proclamation.	Yes. The U.S. was preponderant in 1945, and subsequently bipolarity restrained the U.S. from using its naval dominance against South Americans.
1967	Oceans	Pardo speech; UN became involved.	No. Overall power resources of poor and coastal states did not increase at this time.
1971	Money	Bretton Woods regime collapsed.	No. Changes in overall military power did not lead to the shift, and overall economic power shifts provide only a partial explanation.

but a variable: it is seen as favorable by some actors, unfavorable by others. This distinction is crucial to an understanding of issue structure arguments because different types of power resources — different power structures — will be relevant at this level. If the policy question is no longer how rules should be formulated within the constraints of an international regime, but rather how the regime should be designed, a much wider range of power sources (and therefore of comparative vulnerabilities) becomes relevant. To continue our example of a trade regime, if nondiscriminatory trade is no longer assumed, the ability to impose barriers without effective retaliation becomes an important power resource.

The issue structure approach relies heavily on this distinction. When the underlying distribution of power in an issue area is inconsistent with the effective distribution of power within a regime, the regime is likely to change. States that are strong in the issue area but find themselves disadvantaged by the rules of the international regime will try to undermine or destroy the system. *Incongruity* between underlying power structures and influence within a regime provides the dynamic for change.

International Monetary Issue Area

The issue structure model helps us understand the collapse of the monetary regime in 1931 and makes a major contribution to explaining the breakdown of the Bretton Woods regime in 1971. We have seen that the interwar monetary system based on Britain was weak not only because of the shaky world financial situation of the 1920s, but also because of the overall political structure that could not effectively support the regime. France made a nuisance of herself, and the United States was not prepared to take strong action to help. But there was an inconsistency between the underlying power structure in the issue area and the effects of the rules, which showed itself in two ways. Politically, France resented British preeminence in the international monetary area, which was symbolized and supported by the fact that sterling had been returned to its prewar parity with gold whereas the franc had depreciated many times over. Yet the fact that the franc's value had been set low — indeed, undervalued — ensured that France could put continual pressure on the pound. Thus France had political reasons to snipe at the regime. For Britain, on the other hand, it was difficult at best to maintain the prewar gold parity of the pound; and it became impossible once the banking collapse of 1931 occurred. Thus Britain found that she was helpless within the old rules (because she could not change the value of the pound in terms of gold, but also could not supply sufficient gold or foreign exchange to meet the demand at the current rate). Yet Britain was still a major financial power. Thus when she went off gold and allowed the pound to float (or intervened to manipulate the float), her position immediately strengthened. In 1931 it was this inconsistency between underlying power and the constraints of the regime that proved crucial as Britain abandoned the gold standard.

We can also use our issue structure model to analyze the evolution of the Bretton Woods regime during the 1960s. Under this regime the strength or weakness of one's currency, compared with its par value, and the size of one's international reserves were major sources of political strength or weakness. Within the rules of the regime, the United States was in an increasingly weak position in the 1960s as long as it attempted to avoid a run on the dollar and devaluation. Creditor nations with increasing reserves, such as Germany and Japan, were strong. The United States tried to persuade them not to use the power that their reserves represented. But as German and Japanese reserves increased, although these countries became more powerful within the assumptions of the Bretton Woods system (in which dollars could nominally be freely exchanged for gold), those assumptions became increasingly endangered. Germany and Japan themselves became vulnerable to a dollar devaluation, which would reduce the value of their dollar holdings. As Henry Aubrey pointed out in 1969, "surely a creditor's influence over the United States rests on American willingness to play the game according to the old concepts and rules. If the United States ever seriously decided to challenge them, the game would take a very different course." [11]

By breaking the rules of the old regime, the United States in 1971 threw off the regime's constraints on the exercise of American economic power to influence international monetary politics. It was then able to use its fundamental economic power — its strong economy, its low ratio of foreign trade to national product, and its sheer size — along with its military and political influence — to change the rules of the monetary game. Having suspended the convertibility of the dollar into gold, the United States was no longer hamstrung by the requirements of convertibility, and found itself in a much stronger bargaining position after August 1971 than before.

The difference between changes in the underlying power structure during the fifteen years before the breakdown of the Bretton Woods regime and changes in influence within the regime's constraints can be illustrated by patterns of change in percentage of world trade and financial reserves for major countries during those years. Any figures such as these must be treated with caution as indices of power; they are very rough approximations at best. Nevertheless, within the Bretton Woods regime reserve levels were crucial, because one's currency had to be redeemed at established values for gold or foreign exchange. The alternative of allowing the value of one's currency to change was difficult for any country to accomplish, but effectively impossible (without general consent or a change in the regime) for the United States. After 1971, the specter of trade wars or other forms of competition made underlying measures of power, such as a country's proportion of international trade, more important as power resources.

Table 6.3 presents the relevant figures. The United States' reserve position (indicating its power within the existing regime) dropped much more precipitously than its percentage of world trade (indicating its position in the underlying power structure). Were figures for gross national product to be used, the continued strength of the United States would be even more evident. In the early 1970s the United States still produced between 25 and 30 percent of the world's goods, compared with 13 to 15 percent for the Soviet Union and 7 to 8 percent for Japan.[12] The underlying American position was further strengthened by the fact that trade constituted a much lower proportion of national product for the United States than for its major trading partners. The United States was therefore less vulnerable to disruptions in the international monetary trading systems than its partners were.

These figures reinforce our assertion that inconsistency between underlying power and influence within a regime is a source of regime change. The striking changes in the international monetary system between 1957 and 1972 cannot be accounted for by a simple thesis of decline in the American economy, when that decline only took the United States from 16.6 percent of world trade to 14.4 percent, and left it with over a quarter of world product. Had the American position really become so weak, the

TABLE 6.3   MONETARY POWER RESOURCES: 1957–72

Country	Underlying structure (percentage of world trade)			Regime-determined structure (reserves as percentage of world reserves)		
	1957	1967	1972	1957	1967	1972
United States	16.8	15.3	14.4	40.1	20.0	8.3
United Kingdom	10.1	8.2	6.9	4.2	3.6	3.6
France	5.4	6.1	7.1	1.1	9.4	6.3
Germany	7.7	9.9	11.5	9.1	11.0	15.0
Japan	3.4	5.6	6.9	0.9	2.7	11.6
Eleven major trading states[a]	62.8	67.6	70.0	69.1	70.9	63.5

Source: International Financial Statistics (Washington, D.C.: International Monetary Fund, for years indicated).

a. The five states listed above plus Belgium, the Netherlands, Switzerland, Italy, Canada, and Sweden (Group of Ten plus Switzerland).

United States would not have been able to force a drastic change in the international monetary system in 1971; nor would it have seen its essential views on the nature of a future system prevail in the negotiations leading up to the 1976 agreement to amend the IMF's Articles of Agreement. It is the underlying *strength* of the United States, in the context of its weak position within the pre-1971 regime, that explains the regime change, not American weakness and decline (whether within the issue area or in aggregate power).

Nevertheless, the issue structure explanation is not perfect. During the 1960s the delay in adjusting the regime to the underlying structure was considerable; the issue structure explanation accounts for the removal of inconsistency, but not for its development in the first place. Moreover, the events of 1971 were followed by other events that cannot be explained structurally. The attempt to realign exchange rates at the Smithsonian Institution in December 1971, but to continue with a fixed rate system as under the Bretton Wood regime, failed as transnational money managers lost confidence in the dollar. The magnitude of financial movements, directed first against sterling (June 1972), then against the dollar in February and March 1973, forced a move to de facto floating exchange rates. Eventually, this pattern was legitimized in the new Articles of Agreement for the IMF agreed upon at Kingston, Jamaica, in January 1976, which "embody the most far-reaching changes in the international monetary system since Bretton Woods." [13]

These agreements cannot be accounted for by changes in the structure of power in the issue area, because that did not change greatly among the major industrialized countries during the years in which this agreement was negotiated. In part, the 1976 accord can be accounted for by the economic process model. Transnational organizations in the 1970s control such large amounts of liquid funds, and the mobility of those funds is so great, that pegged exchange rates are extremely difficult, or perhaps even impossible, to maintain. A report for the United States Senate Finance Committee has estimated that in 1971 as much as $258 billion in potentially liquid assets was held by multinational corporations.[14] Richard Cooper has argued that "large-scale changes in exchange rates (as provided for in the Bretton Woods regime) are not compatible with the high mobility of funds prevalent today." [15] Because different patterns of economic change in different countries make permanently fixed rates impossible to maintain, he concludes that some pattern of flexible exchange rates is essential. Thus economic reality sharply constrains political choice.

The economic process model also accounts for some of the incentives that officials had during the 1971–76 period to agree on a new regime. International trade and capital movements are important to all industrialized countries, and some arrangements for regulating those movements were clearly required after the turbulent years of 1973 and 1974. But such incentives existed in 1933 and 1936 as well, and much less was agreed on. It will be useful, therefore, to go beyond both the issue structure and economic process explanations (however useful both are) and to examine the political networks among officials that developed during the Bretton Woods regime. Thus the international organization model will contribute to our understanding of recent international monetary politics.

Oceans Politics

The issue structure model fits quite well with the early eras of oceans politics. Indeed, when the freedom of the seas regime was established there was a multistate balance of power in the overall military system, but naval power was unipolar. In the early nineteenth century, the British navy was larger than all other navies combined, and in 1914, Britain still had nearly as many major warships (192) as the next three naval powers combined (Germany, 89; United States, 67; France, 52). Moreover, Britain was the major user of the sea. In 1886, half the world's merchant tonnage (ships over 100 tons) was British, and in 1914, the British merchant fleet still represented 40 percent of world tonnage (and was four times larger than the second-ranking German fleet).[16] Britain had both the interest to establish a free seas regime (except, as we said earlier, in wartime, which she treated as a special case) and the structural power to enforce it. This did not mean that force was used in the normal course of events, but that its use was not deterred when it was occasionally necessary to preserve the regime. As one writer described the pre–World War I system,

The naval power . . . loudly proclaims that the seas are free in time of peace and that the war problem is therefore the only problem outstanding. This is too strong. Naval domination operates in time of peace in the writing of the law for future wars, in the writing of the laws of navigation, and the law of territorial waters. . . . The minor maritime state receives . . . little attention in the drafting of sea law.[17]

One effect of World War I and the massive American naval building program associated with it (1916–21) was to transform the unipolar prewar naval structure into a bipolar and subsequently tripolar structure, which was formalized in the 5:5:3 ratio of British, American, and Japanese major ships agreed on at the 1922 Washington Naval Conference (see Table 6.4). Britain was no longer able to enforce American adherence to the regime. Moreover, the United States was not as interested in adherence as Britain was. After the Harding administration ended the merchant-marine building program, the American merchant fleet dropped to half of

TABLE 6.4 DISTRIBUTION OF
OCEANS-RELATED CAPABILITIES

Capabilities	Pre-1914	1920–39	1946–65	1966–75
Overall military (measured by expenditures on military force)	Multipolar	Multipolar	Bipolar	Bipolar
Military within issue area (measured by naval force ratios of major naval powers)	Unipolar (U.K.) 2:1	Tripolar (U.K., U.S., Japan) 5:5:3	Unipolar (U.S.) 3:1	Bipolar (U.S., USSR) 1.5:1
Peaceful use: merchant shipping	Unipolar	Multipolar	Multipolar	Dispersed
Peaceful use: fishing	Multipolar	Multipolar	Multipolar	Dispersed

Britain's. Although the United States ranked second in fish catch, its fisheries were, unlike Britain's and Japan's, essentially coastal, not distant-water. Although the United States (and Britain) usually insisted on adherence by lesser states during the interwar period, the United States was imperfect in its own adherence, extending jurisdiction for antismuggling controls in the 1920s and 1930s, exerting strong diplomatic pressure to discourage Japanese fishing on high seas off its coast in the 1930s, and declaring a three-hundred-mile hemispheric neutrality zone after the outbreak of war in Europe in 1939. In 1943, the Roosevelt administration began planning to extend jurisdiction over the continental shelf and fishery conservation zones. Because of the widespread citation of the Truman Proclamation as precedent, this extension proved to be a turning point in the transition from the regime of the first period to the quasi regime of the second.

After World War II and well into the 1950s, the structure of naval power was again unipolar, but with the United States as the preponderant power. The United States had twice as many major surface ships as second-ranking Britain and the third-ranking USSR combined.[18] Even in 1972, after the growth of Soviet naval power, the United States still had one and a half times as many major surface ships and large nuclear submarines as the USSR.[19] When American admirals expressed alarm in 1974 that their navy had "lost control of the seas," Senator Stennis replied that the United States still had over twice the tonnage in major surface ships, with greater range and more weapons than the Soviet navy.[20] In short, at the end of World War II, the United States had more naval power than the rest of the world combined. In this respect, its position was analogous to Britain's in 1914. Even at the beginning of our third period, the United States was the preponderant surface naval power, with twice as many carriers and cruisers (92) as all the other powers combined, and twice as many frigates, destroyers, and escorts (613) as the Soviet Union and Britain combined.[21] For much of the postwar period, the United States had the naval capacity that would have been associated with a hegemonic structure of rule-making power in an earlier period.

The underlying power structure in the oceans issue area was consistent in the 1920s and 1930s with the existing regime. Freedom of the seas was supported by Great Britain, the United States, and Japan, although the United States obtained an exception for measures to curb smugglers. The change in the underlying power structure as a result of World War II — with the United States becoming the dominant naval power — accompanied, although it did not determine, the change from a free seas regime to a quasi regime in 1945, when the United States asserted extended jurisdiction over fishing zones and the continental shelf adjacent to its coasts. American policy reflected a lag in decision-makers' perceptions of their state's role and interest, as we shall demonstrate below; but the United States' ability to make such sweeping claims was undoubtedly facilitated by its dominance in naval power as well as in overall power resources.

The regime change of the post-1967 period, however, is not accounted for by changes in the underlying power structure. New and weak states led the challenge to the strong quasi regime of 1945–67. Both the United States, with its continued dominance in oceans capabilities, and the Soviet Union, with its rapidly increasing capabilities, found themselves on the defensive in negotiations over the governance of oceans space and resources. Issue structure explanations fail to explain the rapid erosion of the old free seas rules since 1967.

Thus for the oceans issue area, changes in international regimes during the last ten years are less well explained by overall or issue structure explanations than previous changes were. The authority of strong states to make the rules for oceans space no longer goes unchallenged as it did in the prewar or early postwar periods. Although the underlying power structure (naval resources) remains concentrated, it has not led to a strong regime in the postwar period. Rather the international regime has become weaker.

Of the nine cases in Table 6.2, an issue structure model helps to improve our explanation of the pre-1920 establishment of the oceans regime and its early erosion in the 1940s, and it accounts for a large part of the regime changes in money in 1931 and 1971, which the overall structure model was unable to explain adequately. Yet neither of the two structural models fits well with the recent regime changes in oceans, and several of our questions about changes in monetary regimes in 1971 and 1976 remain unanswered.

INTERNATIONAL ORGANIZATION AND REGIME CHANGE

How do we account for the failure of basic structural models to explain all cases of regime change well, particularly during the last decade? Their failure is particularly marked for the oceans issue area. How do we account, for instance, for the inability of the preponderant naval state to deter the use of force against its tuna fishermen in a geographic area (Latin America) where its overall hegemonic power was alleged to be great? During the Cold War, bipolarity in the overall power structure provided part of the explanation, but it is not adequate for the period since 1967. How do we account for the fact that tiny Iceland prevailed over Britain in the cod wars? How do we explain the fact that the two preponderant naval powers, the United States and the Soviet Union, have been on the defensive in negotiations over the governance of oceans space and resources?

If power were analogous to money in a domestic economic system, these discrepancies would rarely occur, and when they did, they would not long persist. Actors strong in overall military power resources would redistribute them to achieve equal marginal utility of outputs across issue areas. Similarly, actors with power at the underlying structure level of an issue area would try to make the regimes more consistent with the underlying structure. In political terms these attempts would often take the form of linkages among issues — improving one's position where weak by linking results there to an issue in which one was strong. There would be a tendency toward congruence between structures and regimes — both within issue areas and between overall military structure and various issue areas.

In our monetary cases we found such a tendency toward overall congruence in the 1940s and 1950s, and within the issue area in 1931 and 1971. Yet in monetary politics, and even more in recent oceans politics, incongruities between structure and regime exist. These incongruities suggest that power resources in situations of complex interdependence are neither fully homogeneous nor fungible. Capabilities in one area may not be easily translated into influence in another — or even, under existing regimes and procedures for decision, into influence in the same issue area. One of our most important analytical tasks is therefore to understand the exceptions and limitations to basic structural hypotheses that rest on assumptions about the fungibility of power and predict high degrees of structure-regime congruence. Or, to return to the metaphor we used in Chapter 3, power like water may seek a common level, but the analytical challenge is to understand the heights and strengths of the dikes and dams that maintain separate levels and areas of power in world politics.

The international organization model developed in Chapter 3 helps to account for some of these discrepancies between the underlying power structure (overall or issue-specific) and regime change. It assumes political processes typical of complex interdependence, and an independent effect of rules and norms both within and surrounding an issue area. Regimes established in conformity with the underlying power structure in one period, may later develop lives of their own. Underlying power resources may be immobilized by norms and political processes so long as the regime remains in place. For example, the rules of the Bretton Woods regime immobilized underlying American monetary power in the 1960s, and allowed European countries to put more pressure on the United States through the balance of payments, as De Gaulle did in converting dollars into gold.

According to an international organization model, outcomes are predicted by regime-dependent capabilities; that is, capabilities that are legitimized and made possible by norms and processes that characterize a regime. It should be clear that the power relations in a regime process model are weakly based on sensitivity dependence, and are thus constantly susceptible to being overturned by strong military states or by states that have more power in terms of vulnerability interdependence within the issue area. It is remarkable that states are constrained by regimes and organizations at all. Under realist conditions, the overall or issue structure models should account for regime change, and an international organization model should only help account for regime persistence or lags in the timing of changes.

A major contribution of the international organization model is indeed to explain regime persistence, but one can also derive predictions from it about regime change. In this model, the breakdown or weakening of a regime is explained by changes in the norms and organizational processes of world politics. A regime may be altered by the emergence of new norms in other areas of world politics, which are then transferred to the particular issue area, or by the application of established norms (which operate in other issue areas or in particular organizations) to that issue area. Similarly, a regime may be altered by political bargaining processes that diminish the position of the states with underlying power that gave rise to the regime. Or, the development of networks of political interaction, often centered on international organizations, may facilitate agreement on new principles for an international regime.

As we have seen, if issue structure explanations are added to the overall approach of traditional theory, they (combined with the economic process approach) can explain fairly well three of the four cases of regime breakdown or weakening in Table 6.2. Yet the basic structural explanations do not adequately explain erosion of the oceans regime after 1967.

Oceans Politics

The erosion of the free seas regime since 1967 has been caused largely by the norms and the political processes of the United Nations. As we noted in Chapter 5, the norms and procedures of international organizations in the oceans issue area emphasize sovereignty and state equality. This was true in 1930 and 1958; but force still played a greater role in 1930, and the coalition patterns at the Geneva Conference of 1958 reflected the overall bipolar division of the world. By the mid-1960s, the two naval powers, the United States and Soviet Union, were less antagonistic and were both concerned over possible extensions of coastal states' claims to territorial seas. They discussed the possibility of a narrowly defined conference to deal with the issue. The 1967 speech by the ambassador from Malta, *anticipating* a technological breakthrough that would unlock the treasure chest of the deep seabed, not only speeded up the agenda for the great powers, but also recast the issue more in terms of distributing ocean resources than managing oceans space as a public highway. After the establishment of a Seabed Committee, the linkage of additional issues by weak states, and the General Assembly call for a Conference on the Law of the Sea, oceans issues were determined as much by egalitarian organizational procedures and by confrontation between rich and poor nations as by naval power or oceans capabilities.

The result, according to one observer of the negotiations, was that

> major maritime countries no longer control the process. The process is now controlled by the coalition which largely lacks major ocean-related capabilities yet seeks to redress inequalities in the distribution of world income via the medium of the ocean. Moreover, this coalition was mobilized, some opponents would even say "captured," by two groups: (1) those states pushing the 200-mile territorial sea claims; and (2) those states ideologically seeking a redistribution of resources and therefore income.[22]

Patterns of influence in international organizations and conference diplomacy are often quite different from what one would predict from the underlying structure. Moreover, the broader and more general the forum, the greater the divergence is likely to be. The structure of influence in the International Oceanographic Commission (IOC) or International Maritime Consultative Organization (IMCO), each with about seventy members and a specific functional jurisdiction, is quite different from the structure of influence in a Law of the Sea Conference with twice as many members and a virtually unlimited agenda. Negotiating law of the sea questions in the UN General Assembly resulted in an organization-dependent structure of capabilities resembling that of the United Nations Conference on Trade and Development, in which the coalition of less developed countries (the Group of Seventy-seven) first formed and earned its label. A study of influence in UNCTAD in 1969 found that the correlation between influence in UNCTAD and structural power as measured by a general index of overall power was only .43, and as measured by issue-specific power (based on share of world exports) was only .41.[23] Edward Miles found a similar pattern of regime-dependent influence in the UN Seabed Committee; the Latin American and African groups were most influential, and group cohesiveness was a much more important source of influence than country capabilities or global status.[24]

Not only did international organization create a separate organization-dependent structure of influence among states, but it also weakened the bargaining position of the leading naval power. Potential coalitions at international conferences are not restricted merely to states. Sometimes, subgovernmental agencies' interests are more like those within another country than those of competing domestic agencies. International meetings sponsored by the United Nations provided the physical contact and legitimacy for some of these potential transgovernmental coalitions to become active. The functional clubs at the Law of the Sea negotiations had this effect. As we saw earlier, American fallback positions in bargaining were often disclosed in advance. A particularly important instance was the lobbying by United States Interior Department and oil company officials with less developed countries in favor of broad coastal state jurisdiction over the continental shelf (contrary to then official United States policy) at the Geneva sessions of the Seabed Committee.[25] Besides lobbying governments at international conferences, transnational oil and mining companies have sometimes formed joint ventures in several countries to affect governments' perceptions and definitions of their interests in hitherto uncharted areas. In Chapter 5 we presented further examples of transnational and transgovernmental networks affecting political bargaining. All these cases indicate that some "domestic" interests in the leading naval power were not constrained by national boundaries in their choice of political strategies or coalition partners.

One should remember that the international organization model does not completely ignore the underlying power structure. In oceans negotiations the structure of force lurks in the background. After all, the United States or the Soviet Union could always refuse to ratify the outcome of the conference and could send naval ships to defend, for example, deep-sea mining operations. This possibility enters into the organization-dependent structure of influence that statesmen weigh in conference diplomacy, but force must compete with many other sources of influence peculiar to conference diplomacy. As the politics of rule-making in the oceans issue area worked after 1967, however, naval force played a role only after passing through the distorting prism of international organizations. And regardless of whether the United Nations Law of the Sea Conference will produce a treaty that will be ratified by most states, by 1976 the free seas regime had been permanently altered by the political changes best explained by the international organization model.

Why did the predominant naval power allow these changes to occur? The answer lies mainly in the growth of conditions of complex interdependence. The multiplicity of issues and channels made the United States' "national interest" in freedom of the seas more difficult to define and put into practice. At the same time, the fact that using force was more costly for great powers had a pronounced effect on rule-making in the oceans issue area. Unlike the monetary issue area, in which economic power is the basis of the underlying power structure, in the oceans issue area the traditional underlying structure was based largely on naval force. In recent decades, force, unlike financial power, has become much more costly for great powers to use against small states. Its use, or even the public threat of its use, is highly visible, provokes immediate and intense opposition, and frequently contradicts important domestic values.

This change is not completely new. Early in this century,

little headway in restricting belligerent rights was made until Great Britain, under the pressure of humanitarian considerations, the protests and threats of retaliation by neutrals, complaints from British shipping interests over the uncertainty of their (neutral) rights during the Russo-Japanese War, and other influences, voluntarily began to surrender her more extreme demands.[26]

Changes in public attitudes and interests helped to make force less useful, but the advent of nuclear weapons after 1945 was more important, particularly for the superpowers. As we saw in Chapter 5, as gunboat diplomacy became less usable for the large states, paradoxically, the smaller powers began successfully using gunboats in the postwar (but rarely in the prewar) era. As naval force became more costly for the great powers, they became more willing to tolerate rule-making politics characterized by the organization-dependent power structure rather than resorting to the underlying power structure.

The International Monetary Area

Monetary politics is quite different: issue structure explains the break-down of the regime fairly well, and the new rules that emerged in 1976 were principally determined by the major international economic and financial powers. To some extent the change has been accomplished through the weighted voting system of the IMF; even when votes are not taken, the distribution of voting power affects results. But it has also been done by taking effective power away from the IMF itself, in particular, by the 1962 decision establishing the Group of Ten (of which only indus-trialized countries are members) in conjunction with the General Arrange-ments to Borrow. Working Party Three of the OECD and the Bank for International Settlements in Basle were also influential; and "both groups were almost co-terminous with the Group of Ten." [27] The Smithsonian Agreement that temporarily ended the crisis of 1971 was negotiated by the Group of Ten.

Although the agreements of 1976 were developed formally through committees of the IMF Board of Governors, the major industrialized coun-tries dominated the process. Indeed, the crucial breakthrough was an-nounced in November 1975, after talks between France and the United States at the Rambouillet summit meetings of six major industrialized countries.[28] These were then agreed to by the Group of Ten, and subse-quently by the Interim Committee of the IMF.[29] At the 1976 Jamaica meeting, the less developed countries received some concessions related to borrowing from the fund and proceeds from the sale of gold. Never-theless, they by no means dominated the process of regime change; in-stead, they were somewhat peripheral to it.

The contrast with the Law of the Sea Conference is striking. Financial resources *are* concentrated; policies of the major countries *can* be imple-mented financially, without resort to force, and in incremental, carefully modulated fashion; and the major industrialized countries *could* simply establish their own international monetary system apart from the IMF if that body were to prove too difficult. And in any case, because the Group of Ten countries alone have over 56 percent of the quotas in the IMF (even under the new arrangements to go into effect in 1976) — and there-fore only a slightly smaller percentage of the voting power — considerable control is maintained even within the organization.[30] The general UN norms of one-state-one-vote do not apply.

The international organization model is not, therefore, essential for ex-plaining the breakdown of the Bretton Woods regime; and the new re-gime, developed in January 1976, reflects accurately the underlying domi-nance of major industrial powers. Yet to conclude that a basic structural explanation of the monetary area was entirely sufficient would be to ignore a very important feature of that issue area. "Controversy over the choice of an international monetary regime," Richard Cooper says, involves not only differences over goals and distribution of benefits, but "uncertainty about the trustworthiness of other countries with regard to their behavior within any chosen regime." [31] Despite high-level conflicts, a certain degree of trust was built up at the working level during the Bretton Woods era. An extensive and deep network of relationships developed among finance ministers, governors of central banks, and their subordinates. Transgovernmental policy coordination became frequent, along with close intergovernmental ties. Since 1973, informal coordination among central banks has become much closer, as a means of regulating and modulating a flexible exchange rate system, and the major finance ministries have also been in constant contact. Indeed, the 1976 agreement on regime change (including changes in the IMF articles) depended on the belief that further development of close policy coordination among major countries could moderate the effects of flexible rates. This belief was based on the mutual confidence and close ties that were built up over several years, beginning with the Bretton Woods regime, and that were disturbed but not irrevocably ruptured by the Nixon-Connally actions of 1971. The aftermath of 1971 was very different from the aftermath of 1931. The Interim Committee proposed that

the amended Articles of Agreement should include a provision by which the members of the Fund would undertake to collaborate with the Fund and with other members in order to ensure that their policies with respect to reserve assets would be consistent with the objectives of promoting better international surveillance of international liquidity and making the special drawing right the principal reserve asset in the international monetary system.[32]

Although it is difficult to document the precise importance of these policy coordination networks, participants in the system consider them very significant. Those who ignore the effects of elite networks created under a previous regime risk misinterpreting reality.

In summary, the international organization model is less precisely defined than the basic structural models. Norms and processes that will be effective for all issue areas are difficult to specify in advance. The predictions of the international organization model are more indeterminate, ruling out certain directions but leaving open alternate paths in the directions to which it does point. It is definitely a supplemental approach, to be used when simpler and more determinate structural and economic process models used alone would distort reality. Yet, as we have seen, particularly for the oceans issue area over the past decade, and in some significant ways for monetary politics, the international organization model provides insights that are crucial to understanding the politics of regime change.

LIMITS OF SYSTEMIC EXPLANATIONS: DOMESTIC POLITICS AND LEADERSHIP

Systemic explanations are limited. They cannot explain, for example, why powerful states sometimes do not use their resources to direct or control international regimes, as for instance, in the case of the United States' international financial policy during the 1920s. The theory of eroding hegemony is only a partial explanation. We need to introduce lags in perceptions behind changing events, and such lags can be explained only by taking account of domestic politics in the great powers and the domestic effect of transnational relations. This limitation affects all of our systemic models, but particularly the two structural ones that focus on the basic power capabilities of states. The international organization model at least points us toward the political processes typical of complex interdependence, in which the line between domestic and international politics is blurred.

A theory of leadership lag helps to explain one of our cases — the anomalous case of money after World War I — and also helps us understand the beginning of the erosion of the oceans regime. Charles Kindleberger has suggested that in periods of transition in the underlying power structure of an issue area, a newly powerful state will develop the capability for leadership before it perceives the benefits to be gained and the necessity for its leadership. Furthermore, secondary powers, used to taking leadership for granted, are likely to pursue policies that weaken the system. Thus, between the World Wars, the United States failed to exercise international financial leadership, leaving this task to a weakened Britain; and France "sought power in its national interest, without adequately taking into account the repercussions of its positions on world economic or political stability." [33]

After World War II, however, the United States seized world leadership on international monetary questions. After 1947, this leadership was reinforced by the impact of the Cold War and politico-military bipolarity, as discussed in the previous section. A hierarchy of issues was established, headed by national security. Exercising leadership on international financial issues was part of the overall strategy of building militarily and economically strong allies in Europe and Japan. Building a stable international monetary system was obviously crucial to success in the larger design, and short-term neomercantilist interests were not allowed to interfere, in the first twenty or so years after World War II. By 1971, ambiguity had arisen. While officials in the state and treasury departments were announcing to Congress the subordination of international monetary policy to national security policy, President Nixon was publicly justifying his actions to force devaluation on the grounds of creating jobs. Until at least that point, however, American officials' beliefs in the need to exercise leadership, and to keep the dollar strong, had been strong motivations for using the underlying power resources of the United States to maintain a dollar-centered international monetary regime.

Kindleberger's theory of leadership lag was designed to apply to the interwar monetary system, where it certainly contributes to our understanding of regime change. It also helps to account for American behavior in the oceans issue area at the end of World War II. Throughout the prewar period, Britain had been the leader in preserving the regime structure. The United States had not only been something of a free rider, but had demanded exceptions to the regime when strong domestic interests such as prohibitionists and the Justice Department or West Coast salmon fishermen pressed their demands on Congress and the president. The Truman Proclamations of 1945 arose out of the domestic politics of the fishermen's lobby and the domestic interests of the oil industry in offshore drilling. Leadership was taken by the Interior Department. The published documents indicate that the navy did not play a significant role; and the State Department played only a secondary one.[34] In a sense, the Truman Proclamations were a leftover from the 1930s. In 1945, the United States was the de facto leader, but its leadership perceptions were still those of a free rider until Latin American imitators shocked it into new perceptions of its systemic interest in regime maintenance after 1946.

In both the monetary and oceans issues, attempts to exercise leadership, once the need for it was perceived, were complicated by the diversity of interests involved. In the oceans issue area the diversity of interests increased dramatically after World War II with the growth in its complexity. Whereas fishing and navigation were the major uses of the oceans before the war, after 1945 the rise of new issues such as offshore drilling, deep-sea mining, and ecological protection confronted the United States government with a large array of "domestic" groups and corporations that were concerned about oceans policy. Moreover, one of the new issues, offshore drilling, reinforced coastal rather than high seas interests, and the most valuable American fishing was coastal rather than in distant waters. Unlike Britain leadership, which faced a happy coincidence of its security and economic interests, American leadership of a free seas regime suffered from internal cross-pressures.

In the monetary area, two American policies tended to damage domestic interests: allowing Europe and Japan to discriminate against the dollar, and thus against American goods; and maintaining a stable value for the dollar even as Europe and Japan regained their competitive position. Import-competing industries, and workers in those industries, were particularly hurt by those policies. As the United States balance of trade slipped into deficit and the unemployment rate rose in the late 1960s and early 1970s, protests against this situation rose, although they at first took the form of complaints on the *trade* side, not the monetary side. The AFL-CIO became protectionist; pressures for quotas on textile and steel products increased.

In the face of these pressures, perhaps what is most remarkable, both in oceans and monetary policy, is not the exceptions but the extent to which American policy *was* defined in systemic terms, with the United States cast in the role of leader. On the whole, the navy, distant-water fishermen, and shippers were able to define "the national interest" in oceans policy in a classical maritime fashion between 1947 and 1972. Until 1971, the New York financial community's attitudes, as reflected in the views of the Federal Reserve Bank of New York and a succession of high government officials from Wall Street, were reflected in postwar American international monetary policy. In 1971, however, it was not a banker who advised Nixon to take strong action, but "Mr. Peter Peterson, ex-president of Bell and Howell, a midwest corporation which became a conglomerate by being driven out of its original photographics by Japanese competition." [35] And the treasury secretary was a man who had risen through Texas politics, not the Wall Street financial route.

In both oceans and monetary policy, organizational or economic interest buttressed a case for systemic leadership that was attractive to globally oriented political leaders. It is not that distant-water fishermen, shippers, and the navy determined oceans policy themselves, or that the bankers controlled monetary policy absolutely; but that as long as opposition to these groups was not very strong, they benefited by being able to identify their preferences with contemporary political conceptions of America's role in world affairs. The particular interests of domestic groups and the perceived national interests of the political leadership reinforced each other, although more consistently in international monetary affairs than in oceans policy.

This brings us to the question of domestic actors' political strategies, as they affect international leadership. Different groups have different interests, which in principle are hierarchically organized by policy decisions and dressed up with the cloak called "national interest." However, as we noted earlier, the politics of international organizations and conferences sometimes provide opportunities for de facto or active coalitions of national groups whose mutual interests differ from that hierarchy. Domestic groups compete to allocate issues among international forums; to link or separate issues. In the process they politicize the issues, stimulating the attention of a broader range of interest groups and bureaucracies. As a result, the national strategies of major states may not be shaped simply by perceptions about international system leadership, but by domestic interests. Predictions about congruence between international structure and international regimes may fail because key domestic actors in major states capture the policy process and turn policy toward their interests, and against the politico-military interests or the aggregate economic interests, by which realist theory assumes states are guided.*

In the oceans issue area, domestic actors' strategies, particularly those of prohibitionists and fishermen, had a major effect in the prewar period, but between 1946 and the late 1960s, the navy was more effective, and United States policy was oriented toward leadership of the system.† Since 1967, as Ann Hollick has shown, the politics of rule-making through international organizations and conferences has led from international to domestic politicization of the issue, has aroused and involved a broader range of domestic interests, and has subsequently strengthened the position of coastal interests in the United States.[36] The national interest expressed in the United States policy enunciated in May 1970 largely reflected the view of the navy with its strong emphasis on security and free seas. Subsequently, the American position was considerably transformed as domestic actors with coastal interests interacted with resource-oriented weak states, which promoted broad linkage of issues to improve their bargaining positions. In a sense one can imagine the Law of the Sea negotiations as consisting of national positions, which are cross-cut by two large potential coalitions, one coastal and one maritime. The existence of these potential coalitions influences national positions over time as governmental subunits or nongovernmental actors pursue strategies that stretch and strain the bounds of national policies.

In the international monetary policy issue area, political strategies by domestic groups were more muted. The Treasury and State departments have vied for dominance; and nongovernmental organizations with direct interests in the area, such as banks and multinational corporations, have expressed policy views. But there has been more public controversy about

---

* To some extent this is the old issue of the difference between "systemic" and "national" determinants of international politics. For a general discussion with references, see K. J. Holsti, *International Politics: A Framework for Analysis*, 2d ed. (Englewood Cliffs, N.J.: Prentice-Hall, 1972), pp. 353–400.
† In 1948, fishery interests pressed for the creation of a bureaucratic ally in the State Department. Until recently the resulting position of special assistant for fisheries and wildlife has tended to be held by persons previously associated with distant-water fisheries.

trade issues and the activities of multinational corporations. Monetary issues tend to be more technical than trade questions, and their effects seem less easy to understand or to assess than those of textile imports or a runaway plant. Representatives from labor unions or import competing industries can more readily identify the benefits from import quotas, or an expanded adjustment-assistance program, than from devaluation of the dollar. Analysts often observe that even when, from an economic point of view that takes into account the long-run general interest, political actors ought to be discussing exchange rates, they are in fact talking about restraints on trade or investment.

Economists have used the term *money illusion* to refer to popular attention to wages and prices expressed in monetary rather than real terms. Analogously, and particularly under the stable fixed rate regime of Bretton Woods there has been a political money illusion; political groups have paid less attention to the welfare consequences of monetary policy than to the more readily apprehended trade policy. Whether this political money illusion is weakening after the events of the 1970s and under flexible rates is an important question for the future. Thus far the uncertain effects of monetary changes, particularly for people who do not understand the technicalities involved, provide strong incentives for political actors (who are often oriented toward the short run anyway) to focus on specific trade and investment measures designed to correct immediate problems. Congress, and groups with access to it, usually stress trade and investment policy rather than monetary policy.

We have defined politicization as increasing controversiality and agitation that raises an issue's priority on the policy agenda and the level of government at which it receives attention. Roughly speaking, politicization that leads to top-level attention comes from two directions: from below (domestic politics, whether popular, legislative, or bureaucratic) and from the outside (the activities of other governments and international organizations). The way in which issues become politicized affects the government's ability to adopt an international systemic perspective rather than a domestic perspective. Postwar money and oceans provide an illuminating contrast.

Overall, of course, international monetary policy, as well as oceans policy, has become much more highly politicized in recent years. But in the monetary area, politicization has principally been a result of international systemic crisis, in which conditions for maintenance of an international regime were increasingly inconsistent with economic and political realities. It has not been caused by domestic group strategies. In the oceans policy area, by contrast, politicization was initially a result of other governments' strategies, particularly those of less developed nations, which have opposed the constraints of the old regime and therefore opened the issue area to competing proposals for new sets of rules. Their strategies stimulated the other source of politicization, domestic actors, which responded to their own changing interests and to the new problems and opportunities created by the foreign governments' actions. The combination of foreign and domestic pressures increasingly constrained the United States government from adopting a systemic leadership approach.

Our discussion of international leadership has turned out to be complex. Leadership is affected not only by perceptions of top officials but also by domestic and transnational groups and organizations. In the oceans area, perceptions were slow to change and the Truman Proclamations, which reflected the domestic politics of the 1930s, contributed to a process of regime erosion that worked against the international systemic interests of the United States. As politicians and officials began to view the United States as a system leader, the position of groups and organizations with interests in a free seas regime was reinforced, but their dominance was weakened again in the 1970s as increasing domestic politicization and transnational coalitions brought these policies under attack. In conjunction with the opportunities provided by international negotiations on oceans questions after 1967, the activities of these groups made it more difficult for the United States government to take a coherent stand; thus, it is more difficult for the analyst to predict United States behavior on the basis of a structural model.

CONCLUSION

We said in Chapter 3 that analysis should start with the simplest possible explanations, and add complexity only as necessary to fit reality. Adequate explanation will often require a combination of models. The simplest and most familiar combination is of the economic process and overall structure models. Indeed, this combination underlies many traditional analyses. As Table 6.5 indicates, this combination of models accounts very well for three cases (oceans, 1945–46; money, 1944–48; money, 1958), and quite well for the establishment of the oceans regime before 1920. Yet five cases of regime change, including the three most recent ones, are not well explained by this formulation. Britain's decision to return to gold in 1925 requires one to take domestic politics and leadership lag into account. The collapse of sterling in 1931 was affected by economic processes in the context of political weakness; but it was also strongly influenced by the particular pattern of relationships within the issue area, as a result especially of the undervaluation of the French franc relative to sterling. There was an incongruity between the underlying power of states and the provi-

TABLE 6.5 REGIME CHANGE: ECONOMIC PROCESS AND
OVERALL STRUCTURE MODELS

Date	Issue area	Accounted for by combination of these two models?

Regime Establishment or Reconstitution

Date	Issue area	
Pre-1920	Oceans	Yes. Economic factors explain incentives to act. Overall structure explains Britain's ability to act, with some modification to recognize Britain's particularly strong naval position, as opposed to her overall military position.
1925	Money	No. Postwar American military and economic power would predict an American-centered regime. Perceptions from previous hegemonial situation and leadership lag are necessary for explanation.
1944–46	Money	Yes, particularly by the overall structure model. There is American economic and military preponderance.
1958	Money	Yes. European economic recovery occurs in a context of continued American overall power.
1976	Money	No. The economic process model indicates incentives to agree; but the overall structure model mispredicts results. Analysis of political networks is required.

Regime Weakening or Breakdown

Date	Issue area	
1931	Money	Only partially. One needs to look at power relations *within the issue area*, partly as a result of the undervaluation of the franc in relation to sterling, to get an adequate explanation.
1945–46	Oceans	Yes. The economic process model indicates new problems and incentives for the U.S.; the overall structure model explains why the U.S. had power to take its action; and why it did not stop South American extensions.
1967	Oceans	Partially; perceptions of anticipated benefits due to technological change were important. But the overall structure model fails. Political processes of international organizations are important.
1971	Money	Partially; technological change, and changes in overall economic capabilities, contributed. But one must examine changes in the issue area structure of power, and incongruities between underlying resources and the rules of the regime.

sions of the de facto international regime, which Britain could change by allowing sterling to float. Likewise, the structure of power within the issue area is important for an explanation of the events in 1971. Once again, the rules of the regime were inconsistent with the underlying power structure. In both of these cases, our issue structure model was most relevant.

The combination of overall structure and economic process models also does not explain the shift in the oceans regime after 1967. Here the political processes of international organizations were most important. Finally, the overall structure approach does not adequately explain the reconstitution of the international monetary regime in 1976, since neither overall military nor economic power became much more concentrated between 1971 and 1976. Knowledge of the overall capabilities of major states, and their policy preferences, would have been insufficient to predict the regime outcomes. On the basis of those factors in 1971–72, one should have predicted a restored fixed rate system, with adjustments in exchange rates in favor of the United States. This was the immediate result of the December 1971 Smithsonian accord, but it was incompatible with the rapidly increasing volume of international financial flows and with changes in international banking. Britain's decision to float the pound in June 1972 and the eventual floating of the dollar in March 1973 were prompted by the specter of rapid fund transfers that major central banks did not believe they could contain. The economic process model correctly points to the incentives that governmental officials had for reaching agreement, and American strength in the issue structure of power accords quite well with the outcome. But without an analysis of the political networks among major countries, which developed under the Bretton Woods regime, one cannot explain why these incentives should have been so much more effective in 1971–76 than they were in 1931–36.

Table 6.6 shows how well the overall structure model, combined with the economic process model, explains regime change, under conditions approximating realism and complex interdependence. One can see that the explanatory power of these traditional models is high for situations close to the realist ideal type, but not for conditions closer to complex interdependence.*

Table 6.6 suggests three important propositions, which cannot be definitively proved on the basis of two issue areas, but which are supported by our study of money and oceans.

---

* The full application of Bretton Woods rules after 1958 is possibly a deviant case since force was not directly used and multiple channels existed in the issue area. Table 6.6 assumes, however, that the role of force through linkage to overall American hegemony in the Western alliance — as discussed in the last chapter — represented conditions closer to realism.

1. With respect to *trends in the conditions of world politics* over the past half century, the complex interdependence ideal type seems to be becoming increasingly relevant. The three most recent cases are all closer to complex interdependence than to realism.
2. With respect to the *relevance of theories of world politics,* it seems quite clear that traditional theories based on overall structure models and economic process models explain regime change under realist conditions much better than under complex interdependence conditions. The traditional models are particularly weak for explanations of recent cases in which the conditions of complex interdependence, on the whole, applied.
3. These two propositions together imply that traditional theories of world politics, as applied to oceans and monetary politics, are becoming *less useful,* and that new theories based on issue structure and international organization models will frequently be needed for understanding reality and framing appropriate policies.

Regardless of how well these propositions are substantiated, or how extensively they are qualified, by subsequent studies of other issue areas, we should remember our earlier warning that trends toward conditions of complex interdependence are not irreversible. Not only does the cyclical pattern we discovered in money prove the point, but an intense threat to any major state's military security would undoubtedly affect conditions in many issue areas and increase the relevance of overall structure models.

TABLE 6.6 POWER OF OVERALL STRUCTURE AND
ECONOMIC PROCESS MODELS

	Conditions in the Issue Area	
Explanatory power	*Nearer to realism*	*Nearer to complex interdependence*
High	Oceans, pre-1920 Oceans, 1945–46 Money, 1944–48 Money, 1958	
Low		Money, 1925 Money, 1931 Oceans, 1967 Money, 1971 Money, 1976

Nor does approximation to conditions of complex interdependence imply that the politics of different issue areas will be the same. On the contrary, we found that although aspects of an international organization model help to account for recent changes in the monetary area, an issue structure model explains them most fully. In oceans, this was not the case. As we saw earlier, at both the underlying and regime-determined levels, the distribution of power capabilities in the monetary area remained quite concentrated. In oceans, on the other hand, as underlying power resources (naval force) became constrained under conditions of complex interdependence, the procedures of international organization became more important.

We also found that the patterns of politicization in the two issues were quite different. Much of the politicization in oceans tended to be from "below," inside domestic American politics, thus constraining the freedom of the dominant government actors to implement policy. In money, on the other hand, politicization has generally been from outside, allowing the implementation of a more systematically oriented policy. Because of this pattern, money received more consistent presidential attention than did oceans, and consequently a coherent government policy was easier to maintain.

Finally, management of a stable international monetary system comes close to being a public good, that is, all states can benefit from it without diminishing the benefits received by others. To the extent that states perceive a public good from which they all gain, they tend to be more willing to accept leadership. In earlier eras, when the major use of the oceans was as a public highway, management of oceans space and resources was also frequently perceived as being a public good, as indicated by the British memorandum quoted in Chapter 4. With technological change and the dramatization of oil and mineral resources after 1967, oceans politics focused more on distributional questions and how to fence or prevent fencing off parts of the global commons. Under these conditions, many states no longer saw great power leadership in maintaining a free seas regime as a public good, and thus maintaining the regime became more costly for the great power.

Our conclusion from this comparison of the politics of regime change in oceans and money is not that one simple model can be replaced by another, but that international political analysis will have to become more discriminating. An eminent economist has said that a member of his profession, like a dentist, needs both a bag full of different tools and the discrimination to know which to use at the right time.[37] The same is true of political analysis. Our conclusion is that the traditional tools need to be sharpened and supplemented with new tools, not discarded.

PART III | Regimes and Two Bilateral Relationships

Chapter 7

UNITED STATES RELATIONS WITH CANADA AND AUSTRALIA

The concept of complex interdependence — defined by the absence of force, the lack of hierarchy among issues, and the presence of multiple channels of contact between societies — is an abstraction rather than a description of reality. Insofar as an actual situation approximates these ideal conditions, we expect to find a politics of complex interdependence as outlined in Chapter 2. We found many features of such a politics in the issue areas of oceans and money. Yet neither issue area fit the conditions of complex interdependence perfectly. In the last chapter we discovered that when the conditions of complex interdependence were approximated more closely, the overall structure model was least useful for explanation, and issue structure and international organizational explanations became more useful.

Our approach in this chapter will be different from that in Part II. First, we are cutting into the reality of interdependence from a different direction by comparing relationships between countries rather than global economic issues. Second, we deliberately chose a case — Canadian-American relations — that seemed most likely to fit the three ideal conditions of complex interdependence. We do not consider Canadian-American relations a typical case from which to generalize about world politics. We chose to examine a half century of Canadian-American relations because it would allow us to examine the political processes of complex interdependence in practice: to see how they have changed over time, and how they affect the outcomes of high-level political conflicts in which military force plays no role. If there were no significant effects in such a "most likely case," then, even with qualifications for differences of degree, our expectations about political processes of complex interdependence would probably not be very fruitful for broader analyses of world politics.[1]

We would like to go further and have a series of studies that would allow us to say how broadly the generalizations about complex interdependence in the Canadian-American case could be extended. What are the effects, for example, of political friendship, cultural distance, or different levels of economic development? Such ambitions are beyond the practical scope of this volume. Instead, we chose a second case — Australian-American relations — that would at least allow us to hold some factors constant while we looked at the effects of international differences that help us compare the predictive power of different theories. We chose Australia because of its cultural and political *similarities* to Canada, allowing us (as best one can when the real world is the laboratory) to hold constant the effects of size, general economic characteristics, and domestic political systems, while we look at the effects of differences in the two countries' military security and at the costly effects of geographical distance.[2]

In other words, we have chosen two cases that differ in their approximation of complex interdependence while being as similar as possible in other ways. The Australian case is much further than the Canadian one from complex interdependence. In both cases, political conflicts are resolved without resort to military force. In Australian-American relations, however, military security has clearly dominated the agenda, the protective role of military force has remained crucial, and distance has limited the multiple channels of contact. As one observer has said, "Think of a Canada that had been towed away from where it is, and moored off Africa, and the problem of Australia's physical location becomes clear." [3]

Distance, of course, has other effects as well. The proximity of the United States and Canada has generated issues — such as those having to do with the St. Lawrence Seaway, airborne pollution, and smuggling — that would not be found among more distant partners, no matter how extensive their relations were. Furthermore, in the nuclear era a shared fate binds the United States and Canada. Canada would be severely damaged by an all-out nuclear attack on the United States, regardless of whether she was herself meant to be a target of such an attack. Nevertheless, these cases are matched closely enough to allow us to search for the effects of complex interdependence on bilateral relationships.

Because of the differences between them, we should not be surprised that the pattern of outcomes of interstate conflicts in the Canadian-American case contrasts with that in the Australian-American relationship. We shall show that part of the difference is accounted for by the political processes of complex interdependence present in the Canadian case. At the end of the chapter we shall show how, even in Canadian-American relations, structural and economic process models contribute part of the explanation of outcomes and regime. First we must decide how closely the two cases approximate the conditions of realism and complex interdependence and demonstrate how the political processes predicted by each ideal type affected the pattern of outcomes of political conflicts.

CANADIAN-AMERICAN RELATIONS AND COMPLEX INTERDEPENDENCE

In general, Canadian-American relations fit closely the three conditions of complex interdependence set forth in Chapter 2. Military force plays only a minor role in the relationship.[4] Two early American military invasions of Canada are regarded today as ancient history. Though occasional fears of American military invasion lingered until the eve of World War I, the fear of military threat was probably over by 1871, and certainly by 1895. The last official Canadian military contingency plan for defense against an American invasion was an historical curiosity by the time it was scrapped in 1931.[5]

As we argued in Chapter 2, the absence of military force as an instrument for achieving positive goals does not mean that military force has no role. Since World War II, the Canadian-American military alliance against external threat has been a source of both close cooperation and serious friction. Some of the most far-reaching steps toward continental cooperation occurred during wartime.[6] Similarly, one of the most serious crises in postwar relations, and one that led to the fall of a divided Canadian government, was over the nuclear arming of missiles involved in joint Canadian-American defense against the Soviet military threat. But military threats, or even threats of withdrawing military protection, have not characterized the bargaining process.

We also noted in Chapter 2 that military force can sometimes play a latent role. Its *possible* use can set significant structural limits on the political process. Such limits, if they exist, are extremely broad and not very constraining in the Canadian-American relationship. One might stretch one's imagination and conceive of situations in which military force might be used, but such speculations are hardly credible. They only remind one of the Red Queen telling Alice in Wonderland that she could think of six impossible things before breakfast every day.

Canadian-American relations are also notable for the multiple channels

TABLE 7.1   SELECTED TRANSNATIONAL PROCESSES: UNITED STATES–CANADA

IMMIGRATION

Year	U.S. to Canada	Canada to U.S.
1920	40,000	90,000
1938	6,000	14,000
1953	9,000	46,000
1962	11,000	44,000
1971	23,000	23,000

VISITS (millions)

Year	U.S. to Canada	Canada to U.S.
1920	nd	nd
1938	nd	nd
1953	28	23
1962	32	30
1971	39	34

TRADE ($ millions)

Year	Canadian exports to U.S.	Percentage of total Canadian exports	U.S. exports to Canada	Percentage of total U.S. exports
1920	581	45	921	12
1938	279	33	460	15
1953	2,463	59	2,940	19
1962	3,608	57	3,970	22
1971	11,665	66	10,951	21

INVESTMENT

Year	U.S. long-term in Canada ($ billion)	U.S. as percentage of foreign investment
1920	1.6 (1918)	36
1938	4.2 (1939)	60
1953	8.9	77
1962	19.2	77
1971	28.0 (1967)	81

Source: M. C. Urquhart, ed., Historical Statistics of Canada (Toronto: MacMillan, 1965); Statistics Canada, Canada Year Book (Ottawa: Information Canada, various years); Statistics Canada, Canada's International Investment Position, 1926–67 (Ottawa: Information Canada, 1971); United Nations Statistical Yearbook (New York: United Nations, 1961, 1971).

of contact between the two countries. Each country is the other's most important trading partner. Each year some 38 million Americans travel to Canada and some 34 million Canadians visit the United States. Recently there have been between 20,000 and 30,000 permanent immigrants in each direction. American magazines and television capture a large portion of Canadian attention. In the late 1960s American residents owned about 29 percent (by value) of Canadian corporations involved in manufacturing, energy, mining, railways, utilities and merchandising. In manufacturing, the figure was 44 percent.[7] Moreover, as Table 7.1 shows, many of these societal connections have increased since 1920.

The two governments, as well as the societies, have multiple points of contact. About thirty-one American federal agencies and twenty-one Canadian counterparts deal directly with each other, as do some states and provinces.[8] A study prepared for the Canadian Parliament found that in 1968 there were about 6,500 visits back and forth across the border by government officials from the two countries. Only 139 of these visits were to or from the Canadian Department of External Affairs.[9] The telephone is another channel of direct contact. In one week in November 1972, there was a daily average of 340 calls between the United States and Canada on the United States government's Federal Telephone Service toll-free lines.[10] The classical image of governments interacting through their foreign offices is clearly inappropriate in the Canadian-American case.

Finally, the agenda of Canadian-American relations shows a broad range of issues without a preponderance or domination of military security concerns. Because of the multiple contacts described above, it is virtually impossible to map the entire agenda of relations, but for 1920–46, we can map the relationship described in diplomatic documents (see Table 7.2).

The documents show a high preponderance of economic issues on the interstate agenda (except for the war years); and a tripling in the average number of annual interactions, from 6.4 per year in the 1920s, through 9.2 per year in the 1930s, to 17 per year in the early 1940s. As the agenda became more complex, the proportion of issues coming before the president increased somewhat, but the most dramatic change was the decline in the proportion of issues handled by cabinet officials (primarily the secretary of state) and the rise in the proportion handled by the bureaucracy. If we limit ourselves to the president's public agenda, indicated by *Public Papers of the President,* we find social and economic issues comprising a major portion of the annual references to Canada except in wartime (Table 7.3).

Not only have socioeconomic issues been prominent, but it has often been difficult to establish and maintain a consistent hierarchy among issues. In the experience of an American official,

TABLE 7.2 INTERSTATE INTERACTIONS
WITH CANADA, 1920–46

	1920s (n = 64)	*1930s* (n = 92)	*1940–46* (n = 119)
Issue Area (government objectives)			
Military	3%	5%	44%
Political	8	10	20
Social	16	20	6
Economic	72	65	30
Level of Attention in United States			
President	12.5%	15%	16%
Cabinet officers	75	34	20
Other officials	12.5	50	64

Source: Foreign Relations of the United States (Washington, D.C.: U.S. Government Printing Office, 1920–46).

Neither country has found it possible to list formally, with meaningful consensus, its priorities toward the other in any specific form. It could not be done without simultaneously applying corresponding priorities to aspects of domestic policy, and consequently to constituent groups. . . . "Country papers," "policy analysis and resource allocation papers," and so forth have some disciplining value when the components are principally active in foreign affairs. They can be little more than bureaucratic exercises when intended to discipline as well some of the major "domestic" departments and regulatory boards.[11]

Although high-level attention from the president or a preponderant cabinet official such as Treasury Secretary Connally in 1971–72 can temporarily impose a set of priorities on the agenda's multiple issues, it is almost impossible to maintain the high level of attention necessary to enforce coherence and consistency. Thus the realist assumption of a consistent hierarchy of national goals with security at the top does not fit the Canadian-American case.

Ever since World War II the Canadian-American relationship has been governed by a regime based on alliance, constant consultation, and prohibition of overt linkage of issues. Although the regimes that govern bilateral country relationships are much broader and more diffuse than those which affect the issue areas we discussed in Part II, the weakness of the formal institutions in a relationship such as that between the United States and Canada does not signify the absence of a regime or of international organization in the broad sense in which we have defined it. On the con-

TABLE 7.3 ECONOMIC AND SOCIAL ISSUES AS PERCENTAGE
OF ANNUAL REFERENCES TO CANADA[a]

Period	Total number of references to Canada	Percentage
Roosevelt to 1940	16	80
World War II	16	23
Truman after 1945	36	65
Eisenhower	36	55
Kennedy-Johnson	52	55

Source: Public Papers of the President (Washington, D.C.: U.S. Government Printing Office, 1933-69).

a. Purely pro-forma and goodwill statements were excluded.

trary, diplomats and close observers were quite able to describe the expected procedures and rules of the game. Indeed in 1965, at the behest of President Johnson and Prime Minister Pearson, ambassadors Merchant and Heeney summarized the procedures for consultation within the alliance that came to be called quiet diplomacy.[12] And the avoidance of overt linkage is described in the words of another experienced diplomat: "marginally you may shade a deal to create goodwill, but basically each deal must stand on its own." [13]

This postwar regime is not immutable. In the prewar era, although force was not used and economic issues dominated the agenda, the procedures in the relationship were quite different. Moreover, both sides frequently linked unrelated issues for bargaining purposes, although the Americans did it more successfully. The postwar regime, with its symbolism of a common cause and its constant consultation, developed in response to the German threat in World War II and the subsequent Soviet threat during the Cold War.

Again in the early 1970s, it seemed that the regime norm against linkage would be altered. In the later 1960s, the doctrine of quiet diplomacy had come under considerable criticism from nationalistic elements of the Canadian public. As we shall see, the increasingly nationalistic and assertive Canadian bargaining approach of the 1960s had positive results, at least in the short run. Outcomes of issues increasingly reflected Canada's position. But in response, the United States Treasury in 1971–72 took the lead in "getting tough with Canada," politicizing trade issues, linking them to other concerns, and attempting to control the transgovernmental contacts of other agencies. At the same time, the Canadian government was itself trying to exercise greater control over transnational and transgovernmental relations.[14] Somewhat surprisingly, the efforts on both sides to politicize issues and centralize bargaining did not persist long enough to alter the regime fundamentally. Transgovernmental interactions continued, and overt linkages again became rare. For example, a 1971 effort by the United States Treasury to link American acceptance of Canadian oil to Canadian willingness to renegotiate the auto pact now seems as striking in its rarity as in its ironic timing. We shall explore the relationship between regime and outcomes in greater detail later in this chapter.

AUSTRALIAN-AMERICAN RELATIONS AND COMPLEX INTERDEPENDENCE

Since most Americans — even many American students of international relations — have only a dim awareness of relations with Australia, we begin this discussion of Australian-American relations and complex interdependence with a brief review of these governments' policies toward each other since 1920.

During the 1920s, governmental as well as transnational transactions were rather low, but the 1930s became a period of acrimony in relations across the Pacific. Australia was involved in trade arrangements developed for "imperial preference" within the British Empire. These trade arrangements raised tariff levels for outsiders to encourage intra-Empire or intra-Commonwealth trade.

As a result, Australia built up considerable resentment among European countries that traded heavily with Australia and usually had an unfavorable balance of trade with Australia. . . . Rather than reduce imperial preference margins, however, the Australian government [in 1934] turned to what appeared to be an easier solution. It undertook to completely overhaul United States–Australian trade relations in order to eliminate the roughly six-to-one unfavorable balance of trade.[15]

The result of this initiative was a trade war between Australia and the United States. Australia devised a discriminatory "trade diversion program" against the United States, which refused to yield to pleas for a new bilateral agreement but instead retaliated by blacklisting Australia. Eventually, as British-American relations improved and World War II approached, the Australian government reversed itself under British pressure, and the trade war came to an end. Negotiations for a trade treaty between the United States and Australia were, however, unsuccessful.

War brought the two countries closer together. Before the Japanese attack on Pearl Harbor in 1941, Australia desperately and unsuccessfully sought a security commitment from the United States, but after the Pearl

Harbor attack Australia and the United States became close allies. Many American troops appeared in Australia, and contacts between the two countries multiplied at all levels. But relations were not entirely harmonious. Australia felt that it was not being consulted adequately by the United States on many issues. In 1944, Australia and New Zealand called for a conference on the Southwest Pacific, which was vigorously opposed by the United States. In discussions with Australian representatives, Americans even compared this initiative to Soviet tactics, arguing that regional arrangements should not be made until after global arrangements for security had been made. Clearly, United States officials feared that their delicate negotiations with the Soviet Union on Eastern Europe could be upset by actions that would seem to create "spheres of influence" in the South Pacific.[16]

Australia and the United States remained allies, and on good terms, after the war, although several contentious issues arose while Herbert B. Evatt was foreign minister under a Labour government (1945–49). Australia sought a formal alliance with the United States, but such an agreement — the ANZUS Treaty — was not signed until 1951, during negotiations on the peace treaty with Japan and after the Korean War had begun. By then a conservative government was in power in Australia.

Since 1951, Australia has depended explicitly and formally on American protection. The two allies have cooperated closely on defense, particularly during the long conservative rule in Australia between 1949 and 1972. Australia has been one of the most consistent supporters of American policy, and was one of the few allies of the United States to furnish troops to fight in Vietnam. Its forces rely heavily on American equipment; military officers of the two armed forces maintain close contact; and political leaders have consulted frequently and intimately on a variety of common issues and trouble spots. Our discussion of "conflict issues" between the United States and Australia should be seen in the context of the remarkable amity and warmth of the relationship during the 1950s and 1960s. Australian parliamentary debates during those years often reveal greater agreement, in fact, between the Conservative government of Australia and the United States government, than between the Australian government and its Labour opposition.

Against this background we can consider the conditions of complex interdependence as they apply to the Australian-American relationship, taking up first the role of military force.

There has never been a serious risk of war between Australia and the United States: military force has not been used or threatened by one country against the other. The *protective* role of military force, however, has been extremely important in the relationship. Thus by a very indirect route, *Great Britain's* desire for American military support in the late

TABLE 7.4   SELECTED TRANSNATIONAL PROCESSES:
UNITED STATES–AUSTRALIA

IMMIGRATION

Year	U.S. to Australia	Australia to U.S.
1920	1,709	2,066
1938	2,937	228
1953	(700)[a]	742
1962	1,082	1,878
1971	6,591	1,046

VISITS

Year	U.S. to Australia	Australia to U.S.
1920	nd	nd
1938	nd	nd
1953	nd	nd
1962	nd	nd
1971	85,079	78,777

TRADE (£ millions)[b]

Year	Australian exports to U.S.	Australian imports to U.S.
1920	11 (7.4%)	24 (24.0%)
1938	3 (2.4%)	18 (16.0%)
1953	58 (6.8%)	85 (16.7%)
1962	109 (10.2%)	174 (19.7%)
1971	634 (12.1%)	1,032 (22.1%)

1930s helped to resolve the trade war to the United States' advantage, and after 1939 and particularly 1941, Australia's need for American protection became acute. Since World War II, Australia has continued to rely on the United States. Moreover, the security relationship is highly asymmetrical. America could fail to protect Australia without jeopardizing its own security, but Australia could not defend itself against a powerful attacker without American support.

On the second dimension of complex interdependence, channels of contact between societies, the Australian-American relationship also differs sharply from that between the United States and Canada. The fact that

TABLE 7.4 (*Continued*)

INVESTMENT (*U.S. $ millions*)

INVESTMENT *(U.S. $ millions)*^c

Year	U.S. direct in Australia	Annual flow, U.S. as percentage of total
1920	53	nd
1938	89	nd
1953	324	27.6
1962	1,097	41.6
1971	nd	38.8

Source: Immigration to Australia: Commonwealth Bureau of Census and Statistics, *Yearbook Australia*, various years.

Immigration from Australia to the U.S.: Historical Statistics of the United States (Washington, D.C.: Government Printing Office, 1960) and *Supplements* (Washington, D.C.: U.S. Government Printing Office: 1965); and (for 1971) *Yearbook Australia* (Canberra: Australian government, 1972).

Visits: Commonwealth Bureau of Census and Statistics, *Overseas Arrivals and Departures, 1971* (Canberra).

Trade: Yearbook Australia, various years; for 1971, International Monetary Fund/International Bank for Reconstruction and Development, *Direction of Trade, 1970–74* (Washington, D.C.: IMF/BFD)

Investments: Before 1971, Donald Brash, *American Investment in Australian Industry* (Cambridge, Mass., Harvard University Press, 1966); for 1971 (flows), *Yearbook Australia*, 1972 and Commonwealth Treasury, *Overseas Investment in Australia* (Canberra, 1972).

*Note:*Some discrepancies exist between sources with regard to these figures, but the order of magnitude is in every case the same.

a. This is an estimate, based on the figure for "country of last departure of permanent and long-term arrivals," of 1,409.

b. Figures for 1971 are in U.S. dollars. Numbers in parentheses indicate the percentage of total Australian exports or imports accounted for by exports to or imports from the United States.

c. For investment, 1919 and 1936 are used rather than 1920 and 1938; the figures for 1953 and 1962 are averages for 1952–54 and 1961–63 respectively, due to large annual fluctuations.

Australia lies almost 10,000 miles from the United States makes an enormous difference. In the 1930s, Australia was three weeks' sailing distance from the United States. A pioneering 1940 air flight took over four days. Even today, the air time from Washington to Canberra is nineteen to twenty-one hours.

It is therefore not surprising that transnational links between the United States and Canada are much more extensive than between the United States and Australia, as tables 7.1 and 7.4, taken together, show. In 1971, immigration to Australia from the United States was 28.7 percent of the comparable figure for Canada; and immigration to the United States from

Australia was only 4.5 percent of Canada-to-United States migration. Total visits to and from Australia were only 0.3 percent as great as visits to and from Canada. Australian exports to the United States were only 5.4 percent of the Canadian figure; imports to Australia from the United States were only 9.5 percent of Canadian imports from the United States. American direct investment in Australia was similarly much smaller than American investment in Canada: less than 10 percent of Australian manufacturing industry was controlled in 1962 by American investors, as compared to 44 percent of Canada's.[17]

Thus, even though Australia's economy and population are smaller than Canada's, it is less dependent economically on the United States. Only about 12 percent of total Australian exports in 1971 went to the United States, compared to 66 percent of Canada's. Imports from the United States constituted only about 22 percent of total Australian imports (as opposed to 67.5 percent of Canadian imports).[18] Although trade, direct investment, and migration all increased sharply between 1920 and 1971, they remained much smaller for the Australian-American relationship than for that between the United States and Canada.

Between the governments, there is what one official called "a tremendous network" of contacts. Since 1950, Australian prime ministers have frequently visited Washington; the ANZUS Council meets annually at the cabinet level, and cabinet officials have often met with each other on a variety of questions. Yet most business is still transacted in Washington, where Australia maintains a large and well-staffed embassy. Although data on visits and telephone calls are not available as they were for the United States and Canada, there seems no doubt that such data would show many fewer points of direct contact between American and Australian officials with similar tasks.

The agenda of Australian-American relations, like the Canadian-American agenda, is quite diverse. Yet, unlike the Canadian-American agenda, it has a clear and consistent hierarchy. By far the most attention has been paid, on both sides of the Pacific, to political and military issues relating to the alliance. Memoirs and secondary works on Australian relations with the United States during the 1950s and 1960s overwhelmingly emphasized security questions, and the official record of Australian foreign policy, reflecting Australian parliamentary debates as well as governmental concerns, was preoccupied with them. So was reporting in the press and journals of foreign affairs.[19] Issues such as those of Malaya, Indonesia, and then Vietnam dominated the scene. The contrast with Canada is illustrated by Table 7.5, which indicates the amount of space devoted in the *Public Papers of the President* to politico-military, as opposed to socioeconomic, activities involving Australia since 1945. It therefore reflects what American presidents said publicly about Australia, and can be com-

TABLE 7.5 REFERENCES TO AUSTRALIA, 1945–71

Administration	Politico-military		Socio-economic or other	
	Number of pages	Percentage	Number of pages	Percentage
Truman (1945–53)	0.4	50	0.4	50
Eisenhower (1953–61)	2.8	97	0.1	3
Kennedy-Johnson (1961–69)	41.1	94	2.5	6
Nixon (1969–71)	2.3	92	0.2	8

Source: Public Papers of the President (Washington, D.C.: U.S. Government Printing Office, 1945–71).

pared with Table 7.3, which carries out a similar task, with slightly different techniques, for the Canadian-American relationship. Except for the period in which Vietnam was a major issue, the salience of Australia to American presidents was obviously very low.

Australia's often expressed concerns about military security during the 1950s and 1960s, and its sense of being a rather isolated outpost of Anglo-Saxon economic, political, and cultural institutions, living next door to actually or potentially hostile Asian neighbors, made it quite feasible to establish and maintain this hierarchy of issues with security affairs the most important. After 1969, when our systematic analysis ends, Australian policy changed markedly, under the Labour government that came to power in late 1972 (but lost power in December 1975).[20] Nevertheless, throughout the two decades after 1950, the traditional hierarchy of issues remained intact.

As we shall see, conflicts took place on economic issues, but they were not allowed to disturb the alliance relationship on which the Australians believed their security depended. Furthermore, on economic and social issues Australia was simply not as closely tied to, or dependent on, the United States as Canada was. Not only was there less direct investment, trade, and travel, but mass communications were quite different. American news magazines are sold in Australia, and a number of American television programs appear there; but the effect of American culture is much less pervasive than in the English-speaking areas of Canada. It may be an overstatement to argue that "Australia is still remote and separated from the day-to-day emotions, the drive and braking forces, the flow of life in

America — almost as remote as she was when the only medium of communication was a clipper." [21] Yet the fact that this exaggerated comment could seriously be made indicates the tremendous difference between Australia's relationship to the United States and Canada's. Distance is not entirely an illusion.

It is evident that the basic conditions within which Australian-American relations take place are very different from those for Canadian-American relations. Nonetheless, certain aspects of the regimes governing the postwar relationships are quite similar, particularly alliance consultation and avoidance of overt linkages in bargaining. Between 1950 and 1969, explicit linkages were virtually taboo. Although the Australian decision to sign the Japanese Peace Treaty was clearly connected to the United States decision to agree to the formation of ANZUS, diplomats tried to convince their audiences that the two events were not part of a single bargain.[22] As in the Canadian cases, linkages had not been uncommon before World War I. But in the Australian-American postwar relationship, politicization did not increase and the taboo against linkage was not threatened, because Australia did not, in general, take an assertive stand toward the United States.

Because Australian-American relations approximate realist conditions better than Canadian-American relations, we expect the overall structure model to explain the former better than the latter. We shall show that this is the case: Australian-American relations can be well explained in terms of overall structure, but the outcomes of postwar Canadian-American policy conflicts diverge considerably from expectations based on such a theory. To determine why Canadian-American relations are different we shall examine the political bargaining process. We shall argue that, to a considerable extent, patterns of complex interdependence linking Canada and the United States account for the differences in patterns of outcomes between the Canadian-American and the Australian-American cases.

IDENTIFYING ISSUES AND OUTCOMES: CANADA–UNITED STATES

By and large, traditional approaches have not been very helpful in explaining the politics of Canadian-American relationships. Canadian-American relations have often bored statesmen and scholars who see the world through realist lenses. As one scholar wrote in the mid-1960s, "study of Canadian-American relations tells one almost nothing about the big problems facing the world." [23] Another scholar cited the unguarded border between the two countries as an example of "indifference to power." [24]

However, despite the minor role of military power in the relationship, there are frequent conflicts, and the two governments often exercise their power. But the power games and processes of political bargaining in conditions of complex interdependence are not caught by traditional analyses.

Nor are the outcomes of conflict predicted well. A simple overall structure explanation tells us that in a bilateral system in which one country had thirty-seven times the military expenditures of its neighbor and was twelve times its economic size, the larger country would prevail in more major disputes than the smaller. Moreover, when transnational actors from the hegemonic country penetrate the small country more than vice versa, the distribution of outcomes should favor the large country even more. Indeed, some writers have coined the term Canadianization to refer to such situations.[25] An issue structure explanation would take account of the difficulty of making linkages among issues, but because of the preponderance of American resources in most issues, a simple issue structure analysis would also predict that, in conflicts between the two governments, the United States would most often prevail in the distribution of gains. Alternatively, we can hypothesize that the political processes of complex interdependence, and more particularly the role of transnational and transgovernmental actors, lead to a more equal pattern of outcomes in intergovernmental bargaining than one would predict from the overall structure.

A more sophisticated structural argument would attribute the pattern of outcomes to the structure of the global rather than the bilateral system. Given global bipolarity, the hegemonic leader stabilizes its alliance by allowing its junior partners to win minor conflicts. It is sometimes said, for example, that in the North American relationship, "the Canadians win a good share of the games, but the ball park and the rules of the game are American." As we shall show later in this chapter, this aphorism includes an element of truth. But the Canadians agreed on the ball park during the Cold War; they have won more games over time; and they have made gradual changes in the postwar rules of the game. The cases that we list in tables 7.6–7.9 were all important enough to capture the attention of the American president, and although the United States prevailed in one of the two cases with greatest global strategic consequences — the 1961 conflict over Canada's reluctance to fit nuclear warheads on BOMARC missiles used in joint North American air defense — the conflict over Canada's delay in cooperating with the United States during the Cuban missile crisis was a standoff (see tables 7.8 and 7.9 for brief descriptions of these conflicts). Of course, not all the cases were equally important to Canada. Yet when one analyzes the ten conflicts selected by a panel of Canadian scholars as most important from the point of view of Canadian autonomy, one finds that the United States did somewhat better than the

TABLE 7.6 CONFLICTS ON PRESIDENTIAL AGENDA,
1920–39: CANADA–UNITED STATES

Conflict	First government action	First interstate request	Outcome closer to objectives of
Regulation of fisheries, 1918–37. Canada pressed U.S. for ratification of treaty on fisheries issues, particularly salmon. U.S. delayed on salmon treaty until 1930s when a threat developed from Japanese salmon fishing.	Both	Canada	U.S.
Canadian restriction of pulpwood exports, 1920–23. U.S. successfully protested by threatening "far-reaching retaliation." Canadian objective was to encourage processing in Canada.	Canada	U.S.	U.S.
St. Lawrence Seaway, 1918–41.[a] U.S. pressed for joint navigation and hydroelectric development. Canada reluctant, but agreed to 1932 treaty which then failed in U.S. Senate. U.S. pressed for new agreement. Canada still reluctant but signed in 1941.	U.S.	U.S.	Equal
Control of liquor smuggling, 1922–30. U.S. successfully pressed Canada to take internal measures that would make U.S. enforcement of prohibition laws easier and cheaper.	U.S.	U.S.	U.S.
Chicago water diversion, 1923–28. Canada protested that Chicago's diversion of Great Lakes' water damaged Canadian harbors. U.S. refused to end the diversion.	U.S.	Canada	U.S.
U.S. tariffs, 1928–38. Canada unsuccessfully sought to deter 1930 rise in U.S. tariffs. Canada retaliated and sought alternative trade patterns. By 1933, Canada pressed for trade	U.S.	Canada	U.S.

TABLE 7.6 (*Continued*)

Conflict	First government action	First interstate request	Outcome closer to objectives of
agreement. U.S. delayed, but signed agreements in 1935 and 1938. Canada gave somewhat greater concessions.			
Trail Smelter Pollution, 1927–35. U.S. protested damage done to Washington farmers by fumes from British Columbia smelter and requested referral to International Joint Committee (IJC). Under pressure from farmers, U.S. rejected IJC recommendations and successfully pressed Canada to set up a special arbitral tribunal.	U.S.	U.S.	U.S.
Liquor Tax Bill, 1936.[b] Canada successfully protested a proposed punitive tax designed to force Canadian distillers to come to an agreement with U.S. Treasury. State Department sympathized with Canada and Roosevelt backed State Department.	U.S.	Canada	Canada
Construction of Alaska Highway, 1930–38. U.S. proposed joint construction of a highway through B.C. Canada feared "penetration" and successfully resisted until 1942, when war changed its objectives.	U.S.	U.S.	Canada

Source: Foreign Relations of the United States (Washington, D.C.: U.S. Government Printing Office, annually).

a. Transnational organizations played a significant role in the political process.

b. Transgovernmental relations played a significant role in the political process.

full list indicates, but not dramatically so.[26] (These cases are indicated in the following tables.)

Testing these alternative hypotheses about the outcome of the intergovernmental bargaining process is more complicated than it first appears.

In addition to describing the pattern of outcomes, we also wanted to see whether the processes of complex interdependence, particularly the roles of transnational and transgovernmental actors, had changed. We thus decided to compare bargaining and outcomes in two decades before World War II with two decades after the war.

One of the first obstacles to clear analysis of Canadian-American inter-state bargaining that we encountered was the well-selected anecdote. Each side had its favorite illustrations. Canadians tended to focus on a few specific incidents such as the magazine tax. Canada was concerned about the dominance of the Canadian magazine market by American magazines — particularly the Canadian editions produced by *Time* and *Reader's Digest*. She viewed the issue as one of cultural intrusion rather than of trade, and in 1956 passed tax legislation discriminating against American magazines. The magazines lobbied vigorously on both sides of the border, and the United States government protested the discriminatory treatment. Canada then granted *Time* and *Reader's Digest* exemptions from the legislation. Canadians frequently point to this case as typical of the postwar economic conflicts in which transnational actors and the United States government team up to defeat the Canadian government.

Americans, on the other hand, tend to cite the auto pact as typical of the relationship. In the early 1960s, in an effort to increase production in Canada rather than in the United States, Canada introduced an export subsidy for automobile parts. Rather than simply retaliating by raising a countervailing tariff, the American government suggested an agreement to allow free trade in automobiles between the two countries. Canada agreed to the auto pact, but by bringing pressure to bear on the transnational automobile companies, she was able to ensure that their next major round of investment would take place in Canada, increasing production and providing jobs on the Canadian rather than the American side of the border. Many American officials felt they had been cheated.*

It was almost as if blindfolded men trying to describe an elephant peeked from under their blindfolds in order to seize the part most useful to their different purposes. It is not unusual to hear Canadians claim that they do poorly in bilateral bargaining with the United States, or to

---

* Carl Beigie, "The Automotive Agreement of 1965: A Case Study in Canadian-American Economic Affairs," in Richard A. Preston (ed.), *The Influence of the United States on Canadian Development* (Durham, N.C.: Duke University Press, 1972), p. 118. A Canadian minister went over the head of GM Canada to negotiate directly with General Motors officials in New York. It is said that without the separate side agreements Canada would not have signed the intergovernmental agreement (from interviews in Ottawa). See also testimony in U.S. Congress, Senate, Committee on Finance, *United States-Canadian Automobile Agreement, Hearings Before the Committee on Finance on H.R. 9042*, 89th Cong., 1st sess., September 1965, pp. 153–56.

hear American officials complain that Canadians get away with too much. Such myths are resilient because they are politically useful. But what is useful for statesmen can be obstructive for analysts.

A second problem, as we saw earlier, was the impossibility of mapping the entire agenda of Canadian-American relations. Our solution to these research dilemmas was to focus on significant interstate conflicts that reached the United States' president. This solution has the disadvantage of focusing on only part of the total interstate agenda, and statistically it produced a small number of cases. Nonetheless, it has several redeeming advantages. First, and most important, the presidential conflict agenda offers the best prospect of closing a universe of like cases. Conflictual behavior at the top tends to be better reported by observers and better remembered by participants. Although complete discovery is unlikely, it is probably possible to approach a reasonably complete universe of significant cases. Conflicts that reach presidential attention also tend to be more important than others, so there is an implicit weighting of cases. It is true that summit meetings sometimes produce "agenda-filler" items, but this happens more often with cooperative than with conflictual issues.* Moreover, unlike total bureaucratic resources, presidential attention is a physically restricted and very scarce resource. Because we are interested in how the transnational and transgovernmental aspects of complex interdependence have affected interstate relations over time, it is useful to see their relationship to a fixed resource. Also, by focusing on high politics, the bias we introduce is against our complex interdependence hypothesis that transnational and transgovernmental relations are important. Finally, because the president has the broadest jurisdiction over issues of any governmental actor, it is at the presidential level that we are most likely to find the linkages among issues that are commonly held not to exist in Canadian-American interactions. Despite the statistical disadvantages, we decided to use a procedure yielding a small number of cases whose importance and validity can be justified in terms of our theoretical concerns.

One of the difficulties in identifying cases concerns the boundaries and outcomes of conflicts. By a significant interstate conflict we mean a situation in which one government's request to another is not easily fulfilled, because objectives are incompatible or the means are too costly. Conflict

* One U.S. official, for example, described how he and a Canadian counterpart took the initiative in working out a new approach to a problem of Great Lakes pollution. By the hazards of timing of a summit meeting and the need for "friendly" items for the communiqué, his venture reached presidential attention. It is hard to discover agendas that need conflictual issues to be deliberately added. See also Roger Swanson, *Canadian-American Summit Diplomacy, 1923–1973* (Ottawa: Carleton, 1975).

TABLE 7.7 DYADIC CONFLICTS, 1950s:
CANADA–UNITED STATES

Conflict	First government action	First interstate request	Outcome closer to objectives of
St. Lawrence Seaway, 1945–58.[a] Canada threatened to build alone if U.S. failed to speed decision.	Canada	Canada	Equal
U.S. agricultural import quotas, 1953–mid-1960s. Canada repeatedly protested U.S. protection. U.S. made minor concessions but did not meet basic request.	U.S.	Canada	U.S.
Gouzenko intrerview, 1953. U.S. requested that Canada arrange interview for Senate subcommittee. Canada initially declined but agreed to a second request under certain conditions.	U.S.	U.S.	U.S.
Chicago water diversion, 1954–59.[a] Canada repeatedly and successfully protested pending U.S. legislation to permit Chicago to divert water from Lake Michigan.	U.S.	Canada	Canada
U.S. quotas on lead and zinc imports, 1954–. Canada unsuccessfully protested U.S. restrictions.	U.S.	Canada	U.S.
Columbia River development, 1944–64.[bc] U.S. requested development of Columbia as a system. Canada delayed until compensated for downstream benefits, and until it reconciled internal dispute with British Columbia.	U.S.	U.S.	Equal
Carling Brewery, 1956.[a] Canada protested Maryland discrimination against Canadian corporation. Eisenhower persuaded Maryland to change.	U.S. (state)	Canada	Canada

TABLE 7.7 (*Continued*)

Conflict	First government action	First interstate request	Outcome closer to objectives of
Magazine tax, 1956–65.[bc] U.S. repeatedly protested discriminatory tax treatment of Canadian editions of U.S. magazines. A 1956 law was repealed; and in 1965, *Time* and *Reader's Digest* were exempted.	Canada	U.S.	U.S.
Security information guarantees, 1957.[a] Canada protested Senate subcommittee disclosures that led to suicide of Canadian official. U.S. acceded to Canadian request for guarantees against future misuse of information.	U.S.	Canada	Canada
Exemption from oil import quotas, 1955–70.[bc] Canada successfully protested the illogic of import restrictions against her based on national security grounds, and threatened to pipe Western Canadian oil to Quebec and thus exclude Venezuelan oil.	U.S.	Canada	Canada
Extraterritorial control of corporations, 1956–.[bc] Canada requested U.S. to forego extraterritorial restrictions on freedom of subsidiaries in Canada. U.S. refused to give up principle, but agreed to consultation procedure for exemptions in specific cases.	U.S.	Canada	U.S.

a. Transgovernmental relations played a significant role in the political process.

b. Transnational organizations played a significant role in the political process.

c. Case has major importance for Canadian autonomy.

TABLE 7.8 DYADIC CONFLICTS, 1960s:
CANADA–UNITED STATES

Conflict	First government action	First interstate request	Outcome closer to objectives of
BOMARC procurement, 1959–60.[a] Diefenbaker asked Eisenhower to continue development of BOMARC missile threatened by Defense Department and congressional cutbacks. Funds were restored.	U.S.	Canada	Canada
Nuclear arming of Canadian weapons, 1961–63.[bc] U.S. requested that Canada arm her weapons systems in NORAD and NATO. Diefenbaker's government split and fell. Pearson government armed the systems.	Canada	U.S.	U.S.
U.S. restriction of lumber imports, 1961–64.[a] Canada requested relaxation of administrative restrictions and later veto of highly protective congressional bill. Johnson vetoed bill.	U.S.	Canada	Canada
Seafarer's International Union, 1962–64.[a c] Canada requested that U.S. government restrain AFL-CIO support of the Seafarers' International Union and disruptive boycotts of Canadian shipping. Presidential efforts to influence AFL-CIO were insufficient and the disruption ended only when Canadian government trustees came to terms with SIU. U.S. government objective was to be helpful without antagonizing the AFL-CIO.	Canada	Canada	U.S.
Renegotiation of civil air routes, 1962–1965. Canada requested renegotiation to permit deeper penetration of U.S. by Canadian airlines.	Canada	Canada	Equal

TABLE 7.8 (*Continued*)

Conflict	First government action	First interstate request	Outcome closer to objectives of
Agreement was reached on basis of Galbraith plan treating continent as a unit.			
Extended fishing zones, 1963–. Canada unilaterally declared extended fishing zones and straight baselines. Although Canada made some provision for historic fishing rights, U.S. protested but was unable to deter the Canadian extension.	Canada	U.S.	Canada
Interest equalization tax, 1963.[c] Canada requested exemption from tax on grounds that an integrated capital market existed. U.S. granted exemption for new issues on condition that Canada not increase its reserves through borrowing in U.S. U.S. objectives were to improve its balance of payments position.	U.S.	Canada	Equal
U.S. balance of payments guidelines, 1965–68.[a][c] Canada requested exemptions from U.S. guidelines, voluntary in 1965 and mandatory in 1968, encouraging American corporations to restrict outflows and increase repatriation of capital. Exemptions were granted in return for restrictions on the pass-through of U.S. funds and on the level and form of Canadian reserves.	U.S.	Canada	Equal
Auto pact, 1962–73.[a][c] U.S. threatened retaliation over Canadian export subsidy designed to achieve Canadian objective of increased production in Canada. Pact integrating automobile trade led to joint gain, but Canada	Canada	U.S.	Canada

TABLE 7.8 (*Continued*)

Conflict	First government action	First interstate request	Outcome closer to objectives of
achieved more of the gain in first decade, causing U.S. complaints.			
Arctic pollution zone, 1969.[a][c] U.S. protested and asked Canada to defer extension of jurisdiction to 100 miles following 1969 voyage of tanker *Manhattan*. Canada refused.	Canada	U.S.	Canada

a. Transnational organizations played a significant role in the political process.

b. Transgovernmental organizations played a significant role in the political process.

c. Case has major importance for Canadian autonomy.

in this sense is not necessarily dramatic. Resolution of a conflict need not favor one country over another; within a continuing cooperative relationship, the resolution may benefit both countries.* There may be large areas of mutual compatibility of government objectives; and the major area of incompatibility need not arise out of the preferences or actions of the chief executives. What *is* necessary for a significant interstate conflict to exist, however, is an interstate request that cannot be easily or costlessly complied with by the recipient government. The request need not take a particular diplomatic form, but there must be communication of a mutually understood preference for (or against) a particular course of action.

A conflict begins when the first intergovernmental request is made, and ends when there are no further requests or when presidential attention is no longer devoted to it. A conflict can involve one or many requests. We shall treat a set of requests as a single conflict if the government objectives stated in each are largely the same. Thus the magazine tax case, for example, recurred during three Canadian administrations, but the nature of the American requests (nondiscriminatory treatment of *Time* and *Reader's Digest*) remained essentially the same. On the other hand, Cana-

* There are often Pareto optimal solutions to conflict that make both countries better off. (This is the joint gain component of the solution.) But the exact location on the curve of Pareto optimality is indeterminate. (This is the question of distribution of gain on which we focus in this section.) In some cases, the joint gain may be in some ways more significant than the distribution of gain, but the latter tests hypotheses about interstate bargaining in a situation of asymmetrical penetration by transnational actors.

dian exports of oil to the United States became a different case in the 1970s from what it was in the 1960s because the governments' objectives (and requests) changed from American limitation to American encouragement of imports from Canada.

Scoring the outcomes of conflicts also poses certain problems. In Table 7.6 we examine the range of incompatibility of initial objectives and ask whether the outcome was closer to the objectives of Canada or the United States at the time of the first request, or was roughly equidistant between them. This tabulation does not tell us how harmonious or creative the resolution was: in some cases, both sides may gain from the result. Nor does it imply that the losing side made all the concessions. All it indicates is which country was more favored by the outcome.

When a conflict was not solved by the end of the period under study, or when there was a major delay during which either government's objectives changed, the delaying country is regarded as having achieved its objectives. For example, although the United States eventually changed its treatment of the Chinese People's Republic, it did not do so until some fifteen years after St. Laurent first raised the question with Eisenhower.

Finally, our conclusions do not depend on a judgment about whether the decision-makers held the "right" objectives. One Canadian official told one of us that certain cases were not really conflicts because the American officials did not correctly perceive their own interests. Likewise, Canada's policy on the 1965 auto pact could be criticized on the grounds that it undermined Canadian autonomy. Yet in both cases, whether conflicts "should" have existed or not, they did. Even two observers with different perspectives on proper policy should be able to say which government got more of the objectives it then (perhaps unwisely) held.

Quite obviously, these procedures for identifying and scoring a set of conflicts address only part of the Canadian-American relationship. For example, it is important to realize that some social and economic groups often benefit more than others from intergovernmental agreements, and this socio-structural aspect is not caught by our analysis of intergovernmental bargaining. Canada won great gains from the 1965 auto pact; but one can also view the auto pact as a tacit coalition between the Canadian government, Canadian auto workers, and American auto companies on one side, and Canadian *consumers* and some American auto workers on the other. Moreover, when national legislative remedies in the United States failed, the auto workers' union took a direct transnational route to discourage the export of jobs to Canada by bargaining with the companies for wage parity across the border. Canadian auto workers profited, but it is not clear that other Canadian workers did. And Canadian nationalists regretted the loss of autonomy for Canadian subsidiaries of the multinational auto firms. Similarly, although the bargaining position of the Canadian government may have been strengthened more often than weakened in the cases that we analyzed, losses are often more costly for the penetrated nation.

It is also worth noting that the cases below focus on conflicts at the pinnacle of the intergovernmental process rather than throughout the government. During the prewar period for which the diplomatic documents are available, however, the pattern of outcomes of seventeen conflicts that did not reach the presidential level (nine, United States; six, equal; two, Canada) was similar to the pattern at the presidential level.* For the postwar period it is impossible to make careful comparisons, but impressionistic evidence does not suggest a great difference in patterns of outcomes at different levels.

Another problem is that the approach divides a continuous process into discrete parts and scores the relationship as a sum of parts rather than as a whole. Although this objection has a certain validity, it is interesting to note that many diplomats and politicians themselves often have a rough scoring system in their heads.† As one official put it, "there is a general sense of who has been making more concessions over the past few years." This vague awareness of who has overdrawn his credit in the political bank balances is a subtle but important background link among issues.‡ If issues are closely linked, then an unfavorable outcome for a government on one issue may simply be the price it is paying for a favorable outcome on another. Generally, however, the linkages are not this close.

Finally, generalizations about the entire Canadian-American relationship made on the basis of high-level conflicts do not include conflicts that failed to arise because of the anticipated reaction or because societal or transgovernmental contacts led to a statement of government objectives that diminished the conflict. For example, some Canadian subsidiaries of American firms probably shunned Chinese orders so as not to run afoul of

* The seventeen conflicts were: 1920's — Great Lakes naval limitations, Missisquoi Bay fishing, Roseau River drainage, Canadian peach embargo, U.S. dairy embargo, St. Mary and Milk River diversion, U.S. sinking of *I'm Alone* liquor ship, border crossing privileges, Passamaquoddy Bay power; 1930's — Canadian discrimination against U.S. tugboats, U.S. seizure of Canadian ship, St. Clair River dredging, Canadian seizure of four U.S. fishing boats, consular visits to criminals, Great Lakes cargo, income tax agreements, arms for the Spanish Civil War. We are indebted to Alison Young for research assistance on these cases.

† About thirty present and former officials were asked to comment and correct the description and scoring of conflicts in tables 7.2, 7.3, and 7.4. Only one (Canadian) objected to the procedure of trying to score discrete conflicts (on the grounds that it misrepresented a continuous process).

‡ Different bureaucracies in the same country may keep different scores. U.S. Treasury officials complained more frequently in the early 1970s that Canadians always came out ahead. As one State Department official observed, "In the 1960's the relations among financial officials were so close that we were often shut out of policy. Now their relations are so poor that they complicate policy." (From interview in Washington, D.C., December 1973.)

TABLE 7.9 CONFLICTS INVOLVING RELATIONS WITH
THIRD COUNTRIES, 1950–69: CANADA–UNITED STATES

Conflict	First interstate request	Outcome closer to objectives of
Conduct of Korean War, 1950–53. Canada repeatedly requested U.S. restraint, but without great effect.	Canada	U.S.
Defense of Quemoy and Matsu, 1954–55. U.S. requested Canadian support, but Canada disassociated itself from defense of the islands.	U.S.	Canada
Recognition of Chinese People's Republic, 1954–70. Canada raised the possibility of recognition three times in 1950s, but was deterred, in part, by U.S. inflexibility.	Canada	U.S.
Wheat sales to third countries, 1954–64.[a] Canada repeatedly requested that U.S. restrict dumping of surplus wheat. Agreement was reached on consultation and avoidance of dumping in Canadian commercial markets.	Canada	Canada
Canada and Organization of American States, 1961–63. U.S. requested that Canada join as part of strengthening Latin America against Cuba and communism. Canada did not join.	U.S.	Canada
British entry into EEC, 1961–63. U.S. requested Canadian support for British entry to strengthen Atlantic world. Canada did not support at that stage.	U.S.	Canada
Aid to less developed countries, 1961–63. U.S. requested increased Canadian assistance in strengthening poor countries. Canadian aid decreased.	U.S.	Canada
Disarmament and nuclear test ban, 1962. Canada opposed U.S. atmospheric tests and requested quicker U.S. agreement for a test ban. Little effect on U.S. policy.	Canada	U.S.
Cuban Missile Crisis, 1962.[a] U.S. informed Canada of its actions and expected diplomatic support and military mobilization. Diefenbaker delayed full support, but military mobilization went faster than he authorized.	U.S.	Equal
Conduct of Vietnam War, 1964–73.[b] U.S. requested Canadian aid to South Vietnam. Canada requested U.S. restraint in war. Little effect on policy.	U.S.	Equal

Note: Dates refer to presidential attention to the Canadian-American dimensions of the issue.

a. Transgovernmental relations played a significant role in the political process.

b. We have scored this case differently than Nye did in *International Organization*, Autumn 1974, because we have discovered additional information about it.

TABLE 7.10   PATTERNS OF OUTCOMES IN HIGH-LEVEL
CONFLICT: CANADA–UNITED STATES

| Dates | Favored by Outcome | | | Total |
	U.S.	Canada	Equal	
1920–39	6	2	1	9
1950s	7	6	2	15
1960s	3	8	5	16
Total	16	16	8	40

Note: Conflicts that overlapped decades are listed according to when they began.

extraterritorial restrictions on their trade.[27] Persistent patterns of transnational ties in North America are a socio-structural factor that is bound to affect the way the Canadian government defines its preferences in the first place. But in tables 7.6–7.9, it appears that close transgovernmental contact among fairly autonomous agencies may have led to avoidance of interstate conflict by understating Canadian objectives in two cases: the Columbia River (Table 7.7) and nuclear weapons (Table 7.8). In the latter, a transgovernmental military coalition pressed Diefenbaker into an early acceptance of nuclear weapons, which he later came to regret.* Similarly, Canadian dependence on transgovernmental communication of relevant information can limit Canadian options.[28]

On the other hand, as a glance at tables 7.6–7.9 quickly shows, it is not true that Canada never raised big issues. Indeed, as we shall see later, Canada raised several difficult issues that Australia kept dormant (but not vice versa). And one must beware of spurious causation in considering why certain conflicts were muted. For example, Canada's delay in recognizing the Chinese People's Republic was partly in deference to the United States, but also because of Canadian domestic politics.[29] In other words, one must be careful to read neither too much nor too little into the cases. With these caveats in mind, we summarize nine prewar cases in Table 7.6 and the thirty-one postwar cases in tables 7.7, 7.8, and 7.9 before analyzing them in terms of agenda formation and political process.†

Later we shall analyze these conflicts, comparing them with Australian-American conflicts. At this point, summarizing our findings about

* The pronuclear group in the Progressive Conservative party was reinforced by official and unofficial visits and communications with NATO and NORAD officials (from interviews in Washington, D.C.).

† The procedure for constructing tables 7.7, 7.8, and 7.9 was as follows: A long list of interactions was constructed from all references to Canada in *Public Papers of the*

the pattern of outcomes may be useful. First, the pattern is much more symmetrical than simple structural explanations would predict. Second, Table 7.10 shows a striking change over time. The outcomes were closer to the Canadian government's objectives in only a quarter of the prewar cases but in nearly half the postwar cases. Outcomes were closer to American government objectives in two-thirds of the prewar cases and nearly half the cases in the 1950s, but in only a quarter of the cases in the 1960s. Canada did better in the postwar than in the prewar period, and better in the 1960s than in the 1950s.

IDENTIFYING ISSUES AND OUTCOMES: AUSTRALIA–UNITED STATES

The same procedure was used to generate lists of Australian-American conflict issues. Tables 7.11–7.13 are comparable to tables 7.6–7.9 on Canadian-American relations, since the criteria for including and scoring issues were identical. Likewise similar caveats apply. For the Australian-American case, nonconflicts seem to be more important than in the Canadian case. Australia seems to have refrained from raising certain issues at the presidential level for fear of disrupting the general pattern of relations with the United States. Thus, our data may even *understate* the degree of American dominance in the relationship.*

Presidents of the United States, presidential references in the *Department of State Bulletin,* and the Council of Foreign Relations clippings files (primarily *New York Times, New York Herald Tribune, Financial Post* [Toronto], *Globe and Mail* [Toronto]). Further references were added and interactions not involving significant conflict were removed from the list on the basis of secondary accounts. Particularly useful for 1950 to 1963 were the Canadian Institute of International Affairs volumes on *Canada in World Affairs;* and for the 1960s, the *Canadian Annual Review.* The list was then further refined through interviews with thirty current and former officials and observers. Certain issues (such as DEW Line, ABM, bunkering facilities, Laos) have been excluded as not involving sufficient incompatibility of objectives. Others (such as Cuban trade, Mercantile Bank) have been excluded as lacking direct presidential involvement.

* It is impossible to get a systematic survey of nonpresidential-level conflicts, since many such issues are likely never to appear in documents, reports, or memoirs. (This may be true also for some presidential issues, particularly on highly classified problems, but presumably it will not happen so frequently.) An analysis of five important (so far as the record shows) nonpresidential conflicts between the U.S. and Australia in the years 1950–69 indicates that the outcome was closer to Australia's position in one (wool auctions, 1950–51) and closer to that of the United States in four (U.S. wool tariff, 1960s; U.S. restrictions on dairy products, 1950s; interest equalization tax, 1963; and U.S.–Australian air routes, 1969). This analysis *suggests* that Australia may have done at least as poorly in conflicts with the United States on nonpresidential as on presidential issues, but it should not be taken as either comprehensive or as definitive.

TABLE 7.11 CONFLICTS ON PRESIDENTIAL AGENDA, 1920–39: UNITED STATES–AUSTRALIA

Conflict	First government action	First interstate request	Outcome closer to objectives of
Wheat agreement, 1933. Australia resisted acreage quota at London conference. U.S. threatened to impose quotas only in the midwest, letting western wheat compete with Australia in the Pacific. Australia then agreed to an arrangement regarded by U.S. as a triumph.	Both	U.S.	U.S.
Bilateral trade agreement, 1934–43. Australia pressed unsuccessfully for a bilateral trade agreement. Issue was superseded after 1943 by multilateral GATT negotiations.	Austr.	Austr.	U.S.
Matson Line controversy, 1935–38.[a] Matson Line competition with British ships led Australia to consider preventing it from participating in Tasman trade. U.S. pressure on Australia prevented action.	Austr.	Austr.	U.S.
Trade diversion, 1936–38. In an effort to balance U.S.-Australian trade, Australia imposed discriminatory barriers on U.S. exports to Australia. U.S. retaliated by blacklisting Australian goods. Australia withdrew discriminatory measures.	Austr.	U.S.	U.S.

Source: Foreign Relations of the United States (Washington, D.C.: U.S. Government Printing Office, annually).

a. Transnational organizations played a significant role in the political process.

Australia had a conservative government between 1950 and 1969. Relations with the United States were more acrimonious both under the previous Labour government, which served until 1949, and under the Labour government that came into power in 1972. The Labour opposition during the 1960s, in particular, was highly critical of Australian government policy toward the United States. A Labour government would almost certainly

TABLE 7.12 DYADIC CONFLICTS, 1950–69:
UNITED STATES–AUSTRALIA

Conflict	First government action	First interstate request	Outcome closer to objectives of
Wool tariff. Throughout the 1950s and 1960s Australia protested U.S. wool tariff as set in 1947. U.S. refused to change it, citing congressional pressures. Although some negotiating took place in the Kennedy Round (1967), Australia would not accept U.S. demands for quid pro quo on tobacco.	U.S.	Austr.	U.S.
Lead and zinc quotas, 1958–65. Australia protested U.S. quotas in 1958. Eisenhower indicated willingness to discuss them, but no significant U.S. action followed. Removal of quota restrictions in 1965 was not a result of Australian pressure.	U.S.	Austr.	U.S.
Meat restrictions, 1964–. U.S. urged Australia to agree to voluntary restraints, which was done in early 1964. Senate passed restrictive quota bill in July; Menzies wrote to Johnson threatening retaliation, and a compromise was devised.	U.S.	U.S., then Austr.	Equal
U.S. balance of payments guidelines, 1965.[a] Australia requested an exemption, but U.S. refused. It took unilateral measures; but the issue died because of Australian ability to borrow in Europe and strengthening of Australian reserve position. Capital inflow was not retarded significantly.	U.S.	Austr.	U.S.
F-111 bomber, 1963–. Gorton expressed concern to	U.S.	Austr.	U.S.

TABLE 7.12 (*Continued*)

Conflict	First government action	First interstate request	Outcome closer to objectives of
Nixon in 1969, on price and specifications. Australia demanded renegotiation in 1970 and got a few minor concessions. Australia purchased 24 F-111's for $200 million more than original estimate (160% cost overrun) with delivery taking place in 1973 rather than 1968.			
Sugar quota, 1960s.[b] Australian leaders paid considerable attention to this issue in the early 1960s; Holt was briefed to raise it with Johnson in 1966 or 1967. Quotas for Australia rose rapidly.	U.S.	Austr.	Equal

Source: Materials cited in footnote 19 as well as interviews conducted in Washington, August 1974, with Australian and U.S. officials and former officials.

a. Transnational organizations played a significant role in the political process.

b. Documentary evidence that this case reached the presidential level is lacking, but interviews indicate that it probably did.

have been less acquiescent to American requests to send troops to Vietnam. It would almost certainly have made an issue of the terms on which the United States acquired the use of the Northwest Cape Communications Station (which were renegotiated in 1974 after Labour's return to power); and it might well have raised more questions about American direct investment in Australia. But raising these issues would not have changed the basic asymmetrical structure of the relationship; and as long as a Labour government felt threatened from Asia it would also have felt the need to maintain strong relations with the United States. And in any case, Australia simply did not have the levers of influence over the United States that Canada possessed. A Labour government — given the politics of Australia in the 1960s — could have changed the tone of relations with the United States, but not the essence. Indeed, on some issues, such as meat and sugar, a Labour government might have received less consideration from the United States.

TABLE 7.13   CONFLICTS INVOLVING RELATIONS WITH
THIRD COUNTRIES, 1950-69: UNITED STATES-AUSTRALIA

Conflict	First interstate request	Outcome closer to objectives of
Japanese peace treaty, 1950–51. Australia resisted signing a Japanese peace treaty, but agreed eventually in conjunction with signing of ANZUS agreement.	U.S.	U.S.
ANZUS, 1946–51. Australia pressed for a security agreement with the U.S., which was formally achieved in conjunction with Japanese peace treaty in 1951.	Austr.	Austr.
West New Guinea, 1950–62. Australia repeatedly expressed concern about West New Guinea and adopted a position hostile to Indonesia's. After discussing the issue with Kennedy in 1961, Menzies moderated Australian policies. Reports indicated a clash between U.S. and Australia on the issue.	Austr.	U.S.
SEATO, 1954. U.S. insisted that its commitment be limited to "communist" aggression, although provision was not included in the treaty but appended as a reservation. The U.S. strongly opposed Australia's adding a similar reservation; Australia did not do so.	U.S.	U.S.
Malaya, 1955. Australia tried to get explicit U.S. commitments to Malaya under SEATO but failed; only a general statement resulted.	Austr.	U.S.
Wheat sales to third countries, 1954–59.[a] Australia repeatedly requested that U.S. restrict concessional sales of surplus wheat. Agreement was reached on consultation and avoidance of damage to Australian commercial markets.	Austr.	Austr.
UK application to EEC, 1962. Australia was concerned that the UK entry to the EEC would result in phasing out of Commonwealth preferences, and asked U.S. support to maintain them. U.S. refused to oppose UK entry or try to make it contingent on Commonwealth preferences.	Austr.	U.S.

TABLE 7.13 (*Continued*)

Conflict	First interstate request	Outcome closer to objectives of
Australian troops for Vietnam, 1967. In July, Clifford and Taylor visited Australia, requesting more troops. Holt resisted, but in October agreed to send more forces. (Australian forces were sent originally in 1965, but resistance was not evident until 1967.)	U.S.	U.S.
International wheat agreement, 1968–69. U.S. and Canada argued that Australia was using improper freight rate arrangements to undercut prices in Europe. Australia agreed to reduce "the intensity of its competitive selling," apparently under threat of U.S. and Canadian retaliation.	U.S.	U.S.
Nonproliferation treaty, 1969–73.[a] U.S. requested all allies to sign and ratify the NPT, but Australia had reservations. U.S. did not exert pressure on Australia, which only signed in 1970 and did not ratify until 1973, after Labor government had taken office.	U.S.	Austr.

Source: Materials cited in footnote 19 as well as interviews conducted in Washington, August 1974, with Australian and U.S. officials and former officials.

a. Transgovernmental relations were significant.

Table 7.14 summarizes patterns of outcomes in Australian-American conflicts. In contrast to what we found for the Canadian-American conflicts in Table 7.10, the United States continues to dominate throughout the period. In this relationship, as structural models under realist conditions would predict, the stronger partner predominates.

COMPARING THE POLITICS OF AGENDA FORMATION

Agenda formation is important to the political process. Allocating the scarce resource of presidential attention toward certain issues to the exclusion of others can sometimes be as significant as influence in decision-

TABLE 7.14 PATTERNS OF OUTCOMES IN HIGH-LEVEL
CONFLICT: AUSTRALIA-UNITED STATES

| Dates | Favored by Outcome | | | |
	U.S.	Australia	Equal	Total
1920–39	4	0	0	4
1950s	6	2	0	8
1960s	5	1	2	8
Total	15	3	2	20

Note: Conflicts that overlapped decades are listed according to when they began.

making.[30] The number of conflicts reaching the president approximately
quadrupled between the prewar and postwar periods for both Canadian
and Australian relations with the United States. Further, whereas the
interwar agendas consisted almost entirely of bilateral problems, a third
of the postwar Canadian-American agenda, and 60 percent of the postwar
Australian-American agenda, involved relationships with third countries.
This postwar appearance of third country conflicts reflects responses to a
global structural factor: postwar involvement and alliance ties in contrast
with prewar isolationism for all three countries.[31]

Yet the two postwar agendas were quite different. In particular, the
Canadian-American agenda included more than three times as many bilateral issues. This is partly accounted for by their physical proximity and
the consequent prominence of jurisdictional conflicts in their relationship.
Six of the nine conflicts in the prewar Canadian-American relationship
arose from proximity (St. Lawrence Seaway, trail smelter, fisheries, Chicago
water diversion, liquor smuggling, and Alaska highway), but this was
true of only three of the thirty-one postwar cases (St. Lawrence Seaway,
Columbia River, and Chicago water diversion). Dividing each relationship
into a prewar and postwar era, Table 7.15 compares interstate agendas,
categorizing issues according to the types of objectives pursued by governments.

A Canadian analyst has hypothesized that in an asymmetrical relationship, the smaller state sets the agenda.* At least in the postwar period,

* James Eayrs, "Sharing a Continent: The Hard Issues," in John S. Dickey (ed.), *The
United States and Canada* (Englewood Cliffs, N.J.: Prentice-Hall, 1964), p. 60. Determining the first interstate request is often difficult for the recent period when the
documents are not available; so we have used the source of the *basic* request underlying the conflict. This is sometimes not the same as the first request. For example, in
cases where the U.S. requested voluntary export controls but Canada requested better
access to the American market, it is the U.S. action that generates the issue but the
basic request is Canadian.

TABLE 7.15 INTERSTATE AGENDAS, BY ISSUE AREA

Conflict set	Politico-military[a]	Diplo-matic[b]	Socio-economic	Joint resource problems	Competing sovereignty claims
Prewar					
U.S.–Australia 1920–39	0	0	4	0	0
U.S.–Canada 1920–39	0	0	3	6	0
Postwar					
U.S.–Australia 1950–69	6	3	7	0	0
U.S.–Canada 1950–69	7	6	11	3	4
Total	13	9	25	9	4

a. Force or weaponry involved.
b. Military force not involved.

the smaller states made most of the interstate requests; in each case over 50 percent more than the number of requests made by the United States. In this sense, it was the beaver's agenda. If, however, we ask in which country the first governmental action occurred that led to dyadic interstate conflicts, it was somewhat more clearly the elephant's agenda. The United States originated more conflicts than its partner in both relationships. If we disaggregate the Canadian-American figures, however, we find a different pattern in the 1960s. Canada took the first governmental action in six of ten cases, partly because presidential attention was diverted to problems elsewhere, as in Vietnam, but also because of rising Canadian nationalism and dissatisfaction with the status quo.

When we analyzed these findings by issue area, we found that the smaller countries made the first request most frequently on socioeconomic issues. These were precisely the issues on which the United States most often took the first governmental action. Thus the typical conflict pattern on these issues was for the United States (frequently the Congress) to take a unilateral, often "domestic" action to which the smaller partners tended to respond by demanding redress through diplomatic channels. On other issues, patterns of requests and governmental action were more symmetrical.

On these, the United States made the first request fourteen of twenty-nine times, and took the first governmental action on six of eleven occasions.

Table 7.16 examines another perspective on interstate agendas, by tabulating the number of times that transnational organizations were involved in issues, for the four sets of conflicts under investigation. Three of these agendas look remarkably alike, with transnational organizations playing minor roles in generating conflicts between the governments. It is the Canadian-American postwar agenda that is dramatically different, with ten cases involving transnational organizations. (If we looked at socioeconomic issues alone the difference would be even more pronounced, with almost half the Canadian-American postwar issues involving transnational organizations.) Thus in the postwar Canadian-American relationship — the one that came closest to our model of complex interdependence — transnational organizations are clearly more important in high-level conflicts than they were in the other three relationships.

Transnational organizations played diverse roles in the political processes of agenda formation, including lobbyist, target, catalyst, instrument, and beneficiary of government action. In three cases (civil air routes, oil import quota, lumber import quota) the transnational organizations were minor actors. In only one case did the transnational organization (Boeing) deliberately initiate political activity. When it acted as a target, the issue was politicized as a result of domestic groups appealing to their home government for protection against the activities of the transnational organization. The "catalyst" case was politicized because the Canadian public perceived the voyage of the tanker *Manhattan* as a threat to

TABLE 7.16 INVOLVEMENT OF TRANSNATIONAL
ORGANIZATIONS IN ISSUES

Conflicts	Transnational organizations involved	Transnational organizations not involved
U.S.–Australia 1920–39	1	3
U.S.–Canada 1920–39	1	8
U.S.–Australia 1950–69	1	15
U.S.–Canada 1950–69	10	21

Canadian sovereignty.[32] In two of the "instruments" cases the United States government manipulated corporate subsidiaries to achieve policy goals, but this manipulation in turn stimulated nationalism in Canada. For example, Diefenbaker politicized the extraterritorial controls case in his election campaign in 1957.[*] In 1965, the United States balance of payments guidelines were politicized in Canada through transgovernmental conflict when Eric Kierans, a provincial minister, prodded the Ottawa government out of a complacent acceptance by sending (and publicizing) a letter of protest to the United States Department of Commerce.

Canadians reacted most strongly when multinational firms played important political roles — as targets of government action, catalysts for it, or instruments of United States government policy. More traditional issues of transnational flows, even when multinational firms were involved, rarely stirred such passions.

In summary, one of the major sources of the difference between the prewar and postwar agendas in both relationships was the postwar position of the United States as the leader of a network of alliances. But in the postwar Canadian-American relationship, transnational organizations affected the political processes of agenda formation in a third of the cases. Since the relationship approximates our ideal type of complex interdependence, this is not surprising.

ACCOUNTING FOR DIFFERENCES
IN OUTCOMES

When we compare the outcomes of all high-level conflicts (tables 7.10 and 7.14), the postwar Canadian-American relationship again stands out. In each of the other three relationships, the United States dominated as a simple overall structure model would predict, securing outcomes closer to its objectives at least twice as often as Canada or Australia. In the postwar Canadian-American relationship, however, Canada has a slight edge, which represents its greater success in dealing with the United States in the 1960s. The improvement in Australia's position was much less marked. The postwar Canadian case is an apparent anomaly for a simple overall structure explanation.

Both the Australian-American and Canadian-American postwar relationships involved alliance regimes with norms against overt linkage, yet the

---

[*] In 1957, Diefenbaker charged that the Liberals would make Canada "a virtual 49th economic state." James Eayrs, *Canada in World Affairs, 1955–57* (Toronto: Oxford University Press, 1959), p. 125. In the 1958 election, an alleged refusal by Ford of Canada to sell trucks to China was widely publicized. Trevor Lloyd, *Canada in World Affairs, 1957–59* (Toronto: Oxford University Press, 1968), p. 93.

Canadians were able to reap more gains than were the Australians. Why was Canada more successful? The two major explanations lie in the differences of symmetry in the patterns of interdependence in the two relationships and in the different conditions (realism versus complex interdependence) that affected the bargaining process. In some cases, Canada was able to play on sensitivity interdependence (which was possible only while the regime held), whereas in other cases Canadian success was based on the symmetry of vulnerability dependence. Moreover, the conditions of complex interdependence contributed both directly and indirectly to Canadian success. As we saw above, agenda-setting by transnational actors tended to stimulate Canadian nationalism, which increased the intensity of the Canadian bargaining positions. In at least six cases, moreover, Canadian success depended largely on the direct involvement of transnational and transgovernmental actors in the bargaining process. Table 7.17 summarizes the cases, but we shall now look in greater detail at each of the two major explanations.

First, on several issues, the asymmetry of vulnerability between Canada and the United States is much less than between Australia and the United States. The asymmetry is most striking in alliance defense issues, in which geography gives the Canadians a stronger bargaining position than it gives the Australians. The Australian fear that the United States would withdraw its protective force had only a weak analogue in Canada. On the three conflicts growing out of physical proximity and joint resource issues, Canada's bargaining position was strengthened by the symmetry in legal jurisdiction. And on several economic issues, although Canada was more vulnerable to American actions than Australia was, the United States was more sensitive to Canadian actions than to Australian actions. For example, Canada was granted an exemption from the interest equalization tax in 1963 after Canadian officials showed their American counterparts that the two capital markets had become so integrated that the damaging effects in Canada would feed back into the American economy. So long as the Americans were not provoked to break the issue-specific regime and bring their overall lower vulnerability to bear, the Canadians could play on American sensitivity dependence in certain issues.

You may recall our argument in Chapter 1, suggesting that skillful bargaining may partially compensate for an unfavorable asymmetry in the structure of power resources between partners. Although Canada depended on mutual trade more than the United States (11 percent of GNP compared to 1 percent of GNP), Canadian trade was important enough to the United States (one-fourth of American exports) that Canada had a potential weapon for retaliation. The deterrence value of Canada's ability to inflict pain on the United States would depend on her will to suffer great pain herself. And she was often willing to do that because of asymmetrical

TABLE 7.17   CONFLICTS WITH OUTCOMES CLOSER TO CANADIAN GOVERNMENT OBJECTIVES, 1950–69

Conflict	Juris-diction	U.S. government split?	Low cost or salience to president?	Fear specific retaliation?	Fear link?	De facto transnational ally?	Transnational organization role?	Transgovern-mental role?
Politico-military								
BOMARC	U.S.	Yes	Yes	–	–	Boeing	Boeing	Military
Security information	U.S.	Yes	Yes	Sec. info.	–	–	–	State Dept.
Economic								
Chicago water	Joint	Yes	No	Columbia River	DEW line	Riparian states	–	State Dept.
Carling	U.S.	Yes	Yes	U.S. invest-ment	–	–	–	State Dept.
Oil	U.S.	No	No	Pipeline	Defense	Northern oil refiners	–	–
Lumber	U.S.	No	No	–	–	–	IWA;Crown Zellerbach	–
Auto pact	Joint	No	No	Auto tariff	–	Auto cos.	Auto cos.	–
Totals	4	3	5	2	4	3	4	

salience: the relationship was more important to Canada than to the United States.

Canada indeed proved to be willing in five of the conflict cases in which she was able subtly to hint at possible retaliation. Unless guarantees were received, Canada threatened to cut off cooperation in security information.[33] The possibility of Canada's diverting the Columbia River played a role in the Chicago water case. Possible retaliation against American corporations in Canada played a role in the Carling case.[34] The possibility of building a cross-country pipeline that would result in the exclusion of Venezuelan oil from Eastern Canada was part of the bargaining over exemption from oil quotas; and the possibility of a highly protected automobile industry was hinted at during negotiations on the auto pact.*

Australia was less able to play on American sensitivity. Only in the meat quota case did Australia apply similar tactics. Usually, however, Australia did not protest so vigorously or threaten retaliation for two reasons: there was less economic vulnerability and sensitivity interdependence in the relationship, and she wanted to ensure the maintenance of American security protection. Australia's flexibility in responding to American economic actions was apparent in the aftermaths both of American lead and zinc quotas in 1958 and American balance of payments measures after 1963. After a temporary dip caused by American import quotas, Australia increased lead and zinc exports by value during the quota period (1957–58 versus 1964–65) by about 80 percent.[35] As we said earlier, after 1963, Australia adjusted smoothly to the American interest equalization tax and capital controls, partly because of new revenues from increased mineral exports, and partly because of borrowing in Europe. Even when Australia was hurt by American actions — as on the wool tariff — resort to acrimonious recrimination or retaliatory threats was inhibited by the government's belief, between 1950 and 1969, that the most important goal of Australian foreign policy was to maintain close ties with the United States, in order to receive continued protection. Australia's deference to the United States shows up both in accessions to American requests and in failures to secure American concessions. It reflects the Department of External Affairs' almost exclusive concern with politico-security issues, and the prevailing postwar Australian belief that the priority of foreign policy over domestic interests, and of security over economic objectives, could be maintained. In contrast to the Canadian-American situation, socioeconomic ties were minor enough, and channels of contact sufficiently limited, that this approach could be sustained, at least until the 1970s.[36]

* On replacing Venezuelan oil, see Lloyd, *Canada in World Affairs*, p. 86. During the auto negotiations the Canadians hinted at the possibility of a highly protected market like that of Mexico. As one participant put it in an interview, "we could occasionally point to our sombrero under the table."

Subsequently, it appears that the days of the hierarchy of high and low politics in Australia's foreign relations are ebbing, as security concerns become less acute and economic interdependence and transnational contacts grow.

On several issues, it seems to have been the intensity and coherence of the smaller state's bargaining position that led to different patterns of success. Canada, for example, protested American capital controls much more vigorously than Australia did. Australia did not, as far as the record shows, even protest the interest equalization tax at the presidential level; and after its protests about the 1965 capital controls were rebuffed, the Australian government discovered that it could meet its capital needs in spite of the controls.* Australia's most important success in securing American assent to a request came on the issue of meat import quotas; in this case, Australia was the chief supplier of imported meat to the United States, and Prime Minister Menzies wrote a letter in 1964 to President Johnson hinting strongly that Australia would retaliate against American products if a restrictive bill then before the Senate became law.[37]

Intensity and coherence of bargaining position are also related to the type of politicization that an issue has undergone. Whether it is a spontaneous reaction to transnational processes or a result of manipulation by government leaders, politicization from below involves mobilizing groups to put pressure on the government. That government is placed in a strong position to make demands on the United States, to resist American demands, or even to threaten retaliation (as Australia did in the meat case, or as Canada did over oil and the auto pact) that might from a strictly economic point of view be irrational. By contrast, politicization of issues from below in the United States is carried out by more narrowly based groups, focusing principally on Congress. The United States public does not consider either Canada or Australia important enough to generate broad, popular movements. As a result, politicization from below in the United States (as in the lumber import or meat quota cases) often leads to divisions between Congress — or vocal elements in Congress — and the executive. Thus the pressures of democratic politics usually favor the smaller state in the bargaining process, because for them, politicization from below tends to lead to tough negotiating behavior and coherent stands by government, whereas for the United States such politicization leads to fragmentation of policy. Likewise, these pressures give Canada an advantage over Australia, because the volume of transnational processes that help to stimulate public reaction is so much greater between the

* Australia's mineral export boom of the late 1960s helped, so that by the end of the 1960s Australia could stop borrowing extensively in the U.S. market. See *Australia in Facts and Figures*, various issues. This conclusion was confirmed by discussions with officials in the Australian Embassy in Washington, August 8, 1974.

United States and Canada than between the United States and Australia.

The second major explanation of Canada's greater success in bargaining with the United States lies in the effects of the conditions of complex interdependence on the bargaining process. We observed earlier that the agenda of postwar Canadian-American relations differed from the other three situations partly because transnational organizations were more prominent in its formation. When we examine outcomes, it becomes clear that outcomes on issues involving transnational organizations are more favorable to Canada than on issues not involving transnational organizations: Canada "wins" six and "loses" three, with three equal outcomes.

Table 7.18 indicates the roles played by transnational organizations in the political process and the importance of those roles. In several cases, transnational organizations proved to have interests of their own that did not always coincide with the United States government's. This differentiation meant that the transnational organization sometimes improved rather than weakened the Canadian government's position in bargaining with the United States. As one American official said of the role of the companies in the auto pact, "We knew about the Canadian plan to blackjack the companies, but we expected the companies to be harder bargainers. They didn't have to give away so much. It must have been profitable to them." In the auto pact, the letters of undertaking that Canada solicited from the auto companies helped to ensure her larger share of the joint gains. In the oil case, lobbying in the United States by large northern refiners helped Canada.[38] And in the Arctic pollution case, the fact that Humble Oil needed Canadian approval and support before it could undertake a second voyage greatly strengthened the de facto position of the Canadian claim.[39] On the other hand, in at least two cases (extraterritoriality, nuclear weapons), the United States government's objectives were served by its ability to influence transnational and transgovernmental actors; and in two cases (the magazine tax and Seafarer's International Union) one could argue that American-based transnational organizations were the real winners. Nevertheless, Canada did well, on the whole, in issues involving transnational organizations, even in some of the most crucial issues affecting Canadian autonomy.[40]

Canada did even better in postwar issues involving transgovernmental relations; she came out ahead in five of eight cases in which transgovernmental relations were important, whereas the United States came out ahead only once. For the other relationships, only three cases seemed to include significant transgovernmental politics (liquor tax, Canada, 1936; wheat sales, Australia, 1959; and nonproliferation treaty, Australia, 1969). In each of these, final outcomes were closer to Canada's or Australia's positions than to those of the United States. Governmental cohesion is important in determining outcomes, and in general, the United States

TABLE 7.18 CASES OF TRANSNATIONAL ORGANIZATIONS
(TNOs) IN THE POLITICAL PROCESS:
CANADA–UNITED STATES

Importance of TNO to outcome	Outcome closer to objectives of	TNO lobbied	TNO used by government
Necessary			
Magazine tax	U.S.	*Time, Reader's Digest* in both countries	—
Extraterritorial controls	U.S.	—	U.S.
BOMARC	Canada	Boeing in both countries	—
Seafarer's Union	U.S.	Union in Canada	—
Payments guidelines	Equal	—	U.S.
Auto pact	Canada	—	Canada
Contributory			
Columbia River	Equal	Kaiser in British Columbia	—
Oil import quotas	Canada	Oil companies in U.S.	—
Lumber imports	Canada	Union and corp. in U.S.	—
Arctic zone	Canada	—	Canada
Negligible			
Carling	Canada	—	—
Air routes	Equal	—	—

was less cohesive than Canada and Australia. In part this lack of cohesion is a function of sheer size and of presidential as contrasted with parliamentary government, but it is also a function of asymmetry of attention. The United States government does not focus on Canada or Australia the way that Canada, or even Australia, focuses on the United States. Greater cohesion and concentration helps to redress the disadvantage in size. The Cuban missile crisis and nuclear arms cases are informative exceptions to this rule, in that the ideology of an interdependent defense community faced with a common threat helped to legitimize the successful transgovernmental defense coalition.

In summary, though the patterns of outcomes that we discovered have many causes, our detailed investigation indicates that the political processes of complex interdependence, particularly the activities of transnational and transgovernmental actors, were important. Of the four relationships we examined, the Canadian-American postwar relationship was closest to complex interdependence, and the expected political processes help account for the surprising (from a simple structural point of view) pattern of outcomes. More specifically, the difference between the prewar and postwar Canadian experience showed that complex interdependence was not merely alliance politics or the absence of military force, but that the other defining conditions, particularly multiple channels of contact, were an important causal element.

REGIME CHANGE: ALTERNATIVE EXPLANATIONS

We have seen that the pattern of outcomes in the postwar Canadian-American relationship is not well explained by a theory based on overall political structure. It is clear that some of the characteristics of complex interdependence — particularly the absence of military force and the proliferation of channels of contact between societies — have made it more difficult than it would be under realist conditions for the United States to exercise dominance in the relationship. The United States was constrained, furthermore, by the regime that developed between the two countries after the war, which limited opportunities for linkage among issues and emphasized the virtues of responsiveness and conciliation.

Yet we know that international regimes can be changed if they become intolerable to states that have overwhelming underlying power. Why, then, did the United States not break the regime that has governed Canadian-American relations in the postwar era? Let us look at how well our four models of regime change help to explain the patterns that we have described.

According to our simple economic process model, the dramatic increase in economic sensitivity interdependence between the United States and Canada should have led to a gradual regime change in the direction of increased political integration. For example, George Ball speculated in 1968 that a high degree of political integration would follow from North American economic integration.[41] Certainly economic integration was increasing. Exports to the United States rose from half to over two-thirds of

Canada's total exports between 1948 and 1970. As we saw, each country was the other's largest trading partner, and their exports to each other rose from 26 percent to 36 percent of their total exports during the 1960s. This level of trade integration approached that of the European Common Market, and was greater than in several free trade areas.*

But political integration was limited. We can distinguish three types of political integration: (1) the creation of common institutions; (2) the co-ordination of policies (with or without institutions); (3) development of common identity and loyalty. For voluntary assimilation to occur, all three types must develop. Yet when we look at the Canadian-American case, there is a striking absence of the first and third types. Indeed, one could argue that although there was some increase in the second type, there has been a *decrease* in the third type.

The relationship to the growth of transnational interactions may not be coincidental. Indeed, under conditions of asymmetry rapidly rising trans-national interactions seem to stimulate nationalism.[42] One is tempted to go a step further and speculate that highly visible transnational organizations accentuate this effect. It is intriguing that the growing intensity of Cana-dian nationalism, as shown in public opinion polls,[43] and the gradual de-velopment of government programs for greater control of transnational organizations and communications followed the great economic boom of the early 1950s, when direct investment grew to exceed portfolio invest-ment (1950) and nonresident control grew to more than 50 percent of Canadian manufacturing (1956).[44]

Whatever its causes, rising nationalist attitudes affected Canadian gov-ernment policies in patterns visible in high-level conflicts. As we saw, the agenda switched from one primarily set by American government actions in the 1950s to one reflecting more Canadian government actions in the 1960s. Over the same period, outcomes closer to the Canadian govern-ment's objectives also increased. Perhaps even more indicative is the fact that although several solutions to high-level conflicts in the late 1950s and early 1960s could be called integrative in their effects (oil import exemp-tion, balance of payments measures, air routes, auto pact), these solutions became infrequent in the 1970s.† Societal interdependence and policy in-terdependence did not by themselves create a transnational sense of

---

* The analogous figure for the European Common Market in 1966 was 43 percent; European Free Trade Association, 25 percent; Latin American Free Trade Association, 10 percent.

† This has not been for lack of opportunity. For example, a Canadian regional subsidy to a Michelin tire factory was treated as an export subsidy by the U.S., which imposed countervailing duties. A decade earlier one might have seen an integrative response to this situation of policy interdependence.

political community. Nationalism and the nation-state were not banished from the politics of bargaining in situations of complex interdependence. Quite the contrary: while the elephant roamed abroad, the beaver built dams.

The simple economic growth model does give a reason for the *persistence* of the postwar nonlinkage norm in Canadian-American relations, however. Both governments were aware of the welfare losses they would incur from a disruption of economic integration, and of the necessity of some policy integration — preferably informal — to maintain the economic system. Though unwilling to develop a new regime that would reflect growing integration, both governments drew back from actions that threatened the existing regime with its welfare benefits.

The overall structure explanation is best at explaining the prewar regimes and the *establishment* of the postwar regimes in both cases. In the postwar period, however, it is better at accounting for the Australians' failure to reap greater gains from a regime that discouraged linkage than at explaining the Canadians' postwar gains and the United States' failure to change the regime.

We found that explicit linkages between issues were most significant during the *prewar* period, when isolationism in all three countries made the *bilateral* structure of power more relevant than the global structure. During the 1920s and 1930s the United States frequently linked extraneous issues in order to exert the leverage of its overall preponderance, particularly in trade, against Canada. Against Australia, the United States drew linkages within issue areas, on such issues as wheat exports and trade diversion. The United States consul-general in Australia in the 1930s proposed linking military protection of Australia to Australian concessions on trade issues, but because of the isolationist mood of the times, his proposal was apparently rejected by the State Department.[45] Canada and Australia tried linking issues (Canada linked salmon and halibut fisheries, and Trail Smelter pollution and Detroit air pollution; and Australia linked trade diversion with a trade agreement), but without success, as the Americans refused to accept the linkage.

Before World War II, a sense of common security objectives was absent from both relationships, particularly from that between the United States and Australia. It is therefore not surprising that relations were often acrimonious and that the United States, in particular, felt little need to make concessions to its smaller trading partners on economic issues. The norms that helped to preserve the much more responsive patterns of the postwar relationship arose out of a sense of common interest developed during close wartime and Cold War alliances. Both sides were interested in preserving the alliances and the friendly nature of the relationship. In the United States, the State and Defense departments had the most direct interest in these goals, and sometimes supported Canada or (more rarely) Australia against the Agriculture or Treasury departments.

From an overall structure point of view, however, the relationships were very different. Throughout the two postwar decades under review, Australian governments believed that their country was dependent on American protection to combat threats from Asia, whether from Japan, Indonesia, or China. They, as well as American policymakers, believed that Australia was the more dependent partner, and their bargaining position suffered as a result. Although the United States devoted far less attention to Australia than vice versa, Australia was unable to take advantage of this situation because of its sense of asymmetrical dependence in security issues. In this sense, the outcomes of Australian-American issues in the 1950s and 1960s were largely structurally determined. For Australian governments between 1950 and 1969, the fear of weakening the American protective umbrella as a result of negative linkage to security issues was a pervasive source of concern. Because of the Australian subordination of economic issues to security issues, American diplomats did not have to spell out the consequences for security of a major and acrimonious disagreement on another issue.

In the 1950s Canada defined its security situation and its concern with global order not quite so deferentially as did Australia, but nevertheless in such a way that it seems to have made equal or greater sacrifices to preserve the global structure of relations. By the mid- to late 1960s, the decline in the Cold War's intensity, disillusionment with UN peacekeeping, technological obsolescence of defense against bomber attacks, and the Vietnam War altered Canadian perceptions of security. Combined with rising domestic nationalism, these changes diminished Canadian fear of disrupting either the global or North American pattern of relationships. Inhibitions on bargaining were therefore reduced. The norms and operating strategies of the relationship began to change. Thus, the structural constraints on Canadian policy eroded in the 1960s. Although the United States continued to be much more powerful overall than Canada, the Canadian government had learned how to use growing nationalism and public politicization to achieve greater gains in the bilateral relationship.

But the overall structure explanation does not tell us why the United States did not alter the regime once the Canadians began to depart from the rules of quiet diplomacy. According to the overall structure explanation, the declining security threat and eroding global hegemony should have made the United States less willing to pay the costs of leadership and thus more likely to initiate a change of regime. The diminished importance of Canada in air defense in the 1960s should have reinforced this trend — even though the United States could not, in the nuclear age, ever entirely disassociate itself from the defense of Canada.

But this does not fit the pattern of events. First, despite the symmetry of interdependence in defense in the 1950s, it was Canada more than the United States that restrained its bargaining in order to avoid disrupting the alliance, and it was Canada that first began to change procedures in the 1960s. Second, although Connally's actions in 1971 and 1972 infringed on regime norms in the direction that the overall structure explanation would predict, Connallyism did not last, and the regime has persisted without as large alterations as were expected at the time.

Issue structuralism contributes part of the explanation of persistence, though it does not adequately explain the change in Canadian bargaining in the 1960s. As we have seen, for much of the early postwar period, Canadian tactics on bargaining and on politicization were summed up in the term quiet diplomacy. This is what issue structuralism would expect. It was frequently argued that because of the asymmetry of power, public politicization was more likely to strengthen the American demands, whereas depoliticization would allow the bureaucratic managers of the alliance to relate issues to long-range joint interests.

For example, issue structuralism would predict that the Canadians would try to deal with issues in the International Joint Commission (IJC). The IJC was established by the two governments in 1909 to deal largely with border issues, and has traditionally dealt with issues on their specific merits rather than in terms of national political positions. In eighty cases up to 1970, the IJC's six members (three from each country) divided along national lines in only four.[46] The Canadian government, therefore, often tried to steer cases into the IJC, where it could neutralize American political strength, whereas the American government frequently resisted relegating issues to the IJC. In the 1960s however, on issues such as maritime jurisdictional questions, where it had a revisionist position, the Canadian government avoided bilateral institutions. It took the lead in asserting coastal state rights in the UN Law of the Sea Conference, in which weak states linked issues from below and the United States was in a minority position.[47]

In 1954, Senator Fulbright reflected an overall structure view when he said that he could not conceive of Canada's "becoming powerful enough to be able to be unfriendly." [48] Similar statements are frequently made by Canadians. But friendliness is a question of degree. Contrary to imagined scenarios, during the energy crisis of the early 1970s, Canada was able greatly to change the rules of the game in North American energy trade. Not only did Canada charge OPEC-level prices to American consumers, but she was also able to announce that she would completely phase out petroleum sales to the United States. This unfriendly act did not lead to an American "ultimatum" (the title and expectation of a best-selling Canadian novel in 1973); it led to acquiescence. In the winter of 1974, a number of American legislators proposed that America's economic power be brought to bear on Canada by tariffs or taxes in the broader trade area, but these proposals were not implemented. Part of the explanation is issue-structural: Canada was less vulnerable in the issue area because she was largely self-sufficient in oil. But that is not the entire explanation.

The international organization model contributes an important part of the explanation. Recall that this model does not focus so much on formal international organizations such as the United Nations (which are not particularly important in Canadian-American relations) as on the political processes of complex interdependence, to explain changes in international regimes. Informal patterns of relations — such as transgovernmental networks — are regarded, in this formulation, as important determinants of regime maintenance or change.

The norm of nonlinkage that tends to separate issue areas in Canadian-American relations represents an accommodation of foreign policy to conditions of complex interdependence. When multiple issues and actors are involved, linkage is often too costly in terms of domestic politics. No group wishes to see its interests traded away. Threats of retaliation on an extraneous issue involve mobilization of different sets of actors and promote domestic politicization, which bureaucrats fear may get out of control.

Of course there is bound to be some linkage. Diplomats admit that the overall structure of relations is kept in the back of their minds. They were often concerned for the interaction of issues that were proximate in time (for example, the auto pact and the magazine tax) as well as for the effect on the general climate of relations, but overt bargained linkages were too costly to employ.

Moreover, the transgovernmental networks that were part of the regime process proved to be an important source of regime stability. The efforts at centralization and politicization in the Canadian-American relationship changed the style, but did not curtail transgovernmental networks for very long. Canadian and American officials involved in "managing" the relationship kept in close contact. Even during the 1971–72 period, State Department officials were able to use committees and requests for studies to fend off punitive Treasury measures.[49] Canadian and American counterparts reached informal understandings in such a way that the activities appeared to be domestic matters not requiring central oversight. For example, while oil spills in boundary waters are a heated issue in the politics of ecology, the two coast guards operate under a single commander when on oil spill operations. . . . But if it was presented as an integrated approach here in Washington, everyone from OMB to the State Department and many others might want to become involved. The response in Ottawa would be similar. Thus our contingency plans are co-ordinated, but not integrated. And it's better and easier for everyone concerned.[50]

During and after the energy crisis of 1974, when Canadian curtailment of oil exports to the United States could have been the kind of visible and emotional issue that mobilizes American public demands for the punitive use of our overall power, the transgovernmental network of officials co-operated in managing politicization. Informal transgovernmental inter-actions helped to maintain temporary Canadian oil supplies to the northern tier of American refineries, thus diminishing the points of potential domes-tic American politicization — particularly through the Congress — that might have pressed the American government to resist the Canadian change of the energy ball park.[51] Such cooperation among officials in several agencies on both sides of the border involved decisions that would have been both too frequent and too controversial if carried out in the full glare of publicity that accompanies high-level diplomacy. When faced with a potential politicization crisis, the regime procedures (though not the label) of quiet diplomacy were resurrected to avert the threat.

As we argued in Chapter 3, it is unlikely that any single model (of regime change) will fit all situations, and some situations will require a synthesis of explanations. But we also warned that it is most efficient to start with the simplest structural explanations first and to add complexity only as necessary. Because both prewar relationships and the postwar Australian-American relationship are closer to the conditions of realism than to those of complex interdependence, one should expect the overall structure model to provide a neat and simple explanation for these three cases. The postwar Canadian-American relationship, however, was closer to complex interdependence, and it was necessary to go beyond the over-all structure model in constructing a synthetic explanation. The overall structure model helps to explain the *initiation* of the postwar regime, and the nonlinkage norm in that regime helps to explain why an issue structure model can account for the otherwise surprising Canadian success in sev-eral high-level conflicts. But we needed to add the complexity of the international organization model reflecting a political process associated with complex interdependence in order to explain shifts in the agenda of the relationship, the Canadian successes in at least six of the conflicts, and the *persistence* of the nonlinkage regime. Finally, the economic growth model helped to explain some of the incentives, though not the means, for maintaining the regime.

These findings pertain to policy as well as to theory. As we argued in the first chapter, policy is based on (often implicit) theoretical assumptions. An appropriate policy cannot apply the same theoretical model to all situations without taking changing conditions into account. The postwar Canadian case, though not typical of all world politics, at least demonstrates that an approximation to complex interdependence makes an important difference in the political bargaining process by which potential power is translated into power over outcomes. Thus, for example, as Australia's sense of security threat declines and communications technology reduces the costly effects of geographical distance, one might expect the Australian-American relationship increasingly to resemble the Canadian-American case.

More specifically, the postwar Canadian-American relationship indicates that this type of alliance regime, with its constant consultation and its focus more on the joint gain than the zero-sum aspects of an interdependent relationship, does not rely purely on an outside security threat. It is true that as Soviet-American detente progressed in the 1960s, Canadian bargaining was less structurally constrained and became more assertive, but in the 1970s the regime seems to have been restabilized on the basis of awareness of the potential joint losses from disrupting economic interdependence and acceptance of the important role of informal transgovernmental networks in managing relations under conditions of complex interdependence. Of course this restabilization does not mean that the regime could not be broken by a new threat. Nor does it imply that other aspects of the regime governing the relationship will not be altered; witness Canadian legislation in the 1970s that established more restrictive procedures governing transnational corporate investment and transnational communication through television and news magazines. But the relationship does show that regime stability need not require global hegemony, and that leadership in the maintenance of a regime may be shared.

We are not saying that one can generalize readily from our two cases to all bilateral relations. For example, the United States' relationship to Japan is geographically analogous to that with Australia but cultural distance (not to mention history) must also be taken into account. And although the Mexican-American relationship is analogous in some ways to the Canadian-American one, there is a greater social distance between the countries, both culturally and economically. This chapter should be seen as a *pilot study* generating hypotheses and providing suggestive evidence, as well as testing a methodology for the analysis of bilateral relations. It is not a definitive treatment of the effects of complex interdependence on bilateral relations.[52]

Bilateral relations between countries differ along a variety of dimensions, including cultural apparatus, levels of economic development, and

FIGURE 7.1 Bilateral relations on dimensions of complex interdependence and asymmetry

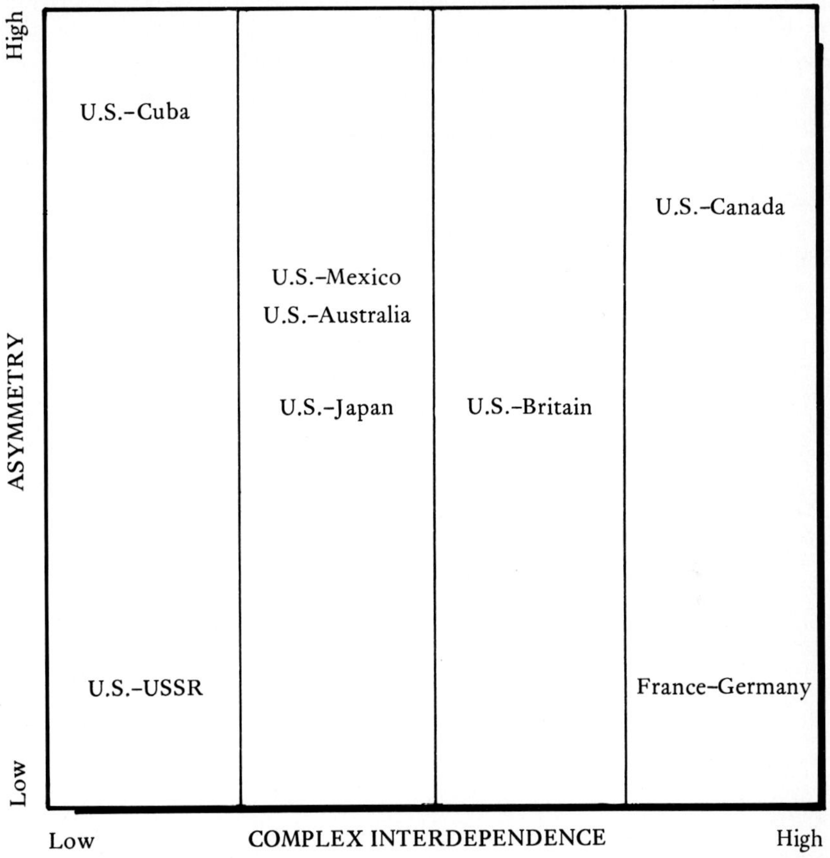

the intensity of transactions. It may help to place the Canadian-American and Australian-American relationships in context, however, to simplify somewhat and think of bilateral relations as placed in two-dimensional space according to (1) the degree to which conditions of complex interdependence are met; and (2) the asymmetry in the relationship. The Canadian-American relationship fits the conditions of complex interdependence and is highly asymmetrical, in terms of the resources available to the two partners. A striking contrast is provided by the Soviet-American relationship, which fits the conditions of complex interdependence very little but is highly symmetrical in capability terms. Figure 7.1 suggests where some other relationships would fit along these two dimensions. Clearly, our two cases do not encompass the full range of variation even on these dimensions. We used them as a *matched pair* differentiated by their approximation to complex interdependence conditions. We cannot attempt to generalize from these cases to all of world politics, or to suggest that Canadian-American relations necessarily reflect the wave of the future. We have, however, gained some insights into the politics of complex interdependence by analyzing them. In the last chapter, we shall look at the problems of coping with complex interdependence and the policy implications for the United States.

PART IV | The United States and Complex Interdependence

Chapter 8 | COPING WITH INTERDEPENDENCE

Interdependence has become a fashionable term, but its rhetorical use can be a source of confusion if we wish to understand world politics or foreign policy. We began this book by examining the rhetoric of interdependence and its implications for policy; but we quickly discovered that we needed to examine the word, interdependence, and to investigate the politics of interdependence before we could make policy judgments. In this final chapter we return to the policy implications.

Although our analysis is not designed to provide precise prescriptions for policy, it does point out two major policy problems: international leadership and organization. Our analysis implies that more attention should be paid to the effect of government policies on international regimes. A policy that adversely affects or destroys a beneficial international regime may be unwise, even if its immediate, tangible effects are positive. Concern with maintenance and development of international regimes leads us to pay more attention to problems of *leadership* in world politics. What types of international leadership can be expected, and how can sufficient leadership be supplied? And focus on contemporary world leadership stimulates increased attention to problems of *international organization,* broadly defined. In this book we have not proposed a set of detailed blueprints for the construction of policy. Rather we have addressed the policy problem at its foundation by analyzing the changing nature of world politics. Without a firm theoretical underpinning, policy constructed in accord with even the best blueprints for peace or world order is like the proverbial house built on shifting sand.

EXPLANATORY MODELS AND CONDITIONS OF WORLD POLITICS

In Chapter 1 we observed that the increasing use of the word *interdependence* reflects a widespread but imprecise feeling that the nature of world politics is changing. We therefore began with conceptual clarification. We defined interdependence in terms of costly effects, distinguished among different types of interdependence, and showed how asymmetrical vulnerability interdependence can be used as a source of power in the traditional game of politics among nations. Then in order to clarify the nature of world politics in this turbulent period, in Chapter 3 we presented (using as few assumptions as possible) an economic process model and three contrasting political power models of how the rules and procedures that govern interdependence change.

In parts II and III we applied these models to four cases over the past half century. We found that the economic model never provided a sufficient explanation, although it was necessary for understanding most of the changes in international regimes with which we were concerned. Our overall structure model was simple enough to produce clear predictions, but, particularly in recent periods, the predictions were often off-target, catching only a small part of the changing reality. A second political model based on the structure of power in specific issue areas sacrificed some of the parsimony of the first model but still yielded clear predictions based on incongruities between power at two different levels within issue areas. Its accuracy was limited, however, by its inability to account for changes in regimes that resulted from changes in the overall power structure or from patterns of international organization, broadly defined. Our third political model, which we called the international organization model, took into account intergovernmental and transgovernmental networks and institutions, and therefore enhanced our ability to explain postwar Canadian-American relations and recent developments in the oceans and monetary issue areas. This result was achieved, however, at a considerable loss of parsimony and predictive power, because the international organization model was more indeterminate than those relying on economic process or underlying political structure.

In developing these models as we did — from the most simple and familiar to the more complex and novel — we sought a systematic rather than an ad hoc approach to theory-building. We tried to see how well one could explain international regime change with simple models before relaxing simplifying assumptions. The more complex models were designed to take into account features of world politics associated with our ideal type of complex interdependence. Nevertheless, we sought analytically to distinguish between the *conditions* of world politics — whether characterized more accurately by realism or by complex interdependence — and our explanatory models.

Ultimately, however, satisfactory explanation involves showing under what conditions one model or another (or a combination of them) will apply. In chapters 6 and 7 we provided some evidence from the oceans and money issue areas, and the United States' relationships with Canada and Australia, that suggested a connection between our two most novel theories (issue structuralism and international organization) and the conditions of complex interdependence. Situations of complex interdependence were not explained well by traditional theories, whereas conditions closer to the realist ideal were. One must be cautious about generalizing these findings. To make more general statements, one would need more information about other issue areas and other country relationships. For the issue areas and relationships considered, however, our research suggests two very important propositions: (1) that issue structure and international organization models are required to explain the politics of complex interdependence; and (2) that the conditions of complex interdependence increasingly characterize world politics in some important issue areas and among some countries. Further research is needed to test these propositions in other cases and explore them with greater precision. Later in this chapter we shall show that there are good reasons to expect aspects of complex interdependence to be important in world politics, in areas other than those we have investigated closely here.

As we indicated earlier, however, our models would not provide the basis for a complete examination of the politics of interdependence, even if we could specify the conditions under which each of them, or each combination of them, would apply. In the first place, they do not focus directly on national policy, but on the development and decline of international regimes. Those who are trying to explain the policies of particular states will find these models too abstract. Our level of analysis is the world system, rather than national policy. To analyze national policies under conditions of complex interdependence, one would need to ask two questions that are quite different from those that we have posed: (1) What range of choice is available to societies confronted with problems arising from interdependence; that is, how severe are the external constraints? (2) What determines the responses that are chosen and their success or failure?

To answer the first of these questions, one would have to analyze the effect of contemporary patterns of interdependence on state autonomy.

The independent variables would be attributes of the system; the question would be how severely they constrained the governments concerned. Our discussion of interdependence and regime change is helpful in defining these systemic independent variables; but it is not very helpful in determining how severely particular governments are constrained by the system. To answer the second question we would require close comparative analysis of the domestic structures and political processes of particular states, and we would need to draw heavily on work in comparative politics.[1]

We do not claim, therefore, to have developed a general theory of world politics under conditions of complex interdependence. Our systemic models would need to be supplemented by analyses of the interplay between international interdependence and domestic politics before such a theory could be constructed. In Chapter 7 we explored that relationship to some degree for Canada and Australia, but hardly more than to suggest some directions for further research.

Our systemic models alone are not adequate to analyze the politics of interdependence. But traditional views of the international system are even less so. Indeed, they fail even to focus on much of the relevant foreign policy agenda — those areas that do not touch the security and autonomy of the state. Moreover, the policy maxims derived from such traditional wisdom will often be inappropriate. Yet the modernists who believe that social and economic interdependence have totally changed the world fail to take elements of continuity into account. As a result, their policy prescriptions often appear to be utopian. All four of our cases confirmed a significant role, under some conditions, for the overall military power structure. Appropriate policies must take into account both continuity and change; they must combine elements of the traditional wisdom with new insights about the politics of interdependence.

POWER IN COMPLEX INTERDEPENDENCE

We particularly need to think carefully about the concept of power under conditions of complex interdependence. Statesmen and scholars often use power to mean an ability to get others to do something they would otherwise not do (and at an acceptable level of cost to oneself), but as we have seen, that kind of power has always been difficult to measure, and has become increasingly so. In the traditionalist view, to know the distribution of the resources that provide power capabilities is to know the structure of world politics; and if we know the structure, we can predict patterns of outcomes. But there are two problems with this approach. First, the resources that produce power capabilities have changed. In the management of the classical eighteenth-century balance of power in Europe, when a good infantry was the crucial power resource, statesmen could calibrate the balance by counting the population of conquered and transferred territories.[2] The industrial revolution complicated such calculations, and nuclear weapons, as a power resource too costly to use except in an extreme situation, further weakened the relationship between military power and power as control over outcomes. For many of the high priority items on the foreign policy agenda today, calculating the balance of military power does not allow us to predict very well the outcome of events.

When we think of asymmetrical interdependence as a power resource in situations of complex interdependence, judgment and measurement are even more complicated. We have seen how being less vulnerable in a situation of mutual dependence can be used as a power resource. But it is difficult to calculate asymmetries and, where there are many of them, to specify the linkages among them. Even if we felt fairly comfortable in our assessment of the power structure, whether based on asymmetries or military resources, we could not be sure of predicting outcomes well.

There is a second problem with the structural approach to power, whether in the overall politico-military system or in the specific issue area. Measurable power resources are not automatically translated into effective power over outcomes. Translation occurs by way of a political bargaining process in which skill, commitment, and coherence can, as we saw in our Canadian and oceans cases, belie predictions based on the distribution of power resources. Thus, traditional foreign policy maxims derived from knowledge of the *structure* of world politics, either at the overall military level or in terms of the asymmetries in an economic issue system, may be seriously misleading. Knowledge of the power structure is the simplest and thus the best starting point for policy analysis. But to predict and understand outcomes, we must give equal attention to the bargaining process in which power resources are translated into effective influence over outcomes.

Bargaining is important no matter what model of the system we use. We must note, however, the ways that the conditions of complex interdependence affect the bargaining process. The minimal role of military force means that governments turn to other instruments, such as manipulation of economic interdependence or of transnational actors, as we saw in the Canadian-American relationship. Similarly, the inapplicability of military force means that considerable incongruity can develop between the structure of overall military power and the structure of power in an issue area. Thus, we found in our study of money and oceans that one of the important questions about bargaining was whether issues would be handled separately or linked to each other and to military security. Linkage among economic issues was one of several tactics for politicizing an issue, thus forcing it to a higher priority on other countries' foreign policy agendas.

If we could assume that linkage and politicization were controlled by rational statesmen in firm control of their governments and societies, then the bargaining process of complex interdependence could be quickly apprehended. But the fact that interdependence has different effects on different groups and that these groups press multiple concerns on their governments and have multiple channels of contact across national boundaries greatly complicates the bargaining process. By reducing the coherence of national positions, this complexity of actors and issues strongly affects the commitment to and credibility of threatened retaliation, which, as we saw in the Canadian and oceans cases, can contradict predictions made simply on the basis of power resources. Similarly, they affect the bargaining process, as we also saw in the oceans and Canada cases, by providing transnational allies, hostages, and instruments of manipulation.

Furthermore, as we saw in both the oceans and money cases, linkage can stimulate domestic politicization, which can then turn the linkages to new purposes. For example, a critic of American oceans policy might say that all that was needed to maintain the free seas regime was a stronger American lead, but this statement belittles the policy problems of complex interdependence. As we saw in Chapter 5, the existence of multiple linked issues and domestic politicization has increased the number and demands of domestic *American* groups favoring extended coastal limits. The international contacts and potential transnational allies for such groups have also increased. Many of the most serious policy problems of complex interdependence result directly from this blurring of the distinction between domestic and international politics. Policy conceived as if the world consisted of billiard-ball states guided by philosopher-kings is not very useful. For international regimes to govern situations of complex interdependence successfully they must be congruent with the interests of powerfully placed domestic groups within major states, as well as with the structure of power among states.

TRENDS TOWARD COMPLEX INTERDEPENDENCE

How prevalent will complex interdependence be in world politics? Is it a temporary aberration, or a permanent feature of world politics? Obviously, we cannot answer these questions on the basis of the four cases in this book. And the differences among these cases should make us aware that any answer must be phrased as a matter of degree. Complex interdependence is less closely approximated in military than in economic or ecological issues and it seems less relevant to communist states and many less developed states than it does to advanced industrial countries. Even among advanced countries, government control of social and economic interactions varies; the United States is characterized by a different relationship between the state and society than is France or Japan.

These caveats notwithstanding, there are reasons to expect that significant aspects of world politics will continue to approximate the conditions of complex interdependence. In some issue areas and some country relationships, complex interdependence is deeply rooted. Although these conditions are not irreversible, major changes would be needed to reverse them. A strong argument could even be made that complex interdependence will *increasingly* characterize world politics, because each of the three conditions of complex interdependence corresponds to a long-term historical change with deep causes of its own.

The multiplicity of goals and difficulty in arranging them hierarchically are results of the long-term development of the welfare state. During this century, governments in nearly all types of countries have increasingly been held responsible for more than military security. Although Israel's situation is obviously different from France's, and although a heightened tension in Soviet-American relations could increase the attention of Western countries to military security, governments will continue to be held responsible for economic welfare.

The multiplicity and lack of hierarchy among goals is further complicated by the many dimensions and definitions of economic welfare, and the contradictory choices about foreign economic policy to which they give rise. One might caricature attitudes toward foreign economic policies among Western states as follows: For classical mercantilists concerned with the power of the state, it was more blessed to export than to import. The classical liberal economists who focused on consumer welfare taught that it was more blessed to import than to export. The twentieth-century political mercantilists who focused on employment (producers' welfare) during the Great Depression again favored exports. More recently, a new school of national ecologists who focus on environmental damage and prefer strip-mining abroad rather than at home, favor (certain) imports over exports.[3] What we find politically however, is not the dominance of one of these economic goals, but their coexistence among powerful groups and a fluctuating pattern of priorities.

The development of multiple channels of contact reflects a long-term historical trend in the technology of communications and transportation. Jet aircraft have brought Asia and America within a day's journey from each other. Synchronous orbit satellites have brought the costs of intercontinental phone calls into the same range as intercity calls. Picturephone transmission and intercontinental computer communications promise to continue to shrink many of the costly barriers imposed by distance. Cheaper and improved communications are not the only cause of transnational organizations or of transgovernmental contacts, but they did contribute strongly to their development. And although, as we indicated in Chapter 2, authoritarian governments can at some cost censor and curtail transnational communications and contacts, transnational communications are likely to continue to create social interdependence among more open societies.

The change in the role of military force is related to trends in the destructiveness of military technology and patterns of social mobilization. As we argued in Chapter 2, the use of force has been made more costly for major states by four conditions: risks of nuclear escalation; resistance by people in poor, weak countries; uncertain and possibly negative effects on the achievement of economic goals; and domestic opinion opposed to the human costs of the use of force. Even those states least affected by the fourth condition, such as those with authoritarian or totalitarian governments, may feel some constraints from the first three. On the other hand, lesser states involved in regional rivalries and nonstate terrorist groups may find it easier to use force than before. The net effect of these contrary trends in the role of force is to erode hierarchy based on military power.

The erosion of international hierarchy is sometimes portrayed as a decline of American power, and analogies are drawn to the earlier decline of British hegemony. Admittedly, from the perspective of a policymaker of the 1950s, there has been a decline. But American power resources have not declined as dramatically as is often supposed. American military spending was roughly a third of the world total in 1950 and still is. Over the same period, the American gross national product has declined from slightly more than a third to slightly more than a quarter of the world total; but the earlier figure reflects the abnormal wartime destruction of Europe and Japan, and the current figure still remains twice the size of the Soviet economy, more than three times the size of Japan's, and four times the size of West Germany's. In power resources, unlike Britain in the late nineteenth century, America remains the most powerful country in the world.

Rather than resorting to historical analogy, we should consider the decline in hierarchy as a systemic change. In terms of our distinction between power over others and power over outcomes, the decline of hierarchy is not so much an erosion of the power resources of the dominant state compared with those of other countries, as an erosion of the dominant state's power to control outcomes in the international system. The main reason is that the system itself has become more complex. There are more issues and more actors; and the weak assert themselves more. The dominant state still has leverage over others, but it has far less leverage over the whole system.

From some points of view, this decline of hierarchy in the international system indicates a desirable trend toward democratization and equality in the world. Some observers have argued that the growth of an "invisible continent of nonterritorial actors" can lead to a world in which "loyalty entropy and geographical entropy will be so high that we very much doubt that major world wars will be feasible." [4] Functionalist theorists who envisaged a transformation of world politics through the coalescing of specific interests — both private groups and public bureaucracies — across national boundaries to such an extent that military capabilities and national sovereignty would gradually wither away could also regard trends toward complex interdependence as proof of progress.[5]

Our view of the future is less sanguine. So long as complex interdependence does not encompass all issue areas and relationships among all major states, the remaining role of military force will require sovereign states to maintain military capabilities. Moreover, so long as the world is characterized by enormous inequality of incomes among states — a condition that cannot be changed quickly even on the most optimistic of assumptions about economic growth — citizens are likely to resist the dismantling of national sovereignty. The increase in complexity and decline of hierarchy may simply result in the absence of any effective leadership in organizing international collective action.

LEADERSHIP IN COMPLEX INTERDEPENDENCE

Leadership, of course, can be a self-serving term used by a dominant state to justify any of its actions. Yet in the organization of collective action to cope with economic and ecological interdependence, leadership is often crucial to ensure that behavior focuses on joint gains rather than the zero-sum aspects of interdependence. As Charles Kindleberger has argued, "If leadership is thought of as the provision of the public good of responsibility, rather than exploitation of followers or the private good of prestige, it remains a positive idea. . . . Leadership is necessary in the absence of delegated authority." [6] And such orderly delegation of authority in world politics is not likely. Leadership can take a variety of forms. In common parlance, leadership can mean: (1) to direct or command; (2) to go first; and (3) to induce. These definitions roughly correspond to three types of international leadership: hegemony, unilateralism, and multilateralism.

We defined hegemonic leadership in Chapter 3 as a situation in which one state "is powerful enough to maintain the essential rules governing interstate relations, and is willing to do so." Clearly, hegemonic leadership is one way in which a public good — responsibility — can be supplied. But the hegemonic leader will constantly be tempted to use its leadership position for the sake of specific, self-oriented gains. Observers and pundits may plead for self-restraint in the exercise of power; but when domestic political pressures, reflected particularly in electoral politics, become acute, such advice will frequently be ignored. In any case, other governments will expect it, at crucial moments, to be ignored, and will endeavor to avoid being put into positions where they are asymmetrically vulnerable, or even very sensitive, to the leader's decisions, when this can be avoided. Willing submission to hegemonic leadership is difficult to maintain for long, because the legitimacy (if not the power) of such leadership tends to erode. What in the eyes of the powerful appears to be policing for the public good may appear in the eyes of weak as imperialist bullying. As such perceptions differ, the need for compulsion in hegemonic leadership increases. As we have seen, under conditions of complex interdependence compulsion becomes problematic.

A second type of international leadership is unilateral initiative that, for better or worse, sets an international example. A large state may not be able or willing to police the behavior of other states, but because of its size and importance, its actions may determine the regimes that govern situations of interdependence, both because of its direct effects and through imitation.

The rules made by the United States — and made in response for the most part to *domestic* political pressures and *domestic* economic and social needs — are almost always much the most important set of national rules affecting operators in international markets. . . . Consider the international repercussions of interest-rate policies pursued by the Federal Reserve Board, of air transport rulings given by the Civil Aeronautics Board, of stock market regulations enforced by the Securities Exchange Commission. They are all much more influential on operational bargaining processes than the rules laid down by any other nation-state [emphasis in the original].[7]

Such leadership may have unintended systemic effects (as Truman's initiative in 1945 led to a weakening of the free seas regime for the oceans) or it may be quite deliberate (as unilateral American suspension of convertibility forced a change of the Bretton Woods regime in monetary affairs).

International leadership as unilateral initiative — going first and setting an example — still exists in complex interdependence. As we have seen, because the American economy is dominant and less vulnerable than those of such countries as Japan, Germany, or France, the United States has more leeway in foreign economic policy than those countries do. Thus it is inaccurate to describe complex interdependence as a completely stalemated system in which every actor has a veto power and collective action is impossible. On the other hand, the initiatives taken by the leading state may not always set a good example from the point of view of creating or maintaining a regime from which all states gain; witness the brief but destabilizing American embargo on the export of soybeans as a response to rising domestic food prices in the summer of 1973.

A third type of leadership is based on action to induce other states to help stabilize an international regime. Leading states forego short-run gains in bargaining in order to secure the long-run gains associated with stable international regimes. Large states are most likely to make such short-run sacrifices, because they are likely to be major beneficiaries of the regime and they can expect their initiatives to have significant effects on world politics. Yet for such leadership to be sustainable under non-hegemonic conditions, other states must cooperate somewhat. If too many middle-level states are free riders, growing resentment among powerful groups within the leading states may diminish those states' willingness to forego short-run gains. Cooperation by middle-level states, however, will depend in turn on the legitimacy of the regime — the widespread perception that it is indeed in the interests of all major parties.

The trends that have eroded hierarchy and that produce complex interdependence do not seem likely suddenly to be reversed. Although the United States still has the most powerful economy in the world, the prospects for American hegemony — to the point of being able to determine and maintain the rules — are slim. The likelihood that any other state will be able to exercise such dominance is almost nil. Unless drastic changes take place in world politics — such as a renewal of a strong Soviet threat to the military security of Western Europe and Japan — hegemonic leadership will therefore be out of the question. The choice will essentially be between nonhegemonic leadership and no effective leadership at all.

Effective nonhegemonic leadership depends to some extent on unilateral initiatives setting good examples, but it also requires cooperation to maintain regimes over the long term. It therefore involves a combination of the second and third types of leadership discussed before. Leadership in these terms does not confer special material benefits, although it may carry high status as well as the ability to shape the agenda for interstate discussions. If nonhegemonic leadership is to be effective, furthermore, all major parties must believe that the regime being created or maintained is indeed in their interests. Any leadership requires legitimacy, which induces willingness to follow and to forego the option of free riding or cheating on the regime that corrodes the incentive for leadership. But legitimacy and willingness to follow is particularly important in nonhegemonic situations, because the coercive element is diminished. Assuring the stability of international regimes under conditions of complex interdependence will require multiple leadership and practices that build legitimacy of regimes.

MULTIPLE LEADERSHIP AND
POLICY COORDINATION

Charles Kindleberger has claimed that effective international leadership must be unitary, not collective: "For the world economy to be stabilized there has to be a stabilizer, one stabilizer." [8] Politically, however, it is extraordinarily difficult for unitary leadership to be effective in the absence of hegemonial power. The leading state may have habits left over from the period of hegemony, and thus assume that it can change or maintain the rules of the game without effective consultation. That assumption can lead to resentment and loss of legitimacy, such as we have frequently seen in American-European relations over the past decade. If, on the other hand, the leading state recognizes that it can no longer exercise hegemonial power, leadership will involve being willing to make the first concessions and to take the most farsighted approach. When its margin of superiority over its partners (and rivals) is diminishing, however, this will be difficult. Finally, no matter how conciliatory the leader is, the patron-client relationships that result from unitary leadership will raise status anxieties on the part of other governments, and foment resentment on both sides.

Unitary leadership under the conditions of complex interdependence is therefore unlikely to be effective. As Kindleberger points out, however, collective leadership has not generally worked in the past. Should we therefore conclude that under complex interdependence, neither type of leadership will be effective?

Clearly, certain well-entrenched patterns of governmental behavior will have to change before collective leadership can be developed. First of all, there will need to be a general acceptance of "collective economic security" as a principle for the conduct of international economic policy.[9] In other words, the preponderant state as well as other major states must be willing to accept mutual surveillance of domestic and foreign economic policies, criticism of these policies by other governments, and coordinated interventions in certain international markets. The illusion that major macroeconomic policies can be purely domestic will have to be discarded, along with the search for total control over one's own economic system. This does not mean that governments will give up control over their economies to international organizations with sovereign power, but that they will accept much more international participation in their decision-making processes than they have in the past. Domestic fiscal and monetary policies, as well as foreign trade, capital, and exchange rate policies, will have to come under surveillance by the international community.

The need for international surveillance and collective leadership is at least as evident in other areas as in macroeconomic policy. If nuclear pro-liferation is to be kept under even a semblance of control, cooperation among suppliers of nuclear equipment and materials will be necessary. Effective action to prevent large-scale famine may, in the future, require similar multinational collaboration. Pollution of the atmosphere and the oceans knows no boundaries; domestic air and water pollution control programs will have major effects on the extent of internationally borne pollution. Already, there is extensive international cooperation for devel-oping and regulating communications satellites.[10]

It is not enough, however, to recommend that leadership be shared. Often, to put a new issue on the interstate agenda or to encourage active consideration of a new proposal, one government will have to take the lead. Yet governments are frequently sensitive about status, as well as about the power and dependence implications of leadership. Thus, in a world of many issues, linked more or less closely to one another but still significantly differentiated, the leader on one issue will need to be a fol-lower on another. More powerful states, such as the United States, will have a greater effect on more issues; but for symbolic as well as substan-tive reasons, several states will need to take leadership roles. This can help to diminish the tendency of middle-ranking states to adopt free-rider strategies. *Multiple leadership* is perhaps a more apt term for this differ-entiated process of initiative-taking than collective leadership.

The leaders on any particular issue should be those with large stakes in a regime and a political and economic situation at home that allows them some leeway for leadership on the issue. If initiatives are left to those gov-ernments that regard themselves as having small stakes and no margin for maneuver, parochial and self-protective responses are likely to result. Thus leadership must be assumed primarily by the powerful and self-confident states.

Even with this acceptance of international surveillance and action, co-ordinating collective leadership will be difficult. Summit conferences will help — as in Europe since 1969 and among the world's major economic powers at Rambouillet during November 1975. The formation of interna-tional cabinet-level committees, and specific international organizations, which are proliferating within the OECD area, should also contribute. Equally important, however, will be the informal networks of working re-lationships at a lower level of the bureaucracy, among like-minded officials and those with similar tasks, networks that we have described as trans-governmental. The convergence of views and perspectives that these mul-tiple contacts can create will be crucial in effectively coordinating policy.

In other words, the very complexity of relationships, and the multiplicity of contacts between societies, can contribute a considerable mutual ad-justment of policy even when conflict exists and formal rules cannot be developed. The trade wars predicted in 1971 have not materialized, and international monetary reform did take place (although after a considerable period of uncertainty). Contrary to the Cassandra-like predictions of the neomercantilists, major developed countries did not initially react to the petroleum crisis by imposing unilateral trade measures or manipulating the values of their currencies. On the contrary, in June 1974 and again in 1975, the OECD countries pledged to avoid solving their energy problems by beggar-thy-neighbor trade policies. Competition for exports, particularly to oil producers, has taken place; and there was some increased protectionism. But the overall response was moderate. The politics of complex interdependence are not neat, but neither have they proved as unstable as many predicted they would be when threatened by economic crisis.

These contacts will usually occur within the framework of international organizations, as will meetings between higher-level officials. As we saw in Chapter 5, an important but little-noticed function of international organizations in world politics is to provide the arena for subunits of governments to turn potential or tacit coalitions into explicit coalitions characterized by direct communication. Thus international organizations can facilitate the informal transgovernmental networks that are required for managing interdependence. International organizations are by no means a substitute for leadership, but they may contribute to its development and nurturing.

We are not arguing for a trilateral oligopoly of the United States, Germany, and Japan, nor for a closed community of rich states. Policy coordination and multiple leadership can more readily be organized among a small number of actors with similar perceptions of legitimacy, but participation in and benefits from such regimes can be made available to others if they so choose. Leadership in our terms does not confer special benefits, but rather implies special obligations to offer the first concessions and to exercise foresight in the interests of the overall structure. This includes a concern for North-South distributional problems. The major industrial countries will need to take the initiative in adapting international regimes to the needs of the Third World by offering substantial concessions and entering into a sustained bargaining process.

BUILDING THE LEGITIMACY OF INTERNATIONAL REGIMES

Problems arising from interdependence and technological change will not be solved at one international conference or even in a cluster of such negotiations over a short time. Indeed, policy coordination should be seen as stretching indefinitely into the future. Responsible leaders will therefore understand that they have a reason for maintaining the good will of other major actors and a constructive problem-solving atmosphere; they will be reluctant to seek short-term victories (either through majoritarian resolutions or unilateral action) if such victories could jeopardize the negotiating process over the long term.

Multiple leadership will be difficult enough among advanced industrialized countries with pluralist political systems. It will be much more difficult, perhaps sometimes impossible, when the Soviet Union and China are involved, or when less developed states are brought into the picture. If international regimes involving these poor states are to become legitimate, industrialized countries must be willing to transfer significant real resources, while allowing these countries the freedom to make internal social and economic changes. The industrialized countries, in turn, will need to be convinced that concessions lead to more than escalated demands, and that the practical arrangements for regulating the world economy will be workable and fairly efficient. The negotiating process must hold out an attractive vision of the distant future (to keep both parties in the game); it also must provide, from time to time, specific payoffs that can be pointed to as evidence that the system works. *Both* sides will require these payoffs, although for the poorer states they may be principally material, whereas for the wealthy ones, improvements in the political climate may be more important.

If bargains between rich and poor are struck, they will have to be largely self-enforcing. Other forms of enforcement will rarely be available, or desirable. Effective strategies will have to appeal to elites' perceptions of their self-interests; appeals to altruism or to concepts of equity or global welfare are unlikely to be sufficient. Government leaders are often capable of learning how to achieve their goals in a more cooperative way; over time, their perceptions of self-interest may change. Such a learning process will be of critical importance internationally in future years.[11]

Although multiple leadership and multiple hierarchies help to spread status and diminish incentives for free-rider strategies among the leading states, the *bottom* of the various hierarchies will usually consist of the same poor weak states. For international regimes to appear legitimate to such states, they must perceive that they are receiving a significant share of joint gains, in relation both to other states and to the transnational actors. They must also perceive the power and status hierarchy of the international system as a relatively open one. As states develop their capabilities, they must be both permitted to share the status and encouraged to share the burdens of collective leadership.

Finally, if poor states are not to perceive international regimes for regulating interdependence as a form of imperialism, they must be free to decide for themselves how much they wish to participate. It has become commonplace to realize that the ideology of free trade in the nineteenth century served the intersts of Britain as the most advanced state, and that there can be economic neocolonialism or an imperialism of free trade (and investment). At the same time, politically autonomous small states can benefit from having the option of an open economic system, when force is not used by powerful states to impose such a system on them.

INTERNATIONAL AND DOMESTIC ORGANIZATION

Organizing for international collective action poses a particular problem for the United States. Americans are so used to being dominant in the world that, when a problem arises about which important groups in domestic politics feel strongly, there is immediate emphasis on unilateral action. The adverse environmental effects of supersonic aircraft are to be dealt with by denying landing rights in the United States to the Concorde; nuclear proliferation is to be controlled by a unilateral ban on the export of material from the United States; the world is to be fed by American wheat exports; and effective population control is to be facilitated by changes in United States foreign aid policies. In each case, the goal is a worthy one — environmental quality, control of nuclear proliferation, alleviation of hunger, limitation of population growth. Yet in a world no longer dominated by American power, unilateral American approaches of this sort may, in the long run, be detrimental even to the goals being sought. If they disrupt cooperative international relationships and cast doubt on American motivations (or create negative reactions to American self-righteousness), such approaches may destroy the basis for legitimate international regimes. Supersonic aircraft can still fly where the United States' writ does not run; other nuclear suppliers can increase their exports of nuclear materials; the United States is unlikely in the long run to be able to feed the world; and American attempts to control population growth abroad may be seen by nationalist leaders as attempts at "genocide." Perhaps the United States should take all of these actions, but within the context of international discussion, bargaining, and (where possible) agreement, rather than unilaterally.

As we have shown earlier, many of the relevant policy decisions in situations of complex interdependence will appear in traditional political perceptions to be domestic rather than foreign. We can think of sensitivity interdependence, whether through a market relationship or a flow of goods or people, as a transnational system crossing national boundaries. To affect such a system, governments can intervene at different policy points:

domestically, at their own borders; through international organization, at another country's border; or inside the domestic jurisdiction of another country. Different points of intervention impose different costs and benefits. Political struggles will arise over who pays the costs of any change. Such leaders as the president or secretary of state will often prefer policies proposing equitable international sharing of costs or even, as a price for retaining international leadership, a disproportionate American share. But leverage over domestic points of intervention will be held by bureaucrats and congressmen whose responsibilities are often to narrower and more immediate interests.

Thus, foreign policy leaders dealing with these new issues will have to pay even more attention than usual to domestic politics. Foreign policy strategy will have to include a domestic political strategy that will permit the United States to focus on its long-term systemic interests. Different issues, for example, trade and money, have different political characteristics. Even though they may have the same effect on employment, trade issues usually involve many political groups, whereas monetary issues rarely do. Foreign policy leaders will have to formulate their strategies in terms of such likely patterns of politicization.

They will have to pay special attention to the way that their international bargaining linkages, threats of retaliation, and choice of international forum affect domestic politics as well as the creation of transnational alliances. They will have to anticipate points of strain. At home, they will have to pay more attention to compensating groups that bear the heaviest costs of adjustment to change. A good example is the comparative generosity of the adjustment assistance in the 1974 trade legislation designed to stave off the restrictive alternative Burke-Hartke bill, compared with the narrow adjustment assistance provision of the Trade Expansion Act that President Kennedy pressed as part of a grand security design in the early 1960s.

Defining national interests is usually difficult, but on issues of economic and ecological interdependence, it becomes even more so. These issues directly affect particular groups, and touch the lives of nearly all citizens. If domestic interest groups are powerful enough to block policies favored by the president — such as the policy of selling large quantities of grain to the Soviet Union in September 1975 — top officials may no longer be able to determine policy. As AFL-CIO President George Meany expressed it at that time, "foreign policy is too damned important to be left to the secretary of state." [12] In such a situation the judgment of top-level officials may no longer be authoritative.

During the Cold War this problem was met by placing economic issues below military security in the foreign policy hierarchy. We saw that distant-water fishermen, representing less than a quarter of the American catch, were able, through an alliance of convenience with the navy, to define American fisheries policy in terms of narrow coastal limits. Similarly, in monetary policy, the United States accommodated its interests to considerations of alliance leadership. After the mid-1960s, the Soviet threat seemed less imminent. In the oceans area, strengthened by the law of the sea negotiations, American coastal fishermen (though representing a minor economic interest) successfully pressed Congress for a 200-mile extension of coastal jurisdiction, over the navy's objections. In monetary policy, our allies themselves seemed to pose an economic challenge, and American interests were defined with less concern for preserving the post-war monetary regime or for European sensibilities. As the symbolism of national security is weakened, it becomes more difficult to establish a political consensus on priorities.

The rhetoric of interdependence and symbols of economic and ecological security are likely, however, to be imperfect substitutes for the traditional military security imagery. Economic interdependence affects different groups in very different ways. Grain sales to the Soviet Union, for instance, may help detente, but they may hurt some of the poorest people in less developed countries. Domestically, such sales boost farmers' (and grain exporting companies') incomes, but have an inflationary effect on food prices that is spread across the population. It is unclear whether grain sales will lead to vulnerability interdependence, which could provide the United States with a useful foreign policy tool in relations with the USSR. If not in the short run, what about the more distant future? Or will the United States be unable to use this potential tool because domestic groups with an interest in the profitable transactions will lobby to maintain the relationship? When the conditions of complex interdependence are uneven, and one society bears more of its marks than another, the vulnerability patterns cannot be determined from simple statistics. When domestic burdens and benefits fall unevenly, leaders will find it difficult to make such subtle calculations and indulge their finely balanced judgments. Ecological dangers, by contrast, would often affect everyone fairly equally. But because they are long-term threats and the short-term costs of ensuring against them are unevenly distributed, "ecological security" is unlikely to be a sufficient symbol around which leaders can build a new foreign policy consensus.

Concern about economic and ecological issues can lead both to independent policies and to greater involvement in international policy coordination. Indeed, it is quite plausible to expect an inconsistent and incoherent pattern of involvement and withdrawal. Isolationist policies will be tempting as responses to the frustrations in dealing with a world no longer under hegemonic control. There will be a tension between the United States' increasing involvement in the world economy and its declining control over that economy. Increasing awareness of the need to coordinate environmental policy internationally will coexist uneasily with the awareness that other governments may have very different priorities and may be extremely difficult to influence.

It is possible to design independent economic strategies by which the United States could reduce its economic vulnerability to external events. Consider, for instance, the often-discussed problem of raw materials. If one were concerned about other countries' refusals (or inability due to declining reserves) to sell energy or materials, one could restrict total imports, diversify sources of supply, build up stockpiles, and design contingency plans for rationing supplies in the event of sudden deprivation. Over the longer run, the United States could invest in technologies to produce new sources and substitutes. Given time, technology can change the seemingly inexorable dependence supposedly implied by figures about known reserves.

Yet the important question is not whether independent security strategies are technologically feasible, but how far they should be followed and the uses to which they should be put. Reducing one's vulnerability to external events can be part of a neoisolationist strategy; but it can also be one element in a strategy of policy coordination and international leadership. If we recall our discussion in Chapter 1 of asymmetrical vulnerabilities as sources of power, we can see why this is so. For policy coordination a state requires power in diverse issue areas, in order to persuade others to compromise, and to make sacrifices. Insofar as one state can limit its vulnerability to actions by others, it will increase its ability to influence international negotiations about *collective* economic and ecological security.

At low levels of cost, efforts to increase self-sufficiency are therefore desirable for a strategy of policy coordination and leadership as well as for a neoisolationist approach. The key question between these two policy orientations turns on how far the development of independence should proceed, and at what costs. Taken separately, each "project independence" that neoisolationists propose to reduce our vulnerability dependence might be tolerable. But when one adds them together, one has a heavy burden to impose on the American people — particularly if many of these costs could be avoided by more effective American leadership in world affairs. Moreover, if the environmental pessimists are even partially correct, the burden will grow heavier. Even when it has the capacity for independent action, the United States continues to have an interest in international policy coordination — over which, in such a situation, it would of course have considerable influence.

For some ecological issues the argument for international action is even stronger. When a collective good, such as the atmosphere or the oceans, is threatened with degradation by pollutants from many countries, action by one state alone is unlikely to solve the problem. Yet here again the point is not simply that ecological dangers or finite resources increase interdependence. The key issue is whether the major countries of the world will have the social and governmental ability to respond in time. Will they plan so that the right technology will be available in time, or so that conservation measures can be put into effect before irreversible damage is done? Will we know enough about the adverse effects of technology, and have sufficient control over its development, that we do not create technological monsters? Will international organizations facilitate effective collaboration among governments on such questions?

If we viewed international organizations as formal institutions whose effectiveness depended on their autonomy, it would be difficult to be optimistic. Very little in the record of the last thirty years suggests that intergovernmental organizations such as the United Nations, or even more successful integrative arrangements such as those of the European Community, will become increasingly autonomous and powerful in world politics. On the contrary, these organizations are often divided by controversy and weakened by lack of governmental support, political as well as financial.

This approach, however, reflects an archaic view of international organizations as incipient world governments. We need to think of international organizations less as institutions than as clusters of intergovernmental and transgovernmental networks associated with the formal institutions. Governments must be organized to cope with the flow of business in these organizations; and as governments deal with the organizations, networks develop that bring officials together on a regular, face-to-face basis. International organizations may therefore help to activate "potential coalitions" in world politics, by facilitating communication between certain elites; secretariats of organizations may speed up this process through their own coalition-building activities.[13] Leadership will not come from international organizations, nor will effective power; but such organizations will provide the basis for the day-to-day policy coordination on which effective multiple leadership depends.

From this perspective it is not surprising that — despite their weakness as "governments writ large" — the number of intergovernmental organizations more than tripled between 1945 and 1965.[14] As Table 8.1 indicates, the United States participated in almost three times as many international meetings in 1975 as in 1950. Between 1964 and 1974, the number of accredited government delegates to international conferences and agencies increased by over 150 percent — and fewer than half of the American delegates in 1968 and 1974 came from the State Department.

Because international organizations and meetings are so important as

TABLE 8.1   UNITED STATES TRANSGOVERNMENTAL CONTACTS

Year	International meetings with official U.S. participation	Accredited government delegates to conferences and agencies	
		Total delegates (46 agencies)	State department delegates as percentage of total
1946	141	—	—
1950	291	—	—
1960	394	—	—
1964	547	2,378	52
1968	588	2,137	48
1974	—	3,656[b]	44
1975	817[a]	—	—

Source: Data supplied by U.S. State Department, Bureau of International Organization.

a. 1975 as percentage of 1960: 207%

b. 1974 as percentage of 1964: 154%

centers of informal networks, the proliferation of international activities by apparently domestic agencies is also a natural development. State Department personnel account for less than a fifth of all Americans in diplomatic missions overseas; the rest come from some twenty-three government agencies. Because many of the issues involved are technically complex, technically sophisticated agencies, which have particular domestic constituencies, must be intimately involved in the process, and they must maintain close ties with their counterparts abroad. Thus miniature foreign offices, which have evolved in many United States domestic agencies, are not mere bureaucratic nuisances but have a positive role in managing interdependence. They need to be sufficiently well controlled that they do not establish separate bureaucratic fiefdoms that form coalitions with counterpart agencies to thwart official government policy; but the transgovernmental policy coordination that they engage in is essential.

Transgovernmental policy coordination is particularly beneficial when officials from technical agencies of different governments work together to solve joint problems, or when interactions facilitate learning. Occasionally, a sense of collegiality leads to especially effective problem-solving behavior. Sophisticated attitudes toward international cooperation, and increased sensitivity to the international aspects of problems, may thereby become increasingly diffused throughout the government. Because international organizations often provide arenas for policy coordination, officials of operating agencies may develop close and mutually beneficial relationships with those organizations, and their secretariats, as well. The function of central foreign policy organs such as the State Department should be to encourage constructive transgovernmental contacts of this type, and to orient the agencies involved toward broader views of world order, rather than toward their narrowly defined problems. There should be no attempt to cut off such contacts; such an attempt would be futile. To destroy such networks would be to weaken international organization.

CONCLUSION

The growth of economic and ecological interdependence does not provide clear, deterministic guidelines for foreign policy. There is still a "necessity for choice." The conditions of complex interdependence make the choices harder. The choices will be about how to organize so that both the "domestic" and "foreign" aspects of interdependence issues receive their share of attention. For the United States, a central issue will be how to exercise international leadership without the capability for hegemony. British hegemony over the world's oceans and monetary systems in the last century rested on the twin pillars of restraining domestic interests and applying preponderant power (including an occasional touch of force) abroad. American leadership will encounter the same need to set a good domestic example, but will find the application of power more difficult. We will have to learn both to live with interdependence and to use it for leadership. From a systemic point of view, the American paradox may be that the United States has too much rather than too little freedom in the short run, and may fail to take the lead on the economic and ecological problems that will be increasingly important.

In any case, an appropriate foreign policy for the most powerful state must rest on a clear analysis of changing world politics. Outdated or oversimplified models of the world lead to inappropriate policies. Our argument in this book is not that the traditional view of world politics is wrong. We believe that several approaches are needed, but to different degrees in different situations. We need both traditional wisdom and new insights. We also need to know how and when to combine them. One of the major problems in understanding world politics is the frequent failure to distinguish among dimensions and areas of the field. This failure is all too often accompanied by a tendency to apply the same simplifications to all aspects of the subject. We have studied the policy implications of interdependence in order to contribute to a differentiated, sophisticated approach to analyzing world politics, not to put forward yet another oversimplification as a guide to reality. Careful analysis is not a mere academic game. It is essential for coping appropriately with the turbulent world of our time. In battle, the sword is mightier than the pen, but over the long run, pens guide swords.

PART V | Second Thoughts on Theory and Policy

Afterword*

As we indicated in our Preface to this edition, we have many observations to make about *Power and Interdependence* and the reception it received in the literature of international relations. Our purpose is not principally defensive: indeed, we were enormously pleased and often flattered by the attention given to our book. Instead, we wish to clarify our position, since misinterpretation by intelligent critics usually reflects confusion or poor statement on the part of authors, and to suggest directions for future research.

We begin in Section 1 by examining the three most important themes of *Power and Interdependence*: the relationship between power and interdependence, the ideal type of complex interdependence, and explanations of changes in international regimes. In Section 2 we offer a critique of our concepts and theories and examine which elements of our argument have been most fruitful for later work. In Sections 3 and 4 we raise questions about concepts, such as those of "systemic political process" and "learning," which we did not explicate clearly in *Power and Interdependence* but which we think suggest fruitful directions for future research.

1. PRINCIPAL THEMES OF *POWER AND INTERDEPENDENCE*

In *Power and Interdependence* we identified "political realism" with acceptance of the view that state behavior is "dominated by the constant danger of

* This Afterword is a revised version of Robert O. Keohane and Joseph S. Nye, *"Power and Interdependence* Revisited," *International Organization* 41, no. 4 (Autumn 1987): 725–753.

military conflict," and we argued that "during the 1960s, many otherwise keen observers who accepted realist approaches were slow to perceive the development of new issues that did not center on military-security concerns" (p. 5). As we had done in our edited volume, *Transnational Relations and World Politics*,[1] we pointed to the importance of "today's multidimensional economic, social, and ecological interdependence" (p. 4). Yet *Power and Interdependence* had a different tone from both our earlier writings and popularizers of economic interdependence. We criticized modernist writers who "see our era as one in which the territorial state, which has been dominant in world politics for the four centuries since feudal times ended is . . . being eclipsed by nonterritorial actors such as multinational corporations, transnational social movements, and international organizations" (p. 3). In our view, to exchange realism "for an equally simple view—for instance, that military force is obsolete and economic interdependence benign—would condemn one to equally grave, though different, errors" (p. 5).

We did argue that the use of force has become increasingly costly for major states as a result of four conditions: 1) risks of nuclear escalation; 2) resistance by people in poor or weak countries; 3) uncertain and possibly negative effects on the achievement of economic goals; and 4) domestic opinion opposed to the human costs of force. But we also noted that the fourth condition had little impact on the policies of totalitarian or authoritarian governments, and we warned that "lesser states involved in regional rivalries and nonstate terrorist groups may find it easier to use force than before. The net effect of these contrary trends in the role of force is to erode hierarchy based on military power" (p. 228).

Upon rereading, we think that the general argument has held up rather well. Vietnam's invasion of Cambodia, Israel's of Lebanon, and the Iran-Iraq war all indicate that force remains an option in regional rivalries between small or middle powers. But systemic constraints continue to limit the superpowers' use of force. Nuclear force remains useful principally as a deterrence to attack. Nationalism has acted as a constraint on the superpowers, as both the failure of Soviet intervention in Afghanistan and the weakness of the American response to Iran's taking of hostages have indicated. Even in Central America the Reagan administration, despite its ideological commitment, has been cautious about introducing United States ground forces. Compare the relatively low cost and effectiveness of the Eisenhower administration's interventions in Iran (1953), Guatemala (1954), and Lebanon (1958) with the more recent difficulties encountered by the United States in Iran, Nicaragua, and Lebanon during the 1980s. The use of force against a narrowly based regime in the ministate of Grenada and the limited air strikes against Libya are the apparent exceptions that prove the rule: Grenada was virtually powerless, and against Libya the United States avoided commitment of ground troops.

Our argument about constraints on the use of military force laid the basis for our analysis of the politics of economic interdependence. This analysis contained three principal themes, which we did not explicitly distinguish from one another:

1. A power-oriented analysis of the politics of interdependence, drawing on bargaining theory;
2. An analysis of an ideal type that we called "complex interdependence" and of the impact of the processes that it encompassed;
3. An attempt to explain changes in international regimes—which we defined as "sets of governing arrangements that affect relationships of interdependence" (p. 19).

Our analysis of interdependence is developed in Chapter 1, which links interdependence to power through the concept of asymmetrical interdependence as a power resource. "It is *asymmetries* in interdependence," we wrote, "that are most likely to provide sources of influence for actors in their dealings with one another" (pp. 10–11, italics in original). This concept, that asymmetrical interdependence is a source of power, can be found clearly in Albert Hirschman's *National Power and the Structure of Foreign Trade*,[2] as well as in Kenneth Waltz's article, "The Myth of National Interdependence."[3]

Our analysis linked realist and neorealist analysis to liberal concerns with interdependence. Realism and neorealism both emphasize states' demands for power and security and the dangers to states' survival; the key difference between them is that neorealism, as in the work of Waltz, aspires to the status of science.[4] (When realism and neorealism make similar claims, we use "realism" only to avoid cumbersome language. When referring specifically to the scientifically formulated theories of Kenneth N. Waltz and scholars with similar views, we use "neorealism.") Military force is for both versions of realism, the most important power resource in world politics. States must rely ultimately on their own resources and must strive to maintain their relative positions in the system, even at high economic cost. Liberalism also examines state action but directs its attention to other groups as well. For liberal thinkers, economic incentives are as important as concerns for security. Among republics, at any rate, military threats may be insignificant, expanding the potential area for cooperation and reducing both the role of force and the emphasis states place on their relative power positions in the international system.

Our respect for the liberal tradition of political analysis reflects our debt to studies of regional integration carried out during the 1950s and 1960s. Karl Deutsch focused on the development of pluralistic security communities—groups of states which developed reliable expectations of peaceful relations and thereby overcame the security dilemma that realists see as characterizing international politics. Ernst Haas focused on the uniting of Europe and the transformation of the Franco-German hostility into a postwar economic and political cooperation. Subsequently, scholars extended these perspectives on economic, social, and political interdependence and integration to other regions.[5] What these studies had in common was their focus on how increased transactions and contact changed attitudes and transnational coalition opportunities, and the ways in which institutions helped to foster such processes. They focused directly on the political processes of learning and the redefinition of national interests.

The development of regional-integration theory outstripped the development of regional communities—although the transformation of Western Europe into a pluralistic security community is an important accomplishment. We felt, however, that many of the insights from integration theory could be transferred to the growing and broader dimensions of international economic interdependence. Our first study in transnational relations and interdependence broadened the conceptions of how national interests are learned and changed, but it was only in *Power and Interdependence* that we explicitly addressed the conditions under which the assumptions of realism were sufficient or needed to be supplemented by a more complex model of change. Our goal was not to discard the insights of realist theory, but to construct a broader theoretical framework that could encompass realist concerns about the structure of power while also explaining changes in the processes of the international system. We sought to account for the anomalies that arose when realism tried to deal with issues of interdependence, and to direct attention to new information and directions for research. We were interested in supplementing realism by encompassing it in a broader theoretical framework, not in trying to destroy it.

The discussion of realism in *Power and Interdependence* was deliberately incomplete. We were less interested in describing the realist tradition than in examining some of its central assumptions and assessing its relevance for our analysis of the politics of interdependence. Some reviewers took us to task for, in K. J. Holsti's words, "attempting to apply old approaches or models to areas for which they were never intended," and therefore "setting up straw men." Stanley J. Michalak commented that our "straw man may well be 'parsimonious' and easy to test, but it has little to do with realism."[6] Liberalism as a traditional theory escaped mention entirely: although our analysis was clearly rooted in interdependence theory, which shared key assumptions with liberalism, we made no effort to locate ourselves with respect to the liberal tradition. We presented a version of regional-integration theory that avoided teleological arguments and took the distribution of military power, economic power, and the role of states fully into account.[7] If we had been more explicit about locating our views in relation to the traditions of realism and liberalism, we might have avoided some subsequent confusion.

Interdependence generates classic problems of political strategy, since it implies that the actions of states, and significant nonstate actors, will impose costs on other members of the system. These affected actors will respond politically, if they are able, in an attempt to avoid having the burdens of adjustment forced on them. From the foreign-policy standpoint, the problem facing individual governments is how to benefit from international exchange while maintaining as much autonomy as possible. From the perspective of the international system, the problem is how to generate and maintain a mutually beneficial pattern of cooperation in the face of competing efforts by governments (and nongovernmental actors) to manipulate the system for their own benefit.[8]

In analyzing the politics of interdependence, we emphasized that interdependence would not necessarily lead to cooperation, nor did we assume that its consequences would automatically be benign in other respects. The key point was not that interdependence made power obsolete—far from it—but that patterns of interdependence and patterns of potential power resources in a given issue area are closely related—indeed, two sides of a single coin. Thus we ought not merely to place realist and liberal perspectives side by side but to link them together in an integrated analysis. As David Baldwin later observed, "It should not be necessary to develop a separate theory to cover each issue-area of international exchange relations."[9]

The concept of "complex interdependence," introduced in Chapter 2, reflected our dissatisfaction with the bargaining analysis of interdependence alone, and our attempt to add insight from theories of regional integration to its spare realist assumptions. It is important to recognize that "complex interdependence," as used in Chapter 2, is very different from "interdependence," as used in Chapter 1. "Interdependence" is a very broad term that refers to "situations characterized by reciprocal effects among countries or among actors in different countries" (p. 8). It is as applicable to the political-military interdependence between the Soviet Union and the United States as it is to the political-economic interdependence between Germany and Italy. "Complex interdependence," by contrast, is an ideal type of international system, deliberately constructed to contrast with a "realist" ideal type that we outlined on the basis of realist assumptions about the nature of international politics. Complex interdependence refers to a situation among a number of countries in which multiple channels of contact connect societies (that is, states do not monopolize these contacts); there is no hierarchy of issues; and military force is not used by governments toward one another (pp. 24–25). We began Chapter 2 by stating that "we do not argue . . . that complex interdependence faithfully reflects world political reality. Quite the contrary: both it and the realist portrait are ideal types. Most situations will fall somewhere between these two extremes" (p. 24).

Like the frequently ignored labels on cigarette packages, our warning at the beginning of Chapter 2 was forgotten by many readers who treated our discussion of complex interdependence as if it were our description of the real world rather than our construction of a hypothetical one. For instance, Robert Art's view of interdependence theorists as claiming that a "nation whose economic interests are deeply entangled with another's *cannot* use force . . . interests intertwined render force unusable . . ." portrays some theorists in the liberal tradition but not us.[10] On the contrary, in Chapter 1 we argued that "it must always be kept in mind, furthermore, that military power dominates economic power . . . yet exercising more dominant forms of power brings higher costs. Thus, *relative to cost*, there is no guarantee that military means will be more effective than economic ones to achieve a given purpose" (pp. 16–17). J. Martin Rochester associates us with a "globalist" or "modernist" view, even though we declared at the beginning of *Power and Interdependence* that "neither the modernists nor the traditionalists have an adequate framework for understanding the politics of global interdependence" (p. 4).[11] In contrast to the modernist position, we disavowed the view that complex interdependence is necessarily the wave of the future (pp. 226–29). Indeed, although we began our research on *Power and Interdependence* largely to confirm the importance of transnational relations, as discussed in *Transnational Relations and World Politics*, our investigations produced a much more qualified judgment.

Chapter 2 of *Power and Interdependence* treats all real situations in world politics as falling somewhere on a continuum between the ideal types of realism and complex interdependence. Thus our emphasis in Chapter 2 is quite different from that in Chapter 1. Instead of explaining bargaining outcomes structurally in terms of asymmetrical interdependence, we ask whether the location of a situation on the realism-complex interdependence continuum can help account for the political processes that we observe. The theoretical lineages of the two chapters are also quite different: Chapter 2 is more indebted to liberal theory in general, and theories of regional integration in particular, than Chapter 1, which relies on modified neorealist analysis. Like regional-integration theory, our discussion of complex interdependence focuses on transnational and transgovernmental as well as interstate relations, and it examines how certain patterns of political processes affect actor behavior rather than employing a structural explanation to account for action.

The third major theme of *Power and Interdependence* concerns international regimes, which we define in Chapter 1 as "governing arrangements that affect relationships of interdependence" (p. 19). Our concept of international regimes is indebted to the work of John Ruggie, who defined regimes in 1975 as "sets of mutual expectations, generally agreed-to rules, regulations and plans, in accordance with which organizational energies and financial commitments are allocated."[12] Despite a claim made by Susan Strange, social scientists did not invent this concept: it has a long history in international law.[13]

Chapter 3 of *Power and Interdependence* elaborates our concept of international regimes and offers four roughly sketched models which purport to account for changes in those regimes. One model relies on economic and technological change. Two are structural: one uses overall power structure to predict outcomes, while the other relies on the distribution of power within issue areas. The fourth is an "international organization model," in which networks of relationships, norms, and institutions are important, independent factors helping to explain international regime change.

The three themes of *Power and Interdependence* are to some degree distinct. Interdependence can be analyzed politically without endorsing the concepts of complex interdependence or international regimes; and the concept of international regimes does not depend for its validity on accepting complex interdependence as a useful simplification of reality. Yet we sought to relate our themes to one another. In particular, we argued that the explanatory power of overall structure theories of regime change would be lower under conditions of complex interdependence than under realist conditions (p. 161). Nevertheless, since our argument was to some extent "decomposable" into its parts, it should not be surprising that some parts of it fared better in the later scholarly discussion than others.

2. THE RESEARCH PROGRAM OF *POWER AND INTERDEPENDENCE:* A CRITIQUE

In *Power and Interdependence*, we sought to integrate realism and liberalism by using a conception of interdependence that focused on bargaining. We were cognizant of the realities of power but did not regard military force as the chief source of power, nor did we regard security and relative position as the overriding goals of states. Ironically, in view of our earlier work on transnational relations, the result of our synthetic analysis in *Power and Interdependence*, and of subsequent work such as Keohane's *After Hegemony*, has been to broaden neorealism and provide it with new concepts rather than to articulate a coherent alternative theoretical framework for the study of world politics. Of the themes discussed in Section 1, those having to do with strategic interdependence and international regimes were both most compatible with neorealism and most highly developed in *Power and Interdependence* and later work. Complex interdependence remained a relatively underdeveloped and undervalued concept.

Interdependence and Bargaining

In our analysis of interdependence, we emphasized that asymmetries in military vulnerability remain important in world politics: "Military power dominates economic power in the sense that economic means alone are likely to be ineffective against the serious use of military force" (p. 16). Nevertheless, since in our view the cost of using military force was rising, "there is no guarantee that military means will be more effective than economic ones to achieve a given purpose" (p. 17).

Indeed, we were so cautious about downgrading the role of force that David Baldwin criticized us for not going further in our rejection of realism: "Although Keohane and Nye are clearly skeptical about the fungibility of power resources, they appear unwilling to place the burden of proof on those who maintain that power resources are highly fungible. . . . Whereas the Sprouts and Dahl reject as practically meaningless any statement about influence that does not clearly indicate scope, Keohane and Nye confine themselves to the suggestion that 'we may need to reevaluate the usefulness of the homogeneous conception of power.'" He further complained that we "sometimes seem to exaggerate the effectiveness of military force as a power resource."[14]

Baldwin was right to point out that *Power and Interdependence* is not a "modernist" manifesto, however much some of our friends would like it to have been one. On the contrary, it consistently asks, without dogmatic presuppositions, *under what conditions* liberal or realist theories will provide more accurate accounts of world political reality. The extent to which military force is important in a given situation is to us an empirical question, not one to be decided on the basis of dogmatic realist or modernist fiat.

Bargaining theory has subsequently clarified some concepts and has qualified the analysis that we, following Hirschman, offered. Baldwin's work has helped to emphasize the difficulties of using tangible resources successfully to "explain" behavior, as well as the theoretical perils of introducing factors such as "intensity," "skills," or "leadership" on a post hoc basis to patch up inadequate accounts. Harrison Wagner[15] has shown that being asymmetrically less dependent than one's partner is neither necessary nor sufficient to exercise influence in a bilateral relationship. It is not necessary because a weaker actor with intense preferences on one issue may make great concessions on other matters to attain its objectives. It is not sufficient because in equilibrium, with the terms of agreements fully reflecting bargaining power, even a more powerful actor will not exercise influence on a particular issue if doing so requires concessions on other issues that outweigh its gains. Nevertheless, we believe that asymmetrical interdependence can still be a source of power in bilateral relationships. As Wagner himself is careful to point out, less dependent actors will be able to make bargaining concessions at lower cost than more dependent actors. Furthermore, relationships between powerful and weak actors are often defined by multilateral rule or convention, without bilateral bargaining. Under such conditions, strong states willing to break the rules or alter the conventions may have unexploited bargaining power.[16]

A bargaining approach to interdependence necessarily raises questions about linkages among issues, since, unless unexploited bargaining power exists, to exercise influence on one issue means making concessions on another. *Power and Interdependence* may have miscategorized this problem by placing its discussion in Chapter 2 (which analyzes complex interdependence), rather than in Chapter 1. After all, many of the highest level issue linkages take place between economic and security affairs in relationships such as the United States' and the Soviet Union's. That is, linkage is a phenomenon of realist international politics as much as of complex interdependence. Indeed, we suggested in Chapter 2 that under conditions of complex interdependence, linkages might become *less* effective than under realism (pp. 30–32).

The lack of extensive analysis of issue linkage in *Power and Interdependence* must have struck some observant readers as one of the oddest aspects of our book. Our analysis of regime change focused on issue-specific sources of power and developed an "issue-structure theory." Yet as Arthur Stein pointed out, "Linkage is the central analytic problem with an issue approach to international politics. Issue compartmentalization only goes so far. . . . Because there are situations amenable to linkage politics, the viability of an issue-area approach to the study of international politics is itself context-dependent."[17] Despite the importance of the subject, we failed to develop any theory of linkage that could specify under what conditions linkages would occur. We argued that under conditions of complex interdependence, a variety of linkages would be made, particularly by weak states (pp. 122–24), but we left the matter there. This was not for lack of effort: the truth is that we drafted a chapter on the subject, but since it turned out to be a collection of vague generalizations and illustrative anecdotes, we consigned it to the wastebasket.

Significant progress has been made on this issue since 1977. In addition to Stein, Kenneth Oye and Ernst Haas have developed typologies of linkage that provide more sophisticated categories for analysis. Of particular interest are Haas' threefold distinction between tactical, fragmented, and substantive issue linkage and Oye's distinction between "blackmailing" (making a threat one does not wish to carry out) and "back-scratching" (offering a quid pro quo bargain). Oye's distinction is paralleled by Stein's distinction between coerced and threat-induced linkage. Both recall Thomas Schelling's distinction between a promise and threat: "a promise is costly when it succeeds and a threat is costly when it fails."[18]

Other work on issue linkage has gone beyond typology by applying a rigorous economic or public-choice approach. The basic insight of this argument is that issue linkage is like economic exchange: up to a point, one can increase one's utility by acquiring more of a scarce good to exchange for a plentiful one. Robert E. Tollison and Thomas E. Willett wrote a pioneering article to this effect in 1979, and James Sebenius has employed game theory and an analysis of negotiations on the law of the sea in an attempt to specify the conditions under which linking issues together can create new possibilities for mutually beneficial bargaining.[19]

It should be noted that this progress has been made at the cost of using simple two-actor models. Yet a key feature of issue linkage in world politics is that it necessarily involves intragovernmental as well as intergovernmental struggles. If a government seeks to make a gain on issue X by linking it to issue Y, it is in effect exchanging some of the good involved in issue Y for that in issue X. For example, if a government seeks to stop nuclear proliferation by threatening to stop a potential proliferator from receiving equipment for nuclear power plants, it sacrifices the goal of expanding exports for the goal of stopping proliferation. This policy is not likely to be welcomed by the governmental agencies charged with the task of export promotion. Indeed, there will probably be intragovernmental conflict over the policy, which may, in some circumstances, become a matter for transgovernmental coalitions. Future work on linkage will need to combine the analytical rigor or rational-choice approaches with insights into the complex multilevel games which typically accompany issue linkage in world politics.[20]

The major contribution of *Power and Interdependence* to the study of interdependence and bargaining was to stress that any analysis of the politics of interdependence requires a sophisticated conception of bargaining, and that patterns of economic interdependence have implications for power and vice versa. We did not successfully develop a theory of linkage, which would indeed have furthered our understanding of world politics. Instead, we simply moved the neorealist research program a little further toward taking into account relationships between political-economic interaction and patterns of military-political conflict. Yet neither of us is satisfied with this, or with neorealism's stress on state interest and power, or its static orientation. Other aspects of our work—for example, interdependence and regime change—cut more sharply against the neorealist paradigm.

Complex Interdependence

The concept of complex interdependence is clearly liberal rather than realist. We made no attempt to integrate complex interdependence with realist conceptions of power and structure—on the contrary, our view of complex interdependence was in opposition to a realist ideal-typical view of world politics. Yet precisely because we insisted that complex interdependence is an ideal type rather than an accurate description of world politics or a forecast of trends, its relevance to contemporary world politics is ambiguous.[21]

We did not pursue complex interdependence as a theory, but as a thought experiment about what politics might look like if the basic assumptions of realism were reversed. We therefore did not draw upon liberal theory as fully as we might have. Had we done so, perhaps the concept would have been better developed and more readily understood. We did, however, carry out quite an extensive set of empirical investigations to explore the political processes of complex interdependence, and we closely examined two issue areas (oceans and international finance, in Chapter 5) and two-country relationships (United States–Canada and United States–Australia, for the period 1920–1970, in Chapter 7). These cases functioned as paired comparisons: for oceans and the United States–Canada relationship, there is much evidence of complex interdependence; for finance (due to its political-economic centrality for governments) and for United States–Australia (due to distance and the primacy of security concerns), complex interdependence was much less evident.

The incompleteness of our treatment of complex interdependence is, we fear, partly responsible for the fact that its theoretical implications have been largely ignored. As mentioned earlier, our discussion in Chapter 2 was organized around the continuum between realism and complex interdependence. In effect, the position of a given situation along this continuum constitutes the independent variable for our analysis. Yet the relationship between this independent variable and what we sought to explain was somewhat muddled. In *Power and Interdependence*, complex interdependence has three main characteristics: 1) state policy goals are not arranged in stable hierarchies, but are subject to trade-offs; 2) the existence of multiple channels of contact among societies expands the range of policy instruments, thus limiting governments' control over foreign relations; and 3) military force is largely irrelevant. Table 2.1 of *Power and Interdependence* (p. 37) lists five sets of political processes that we expect to be different under conditions of complex interdependence from what they would be under realist conditions. These include the goals of actors, instruments of state policy, agenda formation, linkages of issues, and roles of international organizations.

A methodological problem immediately arises. Since we *define* complex interdependence in terms of the goals and instruments of state policy, any general arguments about how goals and instruments are affected by the degree to which a situation approximates complex interdependence or realism will be tautological. Thus our propositions about political processes must be limited to issue linkage, agenda formation, and the roles of international organizations. Since, as we have seen, discussions of linkage are as relevant to a realist world as to one of complex interdependence, we are left essentially with two dependent variables: changes in agendas and changes in the roles of international organizations. Ideally, we would have provided qualifying statements specifying the conditions under which agendas change and international organizations are important. How much progress is actually made on these questions?

Chapter 5 discusses both processes. We argue that agenda change results from "poor operations of a regime in a coherent and functionally linked issue area" (p. 121). But we do not specify any model of agenda change that would permit an observer to anticipate when it would occur, and in what direction. Richard W. Mansbach and John A. Vasquez later made an interesting contribution to the understanding of agenda change by presenting their view of an "issue cycle, involving genesis, crisis, ritualization, dormancy, decision making and authoritative allocations."[22] As in most models of stages, the causal processes at work were not clearly specified by Mansbach and Vasquez—as they point out, the issue cycle is more a framework for analysis than a theory. Nevertheless, it goes beyond the brief observations about agenda change in *Power and Interdependence*.

We had more to say about international organizations, partly because of our "international organization model," and partly because of our earlier work.[23] We viewed international organizations not as sources of definitive law but as institutionalized policy networks, within which transgovernmental policy coordination and coalition building could take place. We observed that in oceans politics, international organizations seemed to have a greater effect on states' agendas and influence over outcomes than on international monetary relations. This perspective on international organizations as facilitators rather than lawmakers has held up well in the intervening decade. Such organizations have proliferated, and the activities of a number of them, such as the International Monetary Fund, have expanded—but they have shown little tendency to develop genuinely supranational capabilities. Keohane's *After Hegemony* integrates this view of international organizations into a broader theory of international regimes.

In the interest of parsimony, we limited our analysis in *Power and Interdependence* to the level of the international system: it was essential, in our view, "to know how much one can explain purely on the basis of information about the international system" (p. viii). We admitted the importance of factors at the domestic level but sought first to sort out the systemic forces at work.[24] As a result of this decision, we had to view interests as formed largely exogenously, in a way unexplained by our theory. Thus, domestic politics and the impact of international relations on domestic politics—what Peter Gourevitch later called "the second image reversed"—were ignored.[25] Yet changes in definitions of self-interest, by the United States and other countries, kept appearing in our case studies—both in oceans politics and monetary relations—without adequate explanation.

An example of this difficulty appears in Chapter 5, which describes the extent to which the ideal type of complex interdependence is approximated in the monetary and oceans issue areas and concludes that its applicability is greater in the latter. From a realist perspective, this evidence might suggest that processes of complex interdependence are irrelevant to issues of great importance for states (such as monetary policy). Furthermore, within the oceans issue area, processes of complex interdependence have been viewed by many observers as shrinking rather than expanding since 1977. (The United States' refusal to sign the Law of the Sea Convention reinforced this perception.) Yet such a quick dismissal of complex interdependence as trivial would be too simple. The original American position in favor of narrow coastal jurisdiction and sharing of seabed resources had been determined by the U.S. Navy on the basis of security interests. But the Navy's position was defeated by transnational and transgovernmental coalitions in the context of the Law of the Sea conferences. The United States changed its priorities before it refused to sign the treaty. For realists to say that the United States refused to sign because of "self-interest" begs the critical question of how such interests are defined and redefined.

Our failure to theorize about the domestic politics of interest formation had particularly serious effects on our analysis of the politics of complex interdependence as defined in terms of the goals and instruments available to governments. Understanding changes in complex interdependence must necessarily involve understanding changes in priorities among state objectives, which could only be achieved through an analysis of relationships between patterns of domestic and international politics. Furthermore, the characteristic of "multiple channels of contact" means that states are not unitary actors—that is, the sharp boundary between what is "domestic" and what is "systemic" breaks down. It is not difficult to see how our acceptance for research purposes of the system-unit distinction weakened the prospects for a deeper analysis of complex interdependence. The concept was left hanging—intriguing to some, misunderstood by many, and incapable of being developed without relaxing the systemic perspective whose theoretical parsimony is so highly valued by students of international relations.

International Regime Change

The alacrity with which the concept of international regimes has been accepted in the international relations literature contrasts sharply with the relative neglect of complex interdependence. The concept of international regimes has proven its value, identifying and clustering together the important phenomena to be explained. It has served as a label for identifying patterns of what John Ruggie called "institutionalized collective behavior"[26] on a variety of subjects. And it has been extended to include the analysis of international security issues.[27] Indeed "regimes" seem now to be everywhere!

Although *Power and Interdependence* did not introduce the concept of international regimes, it showed how the concept could be used in systematic empirical analysis and therefore promoted its widespread employment as a descriptive device to encompass clusters of rules, institutions, and practices. Furthermore, it advanced four models of understanding regime change. During the last ten years, a large body of literature on regimes has followed this line of analysis, which Ruggie pioneered and which we sought to extend. Much of this work has tried to test the theory of hegemonic stability—associating a decline in international regimes with erosion of American hegemony during the last quarter century. The result of this work, on balance, has been to increase skepticism about the validity of the hegemonic stability theory. But the literature on international regimes has not been limited to testing the theory of hegemonic stability: characteristics of international institutions, domestic politics, and learning by elites, as well as shifts in relative power capabilities, can account for the nature of international regimes or for changes in them.

During the last decade, research on international regimes has made substantial progress. A wide consensus has been reached on a definition of international regimes as principles, rules, norms, and procedures around which expectations can converge in a given area of international relations.[28] Problems exist in operationalizing this definition: in particular, when the concept of international regime is extended beyond the institutionalized results of formal interstate agreements, the boundaries between regime and nonregime situations become somewhat fuzzy.[29] Most empirical work on regimes, however, deals with the results of formal interstate agreements and is therefore immune to the charge of operational obscurity sometimes raised against the concept in general.

Questions of definition and operationalization aside, much has been learned from this empirical work about how and why international regimes change—in particular, about conditions under which cooperation is facilitated, and about why governments seek to establish, and are willing to conform to, the rules of regimes.[30] Furthermore, policymakers—not only from Western countries but from the Soviet Union as well—have begun to think and talk about international cooperation in terms of international regimes.[31]

Nevertheless, our understanding of international regimes remains rudimentary. Although we have a clearer idea now than in 1977 of how and why international regimes change, we do not have well-tested empirical generalizations, much less convincing explanatory theories of this process. Nor are we likely to have such theories of change without better incorporation of domestic politics into our models. The nature of international regimes can be expected to affect domestic structures as well as vice versa: the flow of influence is surely reciprocal between international institutions and bargaining on the one hand and domestic politics on the other. Although social scientists can understand some aspects of the operation of international regimes on the basis of stylized systemic theories that are indebted to microeconomics, we are unlikely, without close investigation of domestic politics, to understand how states' preferences change. Yet as long as we continue to regard preferences as exogenous, our theories will miss many of the forces that propel changes in state strategies and therefore in the patterns of international interaction.

We know too little about the effects of international regimes on state behavior. Indeed, students of international regimes often simply assume that regimes make a difference because they can alter actors' calculations of their interests or change their capabilities.[32] This assertion has been elaborated but not rigorously tested. *Power and Interdependence* made some observations about how regimes can alter capabilities, making use of the concept of "organizationally dependent capabilities" (p. 55); later work has focused on the impact of regimes on the self-interests of governments, and therefore on state strategies.[33] According to this argument, the principles, rules, and institutions of a regime may have two effects on strategies. First, they may create a focal point around which expectations converge, reducing uncertainty and providing guidelines for bureaucrats about legitimate actions and for policymakers about feasible patterns of agreement. In the long run, one may even see changes in how governments define their own self-interest in directions that conform to the rules of the regime. Second, regimes may constrain state behavior by limiting access to decision-making and by prohibiting certain actions. Since regimes have little enforcement power, powerful states may nevertheless be able to take forbidden measures; but they incur costs to their reputations, and therefore to their ability to make future agreements.

Arguments such as these emphasize that regimes can be understood within an analytical framework that stresses self-interest: states may conform to the rules and norms of regimes in order to protect their reputations. But neither these works nor other works on regimes have established to what extent, and under what conditions, the impacts of regimes on state interests are significant enough to make much difference in world politics. Our relatively poor understanding of the impact of regimes provides opportunities for future research. In particular, we need more careful empirical work, tracing the behavior of states to see how closely policies follow regime principles, rules, and institutions. Yet this is only a first step, since if our attention remains focused on the level of the system, it may be very difficult for an investigator to ascertain the causal status of the regime—perhaps the states would have followed similar policies in the absence of the regime; or regimes could merely reflect interests, without exerting any impact of their own.

To ascertain the impact of the regime, we must trace internal decision-making processes to discover what strategies would have been followed in the absence of regime rules. We could seek to identify issues on which regime rules conflicted with the perceptions of self-interest held by governments (apart from the regime)—what Keohane has called "myopic self-interest."[34] We would then ask whether the reputational and other incentives to abide by regime rules outweighed the incentives to break those rules. How much impact did the regime rules have? Only by examining internal debates on such issues could the analyst go beyond the self-justificatory rhetoric of governments (which is likely to exaggerate their respect for regimes) to the factors affecting their decisions. If this sort of research were carried out on a number of issues involving fairly well-established international regimes in which the governments under investigation had a range of moderate to substantial incentives to violate the regime rules, we might learn quite a bit about the efficacy of international regimes. And if the research examined how decisions were made to strengthen or enlarge the scope of regime rules over a substantial period of time in a given issue area, it could help to test the notion that regimes themselves help to promote their own growth. It might even yield some insights about the question of whether international regimes help to change governments' definitions of their own self-interests over time.

Admittedly, work has been done on national decisions and international regimes (although not explicitly designed as we have suggested); this work indicates the relative weakness of regimes in situations involving high incentives to break the rules.[35] However, the fact that governments conform to most regimes most of the time suggests that regimes do indeed perform a coordinating function—but it tells us little about their efficacy in altering incentives through effects on governments' reputations or in other ways. We need studies examining a wider range of incentives before we will have a better idea of regimes' efficacy in situations involving different amounts of stress. Little such work has yet been done, but the impact of pioneering research along these lines could be substantial.[36]

In studying changes in international regimes, structural theory remains useful: its very simplifications highlight how self-interest can be consistent with the formation and maintenance of international institutions. But structural theory should not be equated with systemic theory, since systems incorporate not only power structures but political processes, including regularized patterns of practice which we refer to as institutions. Yet these processes are intertwined with domestic politics: once one recognizes the significance of these processes, it becomes clear that systemic theory alone will be insufficient either to explain changes in international regimes over time or to account for their impact on policy. Both structural theory and the broader process-oriented version of systemic theory that we sought to develop in *Power and Interdependence* are therefore inadequate by themselves. What researchers must now do is to link a process-oriented version of systemic theory closely with an analysis of domestic politics without suffering the loss of theoretical coherence that advocates of systemic theory have always feared.

3. LIMITATIONS OF STRUCTURAL THEORY: SYSTEMIC POLITICAL PROCESSES

Although we acknowledged the importance of domestic politics, in *Power and Interdependence* we assumed that we could learn a good deal about world politics by having more subtle and sophisticated understanding of the international system. We argued that systems have two dimensions: structure and process. We used the term "structure" in the neorealist sense to refer principally to the distribution of capabilities among units.[37] "Process" refers to patterns of interaction—the ways in which the units relate to each other. To use the metaphor of a poker game, the structure refers to the players' cards and chips, while the process refers to the relationships among the formal rules, informal customs or conventions, and the patterns of interaction among the players. Variations in the ability of the players to calculate odds, infer the strength of opponents' hands, or bluff are at the unit, or actor, level.

The processes that take place in a system are affected by its structure and by the characteristics of the most important units in the system. The preferences of the states predispose them toward certain strategies; the structure of the system provides opportunities and constraints. One needs information about preferences as well as about structure to account for state action. For example, it is not enough to know the geopolitical structure that surrounded Germany in 1886, 1914, or 1936; one also needs to know whether German strategies were the conservative ones of Bismarck, the poorly conceived ones of the Kaiser, or the revolutionary ones of Hitler. Yet even if we understand both state preferences and system structure, we will often be unable to account adequately for state behavior unless we understand other attributes of the system, such as the character of international and transnational interactions and the nature of international institutions.[38] Examining these systemic processes leads the investigator to look more carefully at the interactions between system and unit characteristics—for example, to examine how actors' preferences are affected by the constraints and opportunities in their environments (and vice versa). That is, focusing on systemic processes directs our attention to the reciprocal connections between domestic politics and international structure—and the transmission belts between them.

Clearly there is a great deal of variance in international political behavior that is not explained by the distribution of power among states. Neorealists do not deny this but assign all other determinants to the unit level.[39] This response, however, is not satisfactory. Factors such as the intensity of international interdependence or the degree of institutionalization of international rules do not vary from one state to another on the basis of their internal characteristics (unlike the degree to which democratic procedures are followed internally, or whether the domestic political economy is capitalist or socialist). These are therefore not unit-level factors according to Waltz's earlier definition. Furthermore, making the unit level the dumping ground for all unexplained variance is an impediment to the development of theory. Not only does it complicate the task of analysis by confusing unit-level factors (such as domestic political and economic arrangements) with international-level factors; it also leads some neorealist analysts to forego the opportunity to theorize at a systemic level about nonstructural determinants of state behavior.

These nonstructural systemic factors affecting state strategies can be placed into two general categories: 1) nonstructural incentives for state behavior, and 2) the ability of states to communicate and cooperate. Nonstructural incentives present opportunities and alter calculations of national interest by affecting expected ratios between benefit and costs or risks, without affecting the distribution of power among actors. For instance, increases in the destructiveness of weaponry may produce incentives for states not to engage in warfare, even if the distribution of military power resources between them is not altered by these technological advances. Or reductions in transportation costs may increase trade benefits and therefore encourage policies of greater economic openness, without altering either the relative bargaining power of the actors or the differences among them at the unit level.

The ability to communicate and cooperate can provide opportunities for the redefinition of interests and for the pursuit of strategies that would not be feasible if the only information available to states were about other states' preferences and available power resources. Just as allowing players in Prisoners' Dilemma to communicate with one another alters the nature of the game, so also institutions that increase the capability of states to communicate and to reach mutually beneficial agreements can add to the common grammar of statecraft and thus alter the results.[40] To return to our poker metaphor, the size of the pile of chips in front of each player matters, but so does whether they agree on the nature and the rules of the game.

Liberals have traditionally emphasized these two aspects of systemic process—nonstructural incentives and variations in the capacity to communicate and cooperate. For example, liberal theorists have stressed (with different degrees of sophistication) the ways in which gains from trade and economic incentives may alter states' behavior. Similarly, liberal theorists often stress the effects of increased transnational (and transgovernmental) contacts on attitudes and communication. And, of course, the role of institutions and norms has always been a preeminent part of liberal theory. All these themes were prominent in integration theory between the late 1950s and early 1970s. They are necessary components of a systemic conception of international relations, lest "system" should become equated with only one of its aspects, system structure—a mistake Waltz makes.

This is not to say that liberals have a monopoly on thinking about systemic processes. Technological changes, for instance, are central to realist thought even when they do not alter the distribution of power. Nor do we argue that all factors emphasized by liberal theory belong at the systemic level. But we do contend that adding the process level to the concept of structure in defining international systems enriches our ability to theorize. This emphasis on process as well as (rather than instead of) structure moves us toward a synthesis of, rather than a radical disjunction between, realism and liberalism. Neorealism is appropriate at the structural level of systemic theory; liberalism is most fruitful at the process level. We aspire to combine them into a system-level theory that incorporates process as well as structure.

This approach toward a synthesis of neorealist and liberal theories does raise a danger of tautological reasoning. If dependent variables are vaguely defined as "how nations behave" and the system-level process *is* how they behave, the tautology involved in "explaining" behavior by reference to process is evident. To guard against this, dependent variables must be defined carefully in terms of specific behavior. In addition, a clearly delineated typology of the causal elements involved at the process level—in terms of factors altering nonstructural incentives and affecting the ability to communicate and cooperate—is also needed. Technological change, economic interdependence, and issue density are among the forces affecting nonstructural incentives.[41] The characteristics of international rules, norms, and institutions—"international regimes"—are crucial in affecting ability to communicate and cooperate. Finally, the causal processes that connect forces affecting incentives and ability to cooperate and communicate on the one hand, and behavior on the other, have to be traced: we cannot be satisfied with correlation alone.[42]

Any system-level analysis will necessarily be incomplete. As we have emphasized, to understand systemic processes such as those of complex interdependence, we need to know how domestic politics affects patterns of interdependence and regime formation. This entails a reciprocal comprehension of how economic interdependence and institutions such as international regimes affect domestic politics. Both structural theory and the broader process-oriented version of systemic theory that we sought to develop in *Power and Interdependence* are inadequate by themselves.

Consider, for instance, the ability of states to communicate and cooperate. Although this depends, in part, on whether they agree on rules governing their interactions, it is also affected by the goals that states pursue; these goals are, in turn, affected by domestic politics. The classic distinction between status quo and revolutionary goals is relevant to understanding the ability to cooperate.[43] When deciding whether a stable or turbulent pattern of behavior exists, we must look at the ways in which states' formulation of their goals affects the process of the system. Changes in goals may arise from the domestic processes of a single state—witness the effects of the French Revolution on the classical eighteenth-century balance of power. Changes in goals may also arise from transnational processes that affect the domestic-politics and foreign-policy goals of a number of states simultaneously—witness the effects of the spread of democratization and nationalism on the nineteenth-century balance of power. To say that the nineteenth-century European system remained multipolar in its structure is true if structure is defined in a strict manner, but the inability of this concept to account for change illustrates the necessity of adding process to structure in the concept of system.[44] Moreover, a focus on the systemic-process dimension of communication and cooperation enriches research programs by directing attention to interactions between system- and unit-level changes.

Such a concern with the ways that state goals affect systemic processes (and vice versa) lets us look anew at questions of perception and learning. While these are not new issues, they have had an ambiguous theoretical status as notable exceptions to realist arguments. Adopting a richer conception of system, involving both structure and process, brings perceptions and learning closer to the theoretical heart of the discipline, and suggests the importance of sharpening our understanding of how political organizations "learn."

4. PERCEPTIONS AND LEARNING[45]

State choices reflect elites' perceptions of interests, which may change in several ways. The most obvious is political change. An election, coup, or generational evolution can lead to a replacement of leaders and thus bring in quite different viewpoints about national interest. The change in "national interest" may not reflect new affective or cognitive views in the society at large. Rather the leadership change may reflect domestic issues or other factors unrelated to foreign policy.

Interests may also be redefined through normative change. Practices or interests that are accepted in one period become downgraded or even illegitimate in a later period because of normative evolution. Changed views of slavery or colonialism are examples.

National interest may also change through learning. In its most basic sense, to learn is to alter one's beliefs as a result of new information—to develop knowledge or skill by study or experience. This is a spare definition and does not imply that the new beliefs lead to more effective policies, much less to morally superior ones. The advantage of this definition is that learning can be identified without having to analyze whether a given set of changes in beliefs led to "more effective" policies, whatever that would mean.

Yet this is not the only possible definition of "learning." Indeed, learning is a slippery concept because it has many meanings. Confusion may derive from the notion that "learning" implies improving the moral quality of one's behavior. But in ordinary usage, people can "learn" to do evil as well as good: to devise blitzkrieg strategies, to build and employ offensive nuclear weapons, to commit genocide. Social scientists who discuss learning need not identify it with morally improved action.

A more serious confusion arises because, in social science, a broad definition of learning coexists uneasily with the spare definition we have offered. In its broader usage, learning carries the connotation of an increased ability to cope effectively with one's environment. It is marked by a shift from overly simple generalizations to "complex, integrated understandings grounded in realistic attention to detail."[46] Ernst B. Haas, who has been the leader in advocating the importance of learning for theories of international relations, sees learning occurring internationally when states "become aware of their enmeshment in a situation of strategic interdependence."[47] When learning occurs, "new knowledge is used to redefine the content of the national interest. Awareness of newly understood causes of unwanted effects usually results in the adoption of different, and more effective, means to attain one's ends."[48]

If we define learning to include more effective attainment of one's ends, new difficulties for research arise. In a complex realm such as international politics, we may not be able to determine, even some time after the event, whether such "learning" took place. Misread "lessons of history" and inappropriate analogies have often caused leaders to fail to attain their goals.[49] Did the lesson Harry S. Truman learned from the experience of Munich—that aggression had to be stopped regardless of where it took place—make him more or less able to make wise decisions when North Korea attacked South Korea in June, 1950? Did the lessons American policymakers learned during the Korean War about the dangers of Chinese intervention make them more effective decision makers when American military forces were sent to Vietnam in the mid-1960s? When critics of arms control in the 1970s learned that the Soviets would not simply imitate United States strategic force structure, did they become more or less able to protect American security and world peace during the Reagan administration? In each case, beliefs were altered as a result of experience, and policymakers became increasingly aware of the networks of strategic interdependence in which they were enmeshed. Whether valuable knowledge or skill was acquired, enabling them to act more effectively, remains a matter of controversy.

In conducting research on learning in international relations, we must specify which definition of learning we are using. We believe that it clarifies thinking to begin with the spare definition—alteration of beliefs through new information—since learning, thus defined, can be identified relatively easily. As Haas suggests, one form of such learning is increasing awareness of strategic interdependence. The question of under what conditions such learning leads to more effective goal attainment then becomes an empirical and theoretical question, as it should be, rather than a definitional one.

When we analyze governmental learning, we have to consider complexities of organizational, political, and psychological processes. Policy-relevant learning is an organizational as well as a psychological phenomenon. Shifts in social structure and political power determine whose learning matters. Furthermore, organizations must have an institutional memory and socialization procedures if lessons learned by one cohort are to be assimilated by another. A critical question for research is how different sets of elites perceive and redefine the constraints and opportunities of the international system and the appropriate goals and means of states. Why did Otto von Bismarck, Kaiser Wilhelm, and Adolf Hitler define such different interests and opportunities for Germany? Why did Presidents Wilson and Coolidge define American interests in Europe so differently—and why was Franklin D. Roosevelt's view on this issue so different in 1940, or even 1936, than it was in 1933? To what extent are interests redefined because of systemic or domestic changes? How much are interests redefined because leaders and their supporting coalitions change, or because the views of people who remain in power change? And if the latter, to what extent do the transnational contacts and coalitions stressed in liberal theories contribute to the learning that we observe?

A key question for future research concerns the impact of international political processes on learning. Some learning is incremental and continuous. Incremental learning occurs when bureaucracies or elites come to believe that certain approaches work better than others for their purposes. International regimes probably play a significant role in incremental learning because in such settings they can 1) change standard operating procedures for national bureaucracies; 2) present new coalition opportunities for subnational actors and improved access for third parties; 3) change the attitudes of participants through contacts within institutions; 4) provide information about compliance with rules, which facilitates learning about others' behavior; and 5) help to delink one issue from others, thus facilitating learning within specialized groups of negotiators. Some learning, by contrast, results from large discontinuous events or crises such as Munich, the Great Depression, or the invasion of Afghanistan. Even crisis-induced learning may be facilitated by institutions; these institutions may include international regimes, domestic political parties, or bureaucracies. Contact facilitated by international regimes—among governments, and between governments and international secretariats—may help spread a common interpretation of large events. Whether learning is incremental or discontinuous, therefore, regimes may play a role by creating, altering, or reinforcing institutional memories. The principles and norms of regimes may be internalized by important groups and thus become part of the belief systems which filter information; and regimes themselves provide information that alters the way key participants in the state see cause-and-effect relationships.

Cooperation can occur without regimes or even overt negotiation. Axelrod has shown that it can evolve as actors define their self-interests and choose new strategies in response to others' strategies of reciprocity.[50] Furthermore, there is no assurance that rules and institutions will promote learning or that, if they do promote learning in one part of a relationship, the learning will spill over beneficially into other areas. But looking at international politics in terms of regimes does suggest fruitful avenues of exploration and important questions that are not always captured by the usual approaches. Why has learning been faster in some areas and slower in others? When has learning led to the development of institutions, such as international regimes, and when has it not? What difference do such institutions make? To what extent are domestic factors facilitating or impeding learning affected by international regimes? Can societies take advantage of crises to create new regimes at crucial moments, thus institutionalizing learning?[51] We do not know the answers to these questions—but the answers matter.

CONCLUSION

The research program suggested by *Power and Interdependence* has been, in our view, a fruitful one. Although we as well as others have occasionally been guilty of exaggeration, stereotyping of opposing views, and vagueness about some of our own theories or evidence, the program we helped to develop has stimulated useful further research. It is now conventional to analyze interdependence as a political, as well as an economic, phenomenon and to examine patterns of interdependence by issue area. The conceptions of bargaining and linkage used by political scientists have become more sophisticated and more sensitive to contextual variations and the limited fungibility of power resources. The concept of international regimes has fostered research on the evolution of rules and institutions in world politics, and, to some extent, on the impact of such rules and institutions on state behavior. There is a widespread (although not universal) view among scholars that structural realism, or neorealism narrowly interpreted, is inadequate as an explanatory framework for contemporary world politics.

Yet there have been failures as well as successes in this research program. It seems difficult to understand changes in regimes and in state policies without having a theory of learning; yet the very concept of learning remains ambiguous, and no one has developed a coherent theory of learning in international politics. Furthermore, less has been done with the liberal than the realist half of our attempted synthesis. We have only partially incorporated the liberal emphasis on institutions, interdependence, and regularized transnational contacts into a sophisticated, systematic analysis of process and structure in world politics. The concept of complex interdependence has been bypassed or misinterpreted; in particular, we have paid too little attention to how a combination of domestic and international processes shapes preference. The need for more attention to domestic politics, and its links to international politics, leads us to believe that research at the systemic level alone may have reached a point of diminishing returns.

We need to concentrate now on the interplay between the constraints and opportunities of the international system, including both its structure and its process, and the perceptions of interests held by influential actors within states. We need to examine how conceptions of self-interest change, as a result of evolving international institutions, individual or group learning, or domestic political change. This effort will require dynamic analysis, buttressed by detailed empirical research; and it will entail the further blurring of boundaries between the fields of international relations and comparative politics. For those willing to take up the challenge, the next decade could be an exciting time for scholarship.

Two Cheers for Multilateralism*

In a unique moment of history after World War II, the United States found itself with an unprecedented power to create rules and organizations—international regimes—that laid down a global framework for international relations while protecting American economic and security interests. Largely because of U.S. enthusiasm, such international regimes as the United Nations, the International Monetary Fund (IMF), the World Bank, and the General Agreement on Tariffs and Trade (GATT) were born. Amid this burst of institutional creativity, publicists spoke of entering "the American Century."

The national mood has shifted. International organizations now seem to some like the sorcerer's apprentice—out of control. Jeane Kirkpatrick, then U.S. permanent representative to the United Nations, voiced this view in the January–February 1983 issue of *Regulation* magazine:

U.N. agencies . . . are the scene of a struggle that we seem doomed to lose. Regulation is the instrument for the redistribution of what is called the world's wealth. The international bureaucracy functions as the "new class" to which power is to be transferred. Global socialism is the expected and, from the point of view of many, the desired result.

The United States has been sharply criticized in the United Nations and has responded in kind. It has withdrawn from the U.N. Educational, Scientific and

*Robert O. Keohane and Joseph S. Nye, "Two Cheers for Multilateralism." Reprinted with permission from *Foreign Policy* 60 (Fall 1985). Copyright 1985 by the Carnegie Endowment for International Peace.

Cultural Organization (UNESCO) and has considered quitting the Food and Agriculture Organization (FAO) and the U.N. Conference on Trade and Development. "Global unilateralists" celebrate the U.S. ability to pursue policies on its own, outside of international organizations and unhampered by demands or complaints from abroad.

For the Reagan administration in 1981, the United States was accepting too much governmental intervention disguised as international policy coordination. It viewed interest- and exchange-rate regulation as the job of the market and the IMF as a self-aggrandizing international bureaucracy. Increasing energy production at home was considered more important than strengthening the International Energy Agency (IEA) and its procedures for international policy coordination. Halting the proliferation of nuclear weapons, candidate Ronald Reagan once contended, was not "any of our business." An imperfect draft Law of the Sea Treaty could be safely abandoned. The administration's solution was not a more vigorous effort at multilateral cooperation, but a recovery of lost military strength and U.S. assertiveness.

"Standing up for America" in international institutions is popular domestic politics and also, in some situations, correct policy. Senator Daniel Moynihan (D.-New York) rightly argued when he was U.S. permanent representative to the U.N. a decade ago that, unless answered, rhetoric in the General Assembly gradually would shape the agenda of world politics. Withdrawal may be the only way to nudge errant organizations like UNESCO on to a more pragmatic course. Yet the United States faces a problem: Neither toughness nor unilateralism alone can deal effectively with complex problems that require international cooperation, often in the form of international organization, for their solution.

Indeed, more interesting than the Reagan administration's initial resistance to international policy coordination and institution building was its return to more traditional policies in the face of reality. A world in which Mexico or Brazil might default on massive debts to U.S. banks proved too risky to America's financial health. Keeping the world safe for capitalism turned out to require the intervention of an important international organization called the IMF, whose resources the administration, in a shift of policy, tried to persuade Congress to increase. Likewise, in another shift of policy, the administration, as it thought through the implications for U.S. security of a spread of nuclear weapons, moved to maintain the nonproliferation regime created by earlier administrations. When the Iran-Iraq war raised the prospect that the Persian Gulf might be closed, administration planners looked more sympathetically at the emergency coordination role of the IEA.

The Reagan administration's grudging acceptance of modest internationalism illustrates the impossibility of any return to unilateralism as the guiding principle of U.S. foreign policy. Even officials who expect little from international institutions discover their value in achieving American purposes.

Self-interest in an interdependent world, rather than a desire to improve the world or an ideology of collectivism, accounts for this change of heart. Unilateralism may lead to occasional foreign-policy triumphs, but it is an inadequate answer to a host of problems that cannot be addressed except through international cooperation.

Unfortunately, acceptance of this point does not advance U.S. foreign policy very far. For the key issue is not belated reliance on the regimes and institutions that exist, but future improvement of those regimes and institutions so that the national interests of participating states will be better served. Acceptance by the Reagan administration of the value of international institutions remains tainted by its fears of the collectivistic and shared-wealth doctrines that emanate from international meetings. These fears prevent the administration from thinking strategically about international regimes. Strategic thinking means focusing on a key question that is rarely addressed in current policy debates: What patterns of international cooperation should the United States wish to establish in a fragmented, heterogeneous world?

Because foreign policy by nature involves responding flexibly to unexpected and contradictory events, it benefits little from detailed blueprints for action in the distant future. Yet without a strategic view, tactics cannot be placed in perspective: Flexible responses to contradictory events will run an administration around in circles. One element of a long-term strategy is contingency planning so that tactical opportunities can be seized. Long-range planning that bars innovative responses to new events becomes a destructive exercise, but a purely tactical approach that ignores the impact of policy choices on the structure and institutions of world politics may waste significant opportunities to alter the framework within which the United States can cooperate with other countries.

THE NEED FOR REGIMES

Clear thinking about the roles of international institutions is possible only if Americans accept that so long as they live in a world of sovereign states, international governance will not look much like domestic governance. Even viewed over a 40-year period, despite the fears of conservatives, U.N. members are not advancing slowly toward world government. Nor should international governance be equated with the various institutions of the United Nations, in which some see only virtues and others only flaws. The U.N. system is only part of the complex set of rules and institutions that affects how states manage their interdependent relationships. International regimes—the rules and procedures that define the limits of acceptable behavior on various issues—extend far beyond the scope of the United Nations. Regimes often include formal organizations, but are not limited to them. Regimes are institutions in a broader sense: recognized patterns of practice that define the rules of the game.

Like the famous character from Molière's comedy *Le Bourgeois Gentilhomme* who did not realize that he spoke prose, the public is often unaware that governments exist in a world of international regimes. Regimes vary greatly in their scope and membership. They deal with subjects ranging from debt and exchange rates to whaling and the status of Antarctica; from the spread of trade barriers to the spread of nuclear weapons. Some are open to all states; others are regional. Many are limited to countries similar in capabilities or interests. Not one, however, can impose its will on members, although governments wishing to receive the benefits of some regimes must accept restraints on their domestic or international behavior. In short, regimes facilitate the cooperative pursuit of governments' objectives. They do not substitute abstract, common interests for national interests.

Small states often welcome international regimes as barriers to arbitrary abuse of power by the strong. But regimes can be equally valuable to great powers, such as the United States, that want to create, but are unable to dictate, the terms of a stable world environment.

In recent decades, for example, regimes have served U.S. interests by helping to inhibit the spread of nuclear weapons, to limit trade protectionism, and to organize the rescheduling of loans to less-developed countries (LDCs). The Non-Proliferation Treaty (NPT), opened for signature in 1968, and the U.N. International Atomic Energy Agency (IAEA), created in 1957, are not the only reasons that nuclear weapons have spread so slowly—to less than one-third the number of countries predicted by President John Kennedy in 1963. Yet the existence of an international regime discouraging proliferation has greatly aided American policy in this area and has made the world a safer place. During the last decade, GATT has not kept liberalism in trade from weakening under the pressures of economic distress and rapid changes in comparative advantage. But reflections on what happened in the 1920s and 1930s suggest that without this essentially liberal regime, trade protectionism might well be spiraling out of control. And the fact that the recent debt crisis of LDCs has not turned into a world financial crash is due largely to elaborate international, transnational, and intranational arrangements permitting the rescheduling of debts and providing incentives for banks to continue to make loans to LDCs.

Not all regimes, of course, contribute so effectively to the management of collective problems. Some regimes enjoy less consensus than others. But those that work well characteristically perform at least four valuable functions.

First, regimes facilitate burden sharing. Often governments will contribute to a collective objective only if others do the same. Further, other states find it harder to evade their obligations when a great power can point to clear rules and procedures. Regimes establish standards that can be applied to all states, large or small.

Second, regimes provide information to governments. Shared information, particularly on issues that easily cross national boundaries—such as controlling the spread of communicable diseases, allocating telecommunications frequencies, and limiting pollution of the atmosphere and the oceans—is essential for effective action. Information encourages cooperation on other issues by governments that might otherwise act unilaterally. And where information reveals substantial shared interests, important agreements may result. International regimes make government policies appear more predictable, and therefore more reliable. Thus the IEA, by monitoring international oil stocks and planning for emergencies, may reduce competitive panic buying by governments and firms. Although unsuccessful in this task in 1979, it may well have played a positive role in 1980.[1] Regimes also may provide information indirectly—for example, by giving government officials access, through negotiations and personal contacts, to each other's policymaking processes. Policymakers involved in debt negotiations, then, know not only each other's policies, but also each other: Through this personal contact, they can anticipate more confidently their partners' reactions to hypothetical future events.

Third, regimes help great powers keep multiple and varied interests from getting in each other's diplomatic ways. As interdependence ties issues together, countries become more likely to trip over their own feet. The United States discovered more than 50 years ago that reciprocal trade agreements with one country could harm trade with many others; it was becoming impossible to deal effectively with each issue except in a framework of rules (institutionalized in unconditional most-favored-nation treatment) within which particular negotiations could be carried on. Likewise, in 1945 the United States unilaterally proclaimed its decision to exercise jurisdiction over fishing and offshore oil activities near U.S. coasts; an escalating series of contradictory demands by other countries for control of a wide variety of ocean resources was the result. Well-designed regimes introduce some order into such situations by clustering issues under sets of rules.

Finally, international regimes introduce into U.S. foreign policy greater discipline, a quality most critics believe it needs in greater measure. Thus, international rules help reinforce continuity when administrations change. And they set limits on constituency pressures in Congress. For example, domestic vintners recently sought to exclude European wines. U.S. wheat farmers, worried about retaliation, were able to defeat this move and buttressed their position by referring to the rules of GATT.

In short, regimes usually are in America's interest because the United States is the world's foremost commercial and political power. If many regimes did not already exist, the United States would certainly want to invent them, as it did.

UNREALISTIC VISIONS

Seven maxims may help the United States develop an effective strategic approach to international regimes.

Do Not Try to Recapture the Past

Nostalgia for a simpler, more neatly arranged world leads Americans periodically to propose "grand designs" to solve foreign-policy problems. But postwar visions are now unrealistic. The U.N. General Assembly, with its one state, one vote rule, is not sufficiently amenable to American influence to be a reliable instrument of foreign policy. And policymakers' recent dreams of a "new Bretton Woods" meeting or of a large conference to rewrite and strengthen the NPT might make matters worse. Even during the period of American dominance, universalistic approaches were often unsuccessful: Myths to the contrary, numerous doctoral dissertations have established that the United States did not have an "automatic majority" in the General Assembly, even during the period before the entry of so many Third World states. The diffusion of power that has taken place in recent years makes large-conference diplomacy even more unwieldy than before and therefore more likely to disappoint. The number of contradictory demands often destroys all possibility of a satisfactory resolution, as the troubled outcome of the Law of the Sea Conference, after more than a decade of effort, demonstrates.

In today's world, universal international organizations are more valuable as sounding boards than as decision-making bodies. If the United States listens carefully, but not naively, these organizations may tell it something about the intensity of, and shifts in, others' views. These forums do influence the agenda of world politics. They may legitimate important decisions reached elsewhere (an example would be some of the arms control treaties negotiated by the United States and the Soviet Union and subsequently blessed by a General Assembly vote). But only rarely are universal international organizations likely to provide the world with instruments for collective action.

Ask Whether the World Really Needs It

Regimes are needed only when uncoordinated behavior by governments has much worse results than coordinated action. Issues lacking serious conflicts of interest may need very little institutional structure. Some international problems are more like the question of whether to drive on the left or the right side of the road than like the issue of which car goes first at an intersection. Once a society has decided on which side cars will drive, practice becomes largely self-enforcing. No one but a suicidal maniac has an interest in deviating from the agreement. Many international regimes are similarly self-enforcing—for example, arrangements for delivery of letters, the location of shipping lanes, or specification of which languages will be used in international air traffic control. No one, after all, has an interest in sending mail to the wrong place, inviting collisions by using the wrong shipping lanes, or suddenly switching to French while landing in Chicago.

The more significant regimes, however, concern subject areas where each government would prefer that everyone cooperate except itself. For instance, when a country default seems likely, the common interest calls for a collective effort to save the system. Nevertheless, it is in the interest of each bank to cease lending or even to close out its loans to questionable borrowers. If each bank acts in this way, default is inevitable and the system will surely collapse. A cooperative regime governing bank lending is therefore desirable to the banks themselves. Likewise, international arrangements for the security of energy consumers may, as mentioned earlier, reduce incentives for countries to bid against one another for oil during a shortage. Regimes for debt and oil resemble the stoplights needed at busy intersections: Without rules, pursuit of self-interest by each leads to disaster for all.

To incorporate explicit provisions for monitoring and enforcing rules, regimes that are not self-enforcing usually require international organizations. Such organizations, however, do not have the capability themselves to enforce rules—this must be done by governments—but rather only to exercise surveillance to identify deviations from previous agreements and to engage in planning so that governments will be better prepared to cope with future emergencies. Often the most effective international organizations are surprisingly small. In 1980 the IMF had a staff of only 1,530 persons and GATT employed only 255 individuals.[2] Yet the IMF and GATT arguably accomplish more than certain other international organizations with more than twice the number of personnel, such as the International Labor Organization, the FAO, and UNESCO. And they compare favorably with a number of national bureaucracies as well.

The key question is how well an international organization and the regime of which it is a part structure incentives for governments. A sophisticated strategic approach to international regimes does not assume that international bureaucracies must be large or directive. On the contrary, sometimes an international organization can be most effective by seeking to provide incentives for governments to rely more on markets than on national bureaucratic management. The GATT trade regime, for example, expands the scope of market forces by restricting unilateral protectionism by governments. The IMF stresses the role of market discipline in countries that borrow heavily from it; in the 1970s it shifted from trying to help manage fixed exchange rates to a loosely defined role in a market-oriented system of flexible rates. International organizations are worthwhile only if they can facilitate bargaining among member states that leads to mutually beneficial cooperation. They are not desirable for their own sake.

Build on Shared Interests

To flourish, regimes must enhance the goals of governments. On many issues, governments may regard their interests as so divergent that no worldwide agreement can possibly be reached. Under these conditions, efforts to negotiate regimes are likely to lead eventually to painful choices between poor agreements and negotiation failure. Deliberations on a new international economic order foundered on the heterogeneity of interests in the world—not only between rich countries and poor countries, but within each of those groupings.

The collapse of various global negotiations, however, does not mean that the era of new regimes has closed. During the last decade a number of new institutions and sets of rules affecting relations among the advanced industrialized countries have emerged. Examples include agreements on export credits negotiated during the late 1970s, various codes agreed upon during the Tokyo Round of trade negotiations, and adaptations in the nuclear proliferation regime in the mid-1970s to establish supplier guidelines for safer nuclear commerce.

These regimes and others, such as the IEA, have two key features. All these regimes were designed to resolve common problems in which the uncontrolled pursuit of individual self-interest by some governments could adversely affect the national interest of all the rest. All these regimes were formed not on a universal basis, but selectively. The export-credit and nuclear-suppliers "clubs," for example, include only countries that are major suppliers of credit or nuclear material; the IEA deliberately excluded nonmembers of the Organization for Economic Cooperation and Development.

When establishing smaller clubs, those participating must consider their effect on the larger regime. Nuclear suppliers, for example, were concerned that formation of their group would exacerbate resentment among other adherents to the nonproliferation regime. Yet sensitivity to issues of exclusion can help resolve these problems. Once they had agreed on export guidelines in 1978, members of the nuclear suppliers group emphasized quiet, bilateral diplomacy in order to maintain broad commitment to the nonproliferation regime.

If a relatively small number of governments have shared interests in a given issue greater than their differences, it can make sense to limit membership, or at least decision-making power, to those countries. Sometimes, meaningful agreements can be reached only by excluding naysayers. Every effort should be made, however, as in the GATT code, to allow for the eventual universalization of the regimes. Further, particular attention should be paid to the long-term interests of developing countries, so that a legitimate desire to make progress on specific issues does not turn into a general pattern of discriminating against the weak.

A crazy quilt of international regimes is likely to arise, each with somewhat different membership. Better some roughness around the edges of international regimes, however, than a vacuum at the center. Poorly coordinated coalitions, working effectively on various issues, are in general preferable to universalistic negotiations permanently deadlocked by a diverse membership.

Use Regimes to Insure against Catastrophe

Insurance regimes are less satisfactory than effective regimes that control events and thereby eliminate adversity rather than simply share its burdens. It is better, other things being equal, to prevent floods by building dams than merely to insure against them. Likewise, IEA members would prefer to prevent oil embargoes than merely to share diminished supplies in response to them. Yet in some situations, having adequate insurance may deter hostile action by reducing the potential gains from "divide and conquer" strategies. And in any event, regimes that are able to control events often cannot be constructed. When this is the case, insurance strategies may be better than relying on unilateral action or merely hoping for the best. In thinking about international cooperation, governments are often well advised to "elevate them sights a little lower," accomplishing what they can rather than bemoaning their inability to do more.

The Best Enforcement Is Self-Enforcement

Centralized enforcement of rules in international regimes through hierarchical arrangements is normally out of the question: There is no police force and only a tiny international bureaucracy. If states are to comply with regime rules, they must do so on the basis of long-term self-interest.

Arranging enforcement is not so difficult as it may seem. The major advanced industrialized countries deal with each other on a large number of issues over an indefinite period of time. Each government could "get away with" a particular violation. But viable regimes rely, in one form or another, on the principle of long-term reciprocity. No one trusts habitual cheaters. Over time, governments develop reputations for compliance, not just to the letter of the law but to the spirit as well. These reputations constitute one of their most important assets. As the economist Charles Kindleberger once remarked, "In economics bygones are bygones, but in politics they are working capital."

Reciprocity is harder to institutionalize in multilateral settings than in bilateral settings. It often is difficult to agree on "equivalent" contributions. When arguing with its NATO allies about burden sharing, for instance, the United States concentrates on financial efforts, while European states stress contributions in kind through expropriated land or national service. Moreover, a tradeoff provided in one context may lead to demands for compensation from other countries or on other issues. Nevertheless, the practice of reciprocity does provide incentives for compliance, and in a well-functioning regime, standards exist to govern reciprocity. The subsidies code devised during the Tokyo Round, for example, not only specifies conditions under which countervailing duties can be applied in response to subsidies, but also sets limits on the severity of such duties.

In the design of institutions, enforcement should rest on provisions for information sharing and reciprocity rather than on nominal powers of coercion through centralized enforcement. Despite extensive voting rules, the IEA has never taken a formal vote, but its members share information about oil-company and government behavior. The IAEA has helped deter misuse of nuclear fuels by threat of discovery through its inspection system rather than by assured sanctions in the event of violation. Other contemporary regimes—whether for surveillance of exchange rates by the Group of Five, for maintaining bank lending to debtor countries, or for export credits—also depend on self-enforcement through the generation and dispersal of information, rather than on the wielding of supranational powers.

Failure to notice this point can lead governments to downgrade what international regimes can do—provide a framework for decentralized enforcement of rules. If countries focus instead on the fact that regimes cannot enforce rules through supranational machinery, the international community may miss opportunities to develop new institutions that, by generating information about reputations, may allow practices of greater reciprocity to evolve in world politics.

Look for the Right Moment

In the life cycles of international regimes, erosion takes place gradually, as governments and transnational actors find loopholes in the rules. Defenders of regimes spend their time putting their fingers in the dike.

Occasionally, crises threaten to burst the dike and destroy the established order. The inadequacy of existing regimes becomes evident; old conceptions of reality are shattered and entrenched interests and coalitions shaken or torn apart. The prospect of a world financial crisis can concentrate a banker's mind.

In periods of crisis, opportunities for the construction of international regimes characteristically arise. "Creative destruction," in the economist Joseph Schumpeter's phrase, can result from the collapse of the presuppositions underlying old regimes or from a shattered complacency about the absence of regimes. Thus the first serious discussions of international monetary coordination, which led eventually to Bretton Woods, took place in the ominous depression years before World War II. Economic crises in the 1970s and 1980s saw not only the collapse or erosion of old regimes, but also the founding of the IEA in 1974, after the oil crisis, and the strengthening of the IMF after 1982, in the wake of threats of default by Third World countries.

The period from 1929 to 1933, however, demonstrates that creative responses to crises are not automatic. During crises, policymakers may not look for innovative solutions but may try to muddle through from week to week. Caught unprepared, they may have no time to draw up well-conceived plans for institutional change. Yet if policymakers have thought through the fundamental issues in advance, they may be able to use the opportunities created by crises to devise immediate solutions that support long-term strategy.

In other words, if American foreign policy is to take advantage of crises rather than merely react to them, there is need to think about the desirable evolution of institutions before lightning strikes. No grand design for a broad array of new rules and institutions is necessary. Grand designs stir up objections from many interests, domestic as well as international. Nevertheless, thinking ahead can be used to turn particular crises, even those limited to particular problems, into openings for constructive change. It may not be possible to create comprehensive regimes with an enormous impact, but partial regimes may emerge with constructive effects in particular areas.

For at least the last 25 years the U.S. government has not been known for effective long-range planning. American policymakers can do better than they have at this task. But much thinking about future regimes will be done outside government; at the same time, the effectiveness of the outsiders' work will depend on the receptivity of insiders. Likewise, executive-branch planning must involve key congressional figures. Such links not only help secure legislative support for foreign-policy initiatives, but also help bring new ideas into the policymaking process.

Use Regimes to Focus U.S. Attention on the Future

In the eyes of its critics, American foreign policy is notoriously unreliable. Does it make sense to talk about strategies for international regimes when America cannot seem to avoid confusing and confounding its allies by engaging in erratic, often ideological behavior?

But these shortcomings in American foreign policy reinforce the need to use crises in a sophisticated way to carry out constructive change. During these crises the president's leeway for getting decisive measures through Congress becomes wider, often dramatically so. The United States has always had difficulty keeping sight of its own long-term interests. The division between executive and legislature and the splits within branches of government make it particularly hard for the United States to pursue far-sighted self-interest. Attempting to lay out the principles of international regimes can clarify the country's long-term, internationalist interests. Like the Constitution, international regimes can remind the country of its fundamental purposes, for they can legitimate a broad conception of the national interest that takes into account others' values and policies.

This effort at long-range planning also helps the United States retain its alliance leadership. Constraints imposed by constructive international regimes make America a more reliable partner internationally than if it followed unilateralist policies. Credible promises can be made and extracted by partners with solid reputations. In addition, regimes often provide leaders of allied countries with opportunities to influence the domestic debates of alliance states by holding each to the regime's standards. This strengthens alliances by giving participating governments the opportunity to exercise "voice," in the economist Albert Hirschman's phrase, rather than simply to "exit." Since America's allies have some influence over its policies, they are more willing to commit themselves to alignments with the United States. The impressive strength and durability of America's alliances can be attributed in part to its commitment to the constructive constraints of international regimes.

REGIME MAINTENANCE

In world politics today actors are many, and a bewildering array of issues overlap. Diffusion of power has reduced America's ability to establish international regimes as it pleases. No matter how high the defense budget, the United States cannot recapture the preponderant position it held in the 1950s. Further, maintaining military strength is only part of a viable foreign policy. As the pre-eminent political and commercial power, America also has a strong national interest in building and maintaining international regimes. Yet recent foreign-policy debates have given little attention to this dimension of national interest.

Major international regimes continue to reflect U.S. interests, by and large because of U.S. influence in establishing and perpetuating them. But unless the United States takes the lead in maintaining them, it is unlikely that other countries will have the interest or ability to do their share. As Great Britain found in the 1930s, when the leading trading country closes its market, the protectionist scramble is on. When Washington extended U.S. jurisdiction over new areas of the seas, as it did in 1945, it should have expected others to go it one better—as several coastal states in Latin America did. If the United States relaxes its standards for nuclear exports, other suppliers will relax theirs, probably even more. American restraint is no longer sufficient to build or maintain rules, but it almost certainly remains necessary.

This U.S. interest in regime maintenance does not mean the United States need remain passive as others in pursuit of narrow national interests chip away at existing rules and arrangements. Indeed, there is much to be said for reciprocity as an effective way to maintain cooperation in world politics. And sometimes reciprocity will entail retaliation, as it does increasingly in international trade. But the ultimate objective of retaliation should be to reinforce compliance by others with general rules, rather than to seek exemptions for oneself—exemptions that will be only temporary and that will contribute to the decline of international order, which all should be striving to avoid. Thus the United States should design its strategies to provide realistic incentives to others, behaving in their self-interests, to support international regimes that the United States finds valuable.

In addition to maintaining existing regimes, Washington should be looking for chances to construct new regimes or to expand old ones when opportunities arise. Following are three areas where substantial progress may be possible in the future.

United Nations Peacekeeping

Peacekeeping is an old subject, to which few scholars or policymakers have paid much attention recently. Yet in the aftermath of the failure of American efforts in Lebanon, the imperfect practice of interposing forces under the banner of the U.N. or regional organizations looks ripe for reinspection. Not only have Americans been chastened by the Lebanese experience, but also there is evidence that the Soviet Union has begun to rethink its opposition to peacekeeping and to realize that both superpowers might be better off if devices could be found to limit intervention in local or regional conflicts. Any efforts at effective peacekeeping, however, would have to be limited and cautious. They must be based on the original U.N. Charter's conception of peacekeeping as a Security Council responsibility to be carried out with the consent of all great powers, rather than on the view, sponsored by the United States in the 1950s and early 1960s, that effective peacekeeping could be undertaken under authority granted by the General Assembly and could be directed even toward a great power or its ally. Limited peacekeeping is worth reconsidering, not the overly ambitious efforts reflected in Korea and the Congo.

International Debt

The regime for international debt has shown itself to be remarkably flexible during the last 3 years: Massive default has been avoided, and several of the major debtors, such as Mexico and Brazil, have taken impressive and painful adjustment measures. Yet crisis management, however clever, cannot create new and lasting arrangements that will avoid both eventual collapse and a repetition of the historical debt cycle, which moves from moderate lending to excessive lending, crisis, and collapse (or near-collapse).[3] There is a good deal to be said for acting now, before memories of the crisis fade, to construct a sustainable set of arrangements that will ensure both a steady flow of resources to developing countries from private and public sources and regular payment of debts that have been incurred.

Exchange Rates

Disillusionment with the current arrangements for floating exchange rates is widespread. Hopes that equilibrium rates would emerge automatically, yielding balanced current accounts, have been dashed by massive capital flows that have led to overvaluation of the dollar. The response has been not only discontent in Europe, led by France, but also increasing pressure for protectionism in the United States, which a recession would only accentuate. Little can be said now for calling a grand public conference such as Bretton Woods—which, it should be recalled, was preceded by many months of intense negotiations. Yet it might be feasible to devise a "deal" linking greater exchange-rate stability, a lower value of the dollar, and the institution of the new round of trade talks desired by the United States. It would be wiser to explore this possibility than to engage in discriminatory action against France—and therefore against the European Community in general—in retaliation for its refusal at the Bonn summit in 1985 to set a date for new trade negotiations. The moment for concerted action on the exchange-rate regime may be arriving; thought should be devoted now to what the character of such a regime should be and to how concessions by the United States could be used strategically to attain U.S. objectives in other areas, such as trade.

Dreams of a slow, even unsteady march toward the world order envisaged by the founders of the U.N. are obsolete. But the United States cannot simply exchange these dreams for the alluring promise of a world without the frustrations of multilateral cooperation. Economic and security interdependence is a reality that cannot be wished away. The United States is not strong enough to be able safely to assume that other countries will acquiesce in its unilateral attempts to reshape the world. Global unilateralism in the 1980s could therefore be as expensive an illusion as isolationism was half a century ago.

What global unilateralism misses is the continuing American interest in international regimes. In addition to worrying about military power and Soviet intentions, the United States needs to be concerned about other dimensions of power and relations with the whole international system. To deal effectively with issues involving international regimes—such as how to deal with UNESCO, what to do about nuclear proliferation, and whether to rescue or abandon the nondiscriminatory provisions of GATT—the United States needs a coherent strategy based on a realistic understanding of the conditions for effective multilateral cooperation. Such a strategy should emphasize reciprocity—which means being tough on rule violators as well as being willing to cooperate with those who wish to cooperate. The United States must support international institutions that facilitate decentralized enforcement of rules, without naively believing that enforcement will be automatic or easy. The United States should reflect, in advance of crises, on how international institutions can help achieve cooperation, and it must be ready, in crises, to put forward proposals that have been devised in quieter times.

Such a combination of institutional strategy and tactical flexibility could be simultaneously visionary and realistic. It would be opportunistic in the best sense: ready to seize opportunities provided by crises to make regimes more consistent with America's interests and values. It is a viable alternative to recurring fantasies of global unilateralism.

Notes

Chapter 1   Interdependence in World Politics

1. Stanley Hoffmann, "Notes on the Elusiveness of Modern Power," *International Journal* 30: (Spring 1975) 184.

2. "A New National Partnership," speech by Secretary of State Henry A. Kissinger at Los Angeles, January 24, 1975. News release, Department of State, Bureau of Public Affairs, Office of Media Services, p. 1.

3. See, for example, Lester R. Brown, *World Without Borders: The Interdependence of Nations* (New York: Foreign Policy Association, Headline Series, 1972).

4. Charles Kindleberger, *American Business Abroad* (New Haven: Yale University Press, 1969), p. 207.

5. The terms are derived from Stanley Hoffmann, "Choices," *Foreign Policy* 12 (Fall 1973): 6.

6. For instance, see Robert Angell, *Peace on the March: Transnational Participation* (New York: Van Nostrand, 1969).

7. John Maynard Keynes, *The General Theory of Employment, Interest and Money* (London: Macmillan, 1957), p. 383.

8. For the classic contemporary formulation of political realism, see the works of Hans J. Morgenthau, particularly *Politics Among Nations: The Struggle for Power and Peace* (New York: Knopf, 1948 and subsequent editions). See also Morgenthau, "Another 'Great Debate': The National Interest of the United States," *American Political Science Review* 46 (December 1952): 961–88; and Morgenthau, *Scientific Man Versus Power Politics* (Chicago: University of Chicago Press, 1946). A different but equally impressive statement of a "realist" position can be found in E. H. Carr, *The Twenty Years' Crisis, 1919–1939*, 2nd ed. (London: Macmillan, 1946). Carr, however, emphasizes economic sources of power more strongly.

9. For some evidence on trends in interdependence, using a variety of measures, see Richard Rosecrance and Arthur Stein, "Interdependence: Myth or Reality," *World Politics* 26, no. 1 (October 1973), and Peter J. Katzenstein, "International Interdependence: Some Long-Term Trends and Recent Changes," *International Organization* 29, no. 4 (Fall 1975).

10. See Robert Engler, *The Politics of Oil: Private Power and Democratic Directions* (Chicago: University of Chicago Press, 1962).

11. Arnold Wolfers' "National Security as an Ambiguous Symbol" remains the classic analysis. See his collection of essays, *Discord and Collaboration* (Baltimore: Johns Hopkins University Press, 1962). Daniel Yergin's study of the emergence of the doctrine of national security (in place of the traditional concept of defense), portrays it as a "commanding idea" of the Cold War era. See Daniel Yergin, *The Shattered Peace: The Rise of the National Security State* (Boston: Houghton Mifflin, 1976).

12. Secretary of State Henry A. Kissinger, Address before the Sixth Special Session of the United Nations General Assembly, April 15, 1974, News release, Department of State, Office of Media Services, p. 2. Reprinted in *International Organization* 28, no. 3 (Summer 1974): 573–83.

13. Alex Inkeles, "The Emerging Social Structure of the World," *World Politics* 27 (July 1975): 479.

14. Hoffmann, "Notes on the Elusiveness of Modern Power," p. 183.

15. Hans J. Morgenthau, "The New Diplomacy of Movement," *Encounter* 3, no. 2 (August 1974): 56. This view — which strikes us as wrong — fits oddly with the tradition of realism!

16. See Jeffrey Hart, "Dominance in International Politics," *International Organization* 30 (Spring 1976).

17. Kenneth Waltz, "The Myth of Interdependence," in Charles Kindleberger (ed.), *The International Corporation* (Cambridge, Mass.: MIT Press, 1970).

18. See Anthony Lanyi, "Political Aspects of Exchange-Rate Systems," in Richard Merritt (ed.), *Communications in International Politics* (Urbana: University of Illinois Press, 1972), for a discussion of a game-theoretical way to deal with such issues, using payoff matrices. For a later effort along similar lines see Richard N. Cooper, "Prolegomena to the Choice of an International Monetary System," *International Organization* 29, no. 1 (Winter 1975): 63–98.

19. See Barbara Haskell, "Recent Swedish-American Relations: Some Analytical Observations," translated as "Det moraliserande Sverige," *Internationella studier* 1 (Stockholm, 1976): 30–32.

20. Susan Strange, "What Is Economic Power and Who Has It?" *International Journal* 30 (Spring 1975): 219.

21. For a review of international regimes in the economic areas, see C. Fred Bergsten and Lawrence B. Krause (eds.), *World Politics and International Economics* (Washington, D.C.; Brookings Institution, 1975), originally published as a special issue of *International Organization* 29, no. 1 (Winter 1975). For a review of international regimes in fields involving science and technology, see the special issue of *International Organization, International Responses to Technology,* edited by John Gerard Ruggie and Ernst B. Haas, 29, no. 3 (Summer 1975).

22. Kenneth N. Waltz, "Theory of International Relations," in Nelson W. Polsby and Fred I. Greenstein (eds.), *Handbook of Political Science,* vol. 8, *International Politics* (Reading, Mass.: Addison-Wesley, 1975), pp. 1–86. See also George Modelski, *World Power Concentrations: Typology, Data, Explanatory Framework* (Morristown, N.J.: General Learning Co., 1974).

Chapter 2 Realism and Complex Interdependence

1. Hans J. Morgenthau, *Politics Among Nations: The Struggle for Power and Peace*, 4th ed. (New York: Knopf, 1967), p. 36.

2. See the material referred to in footnotes 9 and 13, Chapter 1; also see Edward L. Morse, "Transnational Economic Processes," in Robert O. Keohane and Joseph S. Nye, Jr. (eds.), *Transnational Relations and World Politics* (Cambridge, Mass.: Harvard University Press, 1972).

3. Henry A. Kissinger, "A New National Partnership," *Department of State Bulletin*, February 17, 1975, p. 199.

4. See the report of the Commission on the Organization of the Government for the Conduct of Foreign Policy (Murphy Commission) (Washington, D.C.: U.S. Government Printing Office, 1975), and the studies prepared for that report. See also Raymond Hopkins, "The International Role of 'Domestic' Bureaucracy," *International Organization* 30, no. 3 (Summer 1976).

5. *New York Times*, May 22, 1975.

6. For a valuable discussion, see Klaus Knorr, *The Power of Nations: The Political Economy of International Relations* (New York: Basic Books, 1975).

7. *Business Week*, January 13, 1975.

8. Stanley Hoffmann, "The Acceptability of Military Force," and Laurence Martin, "The Utility of Military Force," in *Force in Modern Societies: Its Place in International Politics* (Adelphi Paper, International Institute for Strategic Studies, 1973). See also Knorr, *The Power of Nations*.

9. Henry Brandon, *The Retreat of American Power* (New York: Doubleday, 1974), p. 218.

10. *International Implications of the New Economic Policy*, U.S. Congress, House of Representatives, Committee on Foreign Affairs, Subcommittee on Foreign Economic Policy, Hearings, September 16, 1971.

11. For a more detailed discussion, see Robert O. Keohane and Joseph S. Nye, Jr., "Transgovernmental Relations and International Organizations," *World Politics* 27, no. 1 (October 1974): 39–62.

12. Raymond Bauer, Ithiel de Sola Pool, and Lewis Dexter, *American Business and Foreign Policy* (New York: Atherton, 1963), chap. 35, esp. pp. 472–75.

13. Branislav Gosovic and John Gerard Ruggie, "On the Creation of a New International Economic Order: Issue Linkage and the Seventh Special Session of the UN General Assembly," *International Organization* 30, no. 2 (Spring 1976): 309–46.

14. Robert W. Cox, "The Executive Head," *International Organization* 23, no. 2 (Spring 1969): 205–30.

Chapter 3 Explaining International Regime Change

1. K. W. Rothchild (ed.), *Power in Economics* (London: Penguin Modern Economics Readings, 1971), p. 7. Cited in Susan Strange, "What Is Economic Power, and Who Has It?" *International Journal* 30, no. 2 (Spring 1975): 214.

2. See Peter Bachrach and Morton Baratz, "Decisions and Nondecisions: An Analytical Framework," *American Political Science Review* 57 (1963): 632–42. Reprinted in Roderick Bell, David Edwards, and Harrison Wagner (eds.), *Political Power* (New York: Free Press, 1969).

3. For data, see Peter J. Katzenstein, "International Interdependence: Some Long-

Term Trends and Recent Changes," *International Organization* 29, no. 4 (Autumn 1975): 1021–34.

4. John W. Burton, *Systems, States, Diplomacy and Rules* (Cambridge, Eng.: Cambridge University Press, 1968), pp. 28–31.

5. Richard Cooper, "Trade Policy Is Foreign Policy," *Foreign Policy* 9 (Winter 1972–73).

6. Thucydides, *The Peloponnesian War*, Book V, chap. XVII (Melian Dialogues) (New York: Modern Library, 1951), p. 331.

7. Hans J. Morgenthau, *Politics Among Nations: The Struggle for Power and Peace*, 4th ed. (New York: Knopf, 1967), p. 5.

8. See Charles Kindleberger, *The World in Depression 1929–39* (Berkeley: University of California Press, 1974). Collective action theory also points to this conclusion. See, for a good statement, Mancur Olson, Jr., *The Logic of Collective Action* (Cambridge, Mass.: Harvard University Press, 1965).

9. Kindleberger, *The World in Depression*.

10. For the figures, see John P. McKay, *Pioneers for Profit: Foreign Entrepreneurship and Russian Industrialization, 1885–1913* (Chicago: University of Chicago Press, 1970), table 2, p. 5.

11. David P. Calleo, "American Foreign Policy and American European Studies: An Imperial Bias?" in Wolfram Hanreider (ed.), *The United States and Western Europe* (Cambridge, Mass.: Winthrop, 1974), pp. 56–78.

12. See particularly Charles Kindleberger, "The International Monetary Politics of a Near-Great Power: Two French Episodes, 1926–1936 and 1960–1970," *Economic Notes* (Siena) 1, nos. 2–3 (1972).

13. These are titles of books by Raymond Aron, Amaury de Riencourt, and Henry Brandon.

14. We are indebted to Rob Paarlberg for pointing this out to us.

15. See Robert Gilpin, *U.S. Power and the Multinationals* (New York: Basic Books, 1975). See also C. Fred Bergsten, "Coming Investment Wars?" and Joseph S. Nye, Jr., "Multinational Corporations in World Politics," in *Foreign Affairs* 53, no. 1 (October 1974).

16. See Kenneth W. Waltz, "Theory of International Relations," in Fred I. Greenstein and Nelson W. Polsby (eds.), *Handbook of Political Science*, vol. 8, *International Politics* (Reading, Mass.: Addison-Wesley, 1975).

17. This has been the case for many years. See G. Griffith Johnson, *The Treasury and Foreign Policy* (Cambridge, Mass.: Harvard University Press, 1939), pp. 206–207.

18. See Gardner Patterson, *Discrimination in International Trade: The Policy Issues* (Princeton: Princeton University Press, 1966); and Kenneth W. Dam, *The Law and Politics of the GATT* (Chicago: University of Chicago Press, 1970).

19. See Donald J. Puchala, "Domestic Politics and Regional Harmonization in the European Communities," *World Politics* 27, no. 4 (July 1975): 496–520.

Chapter 4   The Politics of Oceans and Money:
Historical Overview

1. Eyre Crowe, "Memorandum on the Present State of British Relations with France and Germany" (January 1907), reprinted in G. P. Gooch and Harold Termperly (eds.),

British Documents on the Origins of the War, 1898–1914 (London: His Majesty's Stationery Office, 1928), p. 403.

2. Richard N. Cooper, "Prolegomena to the Choice of an International Monetary System," *International Organization* 29, no. 1 (Winter 1975): 66.

3. For a close and detailed analysis of foreign exchange market developments, which illustrates very well the tight linkages among events in the international monetary system, see issues of *World Financial Markets,* published by the Morgan Guaranty Trust Company of New York.

4. Committee on Currency and Foreign Exchanges After the War, *First Interim Report* (Cd. 9182) (London: HMSO, 1918), pp. 3–4, quoted in Leland B. Yeager, *International Monetary Relations,* 2nd ed. (New York: Harper & Row, 1976), p. 304.

5. Arthur I. Bloomfield, *Monetary Policy Under the International Gold Standard* (New York: Federal Reserve Bank of New York, 1959), p. 60.

6. Committee on Finance and Industry, *Report* (The Macmillan Report) (London: HMSO, 1931), p. 125, quoted in Yeager, *International Monetary Relations,* p. 304.

7. See especially Peter H. Lindert, *Key Currencies and Gold, 1900–1913,* Princeton Studies in International Finance no. 24 (Princeton: Princeton University International Finance Section, 1969). This sentence paraphrases his conclusion, summarized on p. 78. For earlier statements, see Alec G. Ford, *The Gold Standard, 1880–1914: Britain and Argentina* (Oxford: Clarendon Press, 1962); and Arthur I. Bloomfield, *Short-term Capital Movements Under the Pre-1914 Gold Standard* (Princeton: Princeton University Press, 1963). For a recent work emphasizing the importance of British rule in India for the prewar international financial system, see Marcello de Cecco, *Money and Empire: The International Gold Standard 1890–1914* (Totowa, N.J.: Rowan and Littlefield, 1975).

8. Lindert, *Key Currencies,* p. 78.

9. Ibid., table 1, pp. 10–11.

10. Ford, *The Gold Standard,* p. 25.

11. Lindert, *Key Currencies,* pp. 14–15, 21–27.

12. Calculated from Lindert, *Key Currencies,* table 2, pp. 18–19.

13. Arthur I. Bloomfield, *Monetary Policy.* See especially his "concluding remarks," pp. 60–62. Lindert quotes Chancellor of the Exchequer Callahan's comment in 1965: "There were no balance-of-payments problems fifty years ago because there were no balance-of-payments statistics." Lindert, *Key Currencies,* p. 36.

14. Ford points out that large landowners, who were the dominant political group in Argentina, manipulated the system to impart a bias toward devaluation of the peso, benefiting them (since they were paid in gold-fixed prices). *The Gold Standard,* p. 91.

15. See Yeager, *International Monetary Relations,* pp. 296–97. Also see Bloomfield, *Monetary Policy;* and Lindert, *Key Currencies.*

16. Bloomfield, *Short-term Capital Movements,* p. 91.

17. William A. Brown, *The International Gold Standard Reinterpreted,* 2 vols. (New York: National Bureau of Economic Resources, 1950). On page 781, he stresses this feature of the post-1919 system.

18. Yeager, *International Monetary Relations,* p. 311.

19. Ibid., p. 319.

20. Ibid., pp. 324–29. See also Stephen V. O. Clarke, *The Reconstruction of the International Monetary System: The Attempts of 1922 and 1933,* Princeton Studies

in International Finance no. 23 (Princeton: Princeton University International Finance Section, 1973).

21. "In the fall of 1923, the rate was stabilized at 1 trillion marks = 23.8 cents." Clarke, *Reconstruction*, p. 5.

22. Yeager takes a different view, blaming governmental ineptitude for the fall in the franc and interpreting the British experience as evidence for stabilizing speculation in the pound. See *International Monetary Relations*, pp. 321, 328.

23. Ibid., pp. 328–29.

24. Clarke, *Reconstruction*, pp. 13–14.

25. See Lindert, *Key Currencies*.

26. Clarke, *Reconstruction*, p. 14.

27. Ibid., pp. 17–18.

28. W. A. Brown categorized the period from 1919 to 1925 as one of restoration, and 1925–31 as one of experimentation. Yeager speaks of the "postwar system" after 1925. Clarke refers to "the achievement of European monetary stability that followed sterling's return to gold in the spring of 1925." See Brown, *International Gold Standard*, p. 180; Yeager, *International Monetary Relations*, p. 330; Clarke, *Reconstruction*, p. 18.

29. D. E. Moggridge, *The Return to Gold, 1925* (Cambridge, Eng.: Cambridge University Press, 1969), p. 88.

30. Ibid., p. 80.

31. Ibid., p. 87.

32. As we shall see in the next chapter, the coherence of United States policy at this time was not high. The United States Treasury was reluctant to be too active in European monetary affairs, and much of the burden, and the influence, fell to the head of the Federal Reserve Bank of New York, Benjamin Strong, and his successor, George Harrison. For a discussion of international pressures on the British, see Charles Kindleberger, *The World in Depression, 1929–1939* (Berkeley: University of California Press, 1973), p. 47.

33. Clarke, *Reconstruction*, p. 24.

34. Kindleberger, *World in Depression*, pp. 202–207; Herbert Feis, *1933: Characters in Crisis* (Boston: Little, Brown, 1966), p. 126.

35. Kindleberger, *World in Depression*, quoting Roosevelt's statement, p. 219.

36. Kindleberger, *World in Depression*, pp. 247–57; Yeager, *International Monetary Relations*, pp. 335–36.

37. Kindleberger, *World in Depression*, p. 259.

38. See Yeager's discussion, *International Monetary Relations*, pp. 335–56. He argues convincingly, against Nurkse, that the failure of the 1930s does not provide strong enough evidence of the alleged impractibility of floating rates.

39. Ibid., p. 377.

40. Alfred E. Eckes, Jr., *A Search for Solvency: Bretton Woods and the International Monetary System, 1941–1971* (Austin: University of Texas Press, 1975), p. 228.

41. The figures for countries at Genoa are found in Dean E. Traynor, *International Monetary and Financial Conferences in the Interwar Period* (Washington, D.C.: Catholic University of America Press, 1949), p. 73. Feis, *1933*, gives the figure for London (p. 245). For the Bretton Woods meeting and preliminary discussion, see J. Keith Horsefield, *The International Monetary Fund, 1945–1965* (Washington, D.C.: IMF, 1969), pp. 3–120.

42. Eckes, *Search for Solvency,* p. 110.

43. Ibid., pp. 60–63.

44. For an extensive and detailed discussion of voting arrangements in the IMF, see Joseph Gold, *Voting and Decisions in the International Monetary Fund, 1945–1965* (Washington, D.C.: IMF, 1972).

45. Horsefield, *IMF 1945–1965,* p. 108.

46. Eckes, *Search for Solvency,* p. 212.

47. For an excellent account, see Richard N. Gardner, *Sterling-Dollar Diplomacy: The Origins and the Prospects of Our International Economic Order* (Oxford: Clarendon Press, 1956; revised ed., New York: McGraw-Hill, 1969). For another point of view, see Joyce Kolko and Gabriel Kolko, *The Limits of Power: The World and the United States Foreign Policy, 1945–1954* (New York: Harper and Row, 1972), esp. chap. 3 (pp. 59–90).

48. For the definitive account, see Horsefield, *IMF 1945–1965,* chap. 18 (pp. 474–94).

49. Fred Hirsch, *Money International* (London: Penguin Press, 1967), p. 241.

50. Ibid., p. 202.

51. Ibid., p. 262.

52. See Robert W. Russell, "Transgovernmental Interaction in the International Monetary System, 1960–1972," *International Organization* 27, no. 4 (Autumn 1973): 431–64.

53. Eckes, *Search for Solvency,* p. 255.

54. Lawrence Krause, "Private International Finance," in Robert O. Keohane and Joseph S. Nye, Jr. (eds.), *Transnational Relations and World Politics* (Cambridge, Mass.: Harvard University Press, 1972), p. 184.

55. Richard N. Cooper, "Economic Interdependence and Foreign Policy in the Seventies," *World Politics* 24, no. 2 (January 1972): 166–67.

56. Eckes, *Search for Solvency,* p. 257.

57. Marina V. N. Whitman, "The Current and Future Role of the Dollar: How Much Symmetry?" *Brookings Papers on Economic Activity* 3 (1974): 539.

58. Susan Strange indicates that in April 1971, foreign official holdings of dollars were $18.5 billion, compared to the official value of the United States gold stock of about $10 billion. See "The Dollar Crisis," *International Affairs* 48, no. 2 (April 1972).

59. For a chronology of major events, see *IMF Survey,* March 1, 1976.

60. Jonathan Aronson's Ph.D. dissertation at Stanford University explores the roles of banks in the international monetary system. For a review of some changes in bank and government positions during the 1970s, see Jonathan Aronson, "Multiple Actors in the Transformation of the International Monetary System," paper presented to the International Studies Association Annual Meetings, February 1976.

61. *The Economist* (London), August 5, 1972, p. 61.

62. Marina V. N. Whitman, "The Payments Adjustment Process and the Exchange Rate Regime: What Have We Learned?" *American Economic Review,* May 1975, p. 144.

63. Ibid., p. 138.

64. See the *New York Times,* June 14, 1974; *The Economist,* June 8, 1974 and November 22, 1975; and the *IMF Survey,* January 19, 1976, for accounts of these events.

65. *New York Times,* January 9, 1976.

66. *New York Times*, January 10, 1976.

67. *IMF Survey*, January 19, 1976.

68. See the *New York Times*, January 9, 1976; and *The Economist*, January 10, 1976.

69. For a recent critical comment indicating doubt about the continued usefulness of the IMF, see *The Economist*, January 17, 1976, p. 81. Another author has recently pointed out that the IMF's resources in 1977 are likely to amount to only about 4 percent of world trade, in contrast to 15 percent in 1948. Thus "a member's access to the Fund's resources, which is limited by its quota, nowadays often amounts only to an insignificant part of the deficit with which the member is faced." See Tom de Vries, "Jamaica, or the Non-Reform of the International Monetary System," *Foreign Affairs* 54, no. 3 (April 1976): 599.

70. "Scramble for the Sea," *The Economist*, March 3, 1976.

71. See Evan Luard, "Who Gets What on the Seabed?" *Foreign Policy* 9 (Winter 1972–73).

72. Edward Wenk, Jr., *The Politics of the Oceans* (Seattle: University of Washington Press, 1972), p. 250.

73. Edward N. Luttwak, *The Political Uses of Sea Power* (Baltimore: Johns Hopkins University Press, 1974), p. 8.

74. Representative Bob Wilson, *Congressional Record*, February 9, 1972.

75. Quoted in Lawrence Juda, *Ocean Space Rights* (New York: Praeger, 1975), p. 99.

76. National Academy of Sciences, *International Marine Science Affairs* (Washington, D.C.: National Academy of Sciences, 1972), p. 82.

77. Louis Henkin, "Changing Law for the Changing Seas," in Edmund Gullion (ed.), *The Uses of the Seas* (Englewood Cliffs, N.J.: Prentice-Hall, 1968), p. 75.

78. Max Sorensen, "Law of the Sea," *International Conciliation* 520 (November 1958): 198, 201.

79. Sayre Swarztrauber, *The Three Mile Limit of Territorial Seas* (Annapolis, Md.: Naval Institute Press, 1972), p. 108.

80. Pitman B. Potter, *The Freedom of the Seas in History, Law and Politics* (New York: Longmans, Green, 1924), p. 249.

81. Swarztrauber, *Three Mile Limit*, p. 111.

82. See Edward M. House, *The Freedom of the Seas* (London: National Council for the Prevention of War, n.d.); and Labour Party, *Freedom of the Seas: Old and New* (London, n.d.).

83. Swarztrauber, *Three Mile Limit*, p. 71.

84. Roland G. Usher, quoted in Benjamin Russell, *Anglo-American Relations* (Boston: World Peace Foundation, 1919), p. 43.

85. Calculated from figures in World Peace Foundation, "The Staggering Burden of Armaments," *A League of Nations* 4 (April 1921): 242.

86. The British government was internally divided on whether to accede to the American demands. *The Times* (London), July 7, 1923.

87. See William E. Butler, *The Law of Soviet Territorial Waters* (New York: Praeger, 1967). This exception was a continuation of a Tsarist policy.

88. Swarztrauber, *Three Mile Limit*, p. 148.

89. C. John Colombos, *The International Law of the Sea* (New York: McKay, 1967), p. 103.

90. See Bobbie Smetherman and Robert Smetherman, *Territorial Seas and Inter-American Relations* (New York: Praeger, 1974).

91. World Peace Foundation, "Staggering Burden of Armaments," p. 244.

92. Sorensen, "Law of the Sea," p. 201.

93. E. D. Brown, "The 1973 Conference on the Law of the Sea: The Consequences of Failure to Agree," in Lewis Alexander (ed.), *The Law of the Sea: A New Geneva Conference* (Kingston, R.I.: Law of the Sea Institute, 1972).

94. Quoted in Elizabeth Young and Brian Johnson, *The Law of the Sea* (London: Fabian Society, 1973), p. 3.

95. Edward L. Miles, "The Dynamics of Global Ocean Politics," in Douglas Johnston (ed.), *Marine Policy and the Coastal Community* (London: Croom Helm, forthcoming).

96. J. E. S. Fawcett, "The Law of the Sea: Issues at Caracas," *The World Today* 30 (June 1974), p. 239.

97. José Ayala quoted in the *New York Times,* January 30, 1976.

Chapter 5   Complex Interdependence in Oceans and Money

1. Edward Luttwak, *The Political Uses of Seapower* (Baltimore: Johns Hopkins University Press, 1974), p. 38.

2. See Michael McGwire, K. Booth, and J. McDonnell (eds.), *Soviet Naval Policy: Objectives and Constraints* (New York: Praeger, 1975).

3. James Cable, *Gunboat Diplomacy: Political Applications of Limited Naval Force* (New York: Praeger, 1971).

4. *Foreign Relations of the United States, 1935,* vol. 1 (Washington, D.C.: U.S. Government Printing Office, 1953), p. 918; *Foreign Relations of the United States, 1936,* vol. 5 (Washington, D.C.: U.S. Government Printing Office, 1954).

5. Robert Osgood, "U.S. Security Interests in Ocean Law," *Ocean Development and International Law* 2 (Spring 1974): 29.

6. Cable, *Gunboat Diplomacy,* p. 226.

7. Jeffrey Hart, "The Anglo-Icelandic Cod War of 1972–73," unpublished manuscript, 1976.

8. McGwire, Booth, McDonnell, *Soviet Naval Policy,* p. 528.

9. Ibid., p. 529.

10. Cable, *Gunboat Diplomacy,* pp. 175ff.

11. Jacob Viner, "International Finance and Balance of Power Diplomacy," in Jacob Viner, *International Economics* (Glencoe, Ill.: Free Press, 1951), p. 85.

12. For the definitive study, see Albert O. Hirschman, *National Power and the Structure of Foreign Trade* (Berkeley: University of California Press, reissued, 1969).

13. See Richard N. Gardner, *Sterling-Dollar Diplomacy: The Origins and Prospects of Our International Economic Order* (Oxford: Clarendon Press, 1956; revised ed., New York: McGraw-Hill, 1969).

14. Hugh Thomas, *Suez* (New York: Harper and Row, 1966), p. 145.

15. Susan Strange, *Sterling and British Policy: A Political Study of an International Currency in Decline* (Oxford: Oxford University Press, 1971), p. 97.

16. Stephen Cohen, *International Monetary Reform, 1964–69: The Political Dimension* (New York: Praeger, 1970).

17. Andrew Boyle, *Montagu Norman* (London: Cassell, 1967), p. 229. See also Stephen V. O. Clarke, *Central Bank Cooperation, 1924–31* (New York: Federal Reserve Bank of New York, 1967), p. 119.

18. Herbert Feis, *1933: Characters in Crisis* (Boston: Little, Brown, 1966), p. 213. Of course, as we saw in chapter 4, the monetary uncertainties of the time were *not* cleared up by the conference.

19. See Ann Hollick, "Seabeds Make Strange Politics," *Foreign Policy* 9 (Winter 1972/73); and H. Gary Knight, "Special Domestic Interests and United States Oceans Policy," in Robert G. Wirsing (ed.), *International Relations and the Future of Oceans Space* (Columbia: University of South Carolina Press, 1974).

20. This process is well described by Ann Hollick, "United States Ocean Policy: 1948–1971," Ph.D. dissertation, Johns Hopkins University, 1971.

21. *Annual Report of the Secretary of the Treasury on the State of Finances, 1972* (Washington, D.C.: U.S. Government Printing Office, 1972).

22. Feis, *1933*, p. 294.

23. J. David Singer and Michael Wallace, "Intergovernmental Organization in the Global System, 1815–1965: A Quantitative Description," *International Organization* 24 (Spring 1970): 239–87.

24. For a discussion see Fred Hirsch, *Money International* (London: Penguin Press, 1967), sec. 4, pp. 219–82.

25. The term has been used by Robert W. Russell, and has also appeared in journalistic discussions of international monetary affairs.

26. Based on interviews.

27. See Edward L. Miles, "Transnationalism in Space: Inner and Outer," in Robert Keohane and Joseph S. Nye, Jr. (eds.), *Transnational Relations and World Politics* (Cambridge, Mass.: Harvard University Press, 1972); and Warren Wooster, "Interaction Between Intergovernmental and Scientific Organizations in Marine Affairs," *International Organization* 27 (Winter 1973): 252–75.

28. J. B. Condliffe, *The Commerce of Nations* (New York: Norton, 1950), p. 447.

29. Clarke, *Central Bank Cooperation*, p. 47.

30. Alice C. Barrass, "Afloat on a Sea of Controls," *The Banker* 123 (June 1973): 613–20.

31. See Robert W. Russell, "The Organization of the International Monetary System: Contributions of Transnational Elite Networks to Rules and Reforms," paper prepared for delivery at the 1973 annual meeting of the American Political Science Association, New Orleans, Louisiana, September 1973.

32. Assistant Secretary of the Navy Robert Frosch quoted in Lawrence Juda, *Ocean Space Rights* (New York: Praeger, 1975), p. 99.

33. "Export Drive," *New York Times*, June 7, 1971. "Typical is Secretary Connally's recent suggestion that the United States should pull the Sixth Fleet out of the Mediterranean to retaliate against Common Market preferential trading arrangements there."

34. Based on interviews.

35. Osgood, "U.S. Security Interests," p. 14.

36. Based on interviews.

37. *The Times* (London), July 7, 1923; *Morning Post* (London), November 3, 1923.

38. Ann L. Hollick, "National Ocean Institutions," *Ocean Development and International Law* 3, no. 2 (1975): 163.

39. See Clarke, *Central Bank Cooperation;* Boyle, *Montagu Norman;* and Lester V. Chandler, *Benjamin Strong, Central Banker* (Washington, D.C.: Brookings Institution, 1958).

40. Clarke, *Central Bank Cooperation*, p. 88.

41. Boyle, *Montagu Norman*, p. 247.

42. Ibid., p. 304. One may not want to give complete credence to Schact's retrospective account, but the story is too good to omit, even if one takes it with a grain of salt.

43. G. Griffith Johnson, Jr., *The Treasury and Monetary Policy, 1933–1938* (Cambridge, Mass.: Harvard University Press, 1939).

44. See for instance, Sir Roy Harrod, *The Life of John Maynard Keynes* (New York: Harcourt Brace, 1951); and J. Keith Horsefield, *The International Monetary Fund* (Washington, D.C.: IMF, 1969).

45. Robert W. Russell, "Transgovernmental Interaction in the International Monetary System, 1960–1972," *International Organization* 27, no. 4 (Autumn 1973): 431–64. See also Hirsch, *Money International,* particularly chap. 11, "Central Bankers International." The personal friendship between Giscard d'Estaing and Helmut Schmidt, developed while they were finance ministers of France and the Federal Republic of Germany, respectively, is well known.

46. Russell, "Transgovernmental Interaction," p. 463.

47. *To Provide for a Modification of the Par Value of the Dollar,* U.S. Congress, House Committee on Banking and Currency, Hearings, 92nd Cong., 2nd sess., on H.R. 13120, March 1, 2, 3, and 6, 1972, pp. 11, 19–20.

48. Anthony Barber at the IMF, *Annual Meeting of the Board of Governors* (Washington, D.C.: IMF, 1971), p. 27, quoted in John Odell, "The United States in the International Monetary System," Ph.D. dissertation, University of Wisconsin, 1976.

49. Richard N. Cooper, "Prolegomena to the Choice of an International Monetary System," *International Organization* 29, no. 1 (Winter 1975): 89.

50. For elaboration of the conditions in more systematic fashion, see Robert O. Keohane and Joseph S. Nye, Jr., "Transgovernmental Relations and International Organizations," *World Politics* 27, no. 1 (October 1974): 39–62.

51. Bobbie Smetherman and Robert Smetherman, *Territorial Seas and Inter-American Relations* (New York: Praeger, 1974), p. 49.

52. *New York Times,* January 16, 1976.

53. For an early but explicit comparison of the two areas, see Johnson, *The Treasury and Monetary Policy,* pp. 206–07. See also E. E. Schattschneider, *Politics, Pressure, and the Tariff* (New York: Prentice-Hall, 1935); and Raymond A. Bauer, Ithiel de Sola Pool, and Lewis Anthony Dexter, *American Business and Public Policy: The Politics of Foreign Trade* (Chicago: Aldine-Atherton, 1963). When one analyzes patterns of attention to trade issues over time in such sources as the *New York Times,* one finds that periods of high attention coincide with attempts, stimulated either by domestic interest groups or the executive branch, to adopt new trade legislation; the pattern of attention is therefore very uneven, depending on whether the issue is before the Congress. In monetary affairs, by contrast, attention tends to build up as international crises develop.

54. "Formulation of United States Policy on the Resources of the Continental Shelf and on Coastal Fisheries," *Foreign Relations of the United States,* vol. 2 (Washington, D.C.: U.S. Government Printing Office, 1945), pp. 1481–1520.

55. Edward Wenk, Jr., *The Politics of the Oceans* (Seattle: University of Washington Press, 1972), p. 284.

56. See for example, the annual reports of 1940 (pp. 119–28); 1955 (pp. 49–52); and 1972 (pp. 58–59).

57. Gardner, *Sterling-Dollar Diplomacy* (1956), p. 204.

58. Richard N. Cooper, "Trade Policy Is Foreign Policy," *Foreign Policy* 9 (Winter 1972/73): 18–36.

59. Henry A. Kissinger, speech, April 23, 1973.

60. Based on interviews.

61. Sayre A. Swarztrauber, *The Three Mile Limit of Territorial Seas* (Annapolis, Md.: Naval Institute Press, 1972), p. 132.

62. J. Galtung, "A Structural Theory of Imperialism," *Journal of Peace Research* no. 2 (1971): 81–118.

63. See John Gerard Ruggie and Branislavs Gosovic, "On the Creation of a New International Economic Order: Issue Linkage and the Seventh Special Session of the UN General Assembly," *International Organization* 30, no. 2 (Spring 1976): 309–46.

64. See Joseph Gold, *Voting and Decisions in the International Monetary Fund* (Washington, D.C.: IMF, 1972).

Chapter 6   The Politics of Rule-Making in Money and Oceans

1. For an excellent discussion, see Charles P. Kindleberger, *The World in Depression, 1929–1939* (Berkeley: University of California Press, 1973).

2. Robert Friedheim and Mary John, "The Soviet Position at the Third U.N. Law of the Sea Conference," in Michael MacGwire, K. Booth, and J. McDonnell (eds.), *Soviet Naval Policy: Objectives and Constraints* (New York: Praeger, 1975), p. 343.

3. William E. Butler, *The Law of Soviet Territorial Waters* (New York: Praeger, 1967).

4. *New York Times,* October 7, 1954; *Christian Science Monitor,* November 30, 1954.

5. *New York Times,* March 15, 1956; *Christian Science Monitor,* April 2, 1956.

6. *New York Times,* July 29, 1956. David C. Loring, "The Fisheries Dispute," in Daniel Sharp (ed.), *U.S. Foreign Policy and Peru* (Austin: University of Texas Press, 1972), p. 73, argues that it was private negotiations between the American Tunaboat Association and Peru that kept the peace until the early 1960s when seining technology made bait unnecessary for tuna fishermen, and they stopped purchasing coastal licenses.

7. T. Orchard Lisle, "Offshore Rights: Freedom of the Seas," *The Oil Forum,* August 1955, p. 288.

8. Richard N. Gardner, *Sterling-Dollar Diplomacy: The Origins and the Prospects of Our International Economic Order* (Oxford: Clarendon Press, 1956), pp. 299–305; 319–325. Joyce Kolko and Gabriel Kolko attempt to argue, in our view with only limited success, that the fundamental motivation for American policy was economic. What they do show is that farsighted American capitalists would have had good reasons to espouse such a policy, and that some of them thought in these terms. See *The Limits*

of Power: The World and the United States Foreign Policy, 1945–1954 (New York: Harper and Row, 1972), esp. chap. 3.

9. Leland B. Yeager, *International Monetary Relations*, 2nd ed. (New York: Harper and Row, 1976), p. 413.

10. U.S. Department of the Treasury *Annual Report, 1950* (Washington, D.C.: U.S. Government Printing Office, 1950), pp. 49–50; and *Annual Report, 1955* (Washington, D.C.: U.S. Government Printing Office, 1955), pp. 49–50.

11. Henry Aubrey, "Behind the Veil of International Money," *Princeton Essays in International Finance* no. 71 (January 1969): 9.

12. For two sets of estimates in the same range, see Ray S. Cline, *World Power Assessment* (Washington: Georgetown University, 1975), p. 145; and Kenneth N. Waltz, "America's European Policy Viewed in Global Perspective," in Wolfram Hanreider (ed.), *The United States and Western Europe* (Cambridge, Mass.: Winthrop Publishers, 1974), p. 13.

13. *IMF Survey*, January 19, 1976.

14. U.S. Congress, Senate, Committee on Finance, *Implications of Multinational Firms for World Trade and Investment and for U.S. Trade and Labor*, Report to the Committee on Finance by the U.S. Tariff Commission, 93rd Cong., 1st sess. (Washington, D.C.: U.S. Government Printing Office, 1973), p. 539.

15. Richard N. Cooper, "The 'System' in Disarray," *Saturday Review/World*, January 26, 1974; reprinted in Cooper's testimony to the Joint Economic Committee in U.S., Congress, Joint Economic Committee, Hearings on *The 1974 Economic Report of the President*, 93rd Cong., 2nd sess., part 2, February 22, 1974, p. 621.

16. Sayre Swarztrauber, *The Three Mile Limit of Territorial Seas* (Annapolis, Md.: Naval Institute Press, 1972), p. 108.

17. Pitman B. Potter, *The Freedom of the Seas in History, Law and Politics* (New York: Longmans, Green, 1924), pp. 184, 193.

18. Swarztrauber, *The Three Mile Limit of Territorial Seas*, p. 171; also, Wilhelm Hadeler, "The Ships of the Soviet Navy," in M. G. Saunders (ed.), *The Soviet Navy* (New York: Praeger, 1958), pp. 140–42.

19. Norman Polmar, *Soviet Naval Power* (New York: National Strategy Information Center, 1972), p. 92.

20. Admiral Zumwalt quoted in the *New York Times*, July 3, 1974; Senator Stennis in the *New York Times*, September 20, 1974. Stennis argued further that the Soviet navy had two severe limitations — lack of aircraft carriers and of an amphibious force — and had no significant capability for operation outside the Mediterranean. The Soviet Union has more submarines than the United States.

21. Swarztrauber, *The Three Mile Limit of Territorial Seas*, p. 172. The only areas in which the United States was not superior was in total number of submarines and patrol craft.

22. Edward L. Miles in Douglas Johnston (ed.), *Marine Policy and Coastal Community* (London: Groom Helm, forthcoming).

23. Joseph S. Nye, Jr., "UNCTAD: Populist Pressure Group," in Robert Cox and Harold Jacobson (eds.), *The Anatomy of Influence* (New Haven: Yale University Press, 1973), p. 361. The measure of association is Kendall's tau beta correlation coefficient which varies from -1.0 to $+1.0$.

24. Edward L. Miles, "The Structure and Effects of the Decision Process in the Seabed Committee and the Law of the Sea Conference," unpublished manuscript.

25. Based on interviews.

26. Potter, *The Freedom of the Seas*, p. 230.

27. Fred Hirsch, *Money International* (London: Penguin Press, 1967), pp. 262–63. See also Robert W. Russell, "Transgovernmental Interaction in the International Monetary System, 1960–1972," *International Organization* 27, no. 4 (Autumn 1973): table 1, p. 436.

28. *The Economist* (London), November 15 and 22, 1975.

29. *IMF Survey*, January 5 and 19, 1976.

30. Quotas are calculated from the proposed quotas listed in the *IMF Survey*, January 19, 1976.

31. Richard N. Cooper, "Prolegomena to the Choice of an International Monetary System," *International Organization* 29, no. 1 (Winter 1975): 69.

32. Interim Committee Communique, in *IMF Survey*, January 19, 1976, p. 19.

33. Kindleberger, *World in Depression*, pp. 302–303.

34. "Formulation of United States Policy on the Resources of the Continental Shelf and on Coastal Fisheries," *Foreign Relations of the United States*, vol. 2 (Washington, D.C.: U.S. Government Printing Office, 1945), pp. 1481–1530.

35. For a discussion along these lines, see Fred Hirsch, "The Politics of World Money," *The Economist*, August 5, 1972, p. 62.

36. Ann Hollick, "United States Ocean Policy: 1948–1971," Ph.D. dissertation, Johns Hopkins University, 1971.

37. Charles Kindleberger quoting Keynes, Conference at Harvard's Center for International Affairs, December 1975.

Chapter 7   United States Relations with Canada and Australia

1. See Harry Eckstein, "Case Study and Theory in Political Science," in Fred I. Greenstein and Nelson W. Polsby (eds.), *The Handbook of Political Science*, vol. 7 (Reading, Mass.: Addison-Wesley, 1975), pp. 78–138.

2. See Henry S. Albinski, *Canadian and Australian Politics in Comparative Perspective* (New York: Oxford University Press, 1973), for a good general discussion.

3. Brian Beedham, "Second to None: A Survey of Australia," *The Economist* (London), March 27, 1976, p. 42.

4. For an introduction to the relationship, see Gerald M. Craig, *The United States and Canada* (Cambridge, Mass.: Harvard University Press, 1968); the special issue of *International Organization* 28 (Autumn 1974); and Donald M. Page, *A Bibliography of Works on Canadian Foreign Relations, 1945–1970* (Toronto: Canadian Institute of International Affairs, 1973).

5. Canada's Defense Scheme #1 against the U.S. was formally cancelled in 1931, but the political sense of security community predated the demise of the military contingency plan. James Eayrs, *In Defence of Canada*, vol. 1 (Toronto: University of Toronto Press, 1964), p. 77.

6. See R. D. Cuff and J. L. Granatstein, *Canadian-American Relations in Wartime* (Toronto: Hakkert, 1975).

7. M. C. Urquhart (ed.), *Historical Statistics of Canada* (Toronto: Macmillan, 1965); Statistics Canada, *Canada Year Book* (Ottawa: Information Canada, various years); Statistics Canada, *Canada's International Investment Position, 1926–67* (Ottawa: In-

formation Canada, 1971); *United Nations Statistical Yearbook* (New York: United Nations, 1961, 1971).

8. "Canada and the United States: Principles for Partnership" (Merchant-Heeney Report), *Department of State Bulletin* 53 (July–September 1965), pp. 193–208.

9. The total is 18,000, but among the 11,500 visits involving National Defence are a number of visits for military training. Department of External Affairs, "Canadian Governmental Instruments for Conducting Relations with the United States," Appendix B (Ottawa, 1969).

10. C. Robert Dickerman, "Transgovernmental Challenge and Response in Scandanavia and North America," *International Organization* 30, no. 2 (Spring 1976): 213–40.

11. Dickerman, "Transgovernmental Challenge," pp. 232–33.

12. "Canada and the United States." Even critics acknowledged the existence of the regime. See Steven Clarkson (ed.), *An Independent Foreign Policy for Canada?* (Toronto: McClelland and Stewart, 1968).

13. Interview, Ottawa, 1973.

14. Dickerman, "Transgovernmental Challenge."

15. Raymond A. Esthus, *From Enmity to Alliance: U.S.-Australian Relations, 1931–1941* (Seattle: University of Washington Press, 1964), p. 13.

16. *Foreign Relations of the United States, 1944*, vol. 3 (Washington, D.C.: U.S. Government Printing Office, 1944), pp. 168–201, esp. 191–94.

17. For a discussion of the Australian figures, see Donald T. Brash, *American Investment in Australian Industry* (Cambridge, Mass.: Harvard University Press, 1966), pp. 28–33.

18. International Monetary Fund/International Bank for Reconstruction and Development, *Direction of Trade, 1970–74* (Washington, D.C.: IMF/IBRD, n.d.). In 1974, 9.3 percent of Australia's exports and 63.7 percent of Canada's went to the United States; 20.8 percent of Australia's imports and 65.1 percent of Canada's came from the United States.

19. Major memoir and secondary sources used in this study were as follows:

Memoirs:

Eisenhower, Dwight D. *The White House Years: Mandate for Change 1953–1956.* Garden City, N.Y.: Doubleday, 1963.

———. *The White House Years: Waging Peace 1956–1961.* Garden City, N.Y., Doubleday, 1965.

Menzies, Robert. *Afternoon Light.* New York: Coward-McCann, 1967.

———. *The Measure of the Years.* London: Cassell, 1970.

Miller, T. B., ed. *Australian Foreign Minister: The Diaries of R. G. Casey 1951–60.* London: Collins, 1972.

Spender, Percy. *Exercises in Diplomacy: The ANZUS Treaty and the Colombo Plan.* New York: New York University Press, 1969.

Biographies:

Crisp, L. F. *Ben Chifley.* London: Longmans, Green, 1960.

Dalziel, Allan. *Evatt the Enigma.* Melbourne: Lansdowne Press, 1967.

Perkins, Kevin. *Menzies: Last of the Queen's Men.* Adelaide: Rigby, 1968.

Tennant, Kylie. *Evatt: Politics and Justice.* Sydney: Angus and Robertson, 1970.

General Works on Australian Foreign Policy or U.S.-Australian Relations:

Esthus, Raymond A. *From Enmity to Alliance: U.S.-Australian Relations, 1931–1941.* Seattle: University of Washington Press, 1964.

Grattan, C. Hartley. *The United States and the Southwest Pacific.* Cambridge, Mass.: Harvard University Press, 1961.

Greenwood, Gordon, and Harper, Norman, eds. *Australia in World Affairs,* vols. 1–3. Vancouver: University of British Columbia, 1957, 1963, 1968.

Harper, Norman, ed. *Pacific Orbit: Australian-American Relations Since 1942.* Melbourne: F. W. Cheshire, for the Australian-American Association, 1968.

Miller, T. B. *Australia's Foreign Policy.* Sydney: Angus and Robertson, 1968.

Moore, John H., ed. *The American Alliance: Australia, New Zealand and the United States 1940–1970.* North Melbourne: Cassell Australia, 1970.

Reese, Trevor. *Australia, New Zealand and the United States: A Survey of International Relations 1941–1968.* London: Oxford University Press, 1969.

Watt, Alan. *The Evolution of Australian Foreign Policy.* Cambridge, Eng.: Cambridge University Press, 1967.

Works Primarily on U.S. and Australian Economic Policy:

Australian Department of the Treasury. *Overseas Investment in Australia.* Canberra: Australian Government Publishing Service, 1972.

Brash, Donald. *American Investment in Australian Industry.* Cambridge, Mass.: Harvard University Press, 1966.

Crawford, J. G. *Australian Trade Policy 1942–1966; A Documentary History.* Canberra: Australian National University Press, 1968.

Evans, John. *The Kennedy Round in American Trade Policy: The Twilight of the GATT?* Cambridge, Mass.: Harvard University Press, 1971.

McColl, G. D. *The Australian Balance of Payments: A Study of Post-War Developments.* Carlton, Victoria: Melbourne University Press, 1965.

Malmgren, Harold, ed. *Pacific Basin Development: The American Interests.* Lexington, Mass.: D. C. Heath, 1972.

Moffatt, G. G. *Import Control and Industrialization.* Carlton, Victoria: Melbourne University Press, 1970.

Patterson, Gardner. *Discrimination in International Trade: The Policy Issues 1945–1965.* Princeton: Princeton University Press, 1966.

Perkins, J. O. N. *Australia in the World Economy,* 2nd ed. Melbourne: Sun Books, 1971.

Preeg, Ernest. *Traders and Diplomats.* Washington: The Brookings Institution, 1970.

Major official sources used in this study were as follows:

Current Notes on International Affairs (1945–70). Published monthly by the Australian Department for External Affairs.

Department of State Bulletin (1945–70). Published weekly by the U.S. Department of State.

Public Presidential Papers (1945–70). Published annually by the U.S. Government Printing Office.

Foreign Relations of the United States (1920–47). Published annually by the U.S. Government Printing Office.

References to Australia in the *New York Times* were systematically checked for the years 1950–70. Also consulted were *The Australian* magazine (March 1965 to February 1966) and *The Australian Journal of Politics and History* (1955–69). Various Australian periodicals and newspapers were consulted as well.

20. For informed and accessible surveys of Australian politics and culture since the beginning of the 1970s, see "surveys" in *The Economist,* June 23, 1973, and March 27, 1976.

21. Robin Boyd, "Mass Communications," in Harper (ed.), *Pacific Orbit,* p. 145. We are grateful to Andrew Farran for pointing out to us the exaggerated nature of this statement.

22. The public sources contain many attempts to argue that ANZUS and the Japanese Peace Treaty were not connected as part of an American-Australian bargain. In April of 1951, however, it was made clear by Australian Minister of External Affairs Spender that it would be unrealistic to consider the tentative American draft treaty with Japan except in the framework of effective security guarantees in the Pacific. (*Current Notes on International Affairs* 22 [1951]: 233.)

23. David Baldwin, "The Myths of the Special Relationship," in Stephen Clarkson (ed.), *An Independent Foreign Policy for Canada?* (Toronto: McClelland and Stewart, 1968), p. 5.

24. Arnold Wolfers, *Discord and Collaboration* (Baltimore: Johns Hopkins University Press, 1962), p. 97.

25. See, for example, Theo Sommer, "The Community Is Working," *Foreign Affairs* 51 (July 1973): 753.

26. We are grateful to Peyton Lyon and Garth Stevenson of Carleton University and John Trent of the University of Ottawa for helping to indicate the cases marked as most important for Canadian autonomy in tables 7.7–7.9.

27. David Leyton-Brown, "Governments of Developed Countries as Hosts to Multinational Enterprise," Ph.D. dissertation, Department of Government, Harvard University, 1973.

28. See General Foulkes, "The Complications of Continental Defense," in Livingston Merchant (ed.), *Neighbors Taken for Granted* (New York: Praeger, 1966), p. 101, where he states: "In the assessment of the threat Canada is dependent upon the United States for virtually all principal intelligence estimates."

29. F. Conrad Raabe, "Canada's Decision to Recognize the Communist Government of China," *Association for Canadian Studies in the U.S. Newsletter* 2 (Spring 1972): 12–20. Also, *Mike: The Memoirs of the Right Honourable Lester B. Pearson,* vol. 2 (Toronto: University of Toronto Press, 1973), p. 195.

30. Peter Bachrach and Morton Baratz, "Two Faces of Power," *American Political Science Review* 56 (December 1962): 947–52.

31. See G. P. de T. Glazebrook, *A History of Canadian External Relations,* vol. 2 (Toronto: McClelland and Stewart, 1966), chaps. 17 and 18; and John B. Brebner, *North Atlantic Triangle* (Toronto: McClelland and Stewart, 1968), chap. 15.

32. Walter Stewart, *Trudeau in Power* (New York: Outerbridge and Dienstfrey, 1971), p. 153; also Bruce Thordarson, *Trudeau and Foreign Policy* (Toronto: Oxford University Press, 1972), p. 186.

33. James Eayrs, *Canada in World Affairs, 1955–57* (Toronto: Oxford University Press, 1959), pp. 153–60; James R. Wagner, "Partnership: American Foreign Policy Toward Canada, 1953–1957," Ph.D. dissertation, University of Denver, 1966, chap. 7.

34. Eayrs, *Canada in World Affairs,* p. 128.

35. See *Australia in Facts and Figures,* various issues.

36. An official discussion of this approach can be found in *Submission by the Department of Foreign Affairs to the Royal Commission on Australian Government Administration* (Canberra: October 1974).

37. See Trevor R. Reese, *Australia, New Zealand, and the United States, A Survey of International Relations, 1941–1968* (London: Oxford University Press, 1969), p. 231. Menzies' letter was discussed in the *New York Times*, August 1964. The issue is discussed frequently in *Australia in Facts and Figures*, especially nos. 81 and 83 (1964), but also subsequently.

38. Lloyd says that the international oil companies provided "mild support," *Canada in World Affairs*, p. 86. Lobbying by northern U.S. refiners was more important. (From interviews in Washington, D.C.)

39. Richard B. Bilder, "The Canadian Arctic Waters Pollution Prevention Act: New Streses on the Law of the Sea," *Michigan Law Review* 69 (November 1970): 4.

40. See the cases marked in tables 7.7–7.9 as discussed in footnote on page 193.

41. George Ball, *The Discipline of Power* (Boston: Little, Brown, 1968), p. 113.

42. See Joseph S. Nye, Jr., *Peace in Parts: Integration and Conflict in Regional Organizations* (Boston: Little, Brown, 1971), chaps. 2 and 3.

43. See John Sigler and Dennis Goresky, "Public Opinion on United States–Canadian Relations," *International Organization* 28, no. 4 (Autumn 1974): 637–38.

44. See Isaiah A. Litvak, Christopher Maule, and R. Robinson, *Dual Loyalty: Canadian–U.S. Business Arrangements* (Toronto: McGraw-Hill, 1971), chap. 1.

45. Nancy Hooker (ed.), *The Moffat Papers* (Cambridge, Mass.: Harvard University Press, 1956), chap. 4.

46. Based on interviews. See also K. J. Holsti and T. A. Levy, "Bilateral Institutions," in *International Organization* 28, no. 4 (Autumn 1974).

47. See Ann Hollick, "Canadian-American Relations: Law of the Sea," *International Organization* 28, no. 4 (Autumn 1974).

48. Wagner, "Partnership."

49. Based on interviews in Washington and Ottawa, 1973, 1975.

50. Quoted in Dickerman, "Transgovernmental Challenge."

51. Based on interviews, Washington and Ottawa, 1975.

52. Further comparable studies are being undertaken at Harvard's Center for International Affairs.

Chapter 8   Coping with Interdependence

1. For an interesting and suggestive exploration of these issues for the United States and France in three issue areas, see Peter J. Katzenstein, "International Relations and Domestic Structure: Foreign Economic Policies of Advanced Industrial States," *International Organization* 30, no. 1 (Winter 1976): 1–46.

2. See Edward V. Gulick, *Europe's Classical Balance of Power* (New York: Norton, 1967).

3. These thoughts were stimulated by Alfred E. Kahn's paper, "The Implications of an Electrification Strategy for Canada and the United States," delivered at Carleton University, Ottawa, October 1975.

4. Johan Galtung, "Nonterritorial Actors and the Problem of Peace," in Saul Mendlovitz (ed.), *On the Creation of a Just World Order* (New York: Free Press, 1975).

5. See David Mitrany, *A Working Peace System* (Chicago: Quadrangle, 1966); and Robert Angell, *Peace on the March: Transnational Participation* (New York: Van Nostrand, 1969).

6. Charles Kindleberger, *The World in Depression, 1929–39* (Berkeley: University of California Press, 1974), p. 307.

7. As Susan Strange points out in "What Is Economic Power and Who Has It?" *International Journal 30* (Spring 1975): 220.

8. Kindleberger, *World in Depression*, p. 305.

9. For an elaboration of the concept of collective economic security, see Lawrence Krause and Joseph S. Nye, Jr., "Reflections on the Economics and Politics of International Economic Organizations," *International Organization* 29, no. 1 (Winter 1975): 323–42.

10. For a discussion of these issues, see Appendix B, "The Management of Global Issues," to the report of the Commission on the Organization of the Government for the Conduct of Foreign Policy (Washington, D.C.: U.S. Government Printing Office, 1975).

11. The neofunctional strategy for European integration supports this argument. For a further discussion, see Robert O. Keohane and Joseph S. Nye, Jr., "International Interdependence and Integration," in Fred I. Greenstein and Nelson W. Polsby (eds.), *Handbook of Political Science*, vol. 8 (Reading, Mass.: Addison-Wesley, 1975), pp. 363–414.

12. Quoted in *The Economist* (London), August 30, 1975, p. 46.

13. For a further discussion in greater detail, see Robert O. Keohane and Joseph S. Nye, Jr., "Transgovernmental Relations and International Organizations," *World Politics* 27, no. 1 (October 1974): 39–62.

14. J. David Singer and Michael Wallace, "Intergovernmental Organization in the Global System, 1815–1964," *International Organization* 24 (Spring 1970): 239–87; and Robert Angell, *Peace on the March*.

Afterword

1. Robert O. Keohane and Joseph S. Nye, Jr. (eds.), *Transnational Relations and World Politics* (Cambridge: Harvard University Press, 1972).

2. Albert O. Hirschman, *National Power and the Structure of Foreign Trade* (Berkeley: University of California Press, 1945).

3. In Charles Kindleberger (ed.), *The International Corporation* (Cambridge: MIT Press, 1970).

4. Kenneth N. Waltz, *Theory of International Politics* (Reading, MA: Addison-Wesley, 1979); see also Robert O. Keohane, ed., *Neorealism and Its Critics* (New York: Columbia University Press, 1986).

5. Karl Deutsch et al., *Political Community and the North Atlantic Area* (Princeton: Princeton University Press, 1957); Ernst Haas, *The Uniting of Europe* (Stanford: Stanford University Press, 1958); Joseph S. Nye, Jr., *Peace in Parts* (Boston: Little, Brown, 1971).

6. K. J. Holsti, "A New International Politics?" *International Organization* 32 (Spring 1978), p. 525; Stanley J. Michalak, "Theoretical Perspectives for Understanding International Interdependence," *World Politics* 32 (October 1979), p. 148. For a *mea culpa* and a systemic attempt to articulate realist and neorealist assumptions, see Robert O. Keohane, "Theory of World Politics: Structural Realism and Beyond," in Ada Finifter (ed.), *Political Science: The State of the Discipline* (Washington: American Political Science Association, 1983), reprinted in Robert O. Keohane, *Neorealism and Its Critics* (New York: Columbia University Press, 1986), pp. 158–203. Keohane's later volume, *After Hegemony: Cooperation and Discord in the World Political Economy* (Prince-

ton: Princeton University Press, 1984), explicitly seeks to build a theory of institutions with what could be considered liberal implications, on premises that are consistent with those of political realism.

7. For our account of the connections between integration theory and theories of interdependence, see our article "International Interdependence and Integration," in Fred I. Greenstein and Nelson W. Polsby (eds.), *Handbook of Political Science*, vol. 8 (Reading, MA: Addison-Wesley, 1975), pp. 363–414. Karl Deutsch's work on regional integration was as important to the field as Haas'; although we discuss both in our 1975 article, our own analysis owes a greater debt to Haas' neofunctionalism.

8. In contrast to this position, Holsti asserts that interdependence does not have a problem focus: "The fact of interdependence," he says, "has to lead to a *problem* before it warrants serious attention, just as concern with war, peace, order and power led to our field centuries ago." K. J. Holsti, *The Dividing Discipline: Hegemony and Diversity in International Theory* (Winchester, MA: Allen and Unwin, 1985), p. 47.

9. David A. Baldwin, "Interdependence and Power: A Conceptual Analysis," *International Organization* 34 (Fall 1980), pp. 471–596.

10. Robert J. Art, "To What Ends Military Power?" *International Security* 4 (Spring 1980), pp. 16–17. Professor Art should be commended, however, for forthrightly acknowledging in print that he had misinterpreted our views. *International Security* 4 (Fall 1980), p. 189.

11. J. Martin Rochester, "The Rise and Fall of International Organization as a Field of Study," *International Organization* 40 (Autumn 1986), note 52, p. 792. A similar mistake occurs in Ray Maghroori and Bennett Ramberg (eds.), *Globalism Versus Realism: International Relations' Third Debate* (Boulder: Westview Press, 1982).

12. John Gerard Ruggie, "International Responses to Technology: Concepts and Trends," *International Organization* 29 (Summer 1975), p. 569; see also Richard N. Cooper, "Prolegomena to the Choice of an International Monetary System," *International Organization* 29 (Winter 1975), p. 64. See this text, p. 20, Footnote 21.

13. Susan Strange, "Cave! Hic Dragones: A Critique of Regime Analysis," *International Organization* 36 (Spring 1982), reprinted in Stephen D. Krasner (ed.), *International Regimes* (Ithaca: Cornell University Press, 1983), where this claim is made on p. 344. For early uses of the regime terminology, see Fernand de Visscher, *Le Regime Nouveau des Détroits* (Brussels, 1924), in *Extrait de la Revue de Droit Internationale et de Legislation Comparée (1924)*, nos. 1–2; L. Oppenheim, *International Law*, 5th ed. (New York, 1937; edited by H. Lauterpacht), vol. 1, pp. 207, 366, on regimes for Luxembourg and the Elbe River; David M. Leive, *International Regulatory Regimes* (Lexington: D. C. Heath, Lexington Books, 1976), 2 vols.; and a variety of articles in the *American Journal of International Law*, including 1) William L. Butler, "The Legal Regime of Russian Territorial Waters," 62 (1968), pp. 51–77, 2) Richard Young, "The Legal Regime of the Deep-Sea Floor," 62 (1968), pp. 641–53, 3) Leo J. Harris, "Diplomatic Privileges and Immunities: A New Regime Is Soon to Be Adopted by the United States," 62 (1968), pp. 98–113, 4) W. Michael Riesman, "The Regime of Straits and National Security," 74 (1980), pp. 48–76, 5) John Norton Moore, "The Regime of Straits and the Third United Nations Conference on the Law of the Sea," 74 (1980), pp. 77–121.

14. David A. Baldwin, "Power Analysis and World Politics: New Trends Versus Old Tendencies," *World Politics* 31 (January 1979), pp. 169, 181.

15. Harrison Wagner, "Economic Interdependence, Bargaining Power and Political Influence," unpublished paper, October 1986.

16. Our analysis (p. 140) of the 1971 change in the international monetary system illustrates this point. We emphasized not American weakness, but the underlying strength of the U.S. position, quoting Henry Aubrey to the effect that "a creditor's influence over the United States rests on American willingness to play the game according to the old concepts and rules." See Chapter 6, footnote 11.

17. Arthur A. Stein, "The Politics of Linkage," *World Politics* 33 (October 1980), p. 81.

18. Thomas Schelling, *The Strategy of Conflict* (New York: Oxford University Press, 1960), p. 177. Oye's discussion of linkage appears in the introduction to Kenneth A. Oye, Donald Rothchild, and Robert J. Lieber, *Eagle Entangled: U.S. Foreign Policy in a Complex World* (New York: Longman, 1979), especially pp. 13–17; see also Ernst B. Haas, "Why Collaborate? Issue-Linkage and International Regimes," *World Politics* 32 (April 1980), pp. 357–402.

19. Robert Tollison and Thomas Willett, "An Economic Theory of Mutually Advantageous Issue Linkage in International Negotiations," *International Organization* 33 (Fall 1979), pp. 425–49; James Sebenius, *Negotiating the Law of the Sea* (Cambridge: Harvard University Press, 1984), especially chap. 6; Sebenius, "Negotiation Arithmetic," *International Organization* 37 (Spring 1983), pp. 281–316.

20. For a brief discussion that draws on empirical work in this special issue of *World Politics*, see Robert Axelrod and Robert O. Keohane, "Achieving Cooperation under Anarchy: Strategies and Institutions," *World Politics* 39 (October 1986), especially pp. 239–43.

21. Considering the fondness for philosophical jargon in contemporary writing on international relations theory, we should refer to this as the "ontological status" of complex interdependence. Somehow we cannot quite bring ourselves to do this.

22. John A. Vasquez and Richard W. Mansbach, "The Issue Cycle and Global Change," *International Organization* 37 (Spring 1983), pp. 257–79, quotation on p. 274. See also Mansbach and Vasquez, *In Search of Theory: A New Paradise for Global Politics* (New York: Columbia University Press, 1981), especially chap. 4.

23. See especially Keohane and Nye, "Transgovernmental Relations and International Organizations," *World Politics* 27 (October 1974), pp. 39–62.

24. As a strategy for research, this approach was probably wise, since it is terribly difficult to link domestic politics and the international system together theoretically without reducing the analysis to little more than a descriptive hodgepodge. Recent efforts to bridge this gap, using the concept of state structure, have made notable progress. See Peter J. Katzenstein (ed.), *Between Power and Plenty: Foreign Economic Policies of Advanced Industrialized States* (Madison: University of Wisconsin Press, 1978); and Peter J. Katzenstein, *Small States in World Markets* (Ithaca: Cornell University Press, 1985).

25. Peter A. Gourevitch, "The Second Image Reversed," *International Organization* 32 (Autumn 1978), pp. 881–912; and *Politics in Hard Times* (Ithaca: Cornell University Press, 1986).

26. Ruggie, "International Responses to Technology."

27. Robert Jervis identified a Concert of Europe regime in the nineteenth century; in his discussion of contemporary international politics, however, he looked for a regime in the central strategic relationship between the United States and the Soviet Union and failed to find one. Robert Jervis, "Security Regimes," in Stephen D. Krasner (ed.), *International Regimes* (Ithaca: Cornell University Press, 1983), pp. 173–94. Janice Gross Stein and Joseph S. Nye, Jr., have focused on narrower realms of activity and have discovered meaningful security regimes in contemporary world politics. See Stein, "Detection and Defection: Security 'Regime' and the Management of International Conflict," *International Journal* 40, (Autumn 1985), pp. 599–627; and Nye, "Nuclear Learning and

U.S.–Soviet Security Regimes," *International Organization* 41, no. 3 (Summer 1987). See also Roger K. Smith, "The Non-Proliferation Regime and International Relations," *International Organization* 41 (Spring 1987), pp. 253–82. Smith makes a number of perceptive criticisms of regime theory.

28. Krasner (ed.), *International Regimes*, p. 2.

29. See Stephan Haggard and Beth Simmons, "Theories of International Regimes," *International Organization* 41 (Summer 1987), pp. 491–517.

30. See Keohane, *After Hegemony*, which discusses money, trade, and oil; the articles in the Krasner volume, *International Regimes*, on trade and the balance of payments, by Charles Lipson, Jock A. Finlayson and Mark Zacher, and Benjamin J. Cohen; and Vinod K. Aggarwal, *Liberal Protectionism: The International Politics of Organized Textile Trade* (Berkeley: University of California Press, 1985). In addition, see articles in *International Organization:* on regimes for Antarctica, "Antarctica: The Last Great Land Rush" 34 (Summer 1980), by M. J. Peterson; on nuclear proliferation, "Maintaining a Non-Proliferation Regime" 35 (Winter 1981), by Joseph S. Nye, Jr.; on civil aviation, "Sphere of Flying: The Politics of International Aviation" 35 (Spring 1981), by Christer Jonsson; on Third World debt, "The International Organization of Third World Debt" 35 (Autumn 1981), by Charles Lipson; on international shipping, "The Political Economy of International Shipping: Europe versus America" 39 (Winter 1985), by Alan W. Cafruny; and on international commodity regimes, "Trade Caps, Analytical Gaps: Regime Analysis and International Commodity Trade Regulation" 41 (Spring 1987), by Mark Zacher. Two recent book-length studies seeking to account for the evolution or persistence of international regimes are Charles Lipson, *Standing Guard: Protecting Foreign Capital in the Nineteenth and Twentieth Centuries* (Berkeley: University of California Press, 1985); and Stephen D. Krasner, *Structural Conflict: The Third World Against Global Liberalism* (Berkeley: University of California Press, 1985).

31. On June 3, 1986, for instance, Soviet First Secretary Mikhail Gorbachev stated in a message to the Secretary-General of the United Nations that "it is quite obvious that there is a practical need to start, without delay, setting up an international regime for the safe development of nuclear energy." *New York Times,* June 4, 1986, p. A12. We do not presume to know what led Secretary Gorbachev to use the language of regimes, although Soviet scholars have informed us that they began to use the term in relation to the Law of the Seas Conference in the 1970s. Personal conversations, Moscow, June 1986.

32. Stephen D. Krasner, "Regimes and the Limits of Realism: Regimes as Autonomous Variables," in Krasner (ed.), *International Regimes*, pp. 355–68. But for an analysis of the impact of several international regimes on relations between rich and poor countries, see Krasner, *Structural Conflict: The Third World Against Global Liberalism* (Berkley: University of California Press, 1985).

33. For an early and insightful attempt, see Oran R. Young, *Compliance and Public Authority* (Washington: Institute for the Future, 1979).

34. Keohane defines myopic self-interest in terms of "governments' perception of the relative costs and benefits to them of alternative courses of action with regard to a particular issue, when that issue is considered in isolation from others." *After Hegemony*, p. 99.

35. On the demise of the Bretton Woods international monetary regime, for example, see Joanne Gowa, *Closing the Gold Window: Domestic Politics and the End of Bretton Woods* (Ithaca: Cornell University Press, 1983); and John S. Odell, *U.S. International Monetary Policy: Markets, Power and Ideas as Sources of Change* (Princeton: Princeton University Press, 1982). On rule evasion and circumvention of textile restraints under the umbrella of the Multi-Fiber Arrange-

ment, see David Yoffie, *Power and Protectionism: Strategies of the Newly Industrializing Countries* (New York: Columbia University Press, 1983).

36. Abram Chayes' study of the role of law in the Cuban Missile Crisis is an exception to the statement about the absence of work on international norms, as embodied, for instance, in international regimes. Chayes does not use the language of regimes, but he discusses the impact of international norms for the peaceful settlement of disputes, as embodied in various international practices and agreements, including the Organization of American States and United Nations Charter. See Abram Chayes, *The Cuban Missile Crisis and the Rule of Law* (New York: Oxford University Press, 1974).

37. Kenneth N. Waltz, *Theory of International Politics* (Reading MA: Addison-Wesley, 1979).

38. For a critique of Waltz's work along these lines, see John Gerard Ruggie, "Continuity and Transformation in the World Polity: Toward a Neorealist Synthesis," *World Politics* 35 (January 1983), pp. 261–85; reprinted in Robert O. Keohane (ed.), *Neorealism and Its Critics* (New York: Columbia University Press, 1986), pp. 131–57. An extended argument to this effect is provided in Keohane, *After Hegemony*, especially chaps. 1, 4–7.

39. Kenneth N. Waltz, "Response to My Critics," in Keohane (ed.), *Neorealism and Its Critics*, pp. 322–46.

40. For discussions about the analogy between grammar and systemic processes which facilitate cooperation, we are indebted to Hayward Alker, Jr.

41. On issue density, defined as the number and importance of issues arising within a given policy space, see Robert O. Keohane, "The Demand for International Regimes," *International Organization* 36 (Spring 1982), reprinted in Krasner (ed.), *International Regimes*. The reference is to p. 155 of the latter volume.

42. On this method of "process tracing," see Alexander L. George and Timothy J. McKeown, "Case Studies and Theories of Organizational Decision Making," *Advances in Information Processing in Organizations* 2 (1985), pp. 21–58; or Alexander L. George, "Case Studies and Theory Development: The Method of Structured, Focused Comparison," pp. 43–68 in Paul Gordon Lauren (ed.), *Diplomacy: New Approaches in History, Theory and Policy* (New York: The Free Press, 1979).

43. There is actually a spectrum of goals between revolutionary and status quo. Moreover, these goals may be affected by the types of means available to states. See Barry Buzan, *People, States and Fear* (Chapel Hill: University of North Carolina Press, 1983).

44. The bipolar-multipolar distinction is emphasized by Kenneth N. Waltz, whose *Theory of International Politics* carefully and systematically develops the notion of political structure whose explanatory inadequacy we are criticizing. For a recent discussion of the nineteenth century, see Paul W. Schroeder, "The 19th Century International System: Changes in the Structure," *World Politics* 39 (October 1986), pp. 1–26. Schroeder emphasizes the development of norms for the protection of small countries. What he calls "changes in structure" would not be considered structural changes by Waltz, and we would refer to them as changes in the process of the international system.

45. We are indebted to William Jarosz and Lisa Martin for insightful comments that helped us to clarify the issues in this section.

46. Lloyd Etheredge, *Can Governments Learn?* (New York: Pergamon Press, 1985), p. 143: also "Government Learning: An Overview," in Samuel Long (ed.), *Handbook of Political Behavior* 2 (New York: Plenum Press, 1981), pp. 73–161.

47. Ernst B. Haas, "Why We Still Need the United Nations: The Collective Management of International Conflict, 1945–1984," Policy Paper in International Affairs, no. 26 (Berkeley: Institute of International Studies, 1986), p. 68.

48. Ernst B. Haas, "Why Collaborate? Issue-Linkage and International Regimes," *World Politics* 32 (April 1980), p. 390. See also John D. Steinbruner, *The Cybernetic Theory of Decision* (Princeton: Princeton University Press, 1974); and Robert Jervis, *Perception and Misperception in International Politics* (Princeton: Princeton University Press, 1976).

49. Richard Neustadt and Ernest May, *Thinking in Time* (New York: The Free Press, 1986).

50. Robert Axelrod, *The Evolution of Cooperation* (New York: Basic Books, 1984).

51. For an argument that this should be a goal of farsighted policymakers, see Robert O. Keohane and Joseph S. Nye, Jr., "Two Cheers for Multilateralism," *Foreign Policy* 61 (Fall 1985), which is reprinted in this volume beginning on page 266.

Two Cheers for Multilateralism

1. For a detailed account, see Robert O. Keohane, *After Hegemony: Cooperation and Discord in the World Political Economy* (Princeton: Princeton University Press, 1984), chap. 10, pp. 217–42.

2. *United Nations Yearbook* 34, 1980 (New York, 1983), pp. 1251–1344.

3. For an excellent historical discussion, published well before the recent crisis, see Charles P. Kindleberger, *Manias, Panics, and Crashes* (New York: Basic Books, 1978).

Index

economic interdependence, 9, 32, 38–42, 63, 247, 281
  nonstructural incentives and, 263
  power and, 254
economics
  changing, 250–251
  competition in, 7
  crises in, 277–278
  growth in, 39, 45
  use of military force and, 250
Ecuador, 93, 95, 101–102, 119, 124
Eisenhower, Dwight D., 189
energy crisis, 213–214, 215
Eurodollars, 81n, 111
Europe, 47–48, 135–136 (*See also* Eastern Europe; Western Europe; *specific countries*)
  uniting of, 247–248
European Community (*See* European Economic Community)
European Economic Community, 20, 26, 47–48, 51, 210, 240, 281
  Monetary Committee of, 109, 118
European Payments Union (EPU), 80, 136
European Recovery Program, 78
Evatt, Herbert B., 173
exchange rate (*See also* Foreign exchange)
  regulation of, 269, 281–282
  stability of, 281
export-credit club, 275

Feis, Herbert, 108
Finance Committee, U.S. Senate, 142
First National City Bank, 111
fisheries, 86–87, 144, 238
Fisherman's Protective Act of 1954, 119, 134
Food and Agriculture Organization (FAO), 269
force (*See also* U.S. military force)
  cost of, 246
  limitations of, 246
  realism and threat of, 23–24, 35, 43–44, 119
  in regional rivalries, 246
foreign exchange, 67, 71
  controls on, 67, 78–79, 83
foreign policy (*See also* U.S. foreign policy)
  domestic policy linked to, 8, 156, 194
  international institutions and, 268–270
Fowler, Henry, 30
France, 27, 45, 70–71, 77–78, 84, 120, 139, 151
Franco-German hostility, transformation of into cooperation, 248
French Revolution, changing goals of, 263
Fullbright, J. William, 213

Galtung, Johan, 124
GATT (*See* General Agreement on Tariffs and Trade (GATT))

General Agreement on Tariffs and Trade (GATT), 20–21, 26, 36, 47, 51, 132, 271
  creation of, 268
  nondiscriminatory provisions of, 281
  size of, 274
General Arrangements to Borrow (1962), 81, 110, 151
Geneva Conference (1958), 97, 100, 148
Genoa Conference (1922), 75–76
Germany, 27, 45, 70–71, 75, 91, 140
  national interests of, 265
  state preferences and system structure of, 261
global negotiations, 275, 276
global unilateralism, 281
  fantasies of, 282
"global village" view, 3
gold standard, 76, 131, 139
  abandoned, 77
  before 1914, 67–72
Gorbachev, Mikhail, 286n
Gourevitch, Peter, 256
government interests, shared, 275–276
governmental intervention, Reagan administration attitude toward, 269
Great Britain, 27
  as monetary leader, 45, 67–73, 104, 131, 137
  and monetary regimes, 13, 78–79, 81, 139
  as naval power, 44, 63, 90–91, 92, 132, 143
  and oceans regimes, 94, 96, 100–101, 145, 154
  U.S. loan to, 6, 135
Great Depression, 266
Grenada, U.S. invasion of, 246
Grotius, Hugo, 90
Group of Ten, 81, 84, 85, 110, 118, 151
Guatemala, 28

Haas, Ernst, 247–248, 251, 264–265
Hague Conference (1930), 93, 97, 124
Harding administration, 143
hegemonic stability theory, 257–258
hegemony, eroding, 42–46, 49, 136, 153
  reasons for, 45–46
Hirsch, Fred, 83
Hirschman, Albert, 247, 252, 279
Hitler, Adolf, strategies of, 261
Holland, 77
Hollick, Ann, 156
Holsti, K. J., 248
Humble Oil Company, 207

IAEA, sanctions of, 277
Iceland, 96, 102
IJC (*See* International Joint Commission (IJC))
IMF (*See* International Monetary Fund (IMF))

structure of, 20, 132–137
United Nations peacekeeping and, 280
universalism of, 275–276
U.S. interests in, 279–280
variations in, 271
international relations
impact of on domestic politics, 256
learning in, 264–265
international rules, degree of institutionalization of, 261
international system, 256
constraints and opportunities of, 267
structure changes in, 287*n*
international trade, liberalism in, 271
international–level factors, 261
interstate relations, 25, 251 (*See also* international relations)
intragovernmental conflict, 254
Iran, 50, 93, 124
Iran–Iraq war, 246, 269
issue areas, defining, 64–65, 87–90
issue cycle, 255–256
issue linkage, 30–32, 48, 105, 122–124, 171–172, 211, 225–226, 252–254, 255, 267
intragovernmental and intergovernmental struggles in, 253–255
issues (*See also* issue areas, defining; issue cycle; issue linkage)
absence of hierarchy a characteristic of complex interdependence, 25–27, 32, 105–109, 227
agenda setting and, 32–33, 96, 120–122, 198–202
Australian-American relations and, 176–178, 193–198, 211–212
Canadian-American relations and, 169–172, 178–193, 199–202, 213–214
depoliticization of economic, 41–42
nonstructural incentives and density of, 263
structural hierarchy and, 49–54, 137–146, 176–178, 213
issue-structure theory, 253
Italy, 70

J. P. Morgan and Company, 111
Jamaica agreements (1976), 137*n*, 142, 151
Japan, 145, 212
economy of, 45, 135, 136, 140
sensitivity dependence of, 12
vulnerability dependence of, 14
Jervis, Robert, 285*n*
Johnson, Lyndon B., 171, 206
Johnson administration, 136

Kennedy, John F. 239
Kennedy administration, 6, 136
Kierans, Eric, 202
Kindleberger, Charles, 45, 153, 229, 232, 276

Kirkpatrick, Jeane, 268
Kissinger, Henry, 3, 26, 28
Korea, 102
Kuwait, 50

labor unions, 41, 155
Law of the Sea Convention, 86, 88, 95, 100, 125, 133, 149, 150, 213, 256
failure of, 273
Law of the Sea Treaty, U.S. refusal to sign, 256–257, 269
leadership
in complex interdependence, 229–231, 232–238
hegemonic, 42–44, 229–230
legitimacy of, 231
multiple, 232–238, 243
nonhegemonic, 231
theory of lag in, 153–154
unilateral, 230–231
League of Nations, 75
learning
defined, 264–265
effects on perceptions of interests, 264–266
international political processes and, 266
in international relations, 264–265
legitimacy of, 231, 234–236
theory of, 267
Lebanon, Israel's invasion of, 246
legitimacy
of leadership, 231
of multiple leadership, 234–236
liberalism
economic incentives and, 247
interdependence theory and, 248
trade and, 271
transnational communication and nonstructural incentives in, 262
Libya, 50
U.S. air strikes against, 246
linkage of issues, 48, 211, 225–226, 252–253, 255, 267
Canadian-American relationship and, 171–172
conflict and, 254
in monetary area, 107–109, 123–124
in oceans area, 105, 122–123
and strategies regarding complex interdependence, 30–32
Lombok, straits of, 101
London, as financial center, 69
London Economic Conference (1933), 77, 104, 131
long-range planning, 278–279

MacDonald, Ramsey, 77
Macmillan Report, 69
mail delivery, 274